BROTHER NUMBER ONE

——————— ■ ———————

Pol Pot in Phnom Penh, December 1978. Photo by Richard Dudman. Courtesy of Sygma. Reprinted with permission. Copyright Sygma and Richard Dudman.

BROTHER NUMBER ONE

∎

A Political Biography of Pol Pot

REVISED EDITION

David P. Chandler

Westview Press
A Member of the Perseus Books Group

Copyright © 1999 by Westview Press, A Member of the Perseus Books Group

Published in 1999 in the United States of America by Westview Press, 5500 Central Avenue, Boulder, Colorado 80301-2877, and in the United Kingdom by Westview Press, 12 Hid's Copse Road, Cumnor Hill, Oxford OX2 9JJ

Library of Congress Cataloging-in-Publication Data
Chandler, David P.
   Brother number one: a political biography of Pol Pot / David P. Chandler — Rev. ed.
      p. cm.
   Includes bibliographical references and index.
   ISBN 0-8133-3510-8 (pbk.)
   1. Pol Pot. 2. Cambodia—Politics and government. 3. Prime ministers—Cambodia—Biography. I. Title. II. Title: Brother number 1.
DS554.83.P65C43 1999
959.604'2'092—dc21
[b]   98-51553
                                                                                  CIP

The paper used in this publication meets the requirements of the American National Standard for Permanence of Paper for Printed Library Materials Z39.48-1984.

10   9   8   7   6   5   4   3   2

Chorus:
Who fights for communism must be able to fight and not to fight,
to say the truth and not say the truth, to render and to deny
service, to keep a promise and to break a promise, to go into
danger and to avoid danger, to be known and to be unknown.
Who fights for communism has of all the virtues only one: that
he fights for communism.
Bertoldt Brecht, *The Measures Taken*

Contents

Illustrations

Preface to the Second Edition

I am grateful to my editors at Westview Press, Rob Williams and Kristin Milavec, the project editor, for encouraging me to prepare a second edition of this book. In bringing the narrative up to date, closing with Pol Pot's death in April 1998, I have invaded the text and the end notes to insert new data and to correct minor errors pointed out by correspondents and reviewers. In addition, I have updated the bibliographical essay at the end of the book. The text has also benefited enormously from Jennifer Swearingen's helpful copy-editing.

In the time between the appearance of the first edition and Pol Pot's death six years later, some interesting new biographical data have emerged, thanks in large part to enterprising research conducted by David Ashley, Chhang Youk, Stephen Heder, and Nate Thayer. I am grateful to these four people for providing me with transcripts or summaries of their interviews, and to Thayer for sending me a copy of Nuon Chea's draft history of the "struggle movement," which he composed in 1997. My own study of the S-21 archive in 1994–1998 revealed some new information about the Vietnamese military base known as "Office 100," where Pol Pot and his colleagues sought refuge from Sihanouk's police in the early 1960s; my interviews with Lim Keuky and a former Chinese diplomat speaking on condition of anonymity provided some insights, respectively, into Pol Pot's early married life and into his friendship with the notorious Chinese official K'ang Sheng. My revision of the final chapter benefited from conversations with Terry McCarthy, Seth Mydans, and Nate Thayer. The new data have altered the chronological outlines of Pol Pot's life by making it four years longer, as I now prefer the birth-date of 1925 to the 1928 one I had supported in the first edition.

Pol Pot wanted to be judged by history, as his interview with Nate Thayer in October 1997 makes clear. Unfortunately from his point of view, perhaps, the material that has emerged about his life since 1992 has not made his personality any more accessible or his career any easier to admire.

David Chandler
Washington, D.C.

Acknowledgments

I am delighted to acknowledge the help and encouragement I've received while working on this book. Research began in 1987, when Sally Furgeson, then with Westview Press, wrote to suggest that I write a biography of Pol Pot. I was attracted by the challenge and accepted it at once, but because of prior commitments I wasn't able to begin writing until 1990. I'm grateful to Ms. Furgeson and to Susan McEachern, who took over the project for Ms. Furgeson, for their patience and support. As the manuscript was being written and later, when she went over it, Ms. McEachern made many helpful suggestions. Deborah Lynes, the book's editor, made helpful comments at several stages, and I benefited enormously from Michele Kendall's fastidious, perceptive copyediting.

The Australian Research Council provided a generous grant, twice renewed, that defrayed the costs of research and overseas travel. At various times, I also received financial assistance from Yale University, the Social Science Research Council (New York), California State University at Long Beach, the Institute of International Strategic Studies, and the outside studies program of Monash University (Australia).

Kate Frieson, Christopher Goscha, Stephen Heder, and Serge Thion read the manuscript and suggested many improvements. My wife, Susan, read three successive versions. Without her insights and editorial skill, the book would be clumsier and more obtuse. Over the years, my work on Cambodia has profited from many discussions with these people, as well as with Nayan Chanda, Justin Corfield, May Ebihara, Claude Jacques, Ben Kiernan, Judy Ledgerwood, Jacques Nepote, Lionel Vairon, and Michael Vickery. Several of these friends have generously provided me with material from their personal archives unavailable elsewhere. My debts to the pioneering work on Cambodian radicalism by Heder, Kiernan, Thion, and Vickery should be apparent in the notes. When the book was nearly complete, I profited from the research in progress of J. Thomas Engelbert and Christopher Goscha; this research, since published, provided many valuable insights.

The collection of material took me to Cambodia, Canada, France, Thailand, and the United States. For hospitality and help in arranging interviews,

I am particularly grateful to Lionel Vairon, Judy Ledgerwood, Mika Levesque, Tom Sakara, Suon Kaset Sokho, Serge Thion, Hin Sithan, Charles F. Keyes, and Vora Huy Kanthoul.

Others who have helped with correspondence, introductions, documents, conversation, and hospitality (in addition to those already listed) include Benedict Anderson, Eliza Anderson, David Ashley, Anthony Barnett, Jacques Bekaert, Elizabeth Becker, Anne Blair, Elaine Blumenthal, Georges Boudarel, Pierre Brocheux, Teri Caraway, Timothy Carney, Chea Samaun, Frances Doggett, Maurice Eisenbruch, Steven Erlanger, Grant Evans, David Feingold, David Garrioch, Marvin Gelfand, James Gerrand, Denis Grey, David Hawk, Murray Hiebert, Mary C. Jackson, Somsak Jeemtearaskul, Julio Jeldres, Justin Jordens, Peter Judd, George Kahin, F. W. Kent, Vorleak Leah, J. D. Legge, Hong Lim, Henri Locard, Mary-Kay Magistad, David Marr, Marie-A. Martin, Angus McIntyre, Chantal Mercier, David Monaghan, Roger Normand, Pham van Luu, Francois Ponchaud, Craig Reynolds, John Rickard, Kelvin Rowley, Jim Scott, Frank Smith, Sok Pirun, Sok Saroeun, Richard Tanter, Keith Taylor, Thel Tong, William Turley, Esta Ungar, and Karin von Strokirch.

The men and women I interviewed more formally are listed elsewhere. Without the help of all these people and institutions, I would never have been able to write this book. And without their enthusiasm and kindness, I would have had less enjoyment writing it.

D. C.
Paris

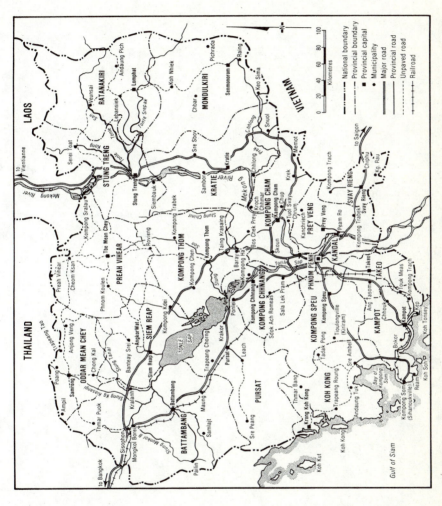

Cambodia. *SOURCE:* David Chandler, *A History of Cambodia,* 2nd ed. (Boulder: Westview Press, 1992). Reprinted with permission.

BROTHER NUMBER ONE

———————— ■ ————————

CHAPTER ONE

—————— ■ ——————

Introduction

On April 17, 1975, Cambodia emerged from five years of invasion, bombardment, and civil war when its capital, Phnom Penh, fell to the guerrilla armies known as the Khmer Rouge or Red Khmer, which had been besieging it since the beginning of the year. The city's population included over one million refugees, driven from their homes in rural areas. During the course of the civil war, perhaps as many as half a million Cambodians had been killed. People in the cities, without knowing much about the Red Khmer, presumed that peace would be better than war and that Cambodians, working together, could reconstruct their country.

What happened next took everyone but the Red Khmer commanders by surprise. Within a week, the people of Phnom Penh, Battambang, and other cities were driven into the countryside by the Red Khmer and told to take up agricultural tasks. Thousands of evacuees, especially the very young and the very old, died over the next few weeks. Some survivors, walking toward regions where they hoped their relatives would welcome them, were on the road for over a month. When they asked questions of the heavily armed young soldiers who accompanied them, they were told to obey the "revolutionary organization" (*angkar padevat*), which would act as their "mother and father." The evacuees were called "new people" or "April 17 people" because they had joined the revolution so late. Residents of the countryside were known as "base people" and were treated less harshly than the others.

After emptying the cities, the revolutionary organization embarked on a program of social transformation that affected every aspect of Cambodian life. Money, markets, and private property were abolished. Schools, universities, and Buddhist monasteries were closed. No publishing was allowed; the postal system was shut down; freedom of movement, exchange of information, personal adornment, and leisure activities were curtailed. Punishments for infractions were severe, and repeat offenders were imprisoned under harsh conditions or killed. Everyone was ordered to perform tasks set

1

for them by the revolutionary organization. For evacuee city dwellers, these tasks seldom had any relation to their training or skills. Instead, nearly all of them became peasants and were made to wear identical black cotton clothing.

The movement's leaders and their rationale remained concealed. To the outside world Cambodia was still ostensibly ruled by the United Front government, founded in Beijing in 1970 when Prince Norodom Sihanouk, Cambodia's chief of state, had been overthrown in a bloodless coup while he was abroad, replaced by a government that sought an alliance with the United States. The prince had been the figurehead leader of the resistance in Beijing. By 1972 the Red Khmer controlled the resistance but for the sake of international respectability continued to operate behind the facade of Sihanouk's coalition.

The charade continued for the remainder of 1975. In January 1976 the revolutionary organization dissolved the United Front, changed the name of the country to Democratic Kampuchea (DK), and promulgated a new constitution. The document praised collective values, identified the revolutionary organization with the people's interests, and formalized the collectivization of Cambodian life. The words *socialism* or *communism* appeared nowhere in the text. Soon after, Radio Phnom Penh announced that elections would be held for a national assembly and broadcast the names of ministers in the new regime. The elections, it seemed, were primarily for overseas consumption. Most "new people" were not allowed to vote; "base people" voted for candidates provided by the organization.

Most of the winners were unknown outside the Red Khmer movement, although some of the new ministers, such as Ieng Sary, Khieu Samphan, and Hu Nim, were prominent leftists who had joined the resistance against Sihanouk in the 1960s. Others elected were identified sooner or later as veteran revolutionaries.

The prime minister, a "rubber plantation worker" called Pol Pot, was impossible to identify. At the moment he took power, just when he might have been expected to step into the open, he concealed himself behind a revolutionary name.

Who was he?

For over a year he revealed almost nothing about himself. When he made a state visit to China in September 1977 and was photographed there, Cambodia watchers identified Pol Pot as a fifty-two-year-old former schoolteacher named Saloth Sar, who had been secretary of the Central Committee of the clandestine Communist party of Kampuchea (CPK) since 1963. Pol Pot had announced the existence of the CPK for the first time in a triumphal speech recorded for Radio Phnom Penh just before he left for China. But very few Cambodians knew that Pol Pot was Saloth Sar. He admitted his former identity only after he was overthrown in 1979.

Mystery clung to him as news of what was happening in Cambodia between 1975 and 1978—the DK period—filtered into the outside world. Most of the news was horrible. Refugees spoke of forced labor, starvation, random executions, and the tyrannical, anonymous "organization."

What did Pol Pot and his colleagues have in mind?

This handful of men and women presided over the purest and most thoroughgoing Marxist-Leninist movement in an era of revolutions. No other regime tried to go so quickly or so far. No other inflicted as many casualties on the country's population.

At one level, the revolution was a courageous, doomed attempt by a group of utopian thinkers to break free from the capitalist world system, abandon the past, and rearrange the future. Many radicals in other countries interpreted events in Cambodia in this way. At another level, the revolution sprang from a colossal misreading of Cambodia's political capacities, its freedom of maneuver vis-à-vis its neighbors, and the interests of the rural poor on whose behalf the revolution was ostensibly being waged. At a third level, Pol Pot and his colleagues displayed a thirst for power and an unlimited capacity for distrust. Believing himself surrounded by enemies, Pol Pot approved the torture and execution of almost fourteen thousand enemies (*khmang*) at the regime's interrogation facility in Phnom Penh, known by the code name S-21. And thousands more died in the regional purges he set in motion in 1977. Most of those put to death at S-21 were loyal members of the party. Victims elsewhere seem, for the most part, to have been innocent of treason.

What were the sources of the revolution and its extraordinary violence? Between 1975 and 1979, those in power in Phnom Penh frequently declared that they followed no foreign models and that the Cambodian revolution was incomparable. In fact, many DK slogans—such as "storming attacks," "leaps forward," "independence-mastery," and "three tons (of rice) per hectare"— came without acknowledgment from Communist China, where the regime, on the eve of Mao Zedong's death in September 1976, was going through a peculiarly radical phase.

What the Cambodian leaders meant by independence, in large part, was that they were different from, and superior to, Vietnam, whose Communist movement had shaped and guided them for many years. Vietnamese guidance began to grate on Saloth Sar and his colleagues in the 1960s, when the Vietnamese treated them not as revolutionaries but as younger brothers in their all-absorbing war against the United States. Fighting between Cambodia and Vietnam erupted in 1977 and culminated two years later in a Vietnamese blitzkrieg that overthrew Pol Pot's regime.

The mayhem that Democratic Kampuchea inflicted on its people led the French author Jean Lacouture to coin the word *autogenocide*—to differentiate events in Cambodia from previous pogroms, holocausts, purges, and vendettas. Lacouture's horror, if not the word he coined, was justified by the facts. In less than four years, more than one million Cambodians, or one in seven, probably died from malnutrition, overwork, and misdiagnosed or mistreated illness. At least one hundred thousand, and probably more, were executed for crimes against the state. Tens of thousands perished in the conflict with Vietnam, almost certainly started by the Red Khmer. But was what happened autogenocide, without forerunners elsewhere? Clear parallels, and probably inspirations, can be found in China's Great Leap Forward in the 1950s, in the Soviet collectivization of Ukraine twenty years before that, and in purges in both countries of "elements" considered dangerous to revolutionary leaders. In a sense, what happened in Cambodia, although more intense, was standard operating procedure in countries whose politics Pol Pot—or "Brother Number One," as he was informally known to subordinates—admired.

The catastrophe of Democratic Kampuchea and its effects encourage an examination of Pol Pot's political career to see what connections can be drawn between the man and what happened in Cambodia between 1975 and 1979, as well as before and since. The outline of his life has been known since the early 1980s, thanks to the path-breaking work of Australian scholar Ben Kiernan and several others. Recently, new sources have come to light that have made possible a longer, more detailed view of Pol Pot's career than Kiernan reached in his book, which dealt primarily with the period before 1975.[1]

Much of what has been written about Pol Pot since his time in power has been reckless and intemperate. This is not surprising in view of the impact of the revolution; but calling him a "moon-faced monster," a "genocidal maniac," or "worse than Hitler" (phrases picked from journalists' reports) has no explanatory power. To understand the man and what happened in Democratic Kampuchea, we need to place him inside a Cambodian context and inside a wider set of influences from abroad.

During my research, I talked with several people who had been to school with Saloth Sar in the 1940s, who had known him in Paris or who had known him as a schoolteacher in Phnom Penh. Those who encountered him during his years in power were more discreet with anecdotal evidence, but from all these sources, as well as printed and archival material, I was able to build a consistent, but rather two-dimensional, picture. This has been enhanced, but not deepened, by interviews conducted by others since 1992.[2]

None of the people I spoke to—including several who live thousands of miles from Cambodia and whose families were savaged by the Pol Pot regime—were prepared to associate the person they had known with the horrors of the 1970s. Victims of Pol Pot's regime, they were unwilling to alter or deny their relatively pleasant recollections of the man.

To his brother and sister-in-law, for example, Saloth Sar was a sweet-tempered, equable child. Schoolmates remembered him as a mediocre student but pleasant company, a reputation that persisted among those who knew him in France. As a teacher, he was remembered as calm, self-assured, smooth featured (*s'aat s'om*), honest, and persuasive, even hypnotic when speaking to small groups. Among his students and his colleagues in the clandestine Communist movement, he seems in these years to have gained some of the moral authority and stature he enjoyed among his followers up to 1997. A man who met him in the late 1950s, for example, said, "I saw immediately that I could become his friend for life." Similar testimony has emerged in confessions from S-21 and in the 1980s and 1990s from Red Khmer defectors who attended Pol Pot's political seminars in Thailand and Cambodia. None of the defectors, although they were free to do so (as those being tortured at S-21 were not), singled out Pol Pot's behavior or personality as a reason for betraying the party or, in the 1980s, for deserting the Communist movement. Instead, most of them came away with memories of a man they regarded almost as a saint.

With witnesses like these, and Pol Pot's own writings, it has been impossible for me to penetrate what may be a facade, a series of masks, or a chosen repertoire of skills to discover a rougher, more diabolical, supposedly more genuine Pol Pot. Throughout his life, the man seems to have tailored his performance to fit the people he was with, making a "genocidal maniac" hard to find. Indeed, the disjunction between his genteel charisma and the death toll of his regime is one of the mysteries that hangs over his career and poses serious difficulties in trying to make sense of his life.

The concealment or absence of conflict in Pol Pot's personal life has also made it difficult to reach sweeping or persuasive psychological conclusions about him. Was he only *apparently* a happy child and an inspiring teacher? Was his kindly manner faked? Was he a cynical political animal, a true believer, or a mélange of both? Was he a paranoid nourished by a sense of betrayal or persecution, or a utopian who saw his vision wrecked by others? Is there a difference? His own writings and speeches, which avoid personal details, provide little information to help us answer any of these questions. Even after his two-hour interview with Nate Thayer in 1997, less than a year before he died, Pol Pot defies analysis.[3]

Pol Pot's lifetime overlaps the story of Cambodian politics since World War II. His revolutionary movement benefited from Vietnamese help during its formative years and during Vietnam's war with the United States. Without the war, Pol Pot's coming to power, like Sihanouk's demise, is inconceivable.[4]

Saloth Sar/Pol Pot was also a product of twentieth-century Cambodian society. From that society, he fought against, and ironically benefited from, a deeply rooted sense of hierarchy that frequently permitted a single man, properly positioned, nicely behaved, and thought to be meritorious, to exercise enormous power. Like most Khmer of his generation, he was incurious about the outside world. He distrusted foreigners and their intentions toward his country. From Cambodian Buddhism, he absorbed the ideas of disciplined personal transformation, rebirth, and enlightenment—found within the privileged, otherworldly communities of monks or Communists—through teaching, "right action," self-denial, and meditation. As a teacher, he automatically enjoyed high status—another legacy of Buddhism.[5]

Although Pol Pot was introspective and xenophobic, his ideas and his career were shaped to a large extent by foreign influences. France, as a colonial power, provided him with seventeen years of formal education and the only foreign language he is known to have spoken. This education introduced him to the idea of progress and the concepts of democracy, imperialism, and revolutionary change. His three years in Paris, where he encountered Marxist-Leninist ideas, led him to adopt a radical alignment—he probably joined the Communist party of France (CPF) in 1952.

When Saloth Sar returned to Cambodia in early 1953, he became a member of the Vietnamese-dominated Indochina Communist party (ICP). For several years he worked from concealment to accomplish its objectives. From his Vietnamese-trained mentors, he learned about party discipline, organization, and theory, as well as the importance of clandestinity and concealment. The Vietnamese, for their part, seem to have assumed that he was loyal to them.

The most important foreign influence on Pol Pot was probably Communist China, which he first visited in 1965–1966. From Mao Zedong's notions of autonomous revolution, voluntarism, and continuous class struggle, Pol Pot drew an inspiring ideology that freed him from what he considered to be the domination of the Vietnamese and that provided a model for Cambodia's transformation. From the high-ranking Chinese official K'ang Sheng, who befriended him in 1965, Pol Pot absorbed the importance of rooting out concealed enemies of the party. The timing of his conversion to a Maoist vision of the world was important. He visited China on the eve of the Cultural Revolution—in other words, before it had turned out to be a disaster—and he came to power in 1975, shortly before Mao's death, during another radical phase of Chinese politics.

These foreign influences and conjunctions are important in understanding Pol Pot's political career, but after taking them into account there is still something elusive about him that makes a biographical inquiry unsatisfactory and incomplete. Often in my research I have had the uneasy feeling that Saloth Sar/Pol Pot was just outside my line of vision observing *me*—an impression confirmed in 1997 when, talking to Nate Thayer, he spoke agreeably about the first edition of this book, while taking issue with some of my phrasing. This elusiveness has been frustrating to me as his biographer but also indicates the kind of impression that this instrument of history—as Pol Pot might call himself—always preferred to leave, or to fail to leave, while proceeding in secret with incandescent revolutionary tasks.

CHAPTER TWO

■

"Original Khmer," 1928–1949

Who Was Pol Pot?

The man known to the world as Pol Pot started life with the name Saloth Sar. Pol Pot was his revolutionary name. When he announced his pseudonym in 1976, he followed precedents set by several Communist leaders, including Lenin, Stalin, Tito, and Ho Chi Minh. Their intentions, when in the underground, were to conceal their true identities from the police and in some cases to inspire their followers ("Stalin," for example, means "steel"; "Ho Chi Minh" means "the enlightened one"). Pol Pot, however, took a new name after he had come to power, concealing his former identity from the nation he was about to govern. The name he chose, although common enough among rural Cambodians (the Khmer), had no independent meaning.

In making this bizarre, self-effacing gesture, Saloth Sar/Pol Pot was behaving true to form. Beginning in the 1950s, he preferred working in secret to living in the open. When Pol Pot came to power in 1976, it took analysts more than a year to identify him with certainty as a former schoolteacher named Saloth Sar who had been the secretary of the Cambodian Communist party since 1963. Pol Pot admitted his original name offhandedly to an interviewer in 1979, several months after he had been driven from power.

Over the years this extraordinarily reclusive figure concealed, clouded, and falsified so many details about his life that it is not surprising that there is even some confusion about his date of birth. North Korean radio announced in 1977 (before Pol Pot had been identified as Saloth Sar) that he had been born in 1925. French colonial records prepared in Cambodia in the 1950s, however, state that he was born on May 25, 1928. The second date, which leaves less time unaccounted for, seemed more plausible than the earlier one to many writers but has been contradicted by Saloth Sar's siblings in recent interviews. Pol Pot himself insisted on the earlier date in his interview with

Nate Thayer in 1997. For these reasons, 1925 is now the preferred year of birth.[1]

Saloth Sar's parents were ethnic Khmer. He was born in the village of Prek Sbauv, less than two miles west of the provincial capital of Kompong Thom, some ninety miles north of Phnom Penh. His father, Pen Saloth, was a prosperous farmer with nine hectares of rice land, several draft cattle, and a comfortable tile-roofed house. Saloth Sar's mother, Sok Nem, was widely respected in the district for her piety and good works. Sar was the eighth of nine children, two of whom were girls. Five of the nine survived into the 1990s.[2]

Palace Connections

What set the family apart from others in the region were its connections with the Royal Palace in Phnom Penh. Saloth Sar's cousin Meak joined the royal ballet in the 1920s in the closing years of the reign of King Sisowath (r. 1904–1927). She soon became a consort of the king's eldest son, Prince Sisowath Monivong, and bore him a son, Kossarak, shortly before Monivong became king in 1927. She held the favored position of *khun preab me neang*—literally, "lady in charge of the women"—from which she controlled the women of the palace. The post was abolished after Monivong's death, but Meak continued to live near the Royal Palace and was attached to the *corps de ballet* as a senior teacher until the early 1970s.

Saloth Sar's family enjoyed other royal connections. In the late 1920s, Sar's older brother Loth Suong went to Phnom Penh to work at the palace as a clerk. Soon after, their sister Saloth Roeung (nicknamed Saroeun) joined the ballet and at some point in the 1930s became a consort of King Monivong. Suong worked in the palace as a clerk until 1975 and in the early 1940s married a dancer, Chea Samy. Saroeun, a favorite consort of the king, returned to Kompong Thom after Monivong's death in 1941 and eventually married a local policeman.[3]

In 1934 or 1935, when Saloth Sar was nine years old, he and his older brother Chhay were sent by their parents to live with Meak and Suong in Phnom Penh. Sar probably would have preferred the relatively carefree life of Prek Sbauv to the more demanding one of being raised by busy relatives in a strange city. Informal adoptions by prosperous relatives are a traditional feature of Cambodian life and therefore should not be taken as indicating estrangement between children and their natural parents. In fact, although Sar's brother and sister-in-law have insisted that Sar got along well with his parents, he is not known to have mentioned them in conversations with other people. This silence, however, may be related to a conscious effacement of personal information rather than to animosity. There is no evidence that he had conflicts with his father of the sort that characterized the adolescent years of Stalin, Mao Zedong, and other prominent political figures. Indeed, his sister told an interviewer in 1997 that Saloth Sar had come back to Prek Sbauv for his father's funeral in the late 1950s and contributed to the cost of erecting a memorial *stupa*. In later life, Sar never mentioned his palace connections. Instead, he tended to emphasize his rural origins.

Soon after arriving in the capital, Saloth Sar spent several months as a novice at Vat Botum Vaddei, a Buddhist monastery near the palace that was favored by the royal family. At such a young age and recently separated from his parents, Sar must have been traumatized by the solemn discipline of the monastery, even though there would have been other little boys with shaven heads wearing yellow robes with him. At the Vat Botum Vaddei he learned the rudiments of Buddhism and became literate in Khmer. Sar was also forced to be obedient. Ironically, for someone who embraced atheism and xenophobia so fervently in later life, this brief period was the only time in his formal education (which lasted until 1952) in which Khmer rather than French was the language of instruction.[4]

Loth Suong and Chea Samy, who looked after Saloth Sar in the 1940s, maintained that he was an even-tempered, polite, unremarkable child. As a primary student, Samy told the Australian journalist James Gerrand, Sar "had no difficulties with other students, no fights or quarrels." In examining his early years, I found no traumatic events and heard no anecdotes that foreshadow his years in power. People who met him as an adult found his self-effacing personality, perhaps a carryover from the image he projected as a child, hard to connect with his fearsome behavior in the 1970s. In Loth Suong's words, "The contemptible Pot [Khmer *a-Pot*] was a lovely child."[5]

Phnom Penh in the 1930s

When Sar was growing up in the 1930s, Phnom Penh was a sleepy, sun-drenched town that had been established as the capital of a French protectorate in 1866. As far as Europe and America were concerned, Phnom Penh was at the back of the world. The city had the form of a rectangle, running north-south along the western bank of the Tonle Sap River, which flowed into the much larger Mekong River at that point. Many public buildings, such as the post office, the library, and the railroad station, were reminiscent of their counterparts in provincial France. So were the tree-lined avenues radiating from the public gardens to the north and the shaded promenades along the river. In 1936, roughly half of its population of 100,000 were immigrant Chinese and Vietnamese, who dominated the commercial sector. Its 45,000 Cambodians lived around the palace, as monks in the monasteries or as bureaucrats, farmers, artisans, and petty traders in the southern and western sectors of the city. There, the Cambodians' bamboo and wooden houses—raised on stilts and surrounded by mango and banana trees, with domestic animals roaming underneath—were indistinguishable from rural dwellings. In those days, most Cambodians chose or drifted into careers in government, farming, or religion, leaving commercial affairs to the Chinese and Vietnamese. Vietnamese immigration into Cambodia was encouraged by the French, who found them more "vigorous" and better educated (in French) than the Khmer and welcomed them into the middle ranks of the colonial civil service.[6]

The center of Phnom Penh contained a bustling commercial quarter of Chinese shops, warehouses, eating stalls, and markets. To the west, parallel to the river, ran shaded streets and boulevards lined with the stucco-covered villas of French civil servants, Chinese businessmen, and the French-educated Cambodian elite. At the northern edge of the city, the small hill (*phnom*) that gave the city its name was crowned by a seventeenth-century monastery and several Buddhist reliquaries (*chedi*). The area had been landscaped by the French into a 25-acre park, with a small zoo, a floral clock, some statuary, a bandstand, and several outdoor cafés.[7]

Roughly half a mile south of the *phnom*, facing the river, was the Royal Palace, whose main buildings had been designed by French architects in a Thai-Cambodian style in the early 1900s. Set back from the foreshore behind manicured lawns, the white and cream buildings, with their green-and-orange-tiled roofs glittering in the sun, resembled the Buddhist temples scattered throughout the city and gave passersby a glimpse of a resplendent, ethereal world.

That world came to life whenever the *corps de ballet* performed for the king and his guests, enacting scenes and stories taken from Indian mythology at a painstakingly slow pace to the music of xylophones, flutes, and Indian-style stringed instruments. Most of the more than three hundred dancers had been recruited into the troupe before they were ten years old; the leading dancers were in their twenties. Some performances were keyed to the Buddhist calendar or to brahmanical ceremonies peculiar to the palace. Others were in honor of important visitors to Phnom Penh. The performances, which lasted for several hours, occurred at night when it was cooler. They depicted a gold-encrusted world of princes and princesses, hermits, demons, and magical beasts. Like the puppet theater in Java, which was also based on classical Hindu stories, the dances had strong religious overtones. Through them, the dancers gained access to the supernatural forces that affected people's lives and were thought to govern the agricultural year.[8]

It is easy to imagine Saloth Sar in the 1930s huddled at the edge of the stage watching the masked and powdered dancers, trained by his cousin and perhaps including his sister and his brother's wife, perform by the light of hundreds of candles (and the moon). Each dance involved thousands of movements, each keyed to moments in a particular story and to the mythological character being portrayed. None of the gestures was improvised. Al-

Chan Chhaya Pavilion, Royal Palace, Phnom Penh. Photo by Bruce Sharp. Copyright 1991 Bruce Sharp.

though some dancers might be more beautiful or more graceful than others, their movements depended on memory, tradition, and practice—in other words, on what they had been taught—rather than on what the individual wanted to express. The dancers were vehicles for tradition rather than its interpreters. Effacing one's creativity by memorizing what the teacher imparts is an integral part of traditional Hindu and Buddhist teaching for vocations as diverse as dancing and monastic life. It also characterizes the painstaking way in which Pol Pot trained his subordinates in the Cambodian Communist party. Pol Pot's modesty as well as his teaching earned his students' admiration. Perhaps this tradition of self-concealment, combined with the costume donning and role playing and the empowerment that came from performing, helped Saloth Sar to shape his public persona—he was perceived by many throughout his career as "clean and smooth," almost as if he were a dancer hiding behind a mask.

The world of the dancers had a less glamorous side. During King Monivong's time, the women lived in an insalubrious warren of huts and cabins inside the royal compound. They passed their time gossiping and scheming, having their fortunes told and playing cards, telling off-color stories and waiting for preferment—frittering away their youth. Some had their children with them, but no nonroyal boys over twelve were allowed to live inside the palace compound. For a few dancers, like Meak, a career in the ballet led to royal patronage, prestige, and financial independence. For those who failed to catch the king's attention, it was an impoverished, unhealthy, dull existence. A dancer's life involved total dedication for limited rewards—a hermetic way of living that resembled the life of a Communist militant adopted by Saloth Sar after he came back to Cambodia from France in 1953.[9]

It is impossible to say which impressions of the palace prevailed among Saloth Sar's memories once he came to power. In the DK period, his policies seemed to reflect a deep resentment at the injustice and exploitation that many Cambodians endured daily. He may have been thinking about the dancers or about the peasants he encountered later on. He may have been thinking of his own uprooted childhood in a potentially hostile city. In any case, he appears to have had no use for the ballet as a cultural institution, perceiving it as a corrupt, counterrevolutionary element of Cambodian life—like money, rank, and property. The *corps de ballet* was disbanded when the Communists came to power.

The Weight of the Past

To the west of the palace not far from Meak's house was the museum of Khmer archaeology, built in Cambodian architectural style and opened in 1920. Here the French had assembled examples of sculpture, pottery, and bronzeware gathered from hundreds of ruined Hindu and Buddhist temples built in what became "Cambodia" between the seventh and sixteenth centuries A.D. This ancient civilization, "rediscovered" by the French, had culminated in the Angkorean empire, which flourished in northwestern Cambodia between the early ninth century A.D. and 1400. For a time, this empire dominated much of what are now southern Laos, eastern Thailand, Cambodia, and southern Vietnam. Near Angkor, the French uncovered impressive waterways and the remains of several hundred Hindu and Buddhist temples. In its heyday, around 1200, the Angkorean region, covering 100 square miles or so, sheltered more people than all of Cambodia did in the 1930s. The twelfth-century temple Angkor Wat, built to honor a Cambodian king, is the world's largest surviving religious building.

When the French naturalist Henri Mouhot was shown some of these ruins by his Cambodian hosts in 1860, he started a love affair between French scholars and Cambodia's medieval past that has lasted to this day. Starting in the 1870s soon after their protectorate had been established, French savants deciphered over one thousand ancient Khmer and Sanskrit inscriptions, named Cambodia's kings, and placed them inside a precise chronology. Although Angkor Wat had been a Buddhist sanctuary for several hundred years, many Cambodians believed that the temples had been built by supernatural creatures rather than by earlier Khmer.

French scholarship gave the Cambodians a prestigious history that as a colonized people they were not prepared to handle. The French stressed the contrast between the glories of the Angkorean empire and what they perceived as its decline in the nineteenth and twentieth centuries, between Angkorean mastery and the protectorate's dependence, between the grandeur of Angkor's kings and the impotence of those like Monivong who were selected by the French to govern colonial Cambodia. These contradictions produced a crisis of identity among educated Khmer in the 1930s and 1940s that acted as a catalyst for Cambodian nationalism. Sovereignty was a major theme in Red Khmer ideology, as it had been for previous regimes. It was thought that because the people who had built Angkor were Khmer, their descendants had extraordinary talents. "If our people were capable of building Angkor," Pol Pot said in 1977, "we can do anything." Since the 1940s, an image of Angkor Wat has appeared on nearly all Cambodian flags.[10]

In his youth Saloth Sar would certainly have been aware of Cambodia's past grandeur and French ideas about it. He would have wandered through the museum more than once. Although he probably did not visit the ruins, he would have known the figures and scenes carved on the temple walls from the gestures and costumes of the royal dancers. The Indian myths the dancers reenacted, such as the *Ramayana* and *Mahabharata*, had been recited and performed since Angkorean times. As he grew up, Sar may also have noticed the gap between the grandeur of Angkor Wat (and these legends, for that matter) and the shabby, crowded quarters of the royal dancers, between the "god-kings" of the Angkorean empire and the middle-aged monarch of the 1930s who often dressed in a French military uniform and who reigned over only a few acres of palace compound.

Phnom Penh was founded in the sixteenth century after the abandonment of Angkor. It flourished as an entrepôt until the late eighteenth century when unrest in Vietnam, dynastic disarray in Cambodia, and Thai invasions ravaged the kingdom. By then, the city had been cut off from the sea and was dependent on Vietnam for trading privileges. The first half of the nineteenth century was chaotic. In the 1840s Cambodia almost disappeared as Thai administrators took charge of much of the country west of the Mekong and the Vietnamese controlled the Cambodian royal family, the capital region, and the eastern part of the country. An uneasy peace concluded between the Thai and the Vietnamese in 1848 left most of Cambodia a Thai protectorate.[11]

The French established themselves in Cambodia in 1863, and during the colonial era, Cambodia's economy was integrated with that of France's new colony in southern Vietnam, Cochinchina. Cambodian exports of rice, corn, dried fish, timber, and other products were handled by Chinese and Vietnamese entrepreneurs in Saigon and its sister city of Cholon, while the rubber plantations established in eastern Cambodia in the 1920s were under French control. Inside Cambodia, Chinese petty traders purchased agricultural products, particularly rice, from Khmer farmers. Chinese entrepreneurs milled the rice and sent it to overseas markets. Profits from these transactions flowed to the Chinese and Sino-Khmer entrepreneurs in Phnom Penh and in provincial towns and then to the French, Chinese, and Sino-Vietnamese export houses in Phnom Penh and Saigon. The French administration levied export taxes on the crops and other taxes on the peasants, whose labor subsidized not only the palace (as it had always done) but also the colonial regime (which was staffed to a large extent by Vietnamese). Years later, spokesmen for Democratic Kampuchea compared Cambodia's tiny capitalist class to the colonial rulers who had "lived off the backs" of Cambodia's rural population.

In the 1870s, as these chains of economic dependency were being forged, the French left the trappings of sovereignty in the hands of Monivong's uncle King Norodom (r. 1860–1904) and his advisers. In exchange for commercial privileges, the French took charge of the country's foreign affairs, finances, and defense. In the 1880s, after an uprising against their rule, the French became more systematic in their control, and royal power was reduced. Taxes were imposed to recoup the costs of the protectorate; French residents were placed alongside Khmer governors in the provinces and superseded them; the king was given a fixed allowance and lost his power to choose and dismiss officials. In this system that paralleled the princely states of India or the regencies in the Netherlands East Indies, the king retained some prestige and some symbolic value but abdicated political control.[12]

When King Norodom died in 1904 he was succeeded by his brother Sisowath, who had cooperated with France in suppressing the Khmer rebellion in the 1880s. By then sovereignty had shifted into French hands. Sisowath was content to be a puppet ruler. He received a cash allowance from the French, who also provided him with high-grade opium to smoke. As "chiefs of state," Sisowath and his son Monivong were patrons of Cambodian Buddhism, acted as hosts for important foreign visitors, and arranged performances of the royal ballet. Although the special vocabulary used to address the king stressed his almost supernatural power, both monarchs enjoyed less freedom than their advisers and had much less power than the French. Monivong resented these conditions but could do nothing to break free. He took refuge when he could in writing poetry, visiting his model farm, and enjoying the company of his entourage.

Cambodians attached to the palace in the 1930s and 1940s, like Saloth Sar and his relations, were insulated from the Chinese and Sino-Khmer commercial sector of Phnom Penh, from the worldwide economic depression, and from the need to grow their own food. Saloth Sar inhabited this elaborate, safe, entirely Cambodian world for many years. He does not seem to have complained about it, and it would be misleading to suggest that boyhood experiences or discomfort with privilege gave birth to his radical ideas. The time he spent in and around the palace may have intensified his sense of being a Khmer, unattached to the Chinese and Vietnamese who made the protectorate a commercial success. He probably absorbed or overheard anti-French sentiments that were widespread among Cambodian officials. These attitudes may have been sharpened by his encountering more French, Chinese, and Vietnamese than he would ever have met in Prek Sbauv. More important, his affectionate family, orderly domestic life, and insulation from poverty may have helped to produce a deceptively smooth psychological surface and an equanimity that impressed observers for the rest of his career.

While Saloth Sar was growing up, few political events occurred in Cambodia. Active resistance to French rule was nonexistent after the 1880s. In the countryside, where nearly all Cambodia's three million people lived, men and women were less concerned with colonial injustice than with raising their families, patronizing the local Buddhist wat, and growing the food they needed to survive. For these Cambodians, the capital and the king were far away. They accepted kingship as a fact of life, like the seasons or exploitation (the Cambodian verb "to exploit," *chi-cho'an*, means literally "to ride and trample"). Some French observers mistook Cambodian acquiescence for affection and Cambodian good manners for respect. Others were more cautious and pointed to undercurrents of violence in Cambodian psychology and rural life, where banditry was widespread and robberies were often accompanied by rape, arson, and murder. By and large, however, Cambodia was a peaceable backwater and a success story for the French, whose rule produced the economic results they desired at a low political cost.

For rural Khmer, the early 1930s were a difficult time. Economic hardship may have prompted Saloth Sar's father to send two of his young children to Phnom Penh. The world price for Cambodian products fell while French taxes—on a per capita basis the highest in Indochina—remained more or less the same. In some parts of the country, undernourishment and underemployment became severe, but no Cambodians complained openly or took up arms.

In Vietnam, on the other hand, economic difficulties and a tradition of resistance to foreign rule had led in 1930–1931 to scattered assassinations of French officials and to several uprisings that were brutally suppressed. One of these, in central Vietnam, involved tens of thousands of peasants. It was instigated by the recently founded Indochina Communist party (ICP). The party had only a handful of Cambodian members before World War II, and although the French watched for evidence of what they called the "virus" of socialism in their Indochinese possessions, Cambodia seemed immune.

The Stirrings of Nationalism

In the late 1930s, when a more tolerant government held power in France, Cambodia felt the first stirrings of what Benedict Anderson referred to as the sense of "imagined community" that characterizes nationalist movements. Anderson argued that this development is nearly always related to the growth of print media and to amplified education emphasizing a community's individuality, expressed in part by representations of its past. His argument holds true in the Cambodian case.[13]

As Saloth Sar was beginning his primary education, three young Cambodians affiliated with the Buddhist Institute in Phnom Penh received permission from the French to publish a Khmer-language newspaper, *Nagara Vatta* ("Angkor Wat"), the first of its kind in Cambodian history. Two of these men, Son Ngoc Thanh and Sim Var, played prominent roles in Cambodian politics later on. The third, Pach Chhoeun, held ministerial posts in the 1940s and 1950s. *Nagara Vatta* reported the activities of Cambodia's elite, reprinted the texts of regulations and decrees, and in editorials urged Cambodians to "awake" and catch up with the Chinese and Vietnamese who dominated commercial life. The paper had a circulation of over five thousand copies. Its weekly readership—particularly among Buddhist monks, who passed copies from hand to hand—was probably much higher.

The French founded the Buddhist Institute in 1930 in an attempt to isolate Cambodian Buddhists from potentially disruptive influences from Thailand. In exchange, the institute exposed intellectuals in Phnom Penh to some of the political currents affecting monks in the Khmer minority in southern Vietnam. The institute acted as a clearinghouse and repository for Cambodian religious and literary texts and as a meeting place for Buddhist intellectuals (most of them monks or former monks). It also coordinated the higher phases of monastic education. The institute's journal, *Kambuja Surya* ("Cambodian Sun"), published poems, novels, proverbs, chronicles, folktales, and religious texts.[14]

When *Nagara Vatta* was founded, its editors sought royal patronage for it, but they were rebuffed by Monivong's eldest son, Prince Sisowath Monireth, who told them brusquely that in his opinion education was a waste of time, because better-educated Khmer would be "difficult to govern." The editors then turned to Monireth's brother-in-law Prince Norodom Suramarit, who agreed to act as a patron for the paper. He remained a close friend of Thanh, Var, and Chhoeun for many years, especially after his son, Norodom Sihanouk, became king in 1941.

The Buddhist Institute was only a few hundred yards from the palace, and Meak, Samy, and Suong probably knew the editors of *Nagara Vatta* by sight, subscribed to the paper, and approved its mildly nationalistic stance. Other readers were concentrated in the Buddhist *sangha* ("monastic order") and among graduates of Cambodia's only high school, the Lycée Sisowath in Phnom Penh. Students at the lycée in the late 1930s included several future prime ministers of Cambodia and an earnest young woman eight years older than Saloth Sar, Khieu Ponnary, the first Cambodian woman to earn a baccalaureate. She and Saloth Sar were married in 1956.[15]

Between 1936 and 1942—coincidentally the lifespan of *Nagara Vatta*—Saloth Sar attended a Catholic primary school near the palace, the Ecole

Miche. The fees were paid by Meak. Most of his classmates were the children of French bureaucrats or Catholic Vietnamese. One of them, brought up near the palace, remembered Sar as "very charming, like his [adopted] mother." No anecdotes about him have survived from this period when he became literate in French, grew familiar with Christian doctrine, and received the rudiments of a classical education. During his final years at the school, however, several events occurred that altered the course of Cambodian history and affected Saloth Sar's career.

The first of these was the Franco-Thai war of 1940–1941, which followed the fall of France to the German army and led to the annexation by the Thai of the northwestern Cambodian provinces of Battambang and Siem Reap. The loss of so much Cambodian territory infuriated King Monivong, who retired to his model farm in Kompong Chhnang. He soon became seriously ill and refused to speak French for the remaining months of his life. Saloth Sar's younger sister, Saroeun, was at the king's bedside when he died at the hill resort of Bokor in April 1941, just as the Japanese, eager to expand southward into Southeast Asia were increasing their military pressure on the French in Indochina.

It was in this intimidating atmosphere, isolated from news from home, that the governor general of French Indochina, Admiral Jean Decoux, in choosing Monivong's successor, bypassed Prince Monireth and plucked the late king's nineteen-year-old grandson, Norodom Sihanouk, from his lycée studies in Saigon to install him on the Cambodian throne.[16]

Moving to Kompong Cham

For several years, the young king was a pliable instrument of French colonial policy. The French were anxious to enhance the prestige of traditional rulers in Indochina without increasing the king's political power. As part of this campaign, they decided to establish a junior high school (collège) in Cambodia's third largest city, Kompong Cham, and name it after the king. The new school replaced a collège in Battambang, which was being administered by the Thai. Battambang was Cambodia's second largest city and its most prosperous province, but Kompong Cham came close behind. In the 1920s the French had established rubber plantations in the province, and farmers had set up profitable market gardens and silkworm hatcheries along the Mekong. Small industries in the region produced silk, tobacco, lumber, and cotton textiles. With its vigorous economy dominated by the Cham, Vietnamese and Chinese minorities, Kompong Cham was also the most cosmopolitan province in the kingdom.

Twenty boys from various Cambodian provinces were selected as the first class to attend the Collège Norodom Sihanouk in 1942. All of them were to be boarders. Saloth Sar was chosen as part of the contingent from Kompong

Thom. Unfortunately, the date of his move to Kompong Cham is unknown, so it is impossible to say if he saw the anti-French demonstration in Phnom Penh on July 20, 1942, a demonstration that was quickly absorbed into Cambodian nationalist mythology. It was the most important political event in Cambodia in the early 1940s and the first mass outburst against the French in over twenty years.

In September 1941, just before Sihanouk's coronation, Admiral Decoux agreed to permit Japanese troops to station themselves in Indochina; in exchange, Japan would allow France to retain administrative control. Encouraged by Japan's triumphant occupation of most of Southeast Asia in the first four months of 1942, and perhaps supported psychologically and financially by Japan's secret police, some Cambodians saw the situation as an opportunity to put pressure on the French for political concessions. In July 1942, two Cambodian monks were arrested by the French for preaching anti-French sermons to the local militia. In their haste to bring the monks to justice, the French failed to have them removed from the sangha, and this sacrilege infuriated Buddhists in Phnom Penh. On July 20, Son Ngoc Thanh and Pach Chhoeun organized a demonstration that involved more than five hundred monks and perhaps as many civilians. Led by Chhoeun, the group marched on the office of the French chief administrator (*résident supérieur*). Thousands—including the French police—watched from the sidewalks of the city's major boulevard. The Japanese, to Thanh's chagrin, gave the demonstrators no support. When Chhoeun presented a petition to the French authorities, he was arrested and bundled off to prison. Over the next few days, a handful of his colleagues were rounded up. Thanh went into hiding and soon escaped to Battambang, where he petitioned the Japanese emperor to be allowed to live in Japan. Permission arrived several months later, and Thanh spent the last two years of the war living in Tokyo under an assumed name.

Whether he had watched the demonstration or not, Saloth Sar would have heard about it from contemporaries and relatives, although politics did not yet preoccupy him or his fellow students. The boys were excited by their new school and formed a tightly knit group. All the classes were conducted in French, and students were discouraged from speaking Khmer among themselves. They studied literature, history, geography, mathematics, science, and philosophy, played soccer and basketball, learned to play musical instruments (Saloth Sar's was the violin), and staged plays. One graduate recalled a production of Molière's *Le Bourgeois Gentilhomme* starring a student named Hu Nim who later joined the Communist party and became minister of information in Democratic Kampuchea. In the class below Saloth Sar, the eldest son of a Kompong Cham judge, Khieu Samphan, was singled out by his contemporaries as intelligent, ambitious, and aloof. After studies in France, where he became a Communist, Samphan became Democratic Kampuchea's ceremonial chief of state. In 1977 he took on the job of supervising the work of the

Communist party's Central Committee. By then he had served the Communist movement faithfully for twenty years. Others who attended the school with Saloth Sar and later became Communists were Hou Youn and Khieu Komar.[17]

The students' favorite teacher in those years was Khvan Siphan, who arrived in 1945 to teach them mathematics, physics, and philosophy. Several former graduates remembered Siphan, then in his twenties, as "honest and inspiring" and singled him out because of his teaching skills, his fondness for the students, and his fair dealings. "He was honest, loving, and helpful," one of them recalled. These traits contrasted sharply with the autocratic demeanor of the French teachers at the school, whose names the graduates failed to mention. In view of Saloth Sar's later success as a teacher and his reputation for fairness, it is tempting to see Khvan Siphan as the first of several role models he chose to emulate.[18]

These young men must have observed the gap between the grandeurs of French history as communicated at school and the beleaguered position of the French themselves in the early 1940s. As the students learned about France's "civilizing mission" (mission civilisatrice), they knew that France was occupied by Germany, that Battambang and Siem Reap had been taken over by Thailand, and that Japanese troops were stationed in Kompong Cham. The once omnipotent French were almost powerless.

Saloth Sar is remembered by contemporaries in Kompong Cham as a mediocre student. "His manner was straightforward, pleasant, and very polite," one of them said. Another recalled that Sar "thought a lot, but said very little," while a third noted that he spent much of his spare time playing basketball and soccer: "He was a pretty good player, but not outstanding." Saloth Sar seemed to have had no clear ambitions. He was content to drift along, enjoying his companions without making a strong impression on them, secure in the knowledge that he was among friends and would always be welcome in Phnom Penh and Prek Sbauv.

Ironically, in view of the paths they followed later, Saloth Sar's closest friend at the school was Lon Non, an official's son from Kompong Cham. Lon Non's oldest brother, Lon Nol, became president of the Khmer Republic in 1970, leading his country to defeat at the hands of the Cambodian Communists, led by Sar, and the Vietnamese Communists. There is no evidence that the friendship with Lon Non survived Sar's politicization in the 1950s. Under the republic, Non was a political troubleshooter for his intellectually limited brother. As defeat loomed in 1975, Lon Non, by then a general, hoped to capitalize on his friendships with the Communists who had gone to school with him in Kompong Cham. He lingered in Phnom Penh after it was captured, certain that these old friends would remember him and that he could reach an arrangement with them. He was executed within forty-eight hours.[19]

In late 1944 the war in the Pacific reached a crescendo, and the students in Kompong Cham experienced some of its effects. Phnom Penh was bombed by Allied aircraft in February 1945, and American bombing of coastal shipping isolated southern Vietnam from the less prosperous north where severe famines killed tens of thousands of people. Communist guerrillas in northern Vietnam, calling themselves the Viet Minh, began to attack isolated Japanese positions. To the west, the Thai government began to drift into the Allied camp. In Europe, where most of France had been liberated from German control, a new French government under General Charles de Gaulle pledged that it would assist Great Britain and the United States in their war against Japan. De Gaulle also promised to restore French rule in Indochina. Sensing a change in the political atmosphere, some French military officers and civil administrators in the colony began working surreptitiously for the Gaullist cause.

The Japanese response to these developments was swift and unexpected. On March 9, 1945, they staged a *coup de force* throughout Indochina, imprisoning French officials and military personnel and placing other French citizens under house arrest. Soon after, the Japanese asked the rulers of Vietnam, Laos, and Cambodia to declare that their kingdoms were independent. King Sihanouk complied on March 11. The French protectorate, considered by nearly everyone in Cambodia to be a fact of life, had been unceremoniously blown away.[20]

For the students in Kompong Cham, the rest of the year was marked by a relaxation of discipline, for their French teachers were interned and less-experienced Khmer teachers like Kvan Siphan took their places. The boys were excited by news from Phnom Penh that Son Ngoc Thanh had returned from Japan in May and that the third anniversary of the monks' demonstration had been celebrated by a parade of more than ten thousand people marching past the Royal Palace. By then, Thanh was acting as Cambodia's foreign minister.

The closing months of 1945 were filled with possibilities for sweeping political change. Among the Vietnamese workforce on the rubber plantations of Kompong Cham and across the border in Vietnam, the Viet Minh recruited followers, distributed arms, and conducted propaganda sessions. There is no evidence that Saloth Sar paid much attention to these developments, but like other students at the collège he would certainly have been aware of them.

In August, just before Japan's surrender, Son Ngoc Thanh became Cambodia's prime minister. For two months he struggled to keep the kingdom independent. In September French military units filtered back into Cambodia, liberated the officials interned in March, and gradually reasserted their control. In October they arrested Thanh, whom they accused of being a traitor. He was tried in Saigon in 1946 and then exiled to France. Faced with widespread violence in Cochinchina and fearful of similar trouble in Cambodia, the French expressed a willingness to deal with the Cambodians face-to-face rather than merely reestablishing the protectorate. After negotiating with Prince Monireth, who had replaced Son Ngoc Thanh, they proposed in early 1946 to grant Cambodia a constitution and to allow political parties to be formed. King Sihanouk, who had enjoyed independence while it lasted, went along with their suggestions.

Back in Phnom Penh

We know nothing of Saloth Sar's activities in 1946. He seems to have left the Collège Sihanouk in 1947, because the following year he was enrolled as a carpentry student at the Ecole Technique at Russey Keo, a northern suburb of Phnom Penh. Several of his fellow students from Kompong Cham, including Hou Youn, Hu Nim, and Khieu Samphan, had gone to the more prestigious Lycée Sisowath. It is unclear whether Saloth Sar genuinely wanted to have a technical education or if, as he admitted in 1978, he had failed to pass the examinations that would have allowed him to pursue a baccalaureate. We know that he took the examinations in August 1948, so the latter explanation seems more likely.[21]

Saloth Sar's stint at the Ecole Technique placed him in contact with less-privileged young people, many of whom were alienated from the French and from the country's traditional elite. As he dirtied his hands, stepping down from his French education and his palace connections, he was still part of a privileged minority. By 1947 only a few thousand other Cambodians had progressed as far as he had in education. In 1948 he was among seventy-seven students in the protectorate who took entrance examinations for the ly-cée system. A year later he was among the first hundred men and women sent to France with government scholarships. His conversion to political activism and socialist ideals occurred against this privileged background and before he had any experience working for a living.

Many of Saloth Sar's contemporaries followed the same path he did, but most of them earned at least one diploma, came from a less-cosseted milieu, and made more of an impression on people than Saloth Sar did. No one I met in the course of my research who knew Saloth Sar before 1952 admitted picking him as a potential leader or professional success. Here again, we encounter the question of Sar's personality. Was he deliberately effacing himself, was he genuinely mediocre, or was he indifferent to making a strong impression?

His classmates at the Ecole Technique were hardly peasants, but they came from lower strata in Cambodian society than did the students in Kompong Cham or at the Ecole Miche. One of them, Sok Knol, was the son of a minor official who later became prominent in the Communist movement before being purged in 1978. With classmates like this, Sar's polite, easygoing manner would not have caused offense, and he may well have found their interests less intimidating than those of his academically gifted friends in Kompong Cham. Unfortunately no anecdotes of his time at the Ecole Technique have surfaced, and even the dates of his enrollment are uncertain, although Loth Suong and Chea Samy stated on several occasions that Sar went there immediately after his time in Kompong Cham.

An important occurrence in these years was Saloth Sar's friendship with Ieng Sary, a student at the Lycée Sisowath. After befriending each other in 1947, Sar received a government scholarship in 1949 and Sary received one in 1951. The two spent time together in Paris, where they became members of the French Communist party. They married sisters, and after Sary returned to Cambodia in 1957 they were Communist militants in Phnom Penh. In 1963 they left the capital together for the maquis. With a handful of close associates, they guided the Cambodian revolution and the affairs of the Communist party of Kampuchea while it was in power.

Ieng Sary was born and raised among the Cambodian minority of Cochinchina. His father, Kim Ream, was a prosperous landowner. When Ream died, Sary, still a young boy, was sent to live with relatives in the Cambodian province of Prey Veng. He was given the name Ieng Sary, which sounded more Khmer than his real name, Kim Trang. He also had his birth date altered to fall within the age limits set by the French for enrollment in primary school. By 1942 or 1943, having done exceptionally well as a student, he went to Phnom Penh for further education. In 1945 Sary was awarded a scholarship at the Lycée Sisowath. He soon attracted attention for his intellectual powers and his interest in political action. In the turbulence of 1945–1946, before Saloth Sar met him, Sary had become a political animal. Like many of Sar's close associates over the years, he made a stronger impression on people than Saloth Sar did. He was the more forthcoming of the two and made friends more easily. Being more abrasive than Sar, he also made more enemies.[22]

Working for the Democrats

Under the agreement reached between Monireth and the French in early 1946, several political parties soon appeared on the Cambodian scene. Only the Democratic party *(Kanakpak procheaneathipdei)* offered an innovative program and had roots in the nationalist traditions of *Nagara Vatta* and the monks' demonstration. Those who supported the party included monks and former monks, teachers, young civil servants, and most graduates of and senior students at the Lycée Sisowath (for example, Ieng Sary). The party was the first political organization in Cambodia to be oriented toward the future and away from the status quo. Other more-conservative parties, one secretly financed by the French, also came into being at this time. They attracted much less support.

The leader of the Democrats, Prince Sisowath Yuthevong, had just returned home after fifteen years in France. He impressed and inspired nearly everyone who met him. He came equipped with doctorates in mathematics and astronomy and with connections to the French Socialist party. Furthermore, his long absence from Cambodia and his estrangement from palace intrigue meant that he was not entangled like so many of his royal cousins in nets of patronage, protocol, and obligation. To the timidity and stagnation of Cambodian politics in 1946, Yuthevong brought new insights and hope.[23] The first test of the Democrats' popularity came in September 1946, when the party fielded candidates for a consultative assembly that was to approve the constitution being drafted. The Democrats won fifty of the sixty-seven seats; the French-sponsored Liberals gained fourteen; the remaining three were won by independents.

Prince Yuthevong and his colleagues redrafted the somewhat royalist text of the constitution until it resembled the French constitution, which granted more power to an elected National Assembly than to the largely ceremonial chief of state. Although Yuthevong died suddenly in July 1947, the Democrats won the elections to the National Assembly held later in the year, capturing fifty-four seats out of a total of ninety. According to Keng Vannsak, who knew Saloth Sar and Ieng Sary in Paris in the early 1950s, the two young men worked for the Democratic party in this campaign.[24]

Between the elections and his departure for France on a scholarship in August 1949, Saloth Sar attended the Ecole Technique and sat for a lycée entrance examination, which he probably failed, in August 1948. This period was one of increasing turbulence on the Cambodian political scene. From 1947 to 1949 Sihanouk and the French became increasingly disenchanted with the Democrats. They suspected, correctly, that the party wanted to govern Cambodia without their supervision or advice. In 1947, before the assembly elections, the French jailed several members of the consultative assembly on trumped-up charges. The men were held for several months and some of them were tortured; they were never brought to trial and eventually were released. In 1948, following scandals involving members of the assembly, Sihanouk dissolved the body and began governing by decree, taking advice from party dissidents and members of parties that had failed to win any seats in 1947.

In the meantime, armed resistance to the French had broken out in the countryside. Some rebel bands were funded by the Thai and called themselves Khmer Issarak ("Liberated Khmers"); others were made up of former bandits and fugitives from the French police. In the areas bordering Vietnam, resistance was coordinated by the Indochina Communist party, which was dominated by the Vietnamese. Although the party had ostensibly been abolished in 1946 as part of a united front strategy to oppose the French, it had remained secretly in existence. As fighting intensified in Indochina, the party sought to enroll members from Laos and Cambodia as well as from Vietnam. Two of its most prominent Cambodian members, who joined the party during World War II, were former monks who took the revolutionary names of Son Ngoc Minh (Achar Mean) and Tou Samouth. Both men had been raised in southern Vietnam and were fluent in Vietnamese. By 1949 Tou Samouth was already playing a major role in the resistance, and he became Saloth Sar's patron when Sar was a Communist militant in the 1950s. For the time being, however, the Democrats rather than the Indochina Communist party, and politics rather than armed struggle, attracted the loyalties of the educated Cambodian elite, including Saloth Sar.[25]

It is unclear why Saloth Sar, with his undistinguished academic record, was awarded a scholarship in 1949 for further study in France. In an interview, his elder brother denied that the offer owed anything to his palace connections. It seems more likely that after working with Ieng Sary he had come to the favorable notice of such Democrats as Chheam Van, Cambodia's new prime minister and the former principal of the Lycée Sisowath, and Ieu Koeuss, who won a landslide victory as a Democratic candidate in Phnom Penh. The Democrats controlled the Ministry of Education, which bestowed scholarships, and many of those sent to France had connections with the party. One of the scholarship students, Mey Mann, gave this explanation to Steve Heder, who interviewed him in 1997. Another explanation for the Democrats' choosing Saloth Sar is that it was Democratic policy, inherited from *Nagara Vatta*, to encourage Cambodians to adopt trades like radio-electricity, carpentry, tailoring, and photography, which had been monopolized by the Vietnamese minority. Saloth Sar, a technical student already fluent in French, was an ideal candidate.[26]

In accepting a scholarship, Saloth Sar again joined an elite—as he had done each time he enrolled at a school. Since 1946, only one hundred Cambodian men and women had been awarded scholarships for tertiary studies in France. Most of them were still there in 1949. The cohort included members of Cambodia's most prominent families as well as several who later became important politicians.[27]

Whether or not Saloth Sar and the others owed their scholarships to Democratic patrons, the party organized a dinner in Phnom Penh in August 1949 to honor the students scheduled to sail for France over the next two months. The dinner took place ten days before Saloth Sar and twenty colleagues were to board the S.S. *Jamaique* in Saigon for the month-long ocean trip. It is tempting to imagine the clamorous Chinese restaurant, cooled by ceiling fans, with Ministry of Education officials toasting these young men and women as the hope of Cambodia, and Saloth Sar's shy smile in response to this attention and at the thought of what lay ahead. Once again, without much effort on his part, he had joined a vanguard. He probably was not looking forward to further studies, but he undoubtedly was thrilled by the prospect of a change of scene.[28]

CHAPTER THREE

— ■ —

Becoming a Communist, 1949–1953

The First Year in Paris

For nearly a month, the *Jamaique* steamed west through the Indian Ocean and the Red Sea, reversing the romanticized voyage to Indochina depicted in many colonial novels. Of the twenty-one Cambodian students aboard, only three were more than twenty-three years old; six were under twenty. Except for one or two who had spent their childhood in Cochinchina, none of them had been outside of Cambodia. This journey was their first adventure. Five of them—Chau Seng, Mey Mann, Mey Phat, Saloth Sar, and Uch Ven—later rose to prominence in the Cambodian Communist movement. They became Communists when it was the popular thing to do—during the early 1950s under the unstable Fourth Republic in France when a Communist-controlled resistance movement in Cambodia bravely confronted the French colonial rulers. This period marked the heyday of the Communist party of France. The Khmer students' time in Paris coincided with the last years of Stalin's life and the apotheosis of the cult of personality surrounding him. The Communist party, one of the strongest in France, was considered the most Stalinist party outside eastern Europe. The years 1949–1953 also marked the victory of communism in China and the confrontation between Communist and anticommunist armies in the Korean War. To many young Khmer and millions of young people in France, communism seemed to be the wave of the future.[1]

During the sea voyage, however, it is unlikely that the young Cambodians gave politics much thought. Most of them probably supported the Democrats at home, and their political views probably mingled hero worship for Son Ngoc Thanh with vague hopes for Cambodia's independence. What preoccupied them was not Cambodia's future, but their own. What would France

25

be like? they asked each other. What will happen to us? Unlike his new acquaintances, Saloth Sar had been uprooted and transplanted several times. Plucked out of his parents' village as a little boy, he had been dropped into a French primary school in Phnom Penh and then sent as a boarder to Kompong Cham. His time at the Ecole Technique had been another readjustment. Therefore, he was probably calmer, more self-assured, and less homesick than the others.

The ship docked in Marseilles in late September. The Cambodians scattered to destinations determined beforehand by the Cambodian Ministry of Education. Most of them traveled from Marseilles by train. To reach the station from the port, they had to climb a wide stairway flanked by giant statues depicting France's overseas possessions in allegorical form. The statues are still there. One of them, "Our Possessions in Asia," is a pubescent girl in Angkorean dishabille (Cambodia) lounging on an elbow as she is offered a Buddha image and some fruit by younger females who are naked to the waist (Laos and Vietnam). The tableau encapsulated three stereotypical views the French had of the Cambodians and Indochinese: They were childish, exotic, and sexually adventurous. Saloth Sar and his friends had been subjected to these stereotypes in school. In the chilly air, they hurried past the statues to catch their trains.[2]

Saloth Sar started out in Paris, as many Cambodian students did, by taking a room in the Indochinese pavilion of the Cité Universitaire, a complex of dormitories for French and foreign students on the southern edge of the city. "In the first year," Pol Pot recalled in 1978, "I worked rather hard. I was a fairly good student." Aside from a few short holidays, he spent more than three years in Paris. We know that he enrolled for courses connected with radio-electricity, and we know where he lived in 1951 and 1952. We have scattered, contradictory impressions from Cambodians who knew him at this time. His academic career made little if any difference to him. He took no examinations and lost his scholarship as a result. By the time he left for home in December 1952 he had gained no formal degree.[3]

The most important event in this period from a biographical perspective was that Saloth Sar became a member of the French Communist party. This move probably occurred in 1952. When he returned to Cambodia, he joined the Vietnamese-dominated Communist resistance against the French and became a member of the Indochina Communist party, since there was not yet an autonomous Cambodian party he could join. These affiliations and Sar's long entanglement with Vietnam colored the rest of his life.

His associations and friendships with other Cambodians studying in Paris also had a decisive influence on his career. His most significant relationships were with radicals Thiounn Mumm and Keng Vannsak, who arrived in Paris in 1946, and with his friend Ieng Sary, who arrived toward the end of 1950.

Thiounn Mumm was a member of the most powerful nonroyal family in Phnom Penh. His grandfather, known merely as Thiounn, amassed a fortune as the minister of palace affairs under Kings Norodom, Sisowath, and Monivong. Mumm's father, Thiounn Hol, was the first Cambodian to earn lycée and university qualifications in France. Mumm, a few years older than Saloth Sar, studied at the University of Hanoi until 1945, when he returned briefly to Phnom Penh. In 1946 he was among the first Cambodian students to be sent to France. Thiounn Mumm specialized in applied science and later had a distinguished academic career. In 1951, it seems, he joined the French Communist party. Mumm was probably responsible for bringing Sar into the party in 1952.[4]

Keng Vannsak's background was less privileged, although he enjoyed some connections with the royal family. During World War II, he attended the Lycée Sisowath, where he excelled in literary studies and befriended the talented young radical Ieng Sary. Vannsak went to France to study Cambodian linguistics. Although drawn toward the left of the political spectrum, he never became a Communist. As an ardent nationalist with antiroyalist leanings, Vannsak was closer to Saloth Sar than Thiounn Mumm was and so helped form some of Sar's political ideas.[5]

The "City of Light" had retained a reputation for over a century as a vibrant intellectual center. In 1949 artists, politicians, writers, philosophers, and musicians mingled in the contending schools of existentialism, postimpressionism, phenomenology, Gaullism, and communism, to name only five. New developments in these fields and many others made Paris an intoxicating place for young people engaged in tertiary study, as did the city's traditions of liberty and revolutionary thought. Political parties, and the newspapers affiliated with them, flourished across the ideological spectrum, giving rise to lively, acrimonious debate. For students of Saloth Sar's generation, the late 1940s and early 1950s were filled with passionate arguments about politics, art, and philosophy, with close friendships and late hours, with a sense of belonging to a world that was opening up in the aftermath of World War II. To understand Saloth Sar's conversion to communism, we must place him among the soot-blackened buildings, leaf-strewn avenues, and smoke-filled cafés of the Latin Quarter among thousands of young men and women who were making similar decisions. By 1951, if not before, he was caught up in a wave of optimism about the potentialities of the Communist movement. Unlike many of his contemporaries, Saloth Sar never abandoned communism or regretted his decision. Instead, he made a life-long commitment to the cause.

To understand the nationalist fervor he brought to this commitment, we must realize how estranged Saloth Sar was from his surroundings. He was not really at home in France. In the cold, crowded streets and cramped student quarters, he often must have felt lonely and disoriented. Although he spoke and read French fluently, he had no connections with the country. Unlike Mumm and Vannsak, who married French women, Sar made little effort to assimilate. Apparently, most of his friends were Khmer. Perhaps in this exile, he became more consciously Cambodian than he had been at home.

His first known action in Paris, however, was surprisingly adventurous. For summer vacation in 1950 he and seventeen other Cambodians volunteered with French students in a labor battalion in the renegade Communist state of Yugoslavia, which had broken off its smothering alliance with the Soviet Union two years before. Sar's decision demonstrates that he was not yet a member of the French Communist party, for party members who traveled to Yugoslavia in July 1950 were summarily dismissed. His action, however, may have been only tangentially political. Becoming a volunteer probably seemed like a pleasant way to pass the summer. Indeed, speaking to Nate Thayer in 1997, Pol Pot recalled, "I went [to Yugoslavia] because it was vacation time and I had no money . . . we went just for pleasure."

Whatever his motives were, Saloth Sar worked for a month as a manual laborer in a Communist country at an exciting stage of its development. The regime was led by the World War II resistance hero Josip (Tito) Broz, who, in breaking with the Soviets, had drawn venomous attacks from the USSR and from other Communist parties in Europe. Between 1948 and the end of 1950, Tito's Yugoslavia stood alone, isolated from the West and expecting a Soviet invasion. To mobilize his people, Tito engaged them in massive construction projects. This nationally based communism, an affront to Stalin, appealed to anticommunist intellectuals in France, including members of the Socialist party, who were dismayed by the French Communist party's subservience to the Soviet Union. In 1949–1950, as Pierre Brocheux has recalled, lycées in Paris became a battleground for Socialists trying to recruit students to work in Yugoslavia and Communists trying to keep the students at home. Sar was probably caught up in this recruitment drive.[6] Twenty-eight years later, he told Yugoslavian journalists that he had spent "more than a month" working as a manual laborer in Zagreb. Smiling, he said, "I had occasion to meet Yugoslavs, and I attended a Yugoslav folklore performance."[7]

It is tempting to speculate about what impressed Saloth Sar while he was in Yugoslavia. Certainly he had never seen social mobilization or public works on such a large scale, nor had he worked so hard as a member of a team. That summer, Yugoslavia was suffering from a severe drought, and famine, food riots, and a Soviet invasion were genuine possibilities. It was a dramatic time. Yugoslavia confronted these challenges much as the Soviet Union had done in the early 1920s during the era of "war communism"—by mobilizing the people's revolutionary will. Sar followed this example when he came to power.

Saloth Sar's response to Yugoslavia was probably similar to that of Ieu Yang, another Cambodian who went there. Yang wrote a letter of thanks to the Yugoslavian authorities in which he described his experiences in glowing terms, using phrases that foreshadowed some of those in favor under Pol Pot's regime twenty-five years later. "Everywhere," Yang wrote, "the People's Federal Republic of Yugoslavia resembles an enormous work site where factories, roads, railways and hydraulic centers are being built. This effort is also worthy of praise because the strength of all the people, united around their leaders, gives them the chance of gaining successive victories, knowing that it is a question of national survival."[8] When Sar returned to Paris to reenroll, the study of radio-electricity must have seemed irrelevant and tame.

Political Developments in Cambodia, 1950–1951

Saloth Sar and the other Cambodian students in France followed political developments at home as closely as they could. In 1950–1951 these consisted primarily of maneuvers among political parties in Phnom Penh and the gradual estrangement of King Sihanouk from the most successful party, the Democrats. Sihanouk's hostility and the Democrats' eclipse narrowed the political options for many Khmer students in Paris. Then, in January 1950, a dramatic event in Phnom Penh shook their faith in orderly procedures and in the Democrats' long-term chances for political power: The party's charismatic leader, Ieu Koeuss, was killed by an assassin. Those who had hired the killer were never identified, but suspicions focused on the French, the king, and the freewheeling prime minister Yem Sambaur, who had taken office after Sihanouk had dissolved the Democrat-controlled National Assembly several months before. Koeuss's funeral drew an enormous crowd—a warning to Sihanouk that the Democrats were still influential.[9]

In February 1950, encouraged by the recent Communist victory in China, the Indochina Communist party, in a secret meeting of its Central Committee, called for "the active construction of independent Lao and Cambodian armies . . . mobilizing the masses . . . to participate in the liberation." The decision paved the way for the formation of rudimentary Communist parties in both countries and inadvertently laid the foundations for Saloth Sar's long career. The three parties, in turn, were to be controlled from the shadows by the Indochina Communist party whose leaders were all Vietnamese. Without the February 1950 decision, it is unlikely that Cambodian communism—or Saloth Sar's rise inside the movement—would ever have made headway.[10]

As a follow-up to this decision, the Indochina Communist party convened a ten-day study session in March at Hatien in southern Vietnam. The meeting drew together party cadre already concerned with Cambodian affairs, and it was later referred to as the meeting at which a provisional revolutionary government for Cambodia was founded. Its high point was a lengthy speech by Nguyen Thanh Son, a middle-ranking official in the Indochina Communist party who had led Vietnamese resistance troops inside Cambodia and had been recruiting Cambodian guerrillas for over a year. The text of his speech fell into the hands of the French; translated, it is over fifty pages long. It was the first detailed discussion of the prospects for revolution in Cambodia by an astute analyst of Cambodian affairs. Son's speech foreshadowed many of the difficulties Cambodian Communists like Saloth Sar would encounter. The most vexing of these, which Son perceived as an advantage to the movement, was the matter of Vietnamese domination.[11]

Son began by charging that Cambodia's political parties were "bred or directed by the French." The Democrats were the most influential. Son said that the French had had Yuthevong and Koeuss ("the last radical element of the Party") killed. Cambodia's principal mode of production, he continued, was "autarchic and family oriented"; also, he found Cambodians "honest, frank, sincere and often impulsive." Most of them were peasants who lived "in the blackest misery. They are awakening slowly but surely. . . . They form the principal force of the Khmer revolution." Son traced Cambodia's revolutionary movement to nineteenth-century resistance to the French led by "feudal or educated people" rather than peasants or workers. The problems with bringing a revolutionary party to power in Cambodia, he noted, were compounded by the fact that so few Cambodians had any Marxist-Leninist training. "The theory of Karl Marx-Lenin [sic]," he said, "must first be spread among the most evolved elements of Cambodia, whose overall cultural, social and economic status remains backward."

Nguyen Thanh Son believed in a worldwide revolution led by the Soviet Union and an Indochinese revolution led by Vietnam. Because there were no progressive Cambodian institutions, Son suggested that local Vietnamese, outnumbered by Khmer seven to one, had key roles to play. "They can bring the Khmer revolution to the same intensity [élan] as the Vietnamese revolution," he said. "They are the motor force that will start up . . . the revolutionary movement." Already the Indochina Communist party inside Cambodia was "composed for the most part of Vietnamese and does not yet have any deep roots among the Khmer people."

Son was not deterred from sponsoring a revolution for Cambodia, even when the materials were so unpromising. He perceived the peasantry on whom the revolution's success would depend as undeveloped, autarchic, disorganized, and *asleep*. The other groups that the Communists might penetrate or convert—the bourgeoisie, the Buddhist sangha, and non-Vietnamese ethnic minorities—were even more conservative. Son was probably counting on the Cambodians' hatred of the French (which in fact was not widespread) and their impatience with oppression to draw them into an armed struggle that would benefit the international Communist movement as well as the Vietnamese. Those Khmer with enough education to absorb "Marx-Lenin" were expected to accept Vietnamese guidance and control. This is precisely what Saloth Sar did when he returned to Cambodia, as a Communist, three years later.

At the beginning of 1951, a year after Son's speech, the Indochina Communist party secretly broke into three parts. The senior partner was the Vietnam Workers' party, which emerged into the open at this time. The Indochina Communist party and the rudimentary parties established in Laos and Cambodia (called People's Revolutionary parties to reflect their lower status) remained hidden. The Cambodian grouping was formally constituted, it seems, in June 1951. Its statutes were drawn up in Vietnamese and then translated into Khmer. Unlike the statutes of the Vietnam Workers' party, the Cambodian statutes failed to mention Marx or Lenin. The Cambodian party's provisional Central Committee included several Vietnamese and was headed by Son Ngoc Minh (a name chosen by the revolutionary activist Achar Mean to give people the idea that he was related to Son Ngoc Thanh). Cambodians joining this secret group were probably told that its aims were to drive the French from Indochina and to cooperate with the Vietnamese. The long-term Communist agenda of the movement was played down.

With hindsight, it is easy to dismiss Nguyen Thanh Son's analysis of Cambodia as contradictory, demeaning, and unworkable and to see the Khmer People's Revolutionary party as a lapdog of the Vietnamese. Given France's refusal to grant independence to Indochina, however, and given the Communist victories in China and eastern Europe, armed struggle was seen as a necessity, and a worldwide Communist victory was thought to be a matter of time. Thus Son's proposals seemed attractive and feasible to his listeners. In 1950–1951 hundreds of Cambodians joined the Khmer People's Revolutionary party, and later, after extensive training, a handful became members of the Indochina Communist party.

Turning to the Left

In the meantime, Saloth Sar had been joined in Paris by Ieng Sary. Sary had been involved in a student strike—labeled "Communist" by panicky French authorities—at the Lycée Sisowath after Sar had left for France. Democratic officials in the Ministry of Education had rewarded Sary and another ringleader, Rath Samoeun, for standing up to the French by giving them scholarships to study in France. One of Sary's first moves when he arrived in Paris was to look up his mentor Keng Vannsak, who helped him get settled. Soon after, Sary introduced Vannsak to Saloth Sar. In early 1951 Vannsak found Sar a furnished room on the rue Letellier, across the street from his apartment in the fifteenth arrondissement. Sar lived there until he returned to Cambodia. Vannsak, who saw a good deal of him, recalled that Saloth Sar "spent most of his time reading." Another contemporary, Mey Mann, said that Sar had "an interest in going to the movies." Pol Pot confirmed Vannsak's recollection when he told Nate Thayer in 1997:

> I looked for secondhand books that were on sale along the Seine, the old books that I loved to read. When I got money for my scholarship, I had to spend it on rent and food, so I only had 20 or 25 francs to spend, but I got a lot of books to read. For example *La grande revolution française*. I didn't understand it all, but I just read. . . . I started as a nationalist and then a patriot and then I read progressive books.[12]

Saloth Sar must also have absorbed a good deal of French literature, for when he became a teacher in Phnom Penh in the late 1950s, he knew enough nineteenth-century French poetry (Hugo, Rimbaud, Verlaine, Vigny) by heart to impress his Cambodian students. One of his favorite authors was the eighteenth-century philosopher Jean-Jacques Rousseau. It would be interesting to know what other writers influenced Sar's thinking, but he never mentioned any, aside from a brief reference to Mao Zedong's writings after Mao was dead. It is likely that, by 1952, Sar received most of his news, and formed many of his opinions, from journals produced by the French Communist party—*Humanité, Les cahiers de communisme*, and so on. He would also have been familiar with Stalin's writings, especially his widely circulated *History of the Communist Party of the Soviet Union*, which took a conspiratorial view of Soviet history and stressed the important role played by Stalin, who controlled the party and the nation but seldom mingled with ordinary people. It is tempting to picture Saloth Sar working through these turgid materials by dim light, absorbing a view of the world that emphasized conspiracies, empowerment, vigilance, and clandestinity. It would probably be misleading, however, to endow his activities at this stage with too much coherence or ambition.

In 1951 Saloth Sar met his first wife, Khieu Ponnary, who had come to France with her younger sister Khieu Thirith. Ponnary came to study Khmer linguistics, and Thirith to study English literature. During World War II, their father, a judge, had run off to Battambang with a Cambodian princess, leaving their mother to raise the family. This action may have hardened the sisters' attitudes toward the raffish Cambodian elite. In any case, they both earned baccalaureates from the Lycée Sisowath, a rare achievement for women at the time. When Ponnary arrived in France, she had already begun a distinguished career as a teacher. Thirith had become engaged to Ieng Sary while they were students in Cambodia; they were married in the summer of 1951 in the *mairie* ("town hall") of the fifteenth arrondissement. The reception drew hundreds of well-wishers, including Khmers of all political persuasions and students of many nationalities. It is tempting to date the start of Sar and Ponnary's romance to their time together in Paris, but this cannot be corroborated.[13]

Soon after their arrival in France, Ieng Sary and Rath Samoeun galvanized Vannsak and others into forming political groups. By the beginning of 1951, several young Khmer began meeting in Vannsak's apartment to discuss Marxist texts. For a while, the discussions were led by either Sary or Samoeun. Some of those who came were members of the Communist party of France, or joined it later. Others, like Vannsak and Saloth Sar, participated because of their friendship with the radicals. Still others dropped in from time to time. Pierre Brocheux, who was a member of the CPF in the 1950s and knew many Cambodians in the Cité Universitaire, called these discussion groups an "outer circle" of Communist activity—that is to say, an activity approved and monitored by the party, but accessible to nonmembers. According to Mey Mann, who took part in the discussions,

> Just as the Marxist circle secretly controlled the student movement from within, the Marxist circle itself was secretly controlled from within by . . . Communist Party members whose . . . membership was kept secret in order to protect them from retaliation by the Cambodian government and also in line with ICP practices.[14]

Others who attended the sessions included Sien An, Yun Soeurn, Hou Youn, Chi Kim An, Thiounn Mumm, and Touch Phoeun, all then or subsequently members of the French Communist party. All of them, except Thiounn Mumm and Mey Mann, were executed sooner or later as traitors in Democratic Kampuchea. Vannsak recalled discussions of such documents as Stalin's "The National Question," Lenin's "On Imperialism," and Marx's *Das Kapital.* The works, or extracts from them, were read in French. The discussions mixed French with Khmer as the young people struggled to express European political terms in their own language.[15]

It is unclear if the texts discussed by these groups were assigned by the French Communist party or if they were agreed upon informally by the group members. The party divided many foreign Communists and Communist sympathizers residing in France into language groups (*groupes des langues)* that could be organized for demonstrations and gathered into smaller discussion groups. Party members, in turn, were organized into three-person cells for discussions, demonstrations, signing petitions, selling party literature, and so on. The "Indochinese" group consisted largely of students housed in the Indochinese pavilion of the Cité Universitaire. Their common language was French. Although the Communist party cells may have included both Vietnamese and Cambodians, the discussion groups at Vannsak's apartment were restricted to Khmer.

Recollections about Saloth Sar's behavior at the meetings are contradictory. In several interviews in the 1980s, after Pol Pot had been identified as Saloth Sar, Keng Vannsak recalled that Sar attended irregularly, kept in the background, and made little impression on his colleagues. In 1975–1976, however, before the Saloth Sar/Pol Pot connection had been made, an un-named source spoke with journalist François Debré. The source, who had at-tended the discussion groups, remembered that Saloth Sar "was the most in-telligent, the most convinced, the most intransigent. It was he who animated the debates and most impressed the newcomers." Debré's source went on to quote Saloth Sar as saying, "Without a solidly built and solidly directed Party, no theory can be applied and the enemies of socialism will profit from these occasions to replace the leadership"—a view that Sar might have found in Stalin's *History of the Communist Party of the Soviet Union*. Sar allegedly con-tinued, "I will direct the revolutionary organization; I will be its secretary general, I will hold the dossiers, I will control the ministers and I will see to it that they don't deviate from the line fixed in the people's interest by the cen-tral committee."[16]

When Debré wrote his book, neither he nor his source knew the identity of Pol Pot. In fact, the source believed Pol Pot to be Rath Samoeun. Consid-ering that Sar's predictions all came true and considering his lifelong fond-ness for concealment, the last quotation, if it is accurate, is extraordinarily re-vealing. If Sar made these remarks in the heat of the moment among friends, they help to explain the long apparent hibernation I have described earlier as well as most of his conduct to April 1976 when he became prime minister of Democratic Kampuchea. Although there was nothing inevitable about his rise inside the succession of parties that constituted the Cambodian Commu-nist movement, the statements recorded by Debré suggest that everything Sar did had been calculated in the early 1950s in terms of his eventually tak-ing command. Sar also saw communism as a set of techniques that would en-able party members to gain independence for their country.

From 1951 to 1952, events in France, Cambodia, Vietnam, China, and Korea had an impact on Cambodian radicals in Paris. In Cambodia, the Democrats were preparing for their electoral campaign. Son Ngoc Thanh was still living in exile in the provincial city of Poitiers, and many of the stu-dents in Paris hoped that he might return home and lead the Democrats to victory. The students were also preoccupied by growing rifts between radi-cals and conservatives within their overseas Cambodian community. By the middle of 1951, Thiounn Mumm and many other Khmer had become Com-munists and had come to see Cambodia's independence struggle in a Marxist-Leninist framework. In August 1951, Mumm and "more than ten" others in the Marxist study group traveled to East Berlin for an International Youth Congress sponsored by the Soviet Union and attended by more than 100,000 delegates from around the world. In this exhilarating, highly orchestrated at-mosphere, the Cambodians learned for the first time of the Khmer Commu-nist resistance and the newly established Khmer People's Revolutionary party. Thiounn Mumm returned excitedly to Paris with a Cambodian Communist flag (five yellow towers on a red field) and literature of various kinds. They had been given the flag by the Viet Minh delegation to the Congress.[17]

At that point, Thiounn Mumm and his friends began working to overthrow the conservative leadership of the Cambodian students in France. They argued with other students about the upcoming elections in Cambodia. Mumm contended that forming a "homogenous minority" of dedicated, reliable radicals in the Cambodian National Assembly was more important than winning the elections. He was probably thinking along the lines of the French Communist party, which placed a higher premium on party loyalty than on compromises with other parties in France.

In 1951–1952 the French party was passing through an identity crisis. Its secretary general, Maurice Thorez, had suffered a stroke and gone to the USSR for medical treatment at the end of 1950. In his absence, which lasted until early 1953, various personalities and factions inside the party jockeyed for position, and some high-ranking members were bloodlessly purged. The party also came under increasing government repression. The leaders were united in their reverence for Stalin, then in his declining years, and in their acceptance of guidance from the Soviet Union. They supported the show trials in Czechoslovakia, where several important party leaders were made to confess, spuriously, to treason. They also opposed U.S. military actions in Europe and Korea and the Franco-American alliance (American money, French troops) that was forming to oppose Communist resistance in Indochina.

The Americans, egged on by the French, had begun to see the war in Indochina as part of a Communist conspiracy against the so-called Free World. Responding to this view, young Cambodians like Thiounn Mumm and Saloth Sar, and thousands of young people from other countries, began to see themselves as part of a revolutionary vanguard, a worldwide brotherhood, destined to fight and overwhelm the United States. A former Communist militant speaking to me in 1988 called the 1950s "the springtime of the people." These young men and, less often, women were buoyed by the huge crowds that some of them melted into in East Berlin and those they joined for manifestations organized by the Communists in Paris. The most massive of these demonstrations, in May 1952, protested against alleged bacteriological warfare by U.S. forces in Korea. Tens of thousands took part, and several hundred were arrested. The momentum of the war in Indochina and the brotherhood enjoined by the Communist party encouraged many Khmer to befriend radical students from Vietnam and elsewhere. Pierre Brocheux recalled that party members from the Indochinese states met frequently for meals in a café in the rue Gît-le-Coeur on the Left Bank.[18]

The Khmer students continued to follow events in Cambodia closely. Until the middle of 1952, many of them placed their hopes in the return to power of Son Ngoc Thanh. Since 1945 Thanh had stuck in their minds as a genuine patriot unjustly imprisoned by the French. In fact, since 1947 he had been living in the provincial city of Poitiers under a benign form of house arrest and had completed a law degree. From time to time, young Cambodians came to pay homage to him. Those who visited him included Hou Youn, Ea Sichau, Keng Vannsak, Saloth Sar, and Thiounn Mumm. Thanh greeted them all politely but made no pledges. To increasingly radicalized students like Mumm, he seemed to have few coherent political ideas. When Mumm visited him in 1951, he noticed that the French editions of Marx's and Engels's works were on his shelves. Taking a volume down, he saw that its pages were uncut.[19]

On several occasions in 1950–1951 Sihanouk pleaded with the French to allow Thanh to return. In late 1951, after the National Assembly elections had been won by the Democrats, the French relented, and Thanh went back to Phnom Penh. He was greeted by an enormous crowd. Sihanouk had probably been under pressure from the Democrats to bring Thanh home, but he may also have thought that the exile's return would split the Democratic party. The king was distressed by the warmth of support for Thanh, interpreting it astutely as expressing disapproval of his own alliance with the French.

In any case, the Democrats' election victory, Thanh's triumphant return, and the subsequent assassination of the French high commissioner in Phnom Penh, Jean de Raymond, by a Vietnamese houseboy seemed, in combination, to mark an acceleration of Cambodia's anticolonial struggle. Many students in Paris thought that Thanh would wrest Cambodia's independence from the French. Their optimism was misplaced. For several months the former prime minister did little. He refused to join the Democratic cabinet and limited his actions to quietly touring the provinces and publishing a nationalist paper, *Khmer Krauk!* ("Khmers, Awake!") whose editorials followed a Democratic line.[20]

In March 1952 the pace of events suddenly altered in a way that no one had foreseen. On the seventh anniversary of the Japanese *coup de force*, Son Ngoc Thanh left Phnom Penh, ostensibly to accompany a colleague to Siem Reap. Before reaching his destination, however, he disappeared. It soon became clear that he had joined forces with noncommunist, anti-French guerrillas operating in the region. Thanh set up a base in the forests of Siem Reap, hoping to draw together the Communist and noncommunist strands of resistance to the French. The move stunned his colleagues and opponents. A handful of young people, many from the Lycée Sisowath, soon followed him into the woods, but the Vietnamese-dominated Communist resistance, after some conversations with Thanh, refused to cooperate with him. By the end of 1952, he had become marginal to the independence struggle.[21]

Sihanouk and his French mentors were unsettled by Thanh's defection. They turned on the Democrats, whom they mistakenly suspected of sponsoring Thanh. Conservatives defeated in the 1951 elections, like Yem Sambaur and Lon Nol, joined the king in his assault. With the connivance of the French, who sent extra troops to Phnom Penh from Saigon at his request, the king dismissed the Democratic cabinet in June 1952, dissolved the National Assembly, and began governing by decree. Sihanouk promised to deliver independence within three years (a program that was later called a "royal crusade for independence"). His bold move marked his entrance onto the political stage. It also marked the end of the Democrats' participation in government, hastened the demise of Son Ngoc Thanh, and closed off a brief era of political pluralism that had begun with the elections of 1946 and 1947. The absolute monarchy that the French had encountered in Cambodia in 1863, and that they had kept under wraps for ninety years, was beginning to reemerge. Ironically, the French still thought that Sihanouk was working in their interests. In fact, he had discovered interests of his own and embarked on a campaign to gain independence for his people. His timing was superb. To many, however, his patriotism seemed belated and opportunistic.[22]

Becoming a Communist

Sihanouk's coup d'état inspired Saloth Sar's first known political writing. An eight-page essay titled "Monarchy or Democracy?" was published in a special issue of the Khmer students' magazine, *Khmer Nisut*, under the pseudonym *Khmer daom* ("Original Khmer"), a term associated by French ethnographers with the Samre and Porr people inhabiting parts of Saloth Sar's native Kompong Thom. Keng Vannsak rushed the issue into print to protest Sihanouk's actions in Phnom Penh.[23] Khmer daom's handwritten article opened by asserting that only the National Assembly and democratic rights "gave the Cambodian people a chance to breathe a little—as in the time of Prince Yuthevong, for example." Khmer daom accused Sihanouk of being an absolute monarch and defined monarchy as "a doctrine which bestows power on a small group of men who do nothing to earn their living so that they can exploit the majority of the people at every level. Monarchy is an unjust doctrine, a malodorous running sore that just people must eliminate."[24]

It is tempting to trace the ferocity of this passage to Saloth Sar's childhood spent among palace dancers exploited by the king and perhaps suffering from venereal infection. In the article Sar went on to say that monarchy was friendly to imperialism but inimical to the people, to Buddhism, and to knowledge. To back up these accusations, he pointed out that Cambodia's recent kings had been appointed by the French, while throughout Cambodia's history the people were "like animals, kept as soldiers *(pol)* or slaves *(knjom ke)*, made to work night and day to feed the king and his entourage"—an eerie foreshadowing of conditions when Saloth Sar himself came to power. To show that the monarchy was the enemy of Buddhism, Sar wrote that Cambodia's kings had placed themselves above religion, but he added that "enlightened monks" had composed a folktale in which Tmenh Chey, a "child of the people," outwits a king. A similar spirit of enlightenment and a hatred of his father's injustice had led the Buddha to desert his own noble family, Sar suggested, so that Buddha could be a "friend to all men, and to teach people to love one another." Sar drew a parallel here to Prince Yuthevong's distancing himself from the royal family so he could "instill democracy in the hearts of the Khmer people."[25]

Turning to a discussion of democracy, Saloth Sar cited revolutions in France, Russia, and China, where the monarchy had been abolished. These movements had been led, he noted, by Robespierre and Danton, Stalin and Lenin, and Sun Yat Sen (intriguingly, not Mao Zedong). In Russia, the "monarchy disappeared without a trace." In France, China, and the Soviet Union the democracy that replaced the kings was a doctrine followed by "people everywhere in the world; it is incomparable and as beautiful as a diamond." Twenty-four years later, as prime minister of Democratic Kampuchea, Saloth Sar's peculiar vision of democracy remained unshaken.

"Monarchy or Democracy?"—like Sar's later writings and speeches—is conversational in tone, overheated in rhetoric, and uncertain in its grasp of history. There is no evidence, for instance, that "enlightened monks" composed "Tmenh Chey" or that the Buddha left home because of his father's behavior—although these may have been stories told by antimonarchic monks and common currency among liberal Khmer. The essay also makes no distinction between the "democratic" regimes of China, France, and the USSR, stressing only that all three had rejected monarchy as an institution. Furthermore, it fails to take sides in the conflict in Indochina. More ominously, "Monarchy or Democracy?" fails to suggest how democracy might take hold in Cambodia, although references to revolutionary leaders (but not to parties or political groups) suggest obliquely that someone as enlightened as Yuthevong, the Buddha, Tmenh Chey, or Robespierre might eventually take command.

In August 1952 Sihanouk's adviser Penn Nouth came to Paris under orders to cut off the scholarships of those associated with the offensive issue of *Khmer Nisut* and other student outbursts that had followed the coup d'état. Keng Vannsak was protected from reprisals because he was related to Cambodia's minister of education, but he was told to return home before he had completed his dissertation. He arrived in Phnom Penh in October 1952.

By the time Saloth Sar was writing "Monarchy or Democracy?" he was no longer enrolled as a student. As he said in 1978, "I neglected my studies, and the authorities took away my scholarship." The government ledger verifying this assertion makes no mention of political activities. Others in the same position, and students whose scholarships were cut off for political reasons, often lingered in France, living by their wits on borrowed money. Three such students were Ieng Sary, Hou Youn, and Son Sen. According to Keng Vannsak, Sar was eager to return to Cambodia to engage in the anticolonial struggle, and his views were shared by several others, including Sien An, Rath Samoeun, Mey Mann, and Yun Soeurn. Vannsak's recollection was corroborated many years later by Mey Mann, when he told Steve Heder:

> Because of our thirst for information, Ieng Sary, Rath Samoeun, and Thiounn Mumm decided in 1952 that some of us would go back to Cambodia to find out more about what was really happening. . . . Saloth Sar was among those designated to go. . . . There was an internal discussion and we were asked to decide and declare whether we were prepared to dedicate our lives to the revolution. Saloth Sar was one who said that he was.[26]

After publishing his essay, however, Sar spent five months in France before returning home. When Vannsak left Paris, the Marxist study group shifted from his apartment to Sary's hotel room on the rue St. André des Arts. It seems likely that Sar joined the French Communist party at this time, perhaps as a candidate member, in preparation for working with the resistance in Cambodia. He may have been sponsored by Thiounn Mumm, the most prominent of the Khmer Communists, but this cannot be corroborated.[27]

Once again, as so often in Saloth Sar's life, mystery shrouds a crucial moment and conceals an important decision—with hindsight, the most important of his life. Several interesting questions remain unanswered: Exactly when did he become a Communist? Before or after the festival in East Berlin? Before or after Sihanouk's coup d'état? And who was his patron inside the party? Who were his immediate superiors? Could they be called role models? Where did he attend cell meetings? What party duties was he asked to perform?[28]

Another question has to do with Saloth Sar's motives for joining the Communist party. His earlier life, as we have seen, revealed few hints of sustained political commitment. His essay in *Khmer Nisut* shows little evidence of systematic reading in Marxism-Leninism, and unlike many of his colleagues he seems to have had no impact on student circles. There is no way of telling if his decision to become a Communist was sudden or came after much reflection. It is impossible to sort out the relative importance of ambition, ideals, group pressure, or inspiring people. What seems to have attracted Sar to the party was its organizational structure and the opportunities for a dedicated person like himself to rise inside it. For the remainder of his life, although the parties he belonged to changed their names or "disappeared," Saloth Sar remained a dedicated Communist and an organization man.[29]

People who knew Sar as a fellow Communist, and who were interviewed in the 1980s after his demonization, have been reluctant to provide biographical

details about this period in his life. The only clues we have come from Debré's book about Cambodian communism, published in November 1976,
which contains the quotations already cited about Sar's persuasive manner
and his ambitions. Aside from the outburst quoted by Debré, Saloth Sar kept
his aspirations to himself, as he admitted to Nate Thayer: "I never talked
about myself," he recalled. "I was taciturn."[30]

His seeming lack of personal ambition—like Stalin and Ho Chi Minh, unlike Lenin and Mao—served his purposes and was consistent with the unruffled persona he always displayed. He wanted his rise inside the movement to
be seen as a response to historical imperatives, patriotism, and the wishes of
others rather than to a strategic plan or calculated moves on his part.

On December 15, 1952, Saloth Sar returned to Marseilles and once again
boarded the *Jamaique*, this time for the journey home. As he crossed the
Mediterranean, the Red Sea, and the Indian Ocean, how did he perceive his
forty months in France? Academically he had earned no qualifications. This
did not upset him. Judging from his conduct when he reached Cambodia, he
had decided that instead of pursuing a career or raising a family, he would allow politics to take command of his life. As a Communist, this meant accepting party discipline and preparing himself and his colleagues for an eventual
seizure of power. More specifically, it meant taking part in armed struggle
against the French. These activities would occur in secret. The odds against
success were high; so were the risks he seemed prepared to take. The rewards, if they came, would be enormous, both for him and for his country.
After almost twenty years of lackluster studies, Saloth Sar must have been
pleased to change direction.

user ID:06413000468792   SINGH, SHA
NDER

        item ID:

                1   item checked out

Brother number one : a political biograp
    due:4/13/2005,23:59

CHAPTER FOUR

———————— ∎ ————————

Multiple Identities, 1953–1963

Joining the Viet Minh

When Saloth Sar returned to Cambodia in January 1953, he stayed for a time with his brother Loth Suong in Phnom Penh. Suong noticed that Sar had become interested in politics. "I think about the people," Sar told him. He also "praised Russia, he bragged about Russia, and talked about working in Yugoslavia." He told Suong how much he had learned from his "teacher" in Paris, Thiounn Mumm.[1] Less than a month later, he left Suong's house to join the resistance. He returned to Phnom Penh from time to time, informing his brother that he had been trying to contact anti-French, noncommunist guerrilla forces commanded by Prince Norodom Chantaraingsey in the nearby province of Kompong Speu or those commanded by Son Ngoc Thanh in the northwest. Sar's brother Saloth Chhay was in touch with both groups. Indeed, Saloth Chhay, when he was interviewed by Steve Heder in 1975, recalled encouraging his brother to work with Chantaraingsey. Saloth Sar told him that he thought Chantaraingsey was "feudal" and spoke vaguely of joining "those engaged in armed struggle"—that is, the Vietnamese-dominated Khmer Issarak. Concealing his intentions from both brothers, Saloth Sar left them with the impression that he was interested in siding with those "most truly interested in democracy."[2]

On a visit to the capital, it seems that Saloth Sar made contact with Pham Van Ba, the local representative of the Indochina Communist party, and asked to be inducted into the party on the basis of his membership in its counterpart in France. Ba told an interviewer in 1981 that he had verified Sar's credentials by communicating with Paris via Hanoi. The procedure took a couple of weeks. Ba then inducted Sar into the ICP, leapfrogging the Khmer People's Revolutionary party. (Steve Heder has accurately referred to this rudimentary Khmer formation as a "secret united front party," semantically a contradiction in terms.) Presumably, Sar's membership in the French

Communist party entitled him to join a grouping with international status—the Indochina Communist party—whose continuing existence was kept secret from noncommunist outsiders.

Sar's initiation probably occurred in eastern Cambodia, which he reached in August 1953. In any case, he was soon absorbed into the Viet Minh–dominated resistance. He worked in a headquarters cell that was half Khmer and half Vietnamese. According to Pham Van Ba, Sar was a "young man of average ability but with a clear desire for power." He went to work in a mass propaganda section and later attended a cadre school.[3]

Years later, after Vietnamese forces had driven Pol Pot into exile, a statement by his supporters complained that in 1953 intellectuals like Sar "were given tasks that had nothing to do with their skills; kitchen chores and the transport of organic fertilizer for crops among other things." Such assignments may have offended Sar's amour propre, but he was never averse to party discipline, and it must have become clear to him that the Vietnamese and their Cambodian colleagues considered him an asset. As an indication of this, Pham Van Ba recalled taking charge of his political training. Because of his background, Sar was ideally suited for united front work bridging gaps between various dissident groups on behalf of the Indochina Communist party. As proof of his usefulness, Sar, who had no combat experience or any competence in Vietnamese, was assigned to the Communists' headquarters along the border rather than to a less prestigious, more vulnerable unit. It appears that the Vietnamese and their Cambodian colleagues were saving him for important work. Sar's time at the headquarters, at the edge of two national struggles for independence, was a kind of entrance examination.[4]

Saloth Sar's value to the Vietnamese sprang largely from the fact that he had links with the urban Cambodian elite, the Democrats, and the Communists in France. His unpretentious manner, his time in Europe, and his willingness to learn made up for his unimpressive academic record, his elite family connections, and his brief exposure to Marxism-Leninism. By walking to the Vietnamese frontier and offering his services he stole the march on better qualified colleagues in France like Ieng Sary, Hou Youn, and Thiounn Mumm and on radicals in Phnom Penh who were still uncertain about communism or unwilling to take risks.

Sar's reaction to his months in the resistance is not recorded. He may have seen the rough-and-ready atmosphere of the headquarters unit as an extension of his militancy in Paris and a welcome immersion among workers and peasants reminiscent of his time in Yugoslavia. He was flattered at being singled out by Pham Van Ba and his Cambodian assistant, Tou Samouth. Perhaps he felt that his life was beginning to gather speed.

He was in little physical danger. By mid-1953 the First Indochina War, at least in the southern parts of Indochina, was dying down. The French were prepared to grant noncommunist components of the federation their independence, while pursuing their anticommunist war, primarily in northern Vietnam. In November 1953 France, pressured by Sihanouk, granted Cambodia its independence. This led Sihanouk to claim that his "royal crusade," set in motion the year before, had been successful. Soon after, fighting between the French and resistance forces died down. Over the next few months, many noncommunist resistance units rallied to Sihanouk's government. Those commanded by the Vietnamese waited on developments.

On the frontier, Saloth Sar continued his political education. His mentor was Tou Samouth, "a wealthy Khmer from Cochinchina" who was less than ten years older than Sar. Samouth had been affiliated with the Buddhist Institute as a monk during World War II. In 1945 he left the monkhood to become a propagandist for the Viet Minh in eastern Cambodia and among the Khmer minority in Vietnam. He joined the Indochina Communist party in 1946. Samouth was a skillful and inspiring orator. One of his former students later said that for "courtesy, modesty and easy-goingness, he was comparable to Ho Chi Minh."[5]

It is tempting to place Tou Samouth beside other role models Sar encountered, beginning in the 1940s with Kvan Siphan and continuing into the 1950s with Ieng Sary, Keng Vannsak, Thiounn Mumm, and Khieu Ponnary. Like them, Samouth was an idealist with a passion for teaching who commanded affection and respect. One difference lay in Samouth's Buddhist rather than French education. This may have appealed to Sar in his apparent eagerness to become less French and more Khmer. A more cynical view would have Sar ingratiate himself to Samouth as a way of rising inside the movement. On balance, it seems likely that Tou Samouth's eloquence, patriotism, and commitment drew the younger man to him as a disciple. They worked together for the next nine years.[6]

In May 1954 a twenty-five-year-old revolutionary named Sok Thuok arrived on the frontier and began a close association with Saloth Sar that ended in 1978 when Thuok, by then a deputy prime minister known as Vorn Vet, was purged at Pol Pot's behest for being "pro-Vietnamese." In his confession, Vet recalled meeting the "brothers from France" in eastern Cambodia and also his political training under Tou Samouth. His enthusiasm for Samouth foreshadows the statements of many who studied under Saloth Sar/Pol Pot: "He made me so happy, and I believed in him *(chhoeou cho't)*. When he opened a study course, I tried hard to understand him, and when he went out on propaganda missions, I followed along after him. This [experience] awakened me to the clear realities of the revolution."[7]

Geneva and the 1955 Elections

By mid-1954 the Viet Minh and their Cambodian colleagues were in a state of suspended animation, awaiting the results of the international conference convened at Geneva to reach a political settlement to the First Indochina War. The conference, in the planning stages for several months, convened soon after the French army suffered a humiliating defeat in northern Vietnam at Dien Bien Phu. The Soviet Union and Great Britain were asked to convene the conference as members of the United Nations Security Council. Both powers were eager to settle the conflict. The conference attendees included France, the United States (which was stubbornly anticommunist), the People's Republic of China (recently at war with the United States in Korea), and the component regimes of Indochina.

The Geneva settlement, concluded in July, provided for the partition of Vietnam at the seventeenth parallel until after national elections and for regroupment areas in Laos for Lao resistance fighters. Those who had fought with the Viet Minh in southern Vietnam could either disarm and reenter civilian life or regroup to the north. For Cambodian fighters, there was no regroupment zone inside Cambodia or any provision for regrouping guerrillas elsewhere. Most of them welcomed independence and chose to return home, but more than one thousand others were evacuated to northern Vietnam. Among those evacuated were such important Khmer Communists as Keo Moni, Sieu Heng, Tou Samouth, and Son Ngoc Minh, as well as three of Sar's friends from Paris, Sien An, Rath Samoeun, and Yun Soeurn. A handful of these Khmer, including Tou Samouth and Sieu Heng, came home in 1955–1956. The rest remained in Vietnam for many years. Other former guerrillas, including Sok Knol and Saloth Sar, were sent to Phnom Penh to work for the Indochina Communist party. Sok Thuok arrived in the capital in October 1954, after Saloth Sar.[8]

For Cambodia, the Geneva agreements stipulated that elections for a National Assembly would be held sometime in 1955. They were to be overseen by an international control group composed of delegates from Poland, India, and Canada. It was hoped that former resistance fighters would thereby be integrated into society by joining political parties or competing with them for people's votes.

Unlike his counterparts in Vietnam and Laos, however, King Sihanouk had become an important political actor. He believed that he had won independence for Cambodia singlehandedly. He wanted to play a larger role in Cambodia than the one allotted him by the constitution, and since he had never respected the National Assembly, he now sought some way of governing unopposed. From his point of view, the elections stipulated at Geneva constituted an obstacle and an opportunity.

The Democrats, still enjoying widespread national support, were eager to campaign. Before Geneva, Keng Vannsak, Ea Shichau, and several others had worked to push the party toward a more radical, anti-American position. Having absorbed anti-American ideas while in France, these men feared that the U.S. "imperialists" would step in to replace the French and that Sihanouk would seek an American alliance or join the anticommunist Southeast Asian Treaty Organization (SEATO) formed at U.S. insistence in the aftermath of Geneva.

Thiounn Mumm, who shared these views, returned to Cambodia in July 1954 and worked closely with Vannsak and Shichau. He also renewed contact with Saloth Sar, then living under an assumed name—the first of many—in the southern part of the city. In January 1955 Mumm, Shichau, and Vannsak staged a bloodless coup in the Democratic party, pushing aside several of its founding members and taking over the executive committee. Saloth Sar continued to operate behind the scenes. Certainly none of the others took the precaution of using a false name. Interestingly, a year later Sar was known to some as "Pol," the nickname he had used on at least one occasion in Paris. He may have been using the name when Thiounn Mumm met him.[9]

No one who recalled seeing Sar at this time knew what he was doing or who was paying him, for he had no visible means of support. As so often in his career, he relished a multiplicity of roles. His work involved carrying out liaison with radical Democrats in Phnom Penh on behalf of the Indochina Communist party (without admitting his affiliation) and making preparations for the 1955 elections. It seems likely that he had been sent to the capital by Tou Samouth and Pham Van Ba to work with his Democratic acquaintances to push the party to the left while also promoting the cause of the Pracheachon Group, a front formation that drew its strength from former guerrillas and that planned to contest the elections. In the months leading to the elections, Sar probably wrote for the radical newspaper *Sammaki* (Solidarity), edited by his brother Saloth Chhay.

Mumm and Sar also shared a specifically Communist agenda. They hoped to lay the groundwork for Communists to seize control in Cambodia, perhaps to coincide with the national elections scheduled for 1956 in Vietnam. These were expected by many, including the Americans, to result in a Communist victory. At the time, the two men accepted Vietnam's guidance of the fledgling Cambodian party, much as their counterparts in France accepted advice from the Soviet Union. Members of the Pracheachon Group also operated under guidelines provided by the Indochina Communist party. Unlike Saloth Sar and Thiounn Mumm, however, these men had peasant or working-class backgrounds, combat experience, and no academic credentials or access to Cambodia's elite.[10]

A former classmate of Saloth Sar, Chhay Yat, recalled meeting him in Phnom Penh in 1954. Yat was working with the Thanhist faction of the Democrats and hoped that supporters of Thanh, like himself, could have some say in Cambodia's future. Chhay Yat was suspicious of Communist strategy, so Saloth Sar tried to reassure him by saying that "the wheel of history" dictated that Cambodians be friendly with Vietnam, "which is so much stronger." Sar also promoted the idea of an Indochinese federation, comparing it favorably to the Soviet Union and its satellites and even to the United States: "Do those states consume each other?" he asked rhetorically.[11]

Keng Vannsak also met Saloth Sar on several occasions in 1954–1955. He was impressed by his former protégé's "measured and intelligent" manner, his seriousness, and his political acuity—characteristics he had not noticed in Paris. The two worked together to radicalize Democratic policy and to educate the electorate. This meant uniting the various strands of opposition to the French—those willing to cooperate with the Vietnamese and those who distrusted them; those ready to continue armed struggle and those unwilling to do so; those who wanted to reform the Cambodian government and those who wanted to overturn it. They were joined in these efforts by Khieu Ponnary, who, upon her return from Paris in 1951, had taken a post teaching Cambodian literature at a collège in Takeo.[12]

The 1955 campaign was the first time that a wide range of political options was available to Cambodia's voters. The occasion did not present itself again until the UN-sponsored elections of 1993. On the left were the concealed Indochina Communist party; its front group, the Pracheachon; and the radical Democrats, led by Thiounn Mumm and Keng Vannsak. In the center were the Thanhist Democrats and other members of that party frightened by radical inroads. Toward the right were those affiliated with the Liberal party and with antidemocratic groupings formed in the early 1950s. The best-organized group was the Democrats, although in some rural areas, particularly in the east and southwest, the Pracheachon, inheriting the popularity of the armed resistance, swiftly struck deep roots.

Most observers believed that the stage was set for another Democratic victory at the polls. The prospect exhilarated Vannsak and his friends, but it distressed members of Cambodia's more conservative elite, who by this time were hitching their political fortunes to the king. These men had no coherent ideology; they were counting on Sihanouk's charisma, his animosity toward the Democrats, and their own support of the king to bring them into power. They came from parties never represented in the National Assembly, and they all resented the Democrats' "monopoly" of power. In December 1954 they joined forces to form a "nonpolitical" grouping that pledged its loyalty to the king. Prominent members of this group included Nhek Tioulong, Sam Sary, Lon Nol, and Sisowath Sirik Matak.[13]

All of the contenders in the elections were optimistic, but only Sihanouk had access to the coercive machinery of the state. This advantage was decisive when combined with his popularity in rural areas and his new political skills. In the end, Sihanouk killed any possibility of political pluralism, forced his opponents into clandestinity, and encouraged the survival of the Cambodian Communist movement, the only political grouping that was prepared to operate in the dark.

Sihanouk's orchestration of the 1955 campaign foreshadowed the methods he used to govern Cambodia for the next fifteen years. In February he sponsored a referendum asking voters to approve his Royal Crusade for Independence. Balloting was open, and those who wished to vote against the king had to discard a ballot with his picture on it, an act of lèse-majesté that was probably grounds for arrest. When over 95 percent of the electorate voted as he had hoped, Sihanouk decided to enter the political arena. As king he had played a ceremonial role restricted by the constitution. To escape this, Sihanouk abdicated the throne, had his father named king, and began to campaign as an "ordinary citizen."

His move took everyone by surprise. As a private citizen, Sihanouk hoped to smash the political parties and impose a Bonapartist consensus on Cambodia. To achieve his goals, he preempted some of the foreign policy positions taken by the Democrats and the Pracheachon. After attending a conference of recently decolonized nations at Bandung in Indonesia in April 1955, where he was lionized by the Chinese premier, Zhou Enlai, Sihanouk announced that he would follow a "nonaligned" foreign policy as the Democrats had demanded. To neutralize conservative opposition, the prince also signed a military aid agreement with the United States.

Sihanouk then formed a national political movement, the Sangkum Reastr Niyum ("Popular Socialist Community"), whose members were not allowed to belong to other political parties. Membership drives swept through the bureaucracy. Hundreds of Democrats working in the government who refused to join the Sangkum lost their jobs, and people working for other political parties were harassed and imprisoned by the police. Radical newspapers were closed down and their editors sent to prison for several months.

As his campaign gathered steam, Sihanouk occasionally accused his opponents of being supporters of communism, a system he believed was alien to most Khmer. After the Sangkum had swept the elections, its journal predicted what Cambodian life would be like if the Communists ever came to power: "There will be no happiness. Everyone will work for the government. No one will ride cars or cyclos, or wear nice clothes; everyone will wear black, exactly alike. There would be no delicious food to eat. If you ate more than allowed, the government would learn about it from your children in secret and you would be taken out and shot."[14] This extraordinary prophecy of socialist practice, self-serving at the time, came to pass in April 1975, when Communist forces liberated Phnom Penh and evacuated its population.

To many Cambodians, the Democrats still offered a feasible alternative to Sihanouk on the one hand and the Vietnamese-dominated Communist resistance on the other. As the electoral campaign gathered momentum, Keng Vannsak and other Democrats spoke out against nepotism and corruption, warning voters of the dangers of an alliance with the United States. Vannsak

Independence Monument, Phnom Penh, 1971. Photo by the author.

Aerial view of Phnom Penh, with the former Royal Palace in the foreground, 1970.
Courtesy of the Khmer Republic Ministry of Information.

also attacked Cambodia's precolonial tradition of absolute kings. Large crowds applauded him. Pracheachon candidates were more prudent than the Democrats, but they emphasized similar issues and commanded widespread support in several provinces.

Since most of the Sangkum candidates were undistinguished, Sihanouk realized that the results he wanted were not guaranteed. Therefore he had his police arrest Keng Vannsak and several others on the eve of the elections. Vannsak was held without trial for several months. Elsewhere, Democratic rallies were broken up and candidates beaten; some campaign workers were killed. Thiounn Mumm, threatened with arrest, returned hurriedly to France. Saloth Sar came to nobody's attention.[15]

Without these tactics, Sangkum candidates would probably have won only two-thirds of the seats in the National Assembly. Because of violence and fraud, however, the Sangkum claimed to have gained all ninety-one seats and 630,000 votes—over 80 percent of those cast. The Democrats officially gained 90,000 votes, and the Pracheachon 30,000. The numbers convinced Sihanouk that Cambodia could now be managed as his personal estate. The elections marked the end of pluralist politics in Cambodia and the beginning of fifteen years of one-man rule.[16]

In September 1977, in a speech tracing the history of Cambodia's Communist movement, Pol Pot looked back on these elections from a different perspective, noting that "the people's forces throughout the country supported the revolution and the progressive side against the reactionaries and U.S. imperialism. But the people were unable to vote for the progressives, because the ruling class resorted to its guns, courts, laws, prisons, and other repressive tools."[17]

Over the next few years, the Sangkum movement and Sihanouk's volatile personality, always on display, came to monopolize politics in Cambodia. Saloth Sar, like many others, shied away from Sihanouk's style of rule. Indeed, Sar's avoidance of the limelight, his neutral style, and his obedience to party discipline were partly in reaction to Sihanouk's flamboyance.

Becoming a Teacher

After the elections, Saloth Sar was at a loose end, and Loth Suong and Chea Samy were worried that he had no job. Sar's friendship with Khieu Ponnary probably became more intense during the campaign—when they both worked closely with Keng Vannsak—and they were married in a quiet ceremony in July 1956. By then Ponnary was in her mid-thirties and had been a schoolteacher for several years. Although deeply respected by her students, some contemporaries found her commitment to her career, her politics, and her austerity unsettling. She was small, neat, even elegant; but she wore no jewelry or makeup, she cut her hair in an "old-fashioned, Chinese style," and she preferred somber clothes. Many Cambodians found her hard to fathom. They called her "the old virgin" behind her back. Lim Keuky, a student of Ponnary's at the Lycée Sisowath in 1956, has recalled that in the months before her marriage to Saloth Sar, the "old virgin" began to wear "lipstick and a little jewelry." For a time, she seemed warmer and more accessible. "She seemed so happy," Lim recalled, "and we were happy on her behalf."[18]

No information has emerged about the couple's courtship or what drew them to each other. Their marriage seems to have taken their mutual acquaintances by surprise. Few Cambodian men marry older women, and women of Ponnary's social class, at least in the 1950s, seldom married men with so few prospects or attainments. Perhaps she and Saloth Sar were drawn together by their shared commitment to utopian politics and the idea of working in secret to transform their country. Perhaps they hoped to team up with Khieu Thirith and her husband, Ieng Sary, soon to return from France, to hasten the revolution. More prosaically, Ponnary might have been charmed by Saloth Sar, like many others before and since, and agreed to share her life with someone whose ideals seemed higher, more integrated, and more exigent than those of most men and women in her circle. Sar, for his part, must have been impressed by Ponnary's intellectual distinction and her elegant demeanor. Chea Samy recalled being delighted by the marriage; she hoped that it would encourage Saloth Sar to settle down.

By then Ponnary was teaching Cambodian literature at the Lycée Sisowath. About this time, Saloth Sar embarked on a career teaching French, history, geography, and civics at a newly established private collège, Chamraon Vichea ("Progressive Knowledge"), in Phnom Penh. This period of his life was the last one he spent in the open, and the impressions he left are the last we have until after 1975, when gnomic, reverent references to him crop up in party documents and confessions. Intriguingly, all the observations convey a similar picture of a self-composed, smooth-featured teacher who was fond of his students, eloquent but unpretentious, honest, humane, easy to befriend—up to a point—and easy to respect. Was the image spontaneous, calculated, or a conscious mixture of both? In what proportions did it spring from his upbringing, his preferences, or his Communist training? Like the issue of his "charm"—by definition something that exists in the eye of the beholder—these questions are crucial to an understanding of Saloth Sar/Pol Pot. They are also impossible to answer. He certainly brought a partially calculated warmth to his personal encounters—here one is reminded of Ho Chi Minh.

Many recollections of Saloth Sar referred to his skills as a teacher. In choosing to play this role, he drew on the reservoir of reverence Cambodians have always had for their teachers, reflecting the centuries in which education was in the hands of Hindu brahmans or Buddhist monks and the high status accorded teachers in the French Third Republic (under which Saloth

Sar was raised). A former engineer told me that "in the Cambodian system, even a mathematics professor teaches ethics." Students traditionally gave respect to their teachers, as they did to elderly relatives, in exchange for moral guidance. Older brothers (*bong*) and teachers who returned this respect with warmth and kindness were rare and doubly honored. After years of failing to catch anyone's attention as a student, Saloth Sar seems to have been an immediate success as a teacher of "progressive knowledge."

In 1959 one of Ponnary's students, You Sambo, decided to visit her informally with several of his friends. By then, Ponnary and Saloth Sar were living in the southern part of the city, not far from Chamraon Vichea. Their Chinese-style house was flush to the ground, and Sambo found the rooms spotlessly clean and the furnishings sparse but neat, with a few books and some unprepossessing "pictures of China" on the walls. Sambo met Saloth Sar that afternoon for the first time. He found him "very clean and well presented (*s'aat s'om*) ... very smooth. ... I could see he was good natured (*chet l'oo*). . . . I could see immediately that he was an attractive figure (*khoonj kuo oy srolanh*) and that I could easily become his lifelong friend." Sar's smooth face, deep voice, and calm gestures were reassuring. He seemed to be someone who could "explain things in such a way that you came to love justice and honesty and hate corruption." On later visits Sambo took part in informal seminars where young people—junior officers in the army, teachers, and students—would discuss their ideals for Cambodia and for themselves. Sambo remembered Saloth Sar leading discussions without revealing his political alignment and attacking dishonesty in government circles.[19]

Chamraon Vichea provided Saloth Sar with a stage for his political talents and a theater for his clandestine party work. Another private collège, Kambuj'bot—almost completely staffed by Communists in the 1950s and 1960s—had been founded by the Democrats in 1952 after Sihanouk's coup d'état. Its name, which means "Son of Kampuchea," had been used by Prince Yuthevong when he was writing for the Democratic press. Both schools catered to students who had failed their examinations for the state-run collège system inherited from colonial times. Those who passed examinations at the end of their collège careers (the ones Saloth Sar failed in 1948) were allowed to enroll in a lycée. The pass rate at private collèges was not especially high, but many parents were willing to take the risk and pay modest annual fees in the hope of guaranteeing their children the government positions that flowed to lycée graduates. About three hundred students attended the four-year course at Chamraon Vichea.[20]

The collège's origins are obscure. Chhay Yat said that it was established with funds provided by Lon Nol, Prince Norodom Chantaraingsey, and others who saw such a school as an investment and as a way of counterbalancing the influence of the Democrats at Kambuj'bot. Sar may have obtained a post there thanks to his schoolboy friendship with Lon Nol's brother Lon Non, and his family connections with Chantaraingsey. Neither man would have known of Sar's Communist affiliations, and even if they had, they would not have taken them seriously. Nevertheless, Chamraon Vichea, like Kambuj'bot, soon became a haven for radicals who lacked credentials to teach in the more prestigious and better-paying state system.[21]

Like so many of Sar's actions—his "selection" of the Ecole Technique, his trip to France, even perhaps his months in the maquis—his decision to become a teacher at Chamraon Vichea seemed to owe more to drift and circumstance than to ambition or choice. He was drawn to a profession, nonetheless, where he could play a variety of roles, concealing his political leanings behind a penchant for moral training and his ambitions behind a taciturn appearance. It is difficult to imagine what other occupation he could have taken up. He was not qualified to teach in the state system. He showed no interest in furthering his education or in being a manual laborer, businessman, or civil servant. Without land or capital, he would find it hard to become a farmer or an entrepreneur. A career in left-wing journalism threatened him with exposure and involved too many risks. Teaching, on the other hand, was congenial and provided the cover Saloth Sar needed to continue his party work and to attract young people to the Communist movement.

He was a talented, popular teacher, gradually earning a reputation similar to those of his mentors, Kvan Siphan and Tou Samouth. A vivid picture of Saloth Sar from this period comes from the novelist Soth Polin, who studied French literature with him in 1959:

> I still remember Pol Pot's style of delivery in French: gentle and musical. He was clearly drawn to French literature in general and poetry in particular: Rimbaud, Verlaine, de Vigny. In Paris many years later I watched him speaking Cambodian on the TV. It was certainly the same person—with his laugh, his manner of choosing his words, his frank appearance. . . . He spoke in bursts without notes, searching a little but never caught short, his eyes half-closed, carried away by his own lyricism. . . . The students were subjugated by this affable professor, invariably dressed in a short-sleeved white shirt and dark blue trousers.[22]

Another student who took Cambodian history from Sar in 1962, and who prefers to remain anonymous, recalled that Sar taught the subject in a manner that Sihanouk would have approved, giving the prince credit for Cambodian independence. This was the view favored in the lycée examinations that students were planning to take. The student remembered that Saloth Sar spoke "gently, slowly, and clearly, in idiomatic French" and that he made an effort to simplify his syntax so that students could understand him and could repeat his exact phrasing in their examinations. "He was popular among the students, a good teacher and very correct in his ways."

A third student, Om Narong, had Saloth Sar as a teacher of French literature in 1959. Narong remembered that Sar "taught because he wanted us to learn." He recalled Sar's frequent smiles and his consistent, unassuming dress: "He always wore a white shirt, with short sleeves reaching to the elbows. His trousers were navy blue. . . . Everyone knew he was Communist," but this was not a distressing thought to students who associated communism with a scrupulous, anti-Sihanouk point of view. In any case, Sar never included radical ideas in his teaching, saving them for more initiated groups. In the 1950s, it seems, the term "Communist" in Cambodia often referred to people who had simple tastes, a good education, and a hatred for corruption. In Narong's words, "They were the only people who cared about the poor."[23]

A Militant for the Party

By 1956 Saloth Sar was already juggling several identities. He was known as "Pol" and probably by other names to members of the Pracheachon and as "Saloth Sar" to his friends outside the movement. He was also working with fellow members of the Indochina Communist party, a much smaller group, to protect its Cambodian leaders Tou Samouth and Sieu Heng and to lay the groundwork, when the time was ripe and permission came from Vietnam, for a larger and better-organized Cambodian Communist party. Whether the Khmer People's Revolutionary party, formed in 1951, continued to function under that name is one of the mysteries that surround the history of the Communists in Cambodia. Mey Mann, a former CPK cadre, told Steve Heder in 1997 that the party in the 1950s "had no name." It seems likely that its role and much of its membership had been absorbed by the Pracheachon. Some of those associated with the Pracheachon, like Keo Meas, would have known about Sar's other political affiliations; many did not. Those who knew the truth about Sar were working undercover themselves. Their world of pseudonyms, secret rendezvous, numbered offices, and safe houses suggests that at a cops-and-robbers level it was exciting to be a Communist in Phnom Penh in the 1950s, particularly for those like Saloth Sar who had elite connections and were immune from police harassment.[24]

After his marriage, Saloth Sar cut himself off from the brother and sister-in-law who had raised him, although he assiduously attended Buddhist ceremonies honoring the dead every September in Prek Sbauv. His last visit there was in 1959 when he attended his father's funeral. Sar also saw less of Keng Vannsak. Part of this aloofness might be traced to the return from Paris of Khieu Thirith and Ieng Sary in early 1957. For a time, the four of them and Sary and Thirith's baby daughter, Vanny, lived together in a rented house west of the palace that belonged to the sisters' family. Neighbors were amazed at the four's refusal to hire domestic servants on ideological grounds. Sary soon began teaching at Kambuj'bot and plunged into secret political work alongside Saloth Sar.[25]

It is hard to say what this political work entailed, how important Saloth Sar was, or where he fit into the Communist chain of command. His name never came up in Sihanouk's speeches or in the government press in connection with the Pracheachon. Although widely known as a progressive, Sar apparently was never questioned by the police, and the U.S. Embassy had no biographical information on him, as it did for hundreds of supposedly Communist figures. Unlike militants in other countries, he never spent a night in jail.

Beginning in 1955, Sar shared much of his secret life with Nuon Chea, a Communist roughly his own age who retained an important position in the movement into the 1990s alongside Saloth Sar/Pol Pot. Nuon Chea was a Sino-Khmer from Battambang, born into a prosperous family in 1927. His name at birth was Lau Ben Kon. During World War II, when Battambang was under Thai control, he went to Bangkok, where he completed his secondary schooling under the name Long Ruot. In 1945 he enrolled as a law student at Thammasat University, also in Bangkok, where he earned an academic scholarship. He soon became a member of the Communist party of Thailand without informing his family. He was probably inspired to do so by his cousin Sieu Heng, who had also spent part of the war in Bangkok and had joined the Indochina Communist party in Battambang in 1945. From that time until the late 1950s, Sieu Heng was a leading figure in the Cambodian Communist movement. Years later, after he had left the party, he told an interviewer that he had admired the Communists in the 1940s because of their "perfect arguments" and because he thought that the Vietnamese could help liberate Cambodia from the French. His young cousin was drawn in by similar ideas and by the flowering of radical politics in Bangkok after World War II.[26]

By 1951 Nuon Chea had joined the Vietnamese-sponsored resistance in Battambang and was a member of the Indochina Communist party. He concealed his affiliations from his family for several years, telling them merely that he was engaged in the struggle against the French. In 1952 he traveled to Vietnam and underwent some political training. In April 1955 he returned to Phnom Penh, where, like Sar, he took a new name and "engaged in secret political work."

It is tempting to speculate that Chea and Sar began to formulate ideas about the party's future and their own while they were working together in the 1950s, when Chea's fortunes were linked to Sieu Heng and Sar's to Tou Samouth. Samouth was in charge of urban work for the party, while Sieu Heng was in charge of the rural sector. It is logical to assume that Chea busied himself with rural matters while Sar had urban responsibilities and that they maintained contact with the zones (Sar with the eastern, and Chea with the northwestern) where their patrons had operated during the war. Indeed, Chea spent some time in the late 1950s in Kompong Chhnang, where he met his wife, allegedly the daughter of illiterate farmers.[27]

Sar's friendship with Chea followed a pattern that began in 1949, when he befriended Ieng Sary, and continued through his relationships with Keng Vannsak, Tou Samouth, and Khieu Ponnary. Except for Sary, each friend was older than Sar. They could all be classified as "intellectuals," a word Saloth Sar probably would not have used about himself. Sary, Vannsak, and Nuon Chea are recalled by many as having forceful, abrasive personalities. No such reputation has clung to Saloth Sar. And yet it was Saloth Sar who became "Brother Number One" in the Cambodian Communist movement. Sar's persona resembles that of Ho Chi Minh and other Communist leaders—artless and kindly at one level; pragmatic, artful, and ambitious at another. One image projected is of still waters running deep. Another is of a romantic radical, happy in concealment, persuasive in small groups, ferociously loyal to the party, whose loyalties and manner allowed him to rise higher than was warranted by his abilities. A third possibility, which fits nicely alongside the others, is that in the 1950s his Vietnamese mentors and Tou Samouth found him a pliable disciple who was easier to work with than other young Khmer like Ieng Sary.

Focusing the Party

Party work in Cambodia in the 1950s involved forming a network of militants and potential cadre who had no mandate for revolutionary action. The network was painstakingly formed by persuasion and education. In Phnom Penh, there were also sporadic attempts to mobilize Cambodia's small proletariat, which included railway workers and longshoremen. Throughout the party's history, the Cambodian Communists insisted that the proletariat made up the vanguard of the revolution, a belief that conformed with Marxist-Leninist teaching. It soon became clear, however, that there were not enough workers to lead a revolution, so they were replaced as the vanguard by members of the Communist party (or whatever the movement called itself at any given time).

The Communists in Cambodia also adopted united front tactics when it seemed appropriate to do so. The governing idea of these tactics was that the Communists would unite temporarily with as many allies as possible to isolate their enemies. Once the Communists had seized power, they could abandon their allies. In Cambodia, the major enemy was thought to be the United States, and so the Pracheachon's newspapers, which Sihanouk did not consider much of a threat, supported the prince's anti-Americanism. Some Communists operated in the open as Sihanouk supporters. These included Khieu Samphan, Hou Youn, and Hu Nim, all graduates of the Collège Sihanouk in Kompong Cham; and Chau Seng, a Cambodian from Cochinchina who had traveled to France with Saloth Sar. Other clandestine members of the party, like the Khieu sisters and Son Sen, pursued careers in the state-run school system.

The Pracheachon retained its legal status through 1962, but the existence of the Indochina Communist party, supposedly dissolved in 1945, was still kept secret. Sihanouk's police concentrated on harassing Pracheachon members. For Communists and their sympathizers, there were frequent study sessions in safe houses in Phnom Penh and in the countryside.

In rural areas, where the movement had been strongest during the First Indochina War, Cambodians in the Indochina Communist party tried to maintain the loyalties of those who had fought the French. Here success was limited because by the late 1950s Sieu Heng had lost his radical zeal. In 1956 he had returned from Vietnam weary with communism; but under Vietnamese orders, it seems, he hung on as leader for two or three more years. This was a period when the Vietnamese Communists urged their Cambodian colleagues to engage in "political struggle" that, in effect, turned militants into targets for the police. Many former resistance fighters, including Sieu Heng, saw no point in attacking Sihanouk's government without weapons and without any assurance that getting rid of him would bring improvements to their material well-being.

Most recruits to the movement in this period—and they were few—were not the rural poor or former militants in the countryside. Instead, they were students in the collèges and lycées, schoolteachers, urban workers, and young Cambodians radicalized during their studies overseas. These men and women joined the Communist movement between 1954 and 1960 because they were inspired by teachers like Saloth Sar, Hou Youn, and Ieng Sary. They were affronted by Sihanouk's dictatorial style and the injustices in Cambodian society; some were admirers of the Chinese revolution. What was required in Cambodia, they thought, was not a liberation from foreign domination and U.S. "puppets" but an overturning and renovation of the Cambodian social arrangements. The United States was the "Number One Enemy" of the revolution, but in Cambodia it shared this position with Sihanouk and all he stood for.

The social composition of new recruits broke with earlier, rural traditions but allowed Cambodia's revolution to follow its own path rather than to respond to Vietnamese military exigencies, as it had done in the early 1950s, when fighting the French had been confined to rural areas. The Cambodian movement could now develop as other revolutions, including Vietnam's, had done. The fledgling party could concentrate on gathering support among the intelligentsia in the towns, targeting schoolteachers, Buddhist monks, and lycée students. This work was ideally suited to Saloth Sar. In 1977, when the party had resurrected its rural orientation with a vengeance, Pol Pot complained that some "90 percent of our revolutionary forces in the countryside" had defected, been arrested, or been killed in 1959. There is no evidence that the leaders of the party, concentrated in the towns, regretted this development. Until it was time to abandon united front tactics and engage in armed struggle, Phnom Penh was where revolutionary battles would be fought and won. It also gave Sar, a lifelong city dweller, the chance to rise inside the movement.[28]

In this context, Sieu Heng's defection was a blessing in disguise. He had not been effective after returning from Hanoi. For a time, he and Tou Samouth lived in adjoining houses in Phnom Penh, protected by young members of the movement. Sieu Heng, a gambler and bon vivant, chafed under these conditions; but because he had been placed in a leadership position by the movement's patrons in Hanoi, Samouth and his colleagues could not replace him. His defection decided the matter for them. Before long, he was back in Battambang engaged in petty trade. For at least two years, Heng led the police nowhere near his former colleagues in Phnom Penh, and the rural sector of the movement declined in importance. The 1973 history of the party noted that "the committee in charge of the urban movement [the group that Tou Samouth, aided by Saloth Sar, led] was named the committee in charge of the country's general affairs." In his 1997 history of the party, Nuon Chea wrote that after Heng's defection, "there was no party secretary, but those who remained continued on their way by relying on awakening the masses."[29]

Sihanouk's tirades against communism were prominent in the 1958 election campaign. They diminished in 1959 when the prince was preoccupied with plots against him orchestrated from South Vietnam and Thailand with the knowledge and connivance of the United States. These plots infuriated the prince, who also resented Thai and South Vietnamese backing for Son Ngoc Thanh. The former prime minister had lived in exile in both countries since 1955 and had built up an anti-Sihanouk paramilitary force with the encouragement of the United States, which was distressed by the prince's "pro-communist" alignment. For Saloth Sar and his colleagues, and especially for Communists operating in the open, Sihanouk's anti-Americanism and his rage at neighboring regimes provided another opportunity to form a united front and operate with Sihanouk's protection.

One result of this alliance was that left-wing newspapers in Phnom Penh not only stepped up their support of Sihanouk's foreign policy; they also toed a pro-Sihanouk line on domestic issues. Leftist intellectuals like Hou Youn, Chau Seng, and Khieu Samphan drew praise from the prince for their patriotism and integrity. Hou Youn was brought into the government as a junior minister, and Khieu Samphan's left-wing newspaper, *L'Observateur*, started publication in September 1959. To the Communists, the atmosphere seemed favorable for the formation of a united front.[30]

By then the Vietnam Workers' party had met twice in Hanoi to discuss requests from Communists in South Vietnam that they be allowed to inaugurate armed struggle against the pro-American Ngo Dinh Diem regime there. At Hanoi's suggestion, South Vietnamese Communists had begun a political struggle that had led to thousands of arrests, imprisonments, and executions. The Vietnam Workers' party gave cautious approval to the requests, as well as to similar ones from Laos, where a pro-Western government had been installed with U.S. assistance. Hanoi was not prepared to back full-scale armed resistance anywhere at this stage, however, and there is no evidence that the Cambodian movement requested or received permission to arm itself. At the same time, the onset of armed struggle in South Vietnam suggested to the Communists in Hanoi that the Cambodian Communists' old alliances and obligations might be reactivated to support the war.[31]

Sihanouk's relations with the left were subject to his volatile moods and to his tactic of playing radicals and conservatives against each other. During the second half of 1960, following his father's death, the prince wanted to install himself as chief of state—a process completed by the end of the year. In making his extraconstitutional moves, Sihanouk felt it prudent to neutralize the left-wing press. When a minor crisis developed over how much time should be devoted to teaching French in Cambodian schools—with Sihanouk taking one position and the left-wing press, including Khieu Samphan's *L'Observateur*, another—the prince wheeled against the left. Samphan was beaten up in the street by plainclothes policemen. In his paper he described the incident as "obviously fascist, with imperialist overtones." In August, after demonstrations organized with Sihanouk's approval condemned the left-wing press, Sihanouk closed the papers down and imprisoned their editors, including Khieu Samphan. The suspects were detained for a month. Their Communist colleagues, of course, had no idea how long they would be held.

Pressure on the Cambodian Communists was also coming from Hanoi, whose support for the armed struggle in South Vietnam meant resuming united front tactics there, combining armed struggle and political struggle, and reconstituting the parties that had been in place in Laos and Cambodia during the First Indochina War. Vietnamese tactics were more complicated this time for two reasons. The first was that most of the fighting would now be in the southern, and not the northern, portion of Vietnam. The second was that the Khmer People's Revolutionary party had to be reconstituted in the context of Hanoi's informal alliance with Sihanouk. In other words, it was to be brought back to life, encouraged to expand, but kept silent and forbidden to engage in armed struggle. These arrangements gave the Cambodians a choice between guidance from Vietnam on the one hand and independence, confrontation, and the possibility of obliteration on the other. Throughout the 1960s the humiliating aspects of the first alternative forced the Cambodian Communists toward the second, with disastrous results. After 1960, when Saloth Sar joined the newly constituted Central Committee of the Cambodian Communist party, these pressures fell on him. They would plague him for the remainder of his career.

A Cambodian Party Takes Shape

In early September 1960 the Vietnam Workers' party convened a congress in Hanoi that resolved to "liberate the South from . . . the American imperialists and their henchmen." The method chosen to achieve this goal was to establish a national front in South Vietnam while inaugurating armed struggle in the countryside. To proceed with the Second Indochina War, the Vietnamese wanted to renew the arrangements of 1950, when they had formed Communist parties in Laos and Cambodia to help their struggle.

Two weeks after the congress, according to Pol Pot and Nuon Chea, twenty-one Cambodian radicals held a secret meeting on the grounds of the Phnom Penh railway station. Thiounn Mumm's brother Thiounn Prasith, who had been active among railway workers, obtained the use of a small building for the meeting. In 1977 Pol Pot described this "Party Congress":

> Among the congress participants were fourteen peasant representatives in charge of work in different rural areas, and seven representatives of the cities, twenty-one delegates in all. . . . The participation of twenty-one representatives at the Party Congress was a life and death struggle. Had the enemy discovered the site of the congress, the entire leadership of the Party would have been destroyed, the line of the Party would never have seen the light of day, the revolution would have been gravely endangered and its future jeopardized.[32]

Considerable controversy surrounds this meeting. After 1975 Red Khmer spokesmen referred to it as the First Congress of the Communist party of Kampuchea, but other documents have called it a second congress, the first having taken place in 1951. Later efforts to play down the 1951 meeting were meant to dissociate the Cambodian movement from its Vietnamese antecedents. None of the documents, however, suggests what seems obvious to a casual observer, namely that the 1960 meeting, like the one nine years before, was convened under orders from Hanoi. The timing of the meeting so soon after the Vietnamese congress is evidence of this. So is the fact that the new Central Committee named at the Cambodian meeting included Son Ngoc Minh, who was in Hanoi, where he had attended the Vietnamese congress incognito. Other members included Tou Samouth, the new secretary of the party (renamed the Workers' party of Kampuchea); Samouth's "assistant," Saloth Sar; and Samouth's deputy, Nuon Chea, who was senior to Sar. These four men, like committee officials Keo Meas and Sao Phim, were already members of the Indochina Communist party. The only member of the committee who had not joined the party was Ieng Sary.[33]

The 1973 party history states that this congress "approved a political line, strategy, stratagems, and Marxist-Leninist statutes for the Party." Members of the Central Committee were given regional responsibilities at this time.

The party's existence and its new name were still kept secret. The Cambodian party's name and its actions over the next twelve years suggest that it remained under Vietnamese supervision and subservient to Vietnamese imperatives. The Vietnamese were certainly resented later on, and their guidance spurned, but before the late 1960s and probably not before 1972–1973 the Cambodian Communist party never adopted an independent line.[34]

It must have been exciting for Saloth Sar, Ieng Sary, and Nuon Chea, all in their early thirties, to be given positions of apparently national responsibility. The appointment of Son Ngoc Minh to the committee was symbolic; Hanoi was in no position to monitor the activities of the new party. Moreover, the younger men had been working closely with Tou Samouth and the other members of the committee for several years. Meanwhile, pressure on radicals diminished, as Sihanouk tempered his anticommunist campaign by making friendly gestures toward leftist intellectuals. In 1962 the prince unwittingly fell in line with the party's united front tactics by inviting several Communists, including Khieu Samphan, to stand for the National Assembly.[35]

The Death of Tou Samouth

After securing the support of leftist intellectuals, Sihanouk spent the first half of 1962 attacking Communists—particularly the Pracheachon Group, whose refusal to dissolve itself enraged him. The group's existence thwarted his demands for total authority and consensus as the National Assembly elections of 1962 approached. In January the Pracheachon's spokesman, Non Suon, and fourteen rural workers for the movement were arrested and held without charges. Chou Chet, the editor of the group's newspaper, *Pracheachon*, was arrested two weeks later, and the paper never reappeared. In May, Non Suon and those arrested with him were tried and condemned to death. The sentences were later commuted to lengthy prison terms. The Pracheachon Group disappeared, as Sihanouk had wished. Tou Samouth and his followers lost their front organization, but now they were no longer obligated to keep in touch with the Communist movement aboveground. This suited their penchant for working in secret. Sangkum candidates in the June 1962 elections were unopposed.[36]

While the Pracheachon Group was being smashed, the Workers' party of Kampuchea remained hidden, its leaders fearful of Sihanouk's vendetta. In 1978 the Vietnamese foreign minister, Nguyen Co Thach, told an interviewer that the Cambodian Communist party had been "paralyzed by mistrust and disorder" between 1960 and 1962. Some of this paralysis can be traced to Vietnamese advice to the Cambodians to continue with political struggle—a line of action that was suicidal. These instructions and Sihanouk's unpredictable conduct knocked the Cambodian party off balance and drove it into a corner.

To make things worse, the party's secretary, Tou Samouth, disappeared in July 1962. Party members assumed that he had been killed by Sihanouk's police. If Lon Nol's agents did arrest Samouth, they probably did not realize who he was. At any rate, they learned nothing from him about the Workers' party, for no arrests of its members followed his disappearance. His colleagues, however, had no way of knowing this. From their point of view, Samouth's disappearance had ominous implications. Nuon Chea wrote years later that "the night Tou Samouth disappeared, I was terrified," while Vorn Vet wrote in his confession, "When Grandfather Tou was captured . . . the Brothers [the leaders of the party] pulled back and went into clandestinity *(dook choul somngat)*, ceased going out, stopped working in the open."[37]

The facts of the matter are still unclear, although since 1979 the Vietnamese have maintained that he was murdered with the connivance of Pol Pot—a view supported by Ben Kiernan, who has called Pol Pot's involvement the "most likely" explanation for Samouth's disappearance. Given Saloth Sar's relatively low status at the time, Samouth's popularity, and the possibility of leaks, Kiernan's argument depends on reading Pol Pot's power and villainy back into 1960. Presumably, Sar would have wanted Samouth killed because Samouth was "pro-Vietnamese" and his removal would clear the way for Sar to rise inside the party. In fact, as we shall see, Saloth Sar himself was assiduously pro-Vietnamese in all his activities before 1967 and retained Vietnamese confidence until the 1970s.

Sihanouk never claimed responsibility for killing Tou Samouth, although in 1990 an informant in Phnom Penh said that it was "well known" in party circles that Samouth had been taken by the police, tied up, weighted with stones, and thrown from a canoe into the Mekong. Two confessions extracted from Samouth's former bodyguards in 1977 and 1978, on the other hand, assert that Samouth was betrayed by Sieu Heng, by then allegedly back in the capital. One of them recalled Heng saying that "if we smash [Tou Samouth], communism will never succeed in Cambodia." Perhaps these two men—who had been Sieu Heng's bodyguards in 1957–1958—knew that Samouth had been abducted and once they were seen as counterrevolutionary for other reasons nearly twenty years later, they were forced to confess their own responsibility to tidy up the file. On balance, it seems unlikely that Saloth Sar was the one responsible for turning Tou Samouth over to the police.[38]

Talking to Monks and Students

After Samouth's disappearance, Saloth Sar became acting secretary of the party's Central Committee, while Nuon Chea remained the deputy. In addition to teaching at Chamraon Vichea, Sar conducted occasional semiclandestine seminars on civic virtue, justice, and corruption that were attended by monks, students, military men, and bureaucrats. Sok Chuon, a Buddhist

monk for ten years, attended one of these seminars in late 1962. Because Saloth Sar went into the maquis a few months later, Chuon's memories are the
last I have been able to obtain about Saloth Sar while he was living a double
existence—known as a progressive schoolteacher to some and an executive of
the Communist movement to others. The seminar was secret; those who
came had been told about it individually. The building was guarded by policemen and "agents" sympathetic to Saloth Sar. The audience consisted of
thirty monks, drawn from three wats in Phnom Penh, and perhaps twenty
others, whom Chuon remembered as "teachers and students."

The highlight of this meeting was Saloth Sar's talk, which, nearly thirty
years later, Chuon remembered vividly. Accustomed to Buddhist sermons,
Chuon judged Saloth Sar's speech as "harmonious and persuasive; he used
examples skillfully. He made himself easy to like." In his talk, Sar asked his
audience to "consider Khmer society." He mentioned that the government
charged Cambodians fees when they were born, when they were married,
and when they died. "No one can do anything," he said, "unless the government gets its fee." Even monks demanded money for their books of sermons
("Did the Buddha sell anything?" he asked rhetorically). Sar suggested that
the government itself was rotten (*puk roluy*) and leading the people into
deeper poverty. He spoke of a "new society" where fees would not be paid
because everyone would be working (he was foreshadowing his years in
power when no one was paid because money had been removed from circulation). To illustrate what was wrong with Cambodia, Sar drew his audience's
attention to royal dancers (*srei suon*) and female hangers-on (*yey akar*) at the
palace, accusing them of "living off the people." He failed to mention the
debt he owed to three of these people for his tranquil, affectionate upbringing. His insensitive choice of targets suggests that by 1962 either Saloth Sar
had rejected his family obligations or he was allowing childhood resentment
at being taken from his parents to break to the surface. To those who knew
nothing of his background, like those attending his talk, he was a heroic, de-
personalized spokesman for a larger cause. His reputation, "whispered"
among the people, had preceded him to the meeting. Chuon remembered
that "he didn't tell us his name, but we all knew already who he was."[39]

These seminars were extensions of Saloth Sar's talks at Chamraon Vichea
and were reminiscent of the discussion groups in Paris and his united front
work in 1954–1955. At the 1962 meeting Sok Chuon attended, no one was
asked to join the Workers' party, and no party officials were mentioned. Instead, Sar tried to raise people's consciousness, develop their perceptions, and
present himself as a model of smoothness, eloquence, and commitment. He
was making similar speeches to his followers in the 1980s and 1990s, after the
collapse of his regime.

The people Saloth Sar addressed in the 1960s were to provide the Cambodian Communist movement with many of its recruits. Monks, teachers, and

students were familiar with Buddhist rhetoric and susceptible to moral sermons. They considered themselves an elite, with high ethical standards. They may have felt superior to workaday Khmers; after all, students and monks did not work for money—monks were not even allowed to touch it. Students and monks also had no families to support. Unlike other public servants, teachers had fewer opportunities for corruption and greater opportunities to influence young people. By and large, monks, teachers, and students were more aware of social issues than others Saloth Sar might have assembled. For these reasons, many of them made ideal recruits.

By the end of 1962, Hou Youn, Khieu Samphan, and others in the party were also running seminars of this kind. They capitalized on a growing impatience with Sihanouk among young people and on a widespread longing for decent government, justice, and social change. They were also on the lookout for recruits. At Chamraon Vichea, a student named Siet Chhae took charge of a student union whose members, he wrote later, "were engaged in revolutionary work." The term probably meant that Siet Chhae, like Sar, was engaged in raising people's consciousness and organizing them into secret, autonomous groups. Chhim Samauk (Pang) had similar duties at the Lycée Yukhanthor. At other lycées, after-school discussion groups sprang up to debate political issues. Some of the meetings were probably known to the police but were considered harmless; others were held in secret.[40]

Efforts like these, carried out by schoolteachers in the party, soon bore fruit. In early 1963, lycée students in Siem Reap, angry at prolonged police harassment, demonstrated outside the police station. Their banners proclaimed that "The Sangkum is rotten!" and "The Sangkum is unjust!" Over the next few days, one student was killed and several were wounded. Similar demonstrations soon broke out in Phnom Penh and Kompong Cham.

Sihanouk was out of the country when he received news of the demonstrations. Angered, he sent a telegram demanding an investigation. Lon Nol saw the prince's request as license to crack down on people Lon Nol viewed as Communists. When Sihanouk returned to the capital in early March, Lon Nol gave him a list of thirty-four men he had decided were subversive. The list was a hodgepodge of journalists, activists, and noncommunist liberals like Keng Vannsak. Alarmingly, it also included the names of Saloth Sar and Ieng Sary—probably because they taught at leftist schools.[41]

By then, Sar and Sary were both high-ranking members of the party. Their positions had been confirmed at a special party congress convened in the wake of the Siem Reap demonstrations, but before Sihanouk's return. At the meeting, Sar replaced Tou Samouth as secretary of the party. Nuon Chea kept the second position, although it is likely that he had hoped to obtain the first; the third position was occupied by either Sao Phim or Ieng Sary. Recent research, based on Vietnamese Communist sources, suggests that Chea was kept out of the top position by rumors, spread by Saloth Sar, that he had recently received a sum of money from his cousin Sieu Heng. Nuon Chea himself, on the other hand, claimed in 1997 that "the Pracheachon group accused me of betrayal because I was a relative of Sieu Heng." Chea went to discuss the issue with Saloth Sar, who "said to let him become secretary and I would be deputy secretary." A 1974 party history noted that the congress had set new tasks and outlined new directions for the party, but this is doubtful, given the constraints of political struggle and the numerical weakness of the party. What was important about the congress was that it locked Saloth Sar, Nuon Chea, and Ieng Sary into positions in the party hierarchy that they retained for many years. Son Sen, who had studied with them in France, joined them on the Central Committee.[42]

Lon Nol's list, therefore, named three party members on the Central Committee (Saloth Sar, Ieng Sary, Son Sen) and two members who were familiar with the organization's inner workings (Chou Chet and Siet Chhae). Chou Chet had already left the city, and Siet Chhae was advised to desist from party business. Saloth Sar and Ieng Sary for their part decided to leave the capital and seek refuge in the eastern part of the country. According to Keng Vannsak, Sar had been eager to leave for some time and had accepted Vannsak's advice to join former Khmer militants near Thboung Khmum in northern Kompong Cham. In fact, he probably concealed his true destination—a Vietnamese military camp known as "Office 100" on the Vietnamese-Cambodian border—from Vannsak, who was not privy to party secrets. Nuon Chea, who knew how to reach the base, transported Sar and other cadre there from Phnom Penh. Talking to Yugoslavian journalists in 1978, Pol Pot said: "In 1963, I could not stay any more in Phnom Penh. I had to join the maquis. I was not very well known to the public. But Lon Nol's police followed my activities. They knew me but they did not know exactly who I was. In Phnom Penh I was the general responsible [for] the movement in the capital; I was also in charge of liaison with the countryside."[43]

When he fled Phnom Penh, Saloth Sar abandoned the double life he had led since he began teaching at Chamraon Vichea and the identities he had adopted since 1953. He was no longer restrained by his career, by his family connections, or by the exigencies of a united front. From this point on he was a full-time revolutionary. His movements were more restricted, but in his own circle he now had greater freedom to develop his views and to plan the party's seizure of power.

As a full-time militant, Sar assumed a new set of identities. After 1963 his personality, statements, and behavior became fused with Cambodia's Communist movement and with his position as "Uncle Secretary" (*om lekha*) or "Brother Number One" (*bong ti muoy*) as he came to be called. His later history suggests that either he kept much of himself hidden or he had a protean personality, revealed in his frequent changes of direction. In any case, after March 1963 Saloth Sar's personality became even more inaccessible and his life story more difficult to write.[44]

CHAPTER FIVE

■

"Red Khmer," 1963–1970

For seven years after his flight from Phnom Penh, Saloth Sar was on the run, hiding in makeshift camps in eastern and northeastern Cambodia. The only respite occurred in 1965–1966, when he spent several months in North Vietnam and China. Most of the time, Saloth Sar, Ieng Sary, and others on the Central Committee were cut off from developments in Phnom Penh and elsewhere in the world, except as filtered through intermittent party couriers (known as *nir'sei*, or "trusted people") and shortwave radio broadcasts from China and Vietnam. This isolation affected their decisions.

After 1963 Sar and his friends met few nonbelievers. They talked continuously to each other, bonding together and reinforcing their paranoia and their self-assurance. They probably spent most of their time identifying "enemies" *(khmang)* and constructing scenarios for the Cambodian people. Gaps between the scenarios and what Cambodians wanted—to say nothing of what was feasible—were numerous and wide. They went unnoticed. When the leaders of the party said that theory was subordinate to practice, what they meant was not that theoreticians had much to learn from ordinary people but that the integrity of the leaders themselves, rather than a theoretical stance, determined which strategies and tactics the party would follow.

For Saloth Sar this period, discouraging as it seemed, probably reinforced his sense of destiny and self-importance. Approval of his ideas came from subordinates in the party who were forced by his status to be deferential. Moreover, with no territories or populations to administer, he made few practical mistakes. Because his realm was insubstantial, his ideas could be utopian. The party members he met were all, in a sense, his students. To extend the metaphor, he ran the school he taught in—a school that had no inspectors, no parents, and no external governing body, except, perhaps, the Vietnam Workers' party in faraway Hanoi.

Isolation, comparative safety, and self-importance were decisive in the formation of the policies that guided the leaders of the Cambodian Communist party when they came to power. Also decisive were events outside the country. Between 1963 and 1970, the leaders did not have to temper or dilute their ideas with practice, compromise, or competition. Although their belief that they would seize power someday fueled their dedication to the party, this belief did not become a possibility until 1970, when Sihanouk was overthrown. Even then, it took five years of fighting for the Red Khmer (*khmer krohom*; in French, *Khmers rouges*)—as Sihanouk had always referred to the movement—to gain control. Their victory in 1975, given their resources and history, was unexpected.[1]

There were several foreign influences on Saloth Sar in this period. The most important intellectual one was probably the so-called Cultural Revolution in China, which broke out in 1966 and continued under various guises until Mao Zedong's death ten years later. This mass movement, largely engineered by Mao himself, was intended to accelerate his idées fixes of continuous revolution, class warfare, and the empowerment of the poor. Society was mobilized to destroy many of the institutions the regime itself had created—including, briefly, the Communist party leadership. When the Cultural Revolution spun out of control, Mao redirected it, but many of his other policies remained unaltered until the early 1980s.

Saloth Sar visited China in the early phase of this revolution. He must have been impressed by what he saw. Some of the measures introduced in China at the time—for example, the partial evacuation of cities, "storming attacks" on economic problems, and the abandonment of differential military ranks—were later adopted by the Red Khmer. Chinese-style purges of "class enemies" were also widespread in Democratic Kampuchea, and Cambodia's economic ambitions were described as the "Great Leap Forward" (*maha lout ploh*), a phrase borrowed from the extravagant industrialization program launched in China in the 1950s. It is uncertain if Sar ever learned that the Cultural Revolution was a disaster. Similarly, he may never have known that the Great Leap Forward had failed—to say nothing of Stalin's collectivization program in the 1930s. A key feature of his 1966 visit was his encounter with K'ang Sheng, a senior Chinese cadre who had often served as the head of Mao's secret police and who befriended Saloth Sar on this occasion.

At home, Saloth Sar was influenced by the shift of his headquarters from Kompong Cham to the remote forested province of Ratanakiri in the northeast. The move occurred after he had returned from China and was probably done with Vietnamese advice and certainly with Vietnamese approval.

The most far-reaching influence on Saloth Sar, however, was the war being waged in Vietnam. The war had at least three effects on Cambodian political life. One was that Sihanouk, half fearing a Communist victory and half desiring one (for he had come to hate the United States), decided that the way to keep Cambodia out of the war and guarantee its survival was to strike up an alliance with North Vietnam and its surrogate in South Vietnam, the National Liberation Front (NLF). In November 1963 Sihanouk rejected any further U.S. military assistance to his regime. He followed this in 1964 with a secret agreement with the Vietnamese that allowed Vietnamese Communist troops to station themselves on Cambodian soil and to move through the country so long as they respected its inhabitants. In exchange, the Vietnamese promised to honor Cambodia's independence and its frontiers when the war was over. As the war intensified, the Cambodian bases became crucial to the Vietnamese, and in late 1966 arms from China began flowing to their forces via the Cambodian port of Sihanoukville (Kompong Som). Thus, in trying to outsmart larger powers and sidestep the conflict, Sihanouk compromised his neutrality and guaranteed that Cambodia would be dragged into the war.

A second effect of the war, and a by-product of Sihanouk's arrangements, was that Cambodian Communists were called by the Vietnamese to provide military and logistical support. Several hundred Khmer Communists traveled to North Vietnam, without Sihanouk's knowledge, for military and political training.

The third effect of the war was a growing malaise among Cambodia's elite. By the late 1960s, they were nervous about Sihanouk's policies and the possibility that Cambodia would be dragged into the war. Many of their children, pouring through an expanded education system, were also unhappy with the prospect of unemployment after they graduated and with Sihanouk's style of rule. Some of them were inspired by radical teachers. Sihanouk's response to the malaise was to crack down on dissidents, a policy that alienated the students even more. By 1969 hundreds of them had left the towns to join the Communist resistance.[2]

A Hostage of the Vietnamese

In late 1963 a Communist militant spotted Saloth Sar in the eastern Cambodian province of Kompong Cham, not far from the Vietnamese border. By the end of 1964 several colleagues had encountered him in an encampment in that region known by the code name "Office *(munthi)* 100." One text locates the encampment inside Vietnam; another places it in eastern Kompong Cham. It seems likely that the base moved back and forth across the border in response to military pressures. Saloth Sar remained there until he traveled to Vietnam and China at the end of 1965. These two years, when he accomplished little and depended on people who later became his enemies, marked a low point in his career.

In late 1964 a young Communist named Chhim Samauk traveled from Phnom Penh to Office 100. Like many of Saloth Sar's close associates, he was later purged by Pol Pot's government at interrogation center S-21 in Phnom Penh. Samauk was one of many "enemies" who left several thousand pages of confessions, extracted under torture, admitting to a range of spurious charges. These documents shed light on details of life in the Communist movement about which the prisoners had no reason to lie. In his confession in 1977, for example, Chhim Samauk remembered:

> I met Brother Number One at Office 100. I was excited and very happy, for I hadn't imagined that he would be there. At that time, I couldn't tell the Brothers [that is, the leading party personalities] apart. After a while, I learned who Brother Number One was and Brother Van [Ieng Sary]. . . . The work was a real struggle. It went on even if you had malaria. I saw the Brothers [Sar and Sary] writing documents, preparing stencils (sdengsil) and printing the documents. I tried very hard to study with them. After a while I was able to help them to an extent, writing and publishing secret documents myself. In Office 100 in 1964–1965 I was very happy. No problems arose to confuse me. I believed that I was building myself [that is, constructing a new, revolutionary personality] and making progress.[3]

Another young party member worked in Office 100 as a paramedic under Ieng Sary. In his confession, he noted that Cambodians had not been allowed outside the base by the Vietnamese who guarded it. The psychological impact of such conditions on these proud men is difficult to measure. In 1964–1965 Office 100 seems to have contained no more than twenty Cambodians at any given time. Only three of them were "military." Those at the base included such party stalwarts as Keo Meas; Ney Saran (Ya); Sok Knol; Sao Phim, a Central Committee member with responsibility for the eastern part of the country; and Chou Chet's wife, Im Naen (Li), who acted as cook for Sar and Sary in Office 100 and who was brought into the party by Sary in 1966 as a reward for her revolutionary zeal.[4]

In spite of these handicaps, Saloth Sar and his colleagues proceeded to plan a revolution. In late 1964 Sar convened a study meeting at the base. A party document from 1978 asserts that the "meeting . . . decided to counter any eventual coup by the Americans"—an opinion confirmed by a former party member interviewed by Steve Heder in 1980. The coup they envisaged would have involved the United States supporting Lon Nol or the exiled Son Ngoc Thanh in a move against Sihanouk. In such an eventuality, the Communists would not be able to count on Sihanouk's alliances with China and Vietnam or his anti-American stance and would have to consider initiating a mixture of armed and political struggle. This was precisely the decision the party reached two years later, shortly before Lon Nol became prime minister in another Sihanouk regime.[5]

Making plans and dreaming of success were as much as the Khmer could do. From Office 100, Cambodia's revolution seemed a long way off. To begin with, the Cambodian Communist party was unarmed. The cramped, malarial conditions under which Saloth Sar, Son Sen, Ieng Sary, and a handful of others lived for two years probably explain Pol Pot's failure to cite any party ini-

tiatives from this time. In his five-hour speech announcing the existence of
the party in 1977, he limited himself to two events in Phnom Penh over
which the party's leaders exercised no control.[6]

He called the first of these "a great event in our struggle." This was Sihanouk's decision to cut off U.S. military aid in November 1963. Sar failed to
mention Sihanouk's name. The second event was the demonstration against
the U.S. Embassy in March 1964, when several thousand students, soldiers in
mufti, and other Cambodians demonstrated against the U.S. bombing of a
Cambodian village near the Vietnamese border. In fact, the demonstrations
had Sihanouk's approval and took the Communists in the capital by surprise.
Vorn Vet, who participated in them, noted later: "I had never imagined that
there could be such a large movement; the revolutionary forces by themselves were incapable of such a thing."[7]

In 1965 Saloth Sar left Office 100 to visit Vietnam and China. He had
probably been asked to make the trip by those in charge of the Workers'
party of Vietnam. He was gone for more than a year. The trip closed off a period in his life that he never mentioned later. At times in Office 100, despite
the brave front he presented to subordinates, he must have come close to de-
spair. He was certainly far removed from his time as a teacher in Phnom
Penh or as a student in Paris, when he had been free to move around, life had
been easier, and continuous conversations made a revolution seem a genuine
possibility.

The Visit to Vietnam

Saloth Sar, Keo Meas, and several other Cambodian Communists, including
Um Neng (Vi), a Pracheachon veteran, visited North Vietnam and China between June 1965 and September 1966. Ieng Sary's wife, Khieu Thirith,
claimed in 1981 that she and her husband had been in the delegation. Their
participation is unlikely.[8]

Saloth Sar and the others were probably summoned north by the Vietnamese to discuss the escalation of the war and the expanded role the Cambodian Communists would be called upon to play. Tactics, as well as a suitable political line, needed to be ironed out. Furthermore, the Vietnamese
wanted to familiarize themselves with Tou Samouth's thirty-seven-year-old
successor; the Cambodian Communists who had resettled in North Vietnam
in 1954–1955 and after were also eager to meet Sar.

When the delegation reached Hanoi, its members were treated with respect. Saloth Sar gave lectures to his countrymen about the situation at
home, and with some of them he discussed "the question of the party's name"
(that it had been changed to the Workers' party of Kampuchea in 1960). He
probably enjoyed meeting with Yun Soeurn and Rath Samoeun, his old
friends from Paris. Another colleague from Viet Minh days, Keo Moni, re-

called that Sar's visit to Vietnam lasted "about nine months" and included several courses of study for the Khmer aimed at bringing the party members in Vietnam and those in Cambodia into agreement. Keo Moni also claimed that Pol Pot had brought documents "dealing with building the party, politics, combat, and economics." When the bonhomie wore off, Saloth Sar and his colleagues must have been intrigued that so many Cambodians like Keo Moni were undergoing political and military training in North Vietnam. They may have wondered what these people were being trained to do and where their loyalties lay.[9]

The delegates also took part in secret talks with Vietnamese Communist party officials, led by the general secretary, Le Duan. For many years, the only record of these talks was in the so-called *Livre noir*, a polemical document written (probably by Pol Pot) twelve years after these events to justify Cambodia's conflict with Vietnam. The book was written in 1978, when Cambodia's relations with Vietnam had reached their nadir. As such, the text is certainly biased, revealing many of Pol Pot's obsessions. However, Vietnamese documents concerning the visit, studied in the 1990s by Thomas Engelbert and Christopher Goscha, reveal that the *Livre noir*'s treatment of events is generally correct.

The *Livre noir* lambastes the party's former patrons in Hanoi. Pol Pot's anger does not necessarily make his allegations false, but he certainly wrote the parts about himself and the delegation in 1965–1966 to make the mission sound more autonomous, successful, and important than it was.[10] The *Livre noir* claims, for example, that Le Duan criticized the Khmer sharply for adopting their own political line. Pol Pot continued: "The Communist Party of Kampuchea had its own political line. Thanks to that line, the revolutionary movement in Kampuchea had taken wing. This disturbed the Vietnamese because . . . if the revolution in Kampuchea developed and strengthened itself independently, they would be unable to control it."

According to the *Livre noir*, Le Duan then presented the Khmer with a document "in the Vietnamese language" that called on them to "renounce revolutionary struggle [on behalf of Cambodia] and wait for the Vietnamese to win." This may well be the document cited by Engelbert and Goscha, which stated that "[Cambodian] independence does not mean breaking off and creating a separate movement; instead Sihanouk could be used to appeal to the people on behalf of the movement or the movement could use the cover of Sihanouk's name to appeal [to the masses], although it would still be led primarily by us."[11]

The *Livre noir* goes on to say that

The conflict on the question of the political line was very bitter. But the Cambodian delegation preserved its calm and did nothing to annoy . . . the Vietnamese. After the departure of Secretary Pol Pot for Kampuchea, the Vietnamese knew that the Communist Party of Kampuchea would maintain its line which was to carry out armed struggle in combination with political struggle.[12]

The *Livre noir* is a mélange of truth, reconstructed history, and wishful thinking. The imposition of a Vietnamese-language text on the Khmer, Le Duan's hectoring, and the Khmer's unwillingness to annoy the Vietnamese sound plausible, but assertions that there was an open "conflict" with Vietnam and that Sar pursued an independent line or that he raised the idea of independence during his visit are contradictory. The Communists' decision to combine armed and political struggle was not taken until late 1967, and no action flowed from the decision until January 1968. In the *Livre noir*, Saloth Sar probably presented the thoughts he had had at the time, but these were heated in retrospect by Vietnam's behavior and his resentment at having been unable to speak out.

The sessions with Le Duan were humiliating to Sar, and there is a poignancy to his bravado twelve years later. His views as the leader of a sovereign party were not solicited or treated with respect by the Vietnamese. He was required to give the same acquiescence that Sihanouk demanded of Lon Nol or that the Vietnamese demanded of their protégé Heng Samrin after 1979. Had Saloth Sar responded as stubbornly as he said he did, the Vietnamese would have found someone else to lead the Cambodian Communist party. They would not have allowed him to visit China. Because he did go to China, and returned home as the party's leader, we can assume that he swallowed his pride and by his silence seemed to accept Vietnamese advice.

The Visit to China

Sometime during his visit to Vietnam, Sar made it known that he wanted to go to China, at that point a strong ally of Vietnam in its war with the United States. Permission from Beijing took several months to arrive. Sar probably filled his time with political and military training (and perhaps language study), which neither he nor the Vietnamese would have been eager to point out after 1977.

The amount of time he spent in China is uncertain. He never mentioned the trip in public. Sources that mention the visit date from 1978 or later and are mostly Vietnamese. These sources, in turn, paint Saloth Sar as having been mesmerized by the "Gang of Four," a group of high-ranking radical Maoists who enjoyed a spectacular spell of power in the 1970s and were imprisoned soon after Mao's death in 1976. These postdated Vietnamese accusations are probably spurious, although a former Chinese diplomat, speaking on condition of anonymity, stated in 1997 that during his 1966 visit Saloth Sar had been befriended by K'ang Sheng, a senior Communist cadre who had often served at the head of Mao's secret police. Since his return from the Soviet Union in 1937, Sheng had earned a reputation for deviousness and for presiding over several ruthless, far-reaching purges. In 1965, one of his duties was to greet visitors to China from friendly and in many cases clandestine Communist parties. Although no record of his conversations with Saloth Sar has survived, it seems likely that Sheng praised the radicalism of Sar's revolutionary stance and pointed out to him the importance of locating and rooting out internal enemies.

In 1966, the political differences between Vietnam and China were not severe, although the Vietnamese, obsessed with fighting the United States, were distressed by differences between Vietnam's major allies, China and the USSR. Chinese help, moreover, was crucial to the Vietnam War, and Saloth Sar visited China not as an independent revolutionary but as a Vietnamese ally paying his respects.

Ironically, those who welcomed him probably included the soon-to-be-discredited "capitalist roaders" Liu Shaoqi and Deng Xiaoping, who were in charge of interparty relations at the time. Liu had recently visited Cambodia to reemphasize China's alliance with Sihanouk. Even more recently, Sihanouk himself had been warmly received on a state visit to China. In this setting, it is unlikely that Saloth Sar was in a position to plead a special case, to argue for armed struggle against the prince, or to ask for Chinese aid.[13]

As far as the Chinese were concerned, Sar was less important than their alliances with Sihanouk and North Vietnam. Perhaps they believed that in a minor way Sar could help the Communists defeat U.S. imperialism in Asia. Cambodia might even become a socialist state later on, and Saloth Sar might come to power under Vietnamese guidance. In the meantime, however, nothing could be gained by encouraging him to take an independent line. Instead, Liu, Deng, and their subordinates probably gave him the same kind of avuncular treatment he had received and resented in Hanoi. They undoubtedly told him to work with Sihanouk, support the Vietnamese, and strengthen the Cambodian Communist party. At the same time, it seems likely that the more radical among them admired his nerve. The Chinese certainly behaved more courteously toward him than the Vietnamese had done. In the back of their minds, they may have seen him as an authentic revolutionary who might be helpful to them later on. K'ang Sheng, who vigorously supported the Gang of Four, would probably have taken this view.

For Saloth Sar, the contrast between China and Vietnam and his reception in both places was probably dramatic. The Chinese revolution had already succeeded and was entering a new phase, while Vietnam was bogged down in its open-ended war with the United States. The crowded, enthusiastic Chinese cities and the highly orchestrated Communist party celebrations that he saw were refreshing after Office 100, Le Duan's hectoring remarks, and the hothouse provincialism of Indochina. Sar must have been as impressed by the scale, autonomy, and momentum of China's social mobilization as he had been by Yugoslavia's in 1950. It was China's triumphant revolution rather than Vietnam's arduous, unfinished struggle, perhaps, that Sar wished to bring back to Cambodia.

In early 1966, while Sar was visiting China, a new edition of Mao Ze-dong's aphorisms—called the *Little Red Book*—was published. The print run was for 200 million copies—another example, if Saloth Sar needed one, of the scale and accessibility of China's revolution. As a Communist, Sar was drawn to Mao's emphases on continuous class warfare, individual revolutionary will, and the importance of poor peasants—ideological areas in which China differed from Vietnam and which were later emphasized in Democratic Kampuchea. Sar may also have been drawn toward the conspiratorial, class-based explanations of politics in China so dear to Mao. As a teacher, Sar probably admired the *Red Book*'s brisk, hortatory style, which was well-suited for memorization by a poorly educated, unquestioning population. Interestingly, either because of the importance of China's alliance with Sihanouk or because the Chinese felt Cambodia had little revolutionary potential, no Khmer language edition of Mao's aphorisms was ever published.

Another document that received attention in China at this time was an address by Vice Premier and Minister of Defense Lin Biao, an ardent Maoist. This wide-ranging speech—published in September 1965 as "Long Live the Victory of People's War!"—offered a defense of several Maoist ideas. Lin suggested, for example, that rural areas throughout the Third World could encircle and suffocate the capitalist cities, just as Chinese Communist armies had done in China in the 1940s. He also argued that Third World revolutions should proceed under their own momentum rather than under the guidance of more powerful and more sophisticated foreign Communist parties. "In order to make a revolution and to fight a people's war and be victorious," he wrote, "it is imperative to adhere to the policy of self-reliance, rely on the strength of the masses in one's own country and prepare . . . to fight independently even when all aid is cut off."[14]

Lin Biao's speech was part of Mao's campaign to regain the upper hand in China, which he had lost following the Great Leap Forward. The speech threw down the gauntlet to "revisionists" like Soviet leader Nikita Khrushchev, who argued for peaceful coexistence with the capitalist world. It had a profound influence on Communist movements as disparate as those in Thailand, Bolivia, and the Philippines. Lin Biao's idea of indigenous revolution (in Cambodia's case, independent of Vietnam's) struck a sympathetic chord in Saloth Sar. The speech must also have distressed policymakers in Hanoi, who needed Chinese and Soviet aid to prosecute Vietnam's war with the United States.

A Change in Tactics

During Sar's absence, the Vietnam War escalated sharply. By the end of 1965 some 300,000 U.S. combat and support troops had poured into South Vietnam, and more were on their way. U.S. and South Vietnamese infantry attacks on Vietnamese Communist forces were accompanied by intense aerial bombardment. Bombing of the Cambodian–South Vietnamese frontier forced Office 100 to shift some fifteen days' march to the north in early 1966, before Saloth Sar came home.[15]

After walking north for fifteen days, Saloth Sar reached the semi-deserted base, code-named Office 102, where Chhim Samauk was waiting for him. Samauk wrote later that "the atmosphere of the camp was very quiet. There was no doctor and no medicine." He nursed Saloth Sar back to health. "I respected and loved him so much," Samauk wrote, "that I would have done nothing to cause him difficulty." When he recovered, Sar moved on to another base in Ratanakiri—Office 104—where he rejoined colleagues from Office 100, including Keo Meas, Sao Phim, Sok Knol, Son Sen, and Ieng Sary. The camp became his headquarters until late 1969, when he traveled to Hanoi.[16]

Soon after Sar reached his new headquarters in Ratanakiri toward the end of 1966, he convened a study session to establish the party's strategy and tactics for the coming year. According to Chhim Samauk, the meeting was frequently disrupted by "enemy" overflights, presumably U.S. spotter aircraft, patrolling the Cambodian–South Vietnamese border. The escalation of the Vietnam War and developments in Indonesia and Cambodia made the 1966 study session a turning point in the history of the Cambodian Communist party because they persuaded Sar that the party's tactics had to be changed.

In September 1965 the Communist party of Indonesia, the largest in the noncommunist world, had been tangentially involved in a coup attempt in which several high-ranking army officers had been killed. The flamboyant Indonesian chief of state, Sukarno, had not been threatened, but the army's response to the abortive coup was harsh. Between October 1965 and March 1966, approximately half a million suspected Communists were massacred by army troops, local militia, and enraged civilians. Thousands of others were imprisoned. Indonesian communism ceased to exist, and Sukarno soon lost his political position. He was replaced by the man who had coordinated the repression, General Suharto.

News of the Indonesian massacres and Sukarno's ouster must have reached Saloth Sar while he was in China and probably made him warier than ever of allying with a charismatic nationalist leader like Sihanouk, who could offer little shelter if the "pro-imperialist" army of Lon Nol decided to crack down. The Vietnamese, however, continued to press this potentially suicidal alliance on Saloth Sar, even though they would be in no position to bail their Cambodian brothers out if they were targeted by Lon Nol. In this connection, it would be intriguing to know what tactics Sar's Chinese hosts suggested. After all, they had been the Indonesian Communists' most ardent backers.[17]

Meanwhile, Cambodians were preparing for the 1966 National Assembly elections, the first since 1951 that were not stage-managed by the prince.

With Sihanouk's encouragement, candidates were allowed to compete for votes. The elections developed a free-for-all character that was later criticized by some writers as showing the dominance of the "right" in Cambodian politics, even though the Communists in the assembly—Khieu Samphan, Hou Youn, and Hu Nim—all won their seats with increased majorities. These elections were significant to the Cambodian Communist party because they resulted in an assembly that did not depend on the prince's patronage and therefore was not under his control.

No longer Sihanouk's rubber stamp, the assembly in October named Lon Nol, the Communists' archenemy, as prime minister. The Communists, of course, soon rejected the notion of building a united front with Sihanouk and the radicals in Phnom Penh. With Nol at the helm, increased government harassment of urban and rural Communists seemed likely.

Developments in Vietnam, Indonesia, and Cambodia dictated the Communists' choice of tactics in 1966–1967 and inspired a contradictory mixture of militancy and prudence. In response to these developments, Sar and the others made two important tactical decisions at the 1966 study session: They changed the party's name from the Revolutionary Workers' party to the Communist party of Kampuchea (CPK), and they moved some of their key personnel to the remote province of Ratanakiri in Cambodia's northeast. Some writers have seen the change of names as a slap at Vietnam, whose Vietnam Workers' party would have dropped semantically to a lower stage of development than the CPK. In fact, the Vietnamese and Cambodians in Hanoi were not informed of the change; in documents sent to Vietnam, the Cambodians used earlier party names. In party circles, the Vietnamese and Cambodians would have referred to themselves and to each other as Communists, and the party flags displayed at their meetings were identical. For Cambodians to declare secretly that they were Communists made no difference to Vietnamese strategy or tactics, but it seems likely that the Red Khmer leaders, in secret, relished their enhanced semantic status.

Bestowing a new name on the party may also have allowed Saloth Sar to reassert his control, which may have weakened while he was traveling, and to draw the dispersed, contentious factions of the organization together. To ensure support for the change, Sar might have told the others that he had suggested it and the Chinese applauded it. In any event, this was the most significant thing he brought back after nearly a year outside the country.

More consequential than the change in party name was the move to Ratanakiri. It was probably made to avoid the U.S. bombing raids and to keep Office 100 from being overrun by South Vietnamese and American forces. In effect, several party leaders were shifted from rural Cambodia, where they worked among Buddhist peasants, into a sparsely inhabited world of tribal minorities who spoke different dialects and engaged in slash-and-burn agriculture.

Over the next four years Ieng Sary and other high-ranking members of the party lived and worked among these people. Over the years, the people of Ratanakiri, Kratie, and Mondulkiri had grown increasingly hostile to the Phnom Penh government as roads, rubber plantations, settlers, and foresters advanced into their lands. "They hated all the Khmer," a party member later recalled. In terms of party history, the years that Sar and Sary spent in that region echoed the years that Ho Chi Minh spent among minority people in northwestern Vietnam in World War II and the ones that Mao Zedong spent in Yanan in 1937–1945. The breathing spell gave the Cambodian Communists time to think about the future. On paper, they were able to carve up the country into numbered administrative sectors (*dombon*) and also devise the number codes for administrative and military units that surfaced in the early 1970s and persisted under Democratic Kampuchea. As time went on, they recruited several hundred tribespeople into the party. "One of their strong points," Siet Chhae remarked, was that "they believed the Revolutionary Organization," as the party came to be known to nonmembers. They probably joined the party because its attacks on the government made sense and because the Communist leaders seemed sincere and sympathetic. In 1968–1970, the northeast was the focus of Communist resistance to the Phnom Penh government.[18]

In Marxian terms, the tribespeople had ideological significance. Without access to money, markets, or the state, they enjoyed what appeared to be deeply rooted traditions of autonomy, solidarity, and mutual aid. To Communist cadre, the Jarai, Tapuon, and Brao peoples, to name just three, participated in "primitive communism," which in Marx's historical schema—later ratified by Stalin—preceded the slave and feudal stages of social development. The tribespeople were "noble savages," uncorrupted by social differentiation or money. They were also, in Maoist terms, "poor and blank" receptacles for Communist teaching. The combination made them role models for the urban intellectuals who dominated the upper reaches of the Communist movement. The relationship between Communists and tribespeople was mutually beneficial. Many tribespeople became trusted bodyguards, messengers, and party members.[19]

The Red Khmer leaders benefited in another way from the time they spent in the forests of Ratanakiri. Consciously or not, Saloth Sar, Ieng Sary, and others in the party were conforming to heroic stereotypes in Hindu and Buddhist mythology—stereotypes embedded in Cambodian popular thought—whereby bandits, exiled princes, and religious ascetics stored up arcane wisdom, merit, and martial skills while living isolated in the forests, only to emerge later as seemingly invulnerable leaders. The Communists were certainly aware of this mythology, but it is impossible to say what influence it had on their behavior. To many Cambodians, forests were also places of illness, danger, and fearsome spiritual power. People who lived in forests (*prey;*

the word also means "wild") or who emerged from them onto the plains were thought to be darker-skinned than most Cambodians and often possessing murderous spiritual gifts. The Red Khmer partook of both traditions when they came to power.[20]

The Samlaut Uprising

In early 1967 harsh government policies ignited a peasant revolt in western Battambang near the village of Samlaut. The trouble began in 1965–1966, when peasants clandestinely sold at least a quarter of Cambodia's surplus rice to North Vietnamese and NLF forces camped along the border. In other words, only three-quarters of the surplus was left for the government to tax for export. Since export taxes were a traditional source of government revenue, Sihanouk was determined to avoid similar losses in 1966–1967. He inaugurated a policy of sending "action teams" with military escorts into the countryside to purchase unmilled rice for the government at prices lower than those paid by the Vietnamese.

In early 1967, while the prince was overseas, Prime Minister Lon Nol decided to concentrate collection efforts in Battambang, which had always had the highest surpluses in the country. His action teams were assiduous and brutal, and clashes soon broke out between farmers and government agents. In some cases, resistance was encouraged by local Communists, who distributed leaflets insulting the Sangkum and accusing Lon Nol and Sihanouk of having "sold out to the United States." In parts of the province that had been anti-French guerrilla strongholds in the 1950s, animosity toward Lon Nol, who had been the governor of Battambang at the time, was deep-seated. Local grievances reinforced negative feelings toward Phnom Penh. The government action teams, for their part, aggravated tensions by looking for "Communists" to rough up.[21]

In early April 1967 over two hundred local people, some bearing anti-American banners, attacked Cambodian army posts near Samlaut. The Communist party leaders in the faraway northeast did not know the attack was going to occur, but undoubtedly the local radicals, exasperated by the government's behavior, encouraged the people to revolt. The insurgents killed two soldiers and made off with some rifles. Violence spread into neighboring villages over the next few days. The army's response was swift. Hundreds of suspects were rounded up, beaten, and interrogated. Hundreds of others fled their homes and took refuge in the forests as army units stormed through their villages, seeking victims, scapegoats, and loot.

When he returned from overseas, Sihanouk approved Lon Nol's repressive tactics and wheeled on leftists operating in the open in Phnom Penh, whom he mistakenly believed had masterminded the uprising. There is some evidence that people like Khieu Samphan, Hu Nim, and Hou Youn had encouraged students to demonstrate against military "oppression" in the northwest, but party members working in secret were probably better informed. There is no evidence that these left-wing intellectuals organized the peasants in Battambang. Sihanouk, who had previously favored the three, now threatened them with arrest. Within a month, Youn and Samphan had fled the capital. Their admirers, particularly in student circles, assumed they had been killed (when Hu Nim joined the other two later in the year, they became known as the "Three Ghosts"), and student opinion hardened against the prince. The Communist party played along with the idea of their martyrdom, keeping them hidden until Sihanouk was overthrown.[22]

Mopping up around Samlaut went on for several months. Combat was especially severe around Vay Chap Mountain, a former guerrilla hideout that had recently been reoccupied by radicals fleeing from Lon Nol. The rebels were pursued into the forest by hundreds of local people who had been given staves and hatchets, formed into militia units, and told to "chase the Reds." Rewards were given for delivering severed heads to the authorities. More than one thousand victims lost their lives. Many of the survivors became permanently embittered. Violence sputtered in the region for the remainder of the year, although Sihanouk declared the rebellion "finished" in July. The killings resembled the massacres in Indonesia (except on a far smaller scale) in that they settled scores against "Communists" and went unpunished.

The Samlaut uprising showed Sihanouk that Cambodian peasants, supposedly his affectionate children, could be goaded to rebellion by oppressive policies and radical propaganda. Because the prince assumed that the Cambodian Communists were puppets of Vietnam, he thought that the uprising had enjoyed Vietnamese support. Sihanouk's opponents among the Phnom Penh elite saw the unrest as proof that he was vulnerable to what they perceived as a genuine Communist threat. The Communist leadership, dispersed and hidden in Phnom Penh, the eastern zone, and elsewhere, interpreted Samlaut in other ways.[23]

As I have noted, local Communists, encouraged by those in Phnom Penh, probably exploited the rebellion in its early phases. The effectiveness of Sihanouk's repression, however, probably convinced the leaders of the party (in Phnom Penh at least, where Nuon Chea remained in charge of party business) that they risked exposure and defeat if they chose to encourage the resistance any further. This interpretation was reinforced by Muol Sambath (Nhim Ros) in his 1978 confession. Sambath was an Indochina Communist party veteran who spent the 1960s as a militant in Battambang. In a laconic chronology prepared for his confession, Sambath wrote:

2/67: The masses exploded and killed police spies. Then enemies attacked the people who were in contradiction with them, until a [full-scale] uprising occurred.

·4–5/67: The Organization [that is, the party leadership] ordered that [the fighting] desist. Brother Kuu, the contemptible Say (Ruos Mau), and the contemptible Suy met in Brother Kuu's house.[24]

In July, Sambath continued, a "brother" (presumably Kong Sopal, a senior revolutionary whose pseudonym was Kuu), who had been sent to the northwest by Nuon Chea in 1965, said that the threat of renewed violence by the enemy would lead to the party's adopting "a policy of armed struggle in 1968." Perhaps hindsight was at work here on Muol Sambath's part, for the decision to change policies was made toward the end of the year, as we shall see.

In the wake of the Samlaut uprising, Sihanouk became distressed by news that the *Little Red Book* was popular in Chinese-language schools and, in French translation, in several monasteries in Phnom Penh. Worried about the possibility of Chinese-sponsored violence against him, Sihanouk had suspected radicals rounded up. Allegedly pro-Chinese students and other activists were killed by the police, and by September 1967 Hu Nim, the last radical in the National Assembly, was driven into the maquis. Over one hundred sympathetic teachers and students followed him before the end of the year. Few of them survived the purges of the DK era.[25]

The Communist party of Kampuchea had now reached a perilous point in its history. The suppression of the Samlaut uprising had been followed by Sihanouk's smashing of the party's urban networks. Faced with obliteration, the party lacked the means to continue political struggle—it had no weapons with which to inaugurate an armed rebellion. In late 1967 its leaders decided to play for time by combining the two forms of struggle—using violence to defend the party's leaders, but continuing their political struggle until the party's forces had increased. In a speech given in September 1977, Pol Pot declared that in 1967 "the enemy [presumably Sihanouk's armed forces] was wavering and incapable of facing the revolutionary forces." In fact, the reverse was true, and Pol Pot admitted as much by connecting this allegedly victorious stage of the revolution with the need for a change in tactics. "If we did not take up armed struggle," he said, "we would be incapable of defending the revolutionary forces."[26]

These contradictions must have been on Saloth Sar's mind when he convened a study session in the northeast toward the end of 1967. The meeting was intended "to organize resistance to the enemies' devious strategy." Those who attended were probably informed of an augmented military role for the Cambodian Communist party in backing up the Vietnamese effort. The meeting also endorsed a policy of mixing armed and political struggle and permitting autonomy to regional commanders. In allowing this freedom of maneuver, Sar was making a virtue of necessity, for he had no way of contacting the other bases, except by messengers moving across the country on foot or by whatever transport they could find. In effect, Sar decided to stay in hiding and to allow the other Red Khmer to carry on as best they could. The first thing these scattered radicals needed to do was to find some weapons.[27]

Armed Struggle, 1968–1970

Communist-led forces frequently clashed with Sihanouk's army, militia, and police in early 1968. In late January, shortly before the Tet Offensive in South Vietnam, several minor clashes occurred in Battambang. One of these, at Bay Damram on January 17, was later celebrated as the birthday of the Revolutionary Army. According to a 1977 document, the incident involved some "10 to 20" combatants. Skirmishes also broke out in the northeast between tribal groups and army units. Similar incidents were reported elsewhere in the country. In most cases, the fights were provoked by government forces, which had been encouraged by Sihanouk and Lon Nol to take the offensive against the Red Khmers. In others, Communist forces ambushed small government units and stole their weapons.[28]

About this time, Saloth Sar convened a specifically military study session, the first of its kind, at his encampment in Ratanakiri. He had no military training or experience, but Lon Nol's troops were nearby and he had to appear as if he knew what he was doing. Two items were almost certainly on the agenda: the party's role in the Vietnamese Tet Offensive, and Sihanouk's drift toward a rapprochement with the United States.

In January 1968 the U.S. ambassador to India, Chester Bowles, had visited Phnom Penh. He was the first high-ranking American to do so since 1964. The Red Khmer in the northeast would not have known of the discussions between Bowles and Sihanouk, which included Sihanouk's allowing American troops in Vietnam to engage in "hot pursuit" of Vietnamese Communist forces across the Vietnamese-Cambodian frontier, but they suspected him of betraying them. The prince's tactics of seeking U.S. friendship as part of his antiradical campaign made him more untrustworthy than ever.[29]

Controversy still surrounds the rationale for the Tet Offensive in Vietnam, which was ostensibly launched by the North Vietnamese and the NLF in February 1968 to set off a nationwide uprising against the United States and the pro-American South Vietnamese regime. The Communists believed that the uprising would succeed and in its wake America would sue for peace.

The offensive, in fact, failed to ignite a national uprising, despite its psychological success in speeding U.S. withdrawal from Vietnam. One of its effects was that NLF forces, cut to pieces in the campaign, were soon replaced in Cambodia by units from North Vietnam, who seemed more foreign to local Khmer and made more demands on them. This development led to increased tension between the Communist forces and Lon Nol's army, on the one hand, and more systematic cooperation between Vietnamese forces and local Red Khmer, on the other.[30]

From the beginning of 1968 to the end of 1969, when Saloth Sar traveled for the second time to Hanoi, he disappeared from view. Siet Chhae, who was in the northeast with him, later recalled that "the Brothers were often away on business for months at a time." If Sar's subsequent conduct is a guide, these trips involved giving talks to cadre and combatants to raise their morale, explain tactics, and clarify strategy.

Sar's forlorn descriptions of this period, which ring true, suggest that he spent much of his time in hiding and on the run.[31] In 1972, for example, he described the odds that his forces had faced in the early phases of combat with Sihanouk's army:

> In some areas where the enemy engaged the people, we were cut off. We lacked personnel. We had no economy. We had no military strength and nowhere to hide. No matter how big the forests were, we found no shelter. No matter how good the people were, the enemy squeezed and manhandled them, and they could do nothing. If people were not good, the enemy controlled and commanded them. The enemy knew the forests. Wherever we came and went, he was aware of us. We had a few weapons here and there, but we had no land, and no people under our control.[32]

As Pol Pot often said, the early stages of the revolution were "waged with empty hands." The phrase is not hyperbolic in view of his assertion in 1977 that the Central Committee in 1968 was protected by four armed men. Although by early 1970 Communist-led guerrilla forces had rendered large parts of the country unsafe for day-to-day administration from Phnom Penh, the military balance of power still favored government forces, and the Communists still depended on captured weapons. It is ironic that the Vietnamese, themselves armed from abroad, should have encouraged a Maoist autonomy for the Khmer as far as weaponry was concerned while insisting on the Khmer's obedience to Vietnam. What drew them to Cambodia (and was later to draw the attention of the United States) were their supply lines into South Vietnam. Insofar as these were threatened by Lon Nol, Sihanouk, and U.S. bombing, the Cambodian Communists and their followers had useful roles to play in providing sentries, laborers, and porters.

The Cambodian Communist party's alliance with Vietnam remained in force. In mid-1968, Keo Meas, a high-ranking Cambodian cadre, was dispatched to Hanoi with documents destined for the Cambodian Communists there. Three of the documents—dealing with Samlaut, the people's war, and perceptions of worldwide revolution—were the subjects of a fifteen-day study session for Cambodian Communists in Hanoi. At the conclusion of the session, a Vietnamese party member told the assembled Khmer that the time was not ripe for them to return home and that the Cambodian revolution would have to wait on the liberation of South Vietnam.[33]

Sihanouk Loses His Grip

It is ironic that while the Red Khmer were struggling to stay afloat, reeling from attacks by Lon Nol's army, their principal opponent, Norodom Sihanouk, was less secure than at any time since 1955. In early 1969 his regime was beset by a range of "contradictions" *(tumnoah)*, and without knowing it, it was subjected to a "rectification campaign" by the Communists. As Ouk Boun Chhoeum told Serge Thion in 1981, "Sihanouk had launched attacks on the movement, officials were expropriating land. . . . We profited from this to make propaganda against him." Armed resistance to Sihanouk's rule led to military repression, which in turn pushed more people into the resistance. Government revenues fell as rubber plantations produced less because of wartime conditions and as more and more rice was sold on the black market. The population and its demands for services continued to rise, while taxes often went uncollected. As the Second Indochina War, which the prince had worked so hard to avoid, spilled over Cambodia's borders, a small guerrilla army was killing twenty to thirty Cambodian soldiers a month. The country had become too complex for Sihanouk to manage. Never a good listener, he responded by talking louder and longer, by making films, and by seeking more allies overseas.[34]

By this time, Sihanouk had hardly any influential friends. A Western diplomat remarked that in his career he had never seen such a wide gap between a ruler and an indigenous middle class. To the Red Khmer, the prince had become indistinguishable from Lon Nol as their "Number One Enemy." Sihanouk's campaigns against radical students, his violent response to the Samlaut uprising, and his diplomatic rapprochement with the United States made the possibility of a united front, in spite of Vietnamese encouragement, remote. In the meantime, elite support for the prince eroded further as Sino-Cambodian businessmen found themselves blocked from participating in the economic boom affecting much of Southeast Asia. Cambodian bureaucrats and army officers felt the pinch of declining revenues. Many of their children, unhappy at Sihanouk's failure to deliver justice or employment, drifted toward the left. Others, less politicized, grew weary of his monologues, his narcissism, and his unsavory entourage.

In the middle of 1969 Sihanouk renewed diplomatic relations with the United States, alienating what little radical support he had retained. He may have hoped that the Americans would provide military aid to turn his army into an effective force and prevent the Vietnamese Communists from encroaching further on Cambodian territory. No such aid was forthcoming. Instead, the new American president, Richard Nixon, had another game plan for the Khmer.

Nixon was committed to withdrawing American troops from Vietnam. To protect this operation he agreed to proposals from his military commanders in Saigon that U.S. B-52 aircraft commence bombing Vietnamese Communist bases and troop concentrations inside Cambodia. News of this bombing, which began in March 1969, was kept from the American people. Whether Sihanouk had authorized it or accepted it as a fait accompli remains unclear. In any case, it continued for more than a year, with over three thousand raids against Cambodian targets. In the eastern part of the country the bombing turned many young men and women into revolutionaries. Between 1968 and 1970, estimates of guerrillas under arms more than doubled; by 1970, some four thousand Cambodians were confronting Phnom Penh's better-armed, but not especially competent, army. Another effect was that Vietnamese forces moved deeper into Cambodia to avoid the bombing. Step by step, Cambodia was entering the Indochina war.

Prime Minister Lon Nol and his ambitious deputy, Prince Sisowath Sirik Matak, supported the bombing campaign. Both men wanted Vietnamese forces to leave Cambodia. In public, Sihanouk and the Vietnamese maintained the charade that the bases were not there. In private they pretended that their alliance remained in force, even as Sihanouk's armed forces, under Lon Nol, attacked Red Khmer and, through them, the Vietnamese. In some areas by early 1970, Red Khmer guerrillas under Vietnamese command were fighting Lon Nol's forces. The United States and North Vietnam, in effect, were waging war on Cambodian soil. Sihanouk's neutralist policy was in tatters. The game he had played since 1955 was lost. Sirik Matak and Lon Nol began plotting to overthrow him.[35]

Saloth Sar Travels North

"Toward the end of 1969," reveals the *Livre noir*, "a delegation of the Communist party of Kampuchea left for Hanoi for discussions with the Vietnamese party." Before leaving, Sar handed his headquarters camp over to Nuon Chea. Several confessions from S-21 corroborate Sar's departure, but none suggests why he took the trip or whose idea it was. It is unlikely that he left Cambodia without being summoned by the Vietnamese, who may have wanted to consult with him about the next phase of the war and the growing hostility they faced from Cambodian government forces. It is also possible that Sar wanted to use this opportunity to ask for help for his guerrillas. Since he would have made the trip on foot, the visit was probably not connected with Ho Chi Minh's funeral in October 1969.[36]

The only detailed evidence for the trip comes from the *Livre noir*. Pol Pot contended that he was summoned north to be told to stop fighting. This does not ring true, but his account suggests that he was more forthright with the Vietnamese this time than he had been in 1965 and that some of his demands—which may have been for more military assistance and increased autonomy—angered his counterparts in Hanoi. The Vietnamese would have rejected both requests, although their failure to imagine an alternative to Sihanouk, now on the ropes, forced them to remain allied with Sar's unsatisfactory party. The *Livre noir* asserts that the Vietnamese in Cambodia "had taken refuge in areas controlled by the Communist party of Kampuchea," a reversal of what Sar and Ieng Sary had done in 1963; this suggests that the Vietnamese needed Cambodian protection more than the Cambodians needed patronage from Hanoi. Although these attitudes were common currency among party faithful by 1978, they had not come into the open at the time of Sar's visit to Hanoi. Had Sar made such demands in 1969, even in the heat of the moment, he would have drawn the angry response he said he drew in the *Livre noir*. Had he made them part of a coherent, independent policy, it is likely that the Vietnamese would have replaced him as secretary of the party. At the same time, it is possible that even a polite request by him for assistance would have been dismissed out of hand. In other words, although it is likely that the *Livre noir* narrative is an accurate description of Sar's psychological state in 1978, and perhaps of his anger in 1969–1970, his conduct and statements until about 1972 cannot be construed as independent or anti-Vietnamese. Indeed, if relations between Cambodia and Vietnam were as poor as the *Livre noir* suggests, it is doubtful that Saloth Sar would have risked a trip to Hanoi or that he would have lingered there as he did for several months. What Sar probably found offensive about his visit was that the Vietnamese, whose thoughts were elsewhere, once again failed to come to grips with his importance, the sufferings of his followers, or the uniqueness of the Cambodian revolution.[37]

Meanwhile, events were moving rapidly in Phnom Penh. In January 1970 Sihanouk left for his annual rest cure in France, unintentionally beginning a life of exile that was to last several years. Before leaving, he had been psychologically bruised by encounters with the hostile National Assembly. Partly to regain control and partly because he was genuinely frightened of Vietnamese incursions, he asked Lon Nol to increase pressure on Communist forces. While the prince was overseas, supplies to the Vietnamese forces in Cambodia were cut off, and government-sponsored riots damaged the diplomatic missions of Vietnamese Communists in Phnom Penh.[38]

On March 19, 1970, Sihanouk was voted out of office by the National Assembly. The coup d'état was bloodless, although later in the month pro-Sihanouk demonstrations were brutally suppressed in several provinces. Two days before the coup, Lon Nol had ordered all Vietnamese forces to leave Cambodia within forty-eight hours. Not surprisingly, there was no response, but the quixotic command reflected widespread popular opposition to the Vietnamese. When the coup took place, the prince was in Moscow on his way home. Half stunned and half enraged, he proceeded as planned on the next leg of his voyage to Beijing.

The coup seems to have taken Saloth Sar and his patrons by surprise, although the *Livre noir* contends that he foresaw the coup six months before it occurred and Nuon Chea, in his 1997 party history, claims that policy since 1967 had been based on the likelihood of a right-wing coup. If Sar indeed foresaw the coup, his long absence from Cambodia in 1969-1970 is difficult to explain. The *Livre noir* also states that in early 1970 Sar had traveled to Beijing from Hanoi "for discussions" and was thus in the Chinese capital when Sihanouk arrived on March 19. It seems more likely that Sar came from Hanoi with the Vietnamese premier, Pham Van Dong, who had been hastily summoned by the Chinese and arrived in Beijing two days after Sihanouk got there.[39]

The *Livre noir* claims that Saloth Sar persuaded the Chinese prime minister, Zhou Enlai, that Sihanouk should adopt an offensive posture toward Lon Nol and, by implication, toward the United States, reinstating an anti-American policy he had abandoned a year before. According to other sources, Pham Van Dong encouraged the prince to resist, promising to return him to power "within forty-eight hours." Thus Sar's advice to Zhou, if it was ever given, was identical to the advice offered to Sihanouk by Pham Van Dong. To keep Sihanouk happy and to protect the Cambodian Communists as a long-term asset, the Chinese and Vietnamese concealed Sar's presence in Beijing from the prince, who did not identify him as the leader of the party for several years.

The anti-Vietnamese rhetoric of the *Livre noir* cannot conceal what must have delighted Saloth Sar in April 1970: His forces were now in a full-fledged military alliance with the Vietnamese. These unevenly endowed allies were dedicated to removing Lon Nol from power. The Red Khmer's hopes were no longer thwarted by the exigencies of a secret, nonviolent Vietnamese-Sihanouk alliance. Instead, that alliance had now come into the open, become warlike, and was recast to include the Cambodian Communist party. The Communists could gain recruits by claiming loyalty to the prince while obtaining arms, training, and experience from Vietnam. Soon after the coup, several hundred well-trained Khmer set off from northern Vietnam to take part in their country's struggle. Many of them had been in exile in Vietnam for fifteen years.[40]

Saloth Sar knew that Lon Nol's army would be no match for the Vietnamese. He also suspected (and may have been told) that the Vietnamese had no intention of reinstating Sihanouk with genuine power when the war was over. For the time being, however, Sar believed that Sihanouk's presence as head of a united, anti-American front would assure the Communists of international support. The crippling contradiction of being allied with Vietnam and opposing "feudalism" in Cambodia had now dissolved. For the first time since he had returned to Cambodia in 1953, Saloth Sar could contemplate actually seizing power. In his years in hiding, he and his associates had lived on hope. The thought of his dream coming true must have exhilarated him as he left Hanoi for Cambodia. After seven years in the wilderness, Saloth Sar was back on the revolutionary path.

CHAPTER SIX

———————————— ■ ————————————

Coming to Power,
1970–1976

The decision to form a National Front with Sihanouk as chief of state had two effects on Saloth Sar's career. One was that after seven years on the run he became, at forty-five, the military commander of the Cambodian Communist component of a popular alliance. Another was that the movement he commanded now benefited from extensive Vietnamese military support. These two factors meant that he could preside over the expansion of the Cambodian Communist party, while his forces could be trained behind a shield provided by the battle-hardened Vietnamese.

Saloth Sar did not emerge from hiding, and it was more than a year before he was even identified as an official of Sihanouk's National Front. Inside the country, authority was supposedly placed in the hands of one of the Three Ghosts—Khieu Samphan—ostensibly working on Sihanouk's behalf. The Vietnamese Communists, for their part, openly admitted their alliance with the prince but said nothing about their relations with the Cambodian Communists or the presence of Vietnamese troops on Cambodian soil.[1]

The model for these bewildering arrangements—aptly described by Elizabeth Becker as a "hall of mirrors"—was provided by the National Liberation Front in South Vietnam, whose socialist agenda and links with North Vietnam were concealed from the Vietnamese public and even from some of the front's most dedicated members. Sihanouk, ensconced in Beijing with an entourage of chefs, courtiers, and hangers-on, was a figurehead from the start, although he vigorously maintained and probably believed that he was beloved by most Khmer and would hold some kind of position when the war was over. His Chinese patrons, including Zhou Enlai, the prime minister, warmly supported him; and the front's publications, financed and printed in China, conveyed the impression that the guerrillas inside Cambodia were fighting on his behalf.[2]

At the time of the coup, U.S. intelligence estimated that the Red Khmers had fewer than three thousand men and women under arms. Not many of these guerrillas were organized into units larger than platoons, and few were trained for combat. Their Marxist-Leninist reading was patchy, and few had any understanding of the international aspects of the movement. In early 1970 they were scattered in small bands in the forested periphery of Cambodia in Kompong Speu, Kampot, Battambang, Kratie, and the northeast.

Saloth Sar Comes Home

While "Brother Number One" was visiting Vietnam and China in 1969–1970, Nuon Chea took command of the party's headquarters in the northeast. Ieng Sary was in charge of a secondary base in Ratanakiri. Shortly after the coup, before Saloth Sar returned home, Vietnamese officers visited Sary's camp asking for Cambodian support. According to Kheang Sim Hon's confession, "They asked for support for their combatants, help with their cadre at all levels, and our help to build a hospital. [Ieng Sary] tried to evade these requests, but it didn't work, and a Vietnamese divisional commander, who claimed to have had a working relationship with Saloth Sar, slept at the base and wouldn't leave."

After acceding to the Vietnamese demands, the Khmer allowed the Vietnamese to train their soldiers. In other parts of the country, the Vietnamese were more abrupt. Without consulting local Cambodian Communists, they mobilized Cambodian villages to "fight for Sihanouk" and took command of the young people they recruited. They hoped to capitalize on people's shock at the coup and Sihanouk's popularity to secure their bases and supply lines in Cambodia. In these early phases of resistance, as Ben Kiernan has written, "revolutionary administration was essentially the creation of Vietnamese Communists and the Khmer working . . . with them."[3]

Meanwhile in Hanoi, according to the *Livre noir*, Saloth Sar and his colleagues, en route to Cambodia from Beijing, were feted warmly by the Vietnamese. Pol Pot later wrote that at a banquet in Hanoi, "the Cambodian delegation was covered with praise from beginning to end. . . . [T]he Vietnamese had a pressing need for Cambodian friendship, aid and assistance." The exact opposite was closer to the truth. In fact, Pol Pot admitted as much when he wrote that the Vietnamese at this stage offered him mixed combat commands, five thousand rifles, and international propaganda support. These were offers he was in no position to refuse. Writing in 1978, however, he said that he had refused to be a client and asserted that he had taken a strong line with the Vietnamese. "For those in charge of Vietnam," he fantasized, "the problem of the liberation of South Vietnam was not their greatest concern. In their eyes, *the problem of Cambodia was much more important*" (emphasis added).[4]

In April 1970 Sar left Hanoi for Cambodia, traveling on the Ho Chi Minh Trail. The journey took a month and a half. As he came south, through North Vietnam, Laos, and northeastern Cambodia, Sar must have been impressed by what he saw. Thousands of trucks lumbered down the trail with weapons, ammunition, and supplies for Vietnamese Communist forces; resting places were set up at regular intervals. Now and then, Sar and his colleagues were able to hitch rides on trucks. At other times, they walked briskly, under forest cover, braving attacks from malaria and U.S. bombers. Chhim Samauk later spoke of camping in "more than twenty places" and of occasionally commandeering elephants from local people for rides. For Saloth Sar, it must have been a thrilling trek. He arrived at the Lao-Cambodian border toward the end of May. According to Chhim Samauk, Sar became ill twice during the trip—first with malaria and then from accidentally eating poisonous "peacock mushrooms" (*psut kngaouk*) in a soup. At the Lao-Cambodian border Sar formally welcomed Cambodian volunteers who had come down the trail with him from Hanoi before proceeding with them to the party's headquarters in the northeast.[5]

The *Livre noir* contends that he spent his first days in Cambodia fending off Vietnamese demands for cooperation. Vietnamese assertions that Ieng Sary had agreed to their requests (confirmed in Kheang Sim Hon's confession) are dismissed by the *Livre noir* as "lies." The weight of the evidence suggests that Sar accepted promises of aid from the Vietnamese officials who welcomed him, agreed to their proposals of mixed commands, and approved Ieng Sary's earlier decision to accept Vietnamese assistance. At this stage of the Cambodian revolution, Sar had no choice. Soon after his arrival at Office 102, Sar sent Ieng Sary back up the trail to become the party's liaison officer in Hanoi, where he joined Keo Meas, sent on a similar mission in 1969. This event, corroborated by many sources, confirms that the Red Khmer were still cooperating fully—tactically and secretly—with North Vietnam.[6]

Immediately after Sihanouk had been deposed, while Saloth Sar was in Beijing, pro-Sihanouk riots—organized and fanned by Cambodian Communists and Vietnamese cadre—broke out in several provincial cities. The demonstrations reflected the genuine shock that many Khmer felt when bereft of the only political leader they had ever known. They were brutally repressed by Lon Nol's army and police. No more demonstrations in support of the prince occurred for the remainder of the war. In the aftermath of the riots, however, hundreds of young Khmer took to the maquis "to fight for Sihanouk." Most of them soon came under mixed Vietnamese-Khmer Communist command.[7]

The U.S.-South Vietnamese invasion of Cambodia in April–May 1970, which brought Cambodia to the attention of television viewers in the United States and set in motion waves of antiwar sentiment there, encouraged Cambodian Communists to increase their anti-American propaganda. The dependence of the Lon Nol regime on the Americans for military equipment and political support played into the Communists' hands. Many noncommunists, particularly in the cities, on the other hand, saw the conflict as stemming from an earlier North Vietnamese invasion of their country. Thousands of young men volunteered for Lon Nol's forces, naively hoping to liberate Cambodia in a few weeks. Hundreds of them were soon killed or wounded. In October 1970 Lon Nol renamed the country the Khmer Republic, ending perhaps two thousand years of monarchic rule. Fighting between his government and the Communists continued for another four-and-a-half years.

Against this background, the Red Khmer moved their headquarters closer to the Vietnamese central command, near Phnom Santhuk on the Kratie–Kompong Thom border. Soon after, Sar summoned cadre from other parts of the country for a study session coinciding with the party's nineteenth anniversary. This session clarified the roles to be played by cadre and discussed the party's alliance with North Vietnam.

A document captured in Kratie that probably emanated from the session consists of notes on such topics as "revolutionary ethics," "short-term strategies," and "solidarity with Vietnam." Under the heading "A Diagram of the Revolution," the document states confusingly that "the revolutionists are in the middle. The revolutionary organizations are behind the revolutionists; and the masses surround the organizations." What the passage probably meant was that the party apparatus—Saloth Sar and his immediate colleagues—were hidden, powerful, and protected. A subsequent section titled "Conduct of a Revolutionist" notes: "A revolutionist should be kind and sympathetic to the people; a revolutionist should always use kind words when talking to the people. These words should cause no harm; make the listeners sympathetic to the speaker; sound polite in all circumstances; be pleasing to everyone; and make the listeners happy." It is tempting to think that these suggestions came from Saloth Sar, whose mannerisms they appear to describe.[8]

The next month, according to the *Livre noir*, Saloth Sar and Nuon Chea were summoned by the Vietnamese Communist high command to discuss "the problem of the development of solidarity and cooperation." These discussions, which allegedly took the form of Vietnamese demands, lasted a week. According to the *Livre noir*, the two Cambodians proudly rejected further Vietnamese aid.[9]

Once again, the *Livre noir*'s account is upside down. In 1970 the Vietnamese increased their support of the Cambodian Communists and were instrumental in eliminating Lon Nol's army as a military force. Through the distorting lenses of the *Livre noir* it is clear nonetheless that by the middle of 1971, if not before, the Red Khmer leaders had grown resentful of Vietnamese advice and their own dependence. Since they were in no position to express these feelings, they continued to mask them. Occasional impromptu clashes had already taken place between Red Khmer and Vietnamese forces, but the former still needed Vietnamese military help and technical assistance. Moreover, the Vietnamese were still much stronger than the Red Khmer and in no hurry to go away.

The National Democratic Revolution

Most of the fighting against Lon Nol in 1971–1972 was carried out by Vietnamese forces or by Cambodians under Vietnamese command. In the process, the Cambodian Communist forces became larger, better organized, and more self-confident than before. In July 1971 a "party school session for the entire country" summoned sixty-odd cadre to the party's headquarters in "the forest in the Northern Zone." Saloth Sar presided over the meeting, which elected an enlarged Central Committee and proclaimed that the Cambodian Communist party had entered a new phase in its history—namely, a national democratic revolution to overthrow feudalism and imperialism.

The meeting provided a forum where the Red Khmer leaders could demonstrate their control over the party and the resistance. Some of the new policies were spelled out later in the year in the party's theoretical journal. The meandering text dealt with the history of "building the party" since 1963, when Saloth Sar had become secretary of the Central Committee. Without mentioning Vietnam, the text noted that the revolution must "be appropriate for our country" and that the party's leaders, also unnamed, were to command "all aspects of the revolution." Delegates later claimed that speeches at the meeting urged rapid collectivization and attacked the Vietnamese. Refugees fleeing southwestern Cambodia into South Vietnam in 1972–1974 reported that beginning in late 1971 more emphasis had been placed by cadre inside Cambodia on "self-reliance" and "Cambodia for the Cambodians."[10]

That Sar could assemble cadre from so many places (Hu Nim and Chou Chet, for example, traveled up from the southwest) suggests that he did not feel threatened by Lon Nol's forces. While the meeting was going on, however, Lon Nol launched an ambitious, though poorly executed, offensive known as "Chenla II," and "all cadres, especially in the military sector, hurried off to fight the enemy." By December 1971 the offensive had collapsed and Lon Nol's forces had been routed. Most of the damage was inflicted by Vietnamese units. After the defeat, Lon Nol's army went on the defensive, freeing the Red Khmer to concentrate on social policies, recruitment, and training.

Several Communist documents written after Chenla II asserted that the Cambodian Communists were winning the war on their own. At a training session in December 1971, for example, a spokesman (perhaps Sar himself) remarked,

If we consider the size of the armed forces, the amount of their power—airplanes, heavy guns, armed riverboats arrayed against us, the enemy was much stronger than we were. Why then did we defeat the enemy [in Chenla II]? This important victory was a victory of the will, transformed into attacks on the enemy. . . . These storming attacks *(vay samrok)* were victories for the combatants, for politics and for economics.

Some of those attending the meeting would have interpreted Sar's failure to mention the alliance with Vietnam as a harmless attempt to praise the Red Khmer's own efforts and build their confidence. Others, however, would have taken his assumption of Khmer prowess at face value and would have endorsed "storming attacks" against enemies, problems, and crises confronting the "revolutionary organization" *(angkar padevat)*, as the party styled itself at this time. This was the audience targeted by Sar. Like Shanouk and Lon Nol, Saloth Sar repeatedly claimed or implied that Cambodians were intrinsically superior to outsiders and immune from foreign influence. This enabled him to shrug off foreign models and to claim that his country's revolution was autonomous and Cambodian as well as Communist and predictable.[11]

As the menace of Lon Nol's army faded, Saloth Sar and the Cambodian Communist party turned to political and organizational matters. Sar wrote in January 1972, "We have the will to win. But this is not enough. We need proper policies, proper politics, and proper methods." Without them, he said, a "revolution was like a blind man moving from place to place." Enrolling and training party members was another urgent need, and so was raising the consciousness of workers and peasants, who were destined to lead the revolution. Other documents at the time suggested that even though 80 to 90 percent of Cambodia's people "loved the revolution," they needed to be taught what was good about it. "Farmers and workers must study," a cadre noted, "so as to fall into step with the wheel of history [*kong pravat'sass*]."

Although cadre were enjoined to behave properly toward the people—who formed "the basis of the revolution"—combatants often behaved abruptly when they moved into villages. Years later, a refugee from Kompong Speu described the process: "In 1972 the Red Khmers took over my village. I don't know how they got there. I just saw them when they came. I don't know where they lived. I just saw them walking around; they didn't tell me where they lived. They would come by and give you a schedule of what to do and how to live. . . . You could not refuse to do anything."[12]

In the meantime, the Lon Nol government entered its decline. As hundreds of thousands of refugees flooded into Phnom Penh, services broke down and the fabric of urban life gave way. In the countryside, several districts near the capital were captured, recaptured, and bombarded by the artillery of both sides in what was becoming a full-scale civil war. Communist troops were more disciplined than those of the Khmer Republic, but both sides robbed, molested, and rounded up civilians. Neither side took prisoners. The lightly populated parts of the country were abandoned to the Communists by the end of 1971, as was the heavily populated southwest. In the dwindling territory controlled by the republic, corruption was widespread. Provincial governors and military officers sold food, arms, and medicine to the enemy. Many of Lon Nol's units padded their payrolls with nonexistent people to capitalize on U.S. aid that provided salaries for the troops. The Communist forces avoided this problem—they were all unpaid.

The United States, for its part, was engrossed with its withdrawal from South Vietnam. Nixon's policies in Cambodia were intended to delay a Communist victory so that American troops could be withdrawn safely. Lon Nol was the man that Nixon had chosen to perform this job, and he was slow and often outmaneuvered. By the end of 1971, the Americans and their allies were losing in Cambodia, but only Cambodians were being killed. The Cambodian elite, powerless in the cities, had lost any grounds for hope; the rural poor were desperate; the economy was in ruins.[13]

After the 1971 study session, Saloth Sar created a special administrative zone, south and west of Phnom Penh, made up of sectors 15 and 25. He placed his old companion Sok Thuok (Vorn Vet) in command of the new zone. In his confession seven years later, Vet suggested that Sar wanted to strengthen Red Khmer authority and lessen the power of Vietnamese cadres and Cambodians trained in North Vietnam. One problem he faced was that well-trained indigenous cadre were scarce.

Party schools were established in the area in 1972, and young men and women were recruited locally as combatants and party members. At the same time, many disillusioned teachers, engineers, and students from Phnom Penh drifted into the "liberated zone" and put themselves at the service of the party. Two young teachers, Ith Sarin and Kuong Lumphon, and French sociologist Serge Thion left valuable eyewitness accounts of conditions in the zone in 1972. While on a short visit, Thion was impressed by much of what he was allowed to see. He was well treated and came away convinced that a genuinely new society was being built. The two Cambodians came away with a different impression of the region. After several months of indoctrination, they returned to Phnom Penh distressed by the rigidity and fervor of their Communist colleagues.[14]

For most of the year, Saloth Sar remained at his headquarters in the north. In March 1972 it was announced in China that he was chief of the military directorate of the armed forces of Sihanouk's National Front. His deputy, Nuon Chea, was named chief of the army's political directorate. Sar's position does not seem to have involved day-to-day military decisions; these were left to the regional commanders. Sar was undoubtedly responsible for strategic decisions, such as rejecting the 1972 cease-fire proposed by North Vietnam and the Khmer Republic, the "strategic storming attacks" on Phnom Penh in 1973–1974, and the final assault on the capital the following year.[15]

After 1971, party documents became more insistent in their class analyses of Cambodian society. They stressed that cadre must be drawn from poor peasant, lower-middle-class peasant, and worker backgrounds—"from deep down in [rural] areas," as one document suggested, "extracted from the earth like diamonds." Relying on these categories, it was thought, guaranteed the disappearance of feudal or capitalist elements. The superiority of workers and peasants, however, like the superiority of communism itself, was an article of faith, even though the prophets of this faith—Marx and Lenin—were never identified and seldom cited. The documents themselves were not expected to generate discussion; rather, they were intended to display the authority of the party. They were memorized and key passages were recited to lower echelons. The documents were the regalia of a new, all-powerful regime that, like many preceding it, enjoyed pretensions of total control. Those in power sprang from segments of society different from those in the past, but they soon behaved in much the same way—for example, people who questioned their authority were often put to death.

The documents were intended to expand the listeners' "revolutionary consciousness." As such, they reflected Saloth Sar's background as a teacher as well as his authority within the party. It is tempting to imagine him at party schools delivering these sermons with subdued eloquence (*voha*) in his low, resonant voice, using few gestures and no notes.[16]

From Cease-Fire to Bombardment

As we have seen, the fortunes of the Red Khmer had always been dependent on events inside Vietnam. Although the war strengthened the Red Khmer, it also deepened their dependency on the Vietnamese. Saloth Sar himself was a creature of an earlier Vietnamese conflict, eased along inside the subsidiary Cambodian movement. Until the end of 1972, his troops were armed, trained, and often led by the Vietnamese. The defeats suffered by Lon Nol in 1970–1971 had been at the hands of Vietnamese regular forces. The Red Khmer's progress, or lack of it, had been calibrated to a large extent by Vietnam.[17]

In the negotiations between the Americans and the Vietnamese in Paris, ongoing since 1968, the Vietnamese delegations now saw short-term advantages in accepting U.S. offers of a cease-fire throughout Indochina. The Americans were eager to reach an agreement before the November presidential election in the United States. For the Vietnamese, time was on their side. Most of the U.S. combat forces had been withdrawn. The remaining ones would pull out as the cease-fire took effect. At that point, the Vietnamese could prepare for an assault on Saigon without facing the threat of American intervention. Until all the Americans were gone—and it would be almost impossible for them to return—the Vietnamese could concentrate on political tactics that would undermine the South Vietnamese regime. Should they refuse a cease-fire, the Americans assured the North Vietnamese, U.S. bombardment would begin again. In January 1973 the Vietnamese agreed to American conditions.

In Cambodia the agreement meant that the Vietnamese would withdraw most of their forces. Those who remained behind, in frontier areas, supported activities in Vietnam rather than the Red Khmer. The Vietnamese urged Saloth Sar to join them in the cease-fire. He almost certainly refused, as he said he did in the *Livre noir*. The Americans put similar pressure on Lon Nol, whose government was reeling from a series of scandals, missteps, and military defeats. Lon Nol reluctantly agreed, hoping to bring the fighting to an end. A temporary cease-fire went into effect at the end of January 1973. It was broken almost immediately.[18]

According to the *Livre noir*, Sar and his colleagues rejected the Vietnamese requests to honor the cease-fire for several reasons. First, they had come to believe that they could win the war themselves. Second, they were unwilling to revert to political struggle without Vietnamese military protection. Doing so would have meant coming into the open against Lon Nol, sharing power with his forces in the countryside, and reviving the fiction that Sihanouk was the leader of the front. Under such an agreement, presumably, Sihanouk would be free to negotiate with Lon Nol. None of these scenarios was palatable to the Red Khmer. They preferred civil war, American bombardment, and operating in secret to reviving a genuine united front.[19]

They also viewed Vietnam's agreement with the United States as a betrayal. Since 1963, after all, they had faithfully performed their duties where the Vietnam War was concerned. Now they were asked to stop fighting or to confront Lon Nol's forces by themselves. They lacked the political cadres to administer the territory abandoned by the Phnom Penh regime and the military staff to coordinate large unit actions. They also lacked the weapons and ammunition to sustain an offensive on Phnom Penh. Their resentment and injured pride are easy to understand. Because they had refused to stop fighting, they were also vulnerable, as their counterparts in Laos and Vietnam were not, to air bombardment by the United States.[20]

The Only Game in Town

As the Vietnamese withdrew from Cambodia, skirmishes broke out between some of their units and Cambodian troops angered that the Vietnamese were removing their equipment as they left. Cambodian cadre from Hanoi, whom the Red Khmer leadership had always suspected of divided loyalties or worse, came under scrutiny. Since 1970 they had been acting as combatants, techni-

cians, and military advisers. In some areas they had carried out useful political work. Starting in 1972, however, many of them were quietly disarmed and
removed from positions of authority. One of them recalled, "At study sessions they would call us 'revisionists.' . . . We were transferred from our jobs;
some of us were sent to grow pepper, or to supervise cattle." Others were ambushed in isolated incidents. In early 1973, some took refuge with Vietnamese units withdrawing from the country. Others were executed by the
Red Khmer.[21]

In early 1973 Cambodian Communist troops attacked government units
throughout the country to extend territorial control and to set their social
programs in motion. The process was closely monitored in the southwest.
Measures adopted there included the introduction of cooperative farms, the
forced movement of some of the population, the repression of Buddhism, the
formation of youth groups whose members were taken from their families,
the extirpation of folk culture, and the imposition of dress codes whereby
everyone had to wear peasant work clothes (black cotton pajamas) all the
time. As a result of the harshness with which these policies were applied,
more than twenty thousand Cambodians sought asylum in South Vietnam.
These policies probably flowed from decisions taken at Saloth Sar's 1971
study session. They certainly had his approval and were introduced nationally after April 1975 with more radical proposals, such as the abolition of
money, markets, and schools and the evacuation of entire towns and cities.[22]

Cambodian Communist stubbornness and the fact that U.S. air power
could no longer be used against Lao and Vietnamese targets encouraged the
United States to bomb the Red Khmer. Cambodia became "the only game in
town," to quote a U.S. official. The bombing campaign began in March 1973
and was halted by the U.S. Congress five months later. During this time a
quarter million tons of explosives were dropped on a country that was not at
war with the United States and that had no U.S. combat personnel within its
borders. Target selection and verification were much less precise than in
Vietnam. Targets were supposedly military complexes and villages where
Communist units were thought to be seeking shelter. The maps used were
outdated, while those depicting the bombing itself show that it was concentrated on the heavily populated approaches to Phnom Penh. The number of
casualties inflicted has never been assessed. Estimates run from thirty thousand to a quarter of a million killed. Over ten thousand of these were insur-
gent troops.

The bombing campaign's effect on rural society is difficult to judge, but in
view of the tonnage involved and Cambodia's unpreparedness it must have
been catastrophic. Some scholars have argued that the bombing helped the
Red Khmer to gain thousands of dedicated, enraged recruits. There is some
corroboration of this. Clearly it also accelerated the collapse of rural society
and eased the way for Communist political control. It also pushed tens of

thousands of rural Cambodians into the cities. These terrified men and women were seen by the Cambodian Communists as "enemies" rather than human beings and the anti-urban bias of the party became even severer than before. The chaotic aftermath of the bombing eventually played into the Communists' hands. In the short term, however, the campaign had the effect the Americans wanted—it broke the Communist encirclement of Phnom Penh. The war was to drag on for two more years.[23]

Sihanouk Visits Saloth Sar

In late February 1973, as the U.S. bombing campaign was gathering momentum, Sihanouk left Beijing and disappeared. Accompanied by his wife, Princess Monique, and Ieng Sary, he went on a month-long trip that took him down the Ho Chi Minh Trail into northern Cambodia and then west to Angkor; he was filmed and photographed by Chinese cameramen along the way. The prince and his wife were in Cambodia for three weeks. The trip was intended by Sihanouk's patrons in Beijing and Hanoi to demonstrate their continuing interest in the prince as a political force. The trip and the films could also be used to raise the front's prestige, to demonstrate its nationalism, and to block the acceptance of the Khmer Republic's credentials in the United Nations. It is possible that the Vietnamese also used the trip to express their disapproval of the independent, anti-Sihanouk policies being followed by the Red Khmer. In any event the prince played the role assigned to him. So did the leaders of the Cambodian Communist party. Looking at the photographs and film footage from the visit, it would be impossible to guess that Sihanouk had ever been their "Number One Enemy," that Saloth Sar was guiding the Communist party, or that the cadre the prince was embracing included men he had condemned to death a few years before. Sihanouk and the Communists, smiling nervously at each other, took the trip one day at a time.[24]

At the Lao-Cambodian border the prince was greeted by the Three Ghosts—Khieu Samphan, Hou Youn, and Hu Nim. They told him that they were in charge of the resistance. Two days later, at the party's headquarters in the northern zone, Sihanouk also encountered Khieu Ponnary; Son Sen; the secretary of the northern zone, Koy Thuon; and Saloth Sar, who mingled genially with his colleagues, giving the prince no hint of his high status. The charade probably amused Sar. He may also have been eager to observe Sihanouk at close range without being questioned or evaluated himself. He was probably beguiled by observing his subordinates and forcing them to act as if he were unimportant.

Saloth Sar and his subordinates and guests posed for photographs at waterfalls, in forest clearings, outside Angkorean temples, and during folklore presentations. The prince and his wife wore freshly laundered peasant costumes.

98

Pol Pot (fourth from left, third row) attending a theatrical performance for Sihanouk (front row, third from left, next to Princess Monique and Khieu Samphan), 1973. *SOURCE:* Official photo of the government of the People's Republic of China.

Pol Pot (fourth from left) and his wife, Khieu Ponnary (eighth from left, with white hair), with Prince Sihanouk at Phnom Kulen, Cambodia, 1973. *SOURCE:* Official photo of the government of the People's Republic of China.

Rebel troops brought into the area for the occasion were enjoined by cadre not to speak to Sihanouk in private. The prince later complained that he had been isolated from his "children" throughout the visit.[25]

Behind the smiles, embraces, and photo opportunities it is hard to imagine what was said. Sihanouk was in no position to ask any probing questions. The party's leaders were unwilling to reveal their social agenda or the names of party officials. Because of Sihanouk's contacts with the outside world, conversations concentrated on the diplomatic aspects of the war. Sihanouk later claimed, for example, that Khieu Samphan had told him that the Vietnamese had recently "dropped" the Cambodian Communists as allies.

To display the liberated zones in a pleasing manner Saloth Sar and his colleagues sponsored concerts of popular music, assembled some monks (or soldiers garbed as monks) for the prince to chat with, housed him comfortably in what his wife called "our White House in the liberated zone," and treated him like a visiting chief of state. Sihanouk may have suspected that the Three Ghosts were a facade and that others less sympathetic to him controlled the party. He may not have believed the Red Khmer as they pledged their allegiance to him and said that the Cambodian people were fighting on his behalf. But he had to pretend that they were telling him the truth. What else could he do? He was at their mercy. There is an eeriness about the visit, as it survives in photographs and films. Nothing was as it appeared; no one could speak his mind. Everyone except a handful of unidentified leaders was being observed, suspected, and used. The visit, in this sense, foreshadowed the political atmosphere of Democratic Kampuchea.[26]

Preparing the Final Assault

After Sihanouk's visit, Saloth Sar was preoccupied with military questions. Operations took the form of three successive storming attacks, in 1973, 1974, and 1975, aimed at capturing Phnom Penh. The first, which was beaten back by U.S. bombing, had been carried out under Saloth Sar's orders. A subsequent assault, on Kompong Cham, was also unsuccessful. Both attacks revealed that the Cambodian Communists had become a disciplined fighting force—estimated at roughly sixty thousand armed men and women—capable of taking heavy casualties and of maneuvering in regimental strength.

The first offensive was costly and dramatic. Between May and July 1973, rebel troops were spurred forward by the vision of liberating Phnom Penh and defeating the United States. The casualties they absorbed, largely from U.S. bombing, were the highest in the war. One aspect of this strategy may have been Sar's desire to embarrass the Vietnamese by taking Phnom Penh before they liberated Saigon. But this is speculation. What is known for certain is that in May 1973 the number of recorded "combat incidents" reached the highest level of the war so far. Most of these were near the capital. In July,

American B-52 bombers from Guam and F-111 fighter bombers from Thailand were attacking targets less than 15 miles from Phnom Penh. The bombing dug a fire trench around the city. Sheltered behind it, Lon Nol's forces fought reasonably well. The bombing could have continued for months, but it was halted by the U.S. Congress, appalled at the senseless destruction and responsive to antiwar sentiment in the United States. When the bombing stopped and as the rains began, rebel units besieging the capital withdrew. In Phnom Penh, there had been little panic. The "collapse of Cambodia"—which dozens of Western reporters had flown in to witness—was, as one writer put it, a "non-event."[27]

The assault on Kompong Cham was probably intended to sustain momentum. Vietnamese forces nearby did nothing to help. At one stage, Communist troops penetrated within a few hundred meters of the center of the town. When they withdrew, they rounded up several thousand local people to take with them, following a pattern of warfare that had been traditional in precolonial Southeast Asia, conforming to their own policies of "drying up the enemies' population base," and foreshadowing what their armies would do in Phnom Penh and other Republican towns and cities in 1975.[28]

The Vietnamese withdrawal of 1972–1973 seems to have intensified anti-Vietnamese feelings among Cambodian Communists. In 1972, in areas where Vietnamese troops had been stationed, demonstrations against them were organized by the Cambodian Communist party. Cadre occasionally referred to the Vietnamese as "hereditary enemies." How closely this campaign was monitored by the Central Committee is impossible to determine, but certainly one committee member, Ta ("Grandfather") Mok, the military secretary in the southwest, was virulently anti-Vietnamese at this time. Others in the region, like Mok's superior Chou Chet, assumed a more moderate stance. On balance, the withdrawal of the Vietnamese made it safe for the Cambodians to attack them verbally and to manhandle and execute Cambodians trained in Vietnam who had remained behind.[29]

On May 20, 1973, at the height of the U.S. bombing campaign, peasants and their farms were collectivized in many Communist-controlled areas. Private property was abolished and people were organized into groups of families to perform tasks set for them by the party. There were several reasons for collectivization: to ensure that enough food was produced for rebel forces; to introduce socialist institutions; and to develop an autonomous revolutionary style. By introducing socialist measures before they came into effect in South Vietnam, the Red Khmer hoped to illustrate the purity of Cambodian communism and the contrast between the storming attacks of the Chinese and the more cautious policies of the Vietnamese.[30]

In early 1974, rebel forces regrouped and formed a noose around Phnom Penh in preparation for their second storming attack. No longer intimidated by the prospect of U.S. bombing, the Communists had begun to initiate more assaults. They failed to capture the capital—the second attack was called off in April 1974—but by the end of the year, they had cut road communication between Phnom Penh and the port city of Kompong Som. Supplies for the capital now had to arrive by air or via the Mekong. Convoys coming upstream were subjected to artillery, mortars, and small-arms fire.

Combat incidents were even higher than in 1973, and Republican forces fought better than they had before. Casualties on both sides were substantial. The rebels faced continuing supply shortages and diminishing political support in areas where they had hastily set in motion severe programs of social control. These programs, like the U.S. bombings in 1973, led thousands of rural people to seek shelter in Phnom Penh, whose population by the end of the year had swelled to over two million.

The twenty-third anniversary of the foundation of the Communist party of Kampuchea was celebrated in Amleang (Kandal Province) on September 30, 1974. The session was monitored by a spy from Lon Nol's government, whose handwritten report surfaced at the former Red Khmer interrogation center known as Tuol Sleng in 1980. The report is of interest for a couple of reasons. First, it states that Saloth Sar (identified as the "secretary of the party") attended the celebration but apparently did not give a speech. The major address was by Hou Youn, who outlined the history of the party, placing its roots in the Democratic party and the Issaraks rather than in the Vietnamese-led resistance to the French. Second, the list of those attending the celebration indicates how confident the Red Khmer had become by September 1974: The party's Central Committee and several of its military commanders assembled at a semipublic meeting within 20 miles of Phnom Penh. The study session that followed the meeting, limited to party members, is not mentioned in the report, presumably because the Republican spy did not attend it.[31]

Soon after the celebration, Saloth Sar became very ill—"numb on one side of his body," Chhim Samauk wrote later, "and also on one side of his face, cold and shivering." The condition persisted for several days. Samauk nursed him back to health as he had done in 1966. Sar fell ill several times a year throughout his time in power, succumbing to bouts of malaria and intestinal disorders.[32]

In 1974 the Red Khmer circulated a revised history of the party. Much of the text was unchanged from a previous history captured by Lon Nol's forces in 1973. Reflecting the growing alienation between the Cambodian Communist party and Vietnam, however, the new document played down the period of Vietnamese influence. References to Tou Samouth and Sieu Heng and to Marx and Lenin were dropped. The revisions stressed the autonomy of Cambodia's revolution, a theme that cropped up often in the party's years in power. Interestingly, Sar's time in Office 100, Vietnam, and China—when the revolution in Cambodia had stalled—was not mentioned in either text, but the "lessons" that concluded both documents are identically worded, suggesting that the tasks that a party history should inspire remained unchanged: organize, educate, raise political consciousness, choose good leaders, and so on.[33]

The Final Assault

Toward the end of 1974, Chou Chet, the secretary of the southwestern zone, met Saloth Sar in rural Kompong Chhnang, where he was coordinating plans for the third storming attack in 1975. Pol Pot declared in 1977 that the Central Committee had decided on this final assault at a meeting in June 1974. "We dared to mount this offensive," he wrote, "because we had completely grasped the enemy's situation and our own"—that is, Lon Nol's government was dead on its feet and the Americans were gone. Not long after the victory, Pol Pot boasted that "in the whole world not a single person believed us. Everyone said that assaulting Phnom Penh wasn't easy, assaulting the American imperialists wasn't easy; [our] guns had no shells or powder: we had shortages like that. No one guessed we could do it."[34]

The final attack was planned for the 1975 dry season. At the end of 1974 Sar visited combat units to "monitor preparations and deployment" for it.[35] His strategy had always been to isolate Phnom Penh before moving in for the kill. Conditions were favorable for this in 1975. By the end of 1974 all roads to the capital were cut, and in the early hours of January 1, rebel forces opened their bombardment. Republican troops on the east bank of the Mekong soon retreated into Phnom Penh. Later in the month, the rebels brought floating mines from China and planted them in the Mekong. After several Republican ships were sunk, the government closed the river to traffic. At this point Sar told units in *dombon* 22 that "the potential existed to win victory over the enemy completely."

About this time, the Central Committee decided what actions the Communists would take following their victory. The most important of these was to evacuate Phnom Penh and all other towns controlled by the Republican regime, driving their populations—well over two million people—into the countryside where they would pose no threat to the party and, in theory, could engage in productive work. This dispersal of "enemies" was breathtaking in its simplicity. At this point, the Central Committee also decided to abolish money, markets, and private property throughout the country. The cadre were not informed of these decisions until the eve of the final assault.[36]

In February and March, U.S. cargo planes airlifted rice and ammunition into the capital, but by the end of March the Phnom Penh airfield had come under rocket and artillery attack and the airlift was halted. Despite lobbying by Nixon's successor, Gerald Ford, the U.S. Congress refused further assistance to the Khmer Republic. Efforts to make a last-minute rapprochement with Sihanouk also failed. In early April, a tearful Lon Nol fled into exile, a casualty of events.[37] A few days later, the U.S. ambassador, John Gunther Dean, his embassy staff, and foreigners who wanted to leave the capital were evacuated by helicopter. In a little over two hours 276 people—82 of them Americans—were taken out. To Saloth Sar and his followers, poised on the outskirts of the city, the evacuation did not represent the departure of a vestigial U.S. mission; rather, it was the definitive defeat of "the largest, most evil imperialist power in the world" at the hands of the Red Khmer. Furthermore, the helicopters came and went more than two weeks before Vietnamese Communist troops produced the same effect in Saigon. The Cambodian Communist party's leaders attributed the victory to their ingenuity, sacrifice, and strength and overlooked American war weariness, Vietnamese help, and the terminal illness of the Khmer Republic.[38]

On April 17, Cambodian Communist troops—heavily armed, silent, many of them alarmingly young—appeared on the boulevards of Phnom Penh and converged on the center of the city. To onlookers crowding the streets to welcome them, the Red Khmer seemed to come from another planet. For their part, the rebel soldiers viewed the city dwellers with smoldering disdain—they were the "enemies" *(khmang)* the rebels had been hearing about, the "capitalists" *(nay tun)* who refused to join the revolution. Within twenty-four hours the young combatants had ordered everyone in Phnom Penh to evacuate the city.

The Red Khmer held that their victory belonged to the army, to the party, and to the workers and peasants. Those who had not taken part in it were enemies. With victory, there was to be no consensus or healing. Psychological wounds on both sides were to be left unbandaged. To those who had welcomed the Communists' victory, this policy of hatred was bewildering. Most of the people in Phnom Penh were poverty-stricken refugees from the countryside. They were ready to help the Red Khmer. Now that the war was over, everyone longed for guidance and support. But as Pol Pot declared in 1977, "class and national hatred" rather than the prospect of building a just and happy country had produced the victory. To follow through, hatred had to be maintained; enemies were to be treated as they deserved. Overnight they became "new people," or "April 17 people"—less than human, without privileges or rights.

Saloth Sar, the architect of the assault on Phnom Penh, was nowhere to be seen. He remained outside the city for a week while the people who might have welcomed him were driven out of sight. This forced evacuation of the cities was the most far-reaching decision any modern Cambodian government ever took. To the leaders of the Red Khmer, it was not so much a cruel and thoughtless tactic as a demonstration of their independence and an extension of their victorious campaign. From that moment on, no foreign aid to feed the people would be allowed into the country. Those who suffered had refused the option of being on the winning side. The city was full of people who had opposed the revolution. They were not to be trusted; they might prove impossible to control. A new Cambodia would therefore start from zero in an empty city.

What happened next has been described by many survivors. Hundreds of thousands of men, women, and children were driven onto the roads to travel on foot, in the hottest month of the year. Thousands died of exhaustion, exposure, or malnutrition over the next few weeks. The very old and the very young were especially vulnerable. In the crush and confusion, family members were separated from each other, sometimes for good. Within a week, there was nobody left in the capital, in Battambang, or in any towns formerly controlled by the Republic.

Saloth Sar Returns to Phnom Penh

Saloth Sar reached Phnom Penh in secrecy on April 23. For the past twelve years, he had waged war against the city and all it stood for. The victory of what the Communists came to call the "glorious 17th of April" had obliterated the authority of Phnom Penh. As he was driven around the capital, with its smoldering garbage, burnt-out cars, abandoned shops, deserted houses, and empty streets, Sar's excitement must have been difficult to restrain. He had stopped imperialism in its tracks. He had driven the Americans away. Two million enemies of the revolution had been dispersed into the countryside. The "CIA agents" and "American puppets" hidden among them had been swept away. For the first time in over twenty years, no one threatened Saloth Sar. His party had come to power. Victory was proof that the strategies and tactics the Communists had followed were correct. Even so, the party secretary remained concealed and on his guard. Sar set up a temporary headquarters in the railway station and established a defense perimeter around the deserted city.[39]

He made no effort, it seems, to find out about his brother Loth Suong and his sister-in-law Chea Samy. As long ago as 1960 they had apparently stopped meaning anything to him. Besides, with victory he had more important work to do. Suong and Samy for their part knew nothing of his eminence; he had disappeared from the city in 1963, and they had heard nothing from him since. On April 18 they had walked with hundreds of thousands of others into exile. Sar's older brother, Saloth Chhay, went with them. They were on the road, heading east and north for over a month. Conditions were appalling, and Chhay, like thousands of others, died on the way. Suong and Samy ended up in their native province of Kompong Thom working as peasants. By keeping their heads down and concealing their palace connections, they managed to survive.[40]

For Saloth Sar, April and May 1975 swept past in a whirl of paperwork, illness, and ceremonial visits abroad. The exercise of power calls for different talents than those needed to seize it, but Saloth Sar believed that the storming attacks and revolutionary zeal that had led him to victory would produce comparable successes in peacetime. Perhaps he also thought that to start a nation from nothing, single-handedly, a person needed superhuman talents. Sar must have smiled, occasionally, as he paused among his dossiers. But the responsibility also wore him down. "The whole day was full of work," Chhim Samauk recalled. "Sometimes it went overtime. Generally at night it went on until eleven or twelve, and sometimes until one in the morning." Communications were primitive, and supplies were lacking. According to Chou Chet, "Flies were everywhere; nobody knew where the water we used came from." Resources, priorities, tasks, and the people to perform them had not been sorted out.

Moreover, Saloth Sar and his associates were still fearful of enemies. They found it impossible to trust "new people," foreigners, or anyone outside the party. To maintain momentum, they wanted to wage a continuous revolution. There was no time for building consensus—who could be trusted?—and little time to lose. Reminders of the past had to be wiped out. In May 1975, over one hundred officers of the Republican army were rounded up in Battambang and told to prepare for Sihanouk's return. They were loaded into trucks, taken into the countryside, and shot. The same fate awaited many officials of the Khmer Republic, including ordinary soldiers. In other parts of the country, particularly in the east, thousands of former officers and officials were imprisoned for more than a year.[41]

The Communist leadership also had other concerns. The Red Khmer army, for example, was still broken into regional commands and had not yet been brought under centralized control. Another problem sprang from the leadership's uncertainty about Vietnamese and Thai intentions. Also, as many as two million April 17 people had to be resettled and controlled. More prosaically, many rural areas were in turmoil just when the rice planting was scheduled to begin. It is amazing that the new regime survived at all.

In May 1975, at the time of the *Mayaguez* incident in which an American freighter was impounded by Cambodian authorities near the coast and released after U.S. bombing of Cambodian port facilities, Sar was "worn out completely with headaches and pains in his ears, his arms and his legs; he was unable to eat." This illness lasted "three or four days" as the *Mayaguez* crisis played itself out.[42]

Soon after, Sar welcomed several hundred Chinese technicians flown in to bolster his regime. Several thousand eventually came to work in Cambodia, but their presence was never openly acknowledged. Sar also visited Hanoi for "five or six days" with Nuon Chea, whose presence suggests that party matters were discussed, as well as the frontiers, economic relations, a friendship treaty, and the withdrawal of Vietnamese troops from Cambodian territory. Chhim Samauk accompanied them. Sar returned briefly to Phnom Penh before setting off for Beijing, where he was photographed with Mao Zedong and told that the Chinese would provide Cambodia with over \$1 billion in economic and military aid. Neither the visits nor Chinese assistance were publicized at the time. From China, Sar made a brief visit to North Korea, where he received promises of military aid. Returning to Beijing, he underwent medical treatment.[43]

For the remainder of 1975 Sihanouk remained the figurehead chief of state; but the party's leaders, who had always distrusted him, made no effort to bring him home. Under pressure from the Chinese, who wanted the prince to be treated fairly, the Red Khmer allowed him to return in September 1975. For awhile, Sihanouk worked assiduously at the protocol tasks assigned to him. A week after his arrival, the Vietnamese reopened their embassy in Phnom Penh. In what they probably considered an inspired move, the man they designated as ambassador was Pham Van Ba, who had enrolled Saloth Sar in the Indochina Communist party twenty-two years before. Pol Pot's reaction to the reappearance of his former supervisor was not recorded.[44]

The Vietnamese had good reason to be conciliatory: Cambodian units had attacked and occupied several Vietnamese islands in the Gulf of Thailand in April and May 1975, perhaps as part of an effort to revise Cambodia's maritime boundaries and lay claim to the oil deposits offshore. The Vietnamese, who had retaliated by occupying at least one Cambodian island, were unwilling to make territorial concessions to the Khmer, but they did not relish an outright confrontation.[45]

In August 1975 Saloth Sar, accompanied by a small entourage, visited a former military workshop west of Phnom Penh. The machinery there was being serviced by former Republican army engineers and some Sino-Khmer artisans—all April 17 people—recruited soon after liberation because of their experience and skills. This recruitment policy remained in effect for several months. One of the artisans recalled the visit vividly in 1989:

> Saloth Sar came into the workplace and asked us to gather round. He asked us if we had any ideas about making new machines, designing them ourselves. He said that because in Cambodia we had an outdated technology, we hadn't yet made new machines. Besides, no one in previous societies could invent them. His manner was honest and kind-hearted. He spoke slowly; he was a straightforward person. He had a small fan in his hand, and from time to time he opened and turned and closed it, like someone in a Chinese opera. He spoke as he walked back and forth, opening out the fan to fan himself—it was so hot! He would open and close the fan [and point it at us] like this, for emphasis. He wore ordinary black clothes; no tie, no scarf.[46]

These remarks echo those of people who knew Sar as a teacher. The way Sar presented himself—the slowly uttered words, the fan, the half-closed eyes—seems theatrical and false, with a straightforward, villainous personality lurking behind the surface. To assume this would be a mistake because it ignores the Khmer tradition of unruffled authoritarianism found in Buddhist and secular teaching, which, when added to Saloth Sar/Pol Pot's apparent warmth, made him so attractive to so many people. His friendly manner and self-control earned him respect and inspired obedience. His recorded statements to small gatherings often sound more brutal than those he made to larger groups, but he never gives the impression that he is raising his voice or losing his equanimity. Thiounn Mumm, who saw him often in this period, described him by quoting G. Axelrod's characterization of Lenin: "He was a revolutionary twenty-four hours a day, and when he slept, he dreamt about revolution."[47]

Inventing Democratic Kampuchea

Revolutionary movements are poorly suited to becoming functioning regimes—the process is painful and contradictory. Revolutionary movements, after all, focus on seizing nations rather than administering them; they are geared toward war. Revolutionaries, for the most part, lack bureaucratic skills and are contemptuous of "government." These impediments to governing properly did not keep Cambodia's leaders from thinking that revolutionary fervor and defeating the Americans were better credentials than any experience as civil servants. Their insistence on prolonging combat and maintaining hatred, when combined with their lack of experience, had disastrous consequences.

It took the Communists more than a year to set up a government. The decisions they made during this time were concealed. Fortunately, however, seventeen crucial texts from this period have come to light: the minutes of party standing committee meetings held between October 1975 and June 1976. Only five copies of the minutes were prepared at the time; the file probably covers less than 10 percent of the meetings that took place in those eight months. Even so, the documents offer a revealing glimpse of Cambodia's tiny governing body and of its modus operandi following the liberation of Phnom Penh.[48]

Most of the texts were triumphalist in tone. At several points Saloth Sar or one of his colleagues spoke of the incomparability of the Cambodian revolution and expressed the hope that larger nations would learn from its revolutionary experience. A corollary of the triumphalism is the lack of information about the outside world. Sar and his colleagues read no newspapers and absorbed little about foreign events. They nourished themselves on their own documents, conversations, and broadcasts and on material produced by other Communist parties. Because they had achieved a revolutionary victory, the Red Khmer assumed that similar ones would occur elsewhere in the world.

On October 9, 1975, the items on the standing committee's agenda were the "allocation of tasks and operational matters"; "overall arrangements"; and "the handling of a number of specific tasks." The party, concealed by the fa-cade of the Revolutionary Organization (the name it had assumed among Cambodians), was still officially hidden behind the National Front, with Si-hanouk ostensibly the chief of state. Layers of disguises, revolutionary names, and secret meetings protected Saloth Sar from the judgment of ordinary peo-ple. Party members who had been assigned new responsibilities took up their work in secret, disguised by revolutionary names. The complex charade hid the real division of spoils, whereby high-ranking members of the party carved out areas of patronage and control.[49]

At the October 1975 meeting, eleven men and two women had been as-signed protoministerial positions. The "comrade secretary," Saloth Sar, took charge of the economy and defense; the "comrade deputy secretary," Nuon Chea, was responsible for party organizational work and education; and Ieng Sary was to handle foreign affairs for the state and the party. Khieu Samphan remained as liaison officer with the National Front—that is, with Sihanouk. He was also given the tasks of "the accountancy and pricing aspects of com-merce," recalling his cabinet post in the 1960s. Koy Thuon took charge of domestic and foreign trade, while Son Sen was in command of security and the military General Staff. Others to receive positions included Vorn Vet, in charge of industry, railways, and fisheries; Soeu Va Si, in charge of the Cen-tral Committee's political office; Non Suon, in charge of the agriculture portfolio; and Chhim Samauk, in charge of the prime minister's office. Seum Son, later ambassador to North Korea, was responsible for the information section of the Central Committee. Ieng Sary's wife, Khieu Thirith, received the social welfare portfolio; and Son Sen's wife, Yun Yat, was in charge of cul-ture, education, and propaganda.[50]

The revolutionaries seem to have divided the "ministries" along prerevolu-tionary lines, and although eight of the thirteen officials survived in positions of authority in Pol Pot's movement into the 1990s, five were purged between 1976 and 1978. In other words, Saloth Sar/Pol Pot saw to it that close to a third of his cabinet were executed over the next three years—an indication of the volatility of his years in power. Some of those killed, like Chhim Samauk and Vorn Vet, had been his intimate associates for many years.

The rest of the October 1975 minutes discussed the monitoring role to be played by the standing committee of the party. It underscored the need to "build and defend" (*kosang nung kapea*) the country, the need to organize a national army, and the desirability of sending people abroad for technical training. Although Vietnam and Thailand were not mentioned, the minutes stressed the importance of guarding Cambodia's land and sea frontiers against invasion and protecting the party against its enemies.[51]

Sihanouk's role within this new government was ambiguous; but as long as the Chinese supported the prince, it was hard for the Red Khmer to move against him. In January 1976, however, Sihanouk's most enduring patron, the Chinese prime minister, Zhou Enlai, died in Beijing after a long illness. By then, the Constitution of Democratic Kampuchea and new statutes for the party had been promulgated, although the new government had not yet taken office. Sihanouk's position became uncertain.

In early March, the prince submitted his resignation without being asked to do so, and the standing committee met to decide his future. That same day, its members also discussed the problem of the "eastern frontier." The two documents make interesting reading.[52] Khieu Samphan opened the discussion about Sihanouk by saying that the prince had just addressed two letters in French to the "organization." One proposed that he resign from office for health reasons; the other, addressed to the Cambodian people, dated his resignation from March 20, 1976, the date scheduled for elections to the national deliberative body known as the People's Representative Assembly.

The prince's spontaneous gesture, probably aimed at pleasing the Red Khmer, angered their leader, who presumed he was upstaging them. The "Comments from the Organization" that followed Samphan's remarks offer a rare glimpse of "Brother Pol" with no mandate to be polite. The resignations, Sar said, were meaningless. After all, "Sihanouk isn't resigning now; he did that already in 1971"—that is, when Ieng Sary had gone to Beijing to supervise the prince. Sar saw two reasons for removing Sihanouk from office. One was "the class contradiction between him, his wife and the revolution. He can't live with us." The second reason was that the prince's presence was a continuing embarrassment to the Red Khmer. The party had no need for Sihanouk anymore, Sar said, and the prince himself realized he was "finished." On the other hand, Sar mused, keeping the prince in Phnom Penh could be a way of getting back at the Vietnamese, "who tell us that we are leftist." If Sihanouk departed the country on his own, Sar said, this would "confuse the Chinese"; but if he stayed, his complaints could be muffled within a month. After all, the prince was a "patriot," Sar maintained, even though his wife was not. Sar proposed that Samphan arrange a meeting with Sihanouk at which he could be praised deceptively and told to withdraw his resignation until it was demanded. It was essential to the party that the prince remain silenced in Phnom Penh.

Two days later, Samphan reported that Sihanouk had "crawled and begged" for permission to resign and had said that his unsolicited letters had not been intended to embarrass the organization. The prince was terrified. Sensing victory, Saloth Sar proposed that Sihanouk not be allowed to leave the country; instead, a meeting of the National Front's Council of Ministers would ratify his resignation and the prince should be given a tape recorder on which to register statements in support of the regime. Sihanouk was an "old tiger, still frightening to some," Sar admitted, but because he had joined the revolution, he would not be killed. Sihanouk resigned in April 2, 1976. He spent the next thirty-three months under house arrest on the grounds of the Royal Palace in Phnom Penh.[53]

Between meetings about Sihanouk, the standing committee met to discuss Vietnam, whose troops still occupied Cambodian territory in the northeast. The party's leaders were distressed by these incursions, not because of legal implications about the frontiers (which the Vietnamese claimed had been drawn by the "imperialists"), but because the Vietnamese habitually violated Cambodian territory. The Lao precedent ("Vietnam controlled the Lao revolution and has taken Lao land; we have learned many lessons from the Lao") was discouraging to the Khmer, but for the time being, a fragile peace prevailed.[54]

At this meeting a speaker remarked that Sihanouk had become entangled with France, the United States, and China and had been "unable to pull out" (doh min ruoc). The same situation applied to Cambodia after liberation ("We have not yet pulled out"), although the entangling patron (probably Vietnam) was not named. The solution, the speaker said, was for Cambodia to seek clients of its own, "in Africa, for example. In a short while, we will be much stronger, and the revolution in Southeast Asia will be much stronger. We can solve the issue [of Vietnam]. If the revolution in Southeast Asia succeeds, we can compete [for leadership?]. Our friends understand us thoroughly. They assist us. If we proceed correctly, we will have an influence over countries that lack our Party's achievements." The "friends" in this fantasy were those in China and North Korea advocating accelerated, autonomous revolutionary wars in Thailand, Burma, and Malaysia. If they were victorious, as Sar believed they would be, Vietnam would be surrounded. The alternative was for Vietnam to dominate the region. Happily, "at the moment," Saloth Sar said, "Vietnam is very confused," and so Cambodia was "proceeding more quickly" along the revolutionary path than Vietnam. Sar's optimism about other Communist movements in Southeast Asia shows how narrow a band of information he and his colleagues were receiving. What passed through to them was Communist-generated material suggesting that all of Southeast Asia, like the rest of the world, was on the march. In fact, the Communist movements whose support Saloth Sar seems to have expected were weak, disorganized, and marginalized by the armed forces of the regimes they forlornly hoped to overturn.

The Emergence of Pol Pot

A few days before these discussions, the Central Committee had met to discuss the elections scheduled for the People's Representative Assembly. Saloth Sar noted that the elections, although modeled on capitalist ones, were being held primarily so that "our enemies can't take advantage of us." The elections were for overseas consumption. No benefits accruing to the people from the elections, or from the assembly, were mentioned.[55]

April 17 people were not allowed to vote, and the 250 candidates were named from slates of peasants, soldiers, and workers rather than from particular districts. The job attributions of some figures were bizarre, as when Khieu Thirith and Yun Yat called themselves "Phnom Penh factory workers." Representing "rubber workers" was an otherwise unidentifiable figure, Pol Pot, soon to be named prime minister of Democratic Kampuchea.

Although Saloth Sar is known to have used the pseudonym "Pol" in the 1950s, and was using it again in 1975 when he convened meetings of the Central Committee, no pre-1976 references to "Pot" have come to light, and the election announcement marked the first public appearance of "Pol Pot" as a person and as a name. It is unclear how thoroughly his colleagues in the party had been prepared for the new man or for Saloth Sar's disappearance. In Paris, Pol Pot's old friend Thiounn Prasith told supporters of the new Cambodian regime that "Pol Pot" had been born along the Vietnamese frontier, had fought against the Japanese, and had worked in the Memot rubber plantation. While it is tempting to view this explanation as an attempt to throw people off the trail, it is possible that Prasith, without better information, was fabricating the biography. More likely, he had been given the cover story without being told the truth. In that case, it is intriguing that Sar chose to provide details of his life not known to many—such as his time on the eastern border in 1953–1954 and his two years as a semihostage of the Vietnamese in Office 100, adjoining the plantation at Memot—while concealing his original name and his activities as leader of the Cambodian Communist party. The new name was probably chosen to hide Saloth Sar and to celebrate a rite of passage. In 1977 the Cambodian ambassador in Beijing told a visitor that "Comrade Pot has always used that name; Comrade Saloth Sar perished during the war."[56]

It is baffling but consistent for Saloth Sar to assume a pseudonym at precisely the moment when he might have been expected to step into the open, using his own name or a revolutionary one that ordinary people would have known (like "Ho Chi Minh"). None of the other members of the government would take new names at this time, although they did not reveal their nonrevolutionary ones. Pol Pot's fondness for obscurity may have sprung from a conscious drive to build a humble, bleached persona, like Stalin's or Ho Chi Minh's—men who forsook everything, including their personalities, for the revolution. "Pol Pot" was a personification of the revolution, a revolutionary name (like "Ho" or "Stalin") without a personal past.

The People's Representative Assembly met in mid-April 1976, approved the new government of Democratic Kampuchea, and dissolved sine die.[57]

As he stepped up to govern Democratic Kampuchea, Pol Pot must have felt as if his destiny had been fulfilled. He had gained everything he had dreamed of when he first became a Communist in 1952. He may have felt invincible; he may also have been frightened by what lay ahead for him. He had certainly reached the limit of his abilities, which had served him well in small groups whose members were, like him, poorly read and inexperienced in government and technology. Nevertheless, Pol Pot and his colleagues in the collective leadership enthusiastically embarked on a program to transform their country. In April 1976 the disasters that would befall the regime and millions of Khmer had not yet come into view.

CHAPTER SEVEN

■

Prairie Fire, 1976–1977

Few survivors of the period from 1975 to 1979 refer to it nowadays as "Democratic Kampuchea." Instead, they speak of *samai a-Pot* ("the era of the contemptible Pot"), giving the period an ex post facto personal tinge. It is important to place this tendency to personalize Pot's reign alongside his own attempts to depersonalize his leadership of the party.[1]

In 1976 and 1977, Pol Pot concentrated on retaining power, which meant changing some of the tactics that had helped him overthrow the Khmer Republic; but he also remained wary and assumed even with victory that enemies were everywhere. To emerge into the open, he thought, was to become endangered. There was no question of catching him off duty or off guard. In DK documents we overhear none of his informal arguments, table talk, or snatches of conversation. Minutes of standing committee meetings, so helpful for 1975 and the first half of 1976, are not available later on. After September 1976, Pol Pot and his colleagues became increasingly fearful of plots being mounted against them. Their response was to become even more remote.[2]

The picture of the man that emerges from this period, however, is consistent with those from earlier times. As before, Pol Pot excelled in dealing with small groups, but colleagues of inferior rank now encountered him more rarely. With the Communist victory, "Brother Pol" had become prime minister. For all the talk of collectivism in Cambodia, this made him "Brother Number One." From a Communist standpoint, victory proved his correctness; from a Buddhist one, his new status demonstrated the meritoriousness of his achievements. From either perspective, he rose in prestige and became more difficult to reach.

Secrecy remained attractive to Pol Pot. It was also seen as an essential ingredient of party life. Nuon Chea expressed this view to a Danish Marxist-Leninist delegation that visited Phnom Penh in 1978. Chea's frankness can be traced to the fact that he considered his remarks confidential and never expected them to be published. "Secret work," he said, "is fundamental in all that we do. For example, the elections of comrades to leading work are secret. The places where our leaders live are secret. . . . As long as there is class struggle or imperialism, secret work will remain fundamental. Only through secrecy can we be masters of the situation and win victory over the enemy who cannot find out who is who."[3]

In 1976–1977 Pol Pot concentrated on the "Four Year Plan to Build Socialism in All Fields" and the purging of "enemies," which was carried out in large part at the party's interrogation center known as S-21 in the Phnom Penh suburb of Tuol Sleng. These programs fit with his priorities of "building and defending" the country. To build the country it was essential to take charge of its economic activities; to defend it, it was essential to eliminate enemies of the state. Pol Pot later blamed the uneven results of his all-embracing, radical Four Year Plan on "enemies" just as Stalin and Mao Zedong had done when their grandiose economic plans ran into trouble. The speed with which the Cambodian plan was set in motion, moreover, was traced to the urgency of defeating the "enemies" before they could sabotage it. In Pol Pot's words, "Enemies attack and torment us. From the east and from the west, they persist in pounding us and worrying us. If we are slow and weak, they will mistreat us."[4]

The plan and the purges can also be linked to Cambodia's intensifying confrontation with Vietnam. This smoldering conflict, fanned by Cambodian cross-border raids in 1975 and 1976, burst into flame in April 1977 and led to successive Vietnamese incursions. Contradictory evidence suggests that Pol Pot, always distrustful of Vietnam, did not desire a full-scale war and that he hoped Vietnam would leave Cambodia alone. He was drawn toward confrontation, however, by his military commanders, by Vietnamese intransigence on the frontier issue—which matched his own—and by his patrons in Beijing, who saw Vietnam as a Soviet satellite, a thorn in their side, and an ungrateful client. The ensuing military hostilities, as well as the plan's shortcomings, kept it from working and accelerated the purges. In 1976–1977 Pol Pot saw the plan and the purges as the best way of building a society that could withstand the Vietnamese.

The Four Year Plan

On August 21, 1976, Pol Pot convened a meeting of the "party center" (Central Committee) to introduce the Four Year Plan to build socialism in agriculture, industry, health and welfare, education, and so on. It was scheduled to take effect at the beginning of 1977. The plan had been actually inaugurated at an "agricultural meeting" at the end of 1975 following consultations between the party center and the various zones. It had been unveiled again at a longer meeting convened in late July. On both occasions Pol Pot had presented the plan as a fait accompli; discussion of its provisions was muted or nonexistent.

In essence, the plan sought to achieve socialism in Cambodia within four years by collectivizing agriculture and industry and by spending money earned from agricultural exports to finance agricultural production, light industry, and eventually heavy industry as well. Capital accumulation, ironically, was to occur in a society in which money, markets, and private property had been abolished.

The plan embodied four of Pol Pot's idées fixes—collectivism, revolutionary will, autarky, and the empowerment of the poor. Pol Pot saw the document as the means by which Cambodia could accelerate toward socialism. The unreality and sloppiness of most of its proposals reveal a blind faith in the possibilities of success. When these proposals were applied at great speed by a self-absorbed regime, they led to the deaths of tens of thousands of citizens. As lower ranking cadre and officials, fearful of reprisals, struggled to apply what they took to be the exigencies of the plan, they made unworkable demands on the people under them on whose behalf the revolution was ostensibly being waged.

The plan's database derived from the 1960s. No attention had been paid to demographic or ecological changes since then or to the devastations of the civil war. The plan owed nothing to sustained research. Instead, it seemed to reflect the remark of a Cambodian official in late 1975: "When a people is awakened by political consciousness, it can do anything. . . . Our engineers cannot do what the people can do." Achieving the plan's goals would be easy, its implementers believed, for a people who had defeated American imperialism. One "storming attack" was as good as another.[5]

After April 1975 Cambodians were repeatedly encouraged to "build and defend"(*kosang nung kapea*) their country. The word "independence" (*aekareach*) was often coupled with "mastery" (*mochaskar*) to form a phrase that constituted a national ideal. To tens of thousands of Cambodians under thirty the notions of "independence-mastery"—taking charge of their future and renouncing the past—were undoubtedly appealing. So was Cambodia's new sense of dignity and importance. With its overwhelming victory, Cambodia had become incomparable and foreign models inappropriate. Speaking to a Lao delegation in December 1975, Ieng Sary remarked pointedly, "At present our Cambodian people control their own destiny, firmly grasping in their own hands the revolutionary administration and building a new society." Cambodia's superiority to Laos, which was linked closely with Vietnam and Vietnamese communism, was clear.[6]

In Pol Pot's view, independence-mastery would grow out of economic independence. This would come, he thought, from earning foreign exchange by selling agricultural products overseas. To cynics this might seem like the colonial prescription without the material incentives connected with profit, markets, land ownership, and money. The difference in theory was that the transactions would not benefit oppressive merchants and landlords, as in the past, but the poor and landless peasants who grew the crops and had become the masters of the country. Because money had been abolished, all foreign exchange, it was thought, would directly benefit the people. The "vestiges of capitalism" (and inequality) would not survive without money in circulation.[7]

Pol Pot wanted to set this process in motion immediately within the framework of a national plan. To allow economic activity to occur for even a year without control, he thought, would revive capitalism, which was unthinkable. In the preamble to the plan, Pol Pot brushed aside conceivable objections, including the benefits of moving more slowly, declaring that "we mean to build the country quickly, and build socialism quickly." Cambodia was not comparable to more cautious countries. "We have a different character from them," he said. "We are faster than they are."[8]

All the same, there were many obstacles to achieving independence-mastery. Cambodia had no exportable minerals, few skilled workers, even fewer technocrats, and an insignificant industrial sector. Exports were limited to agricultural products. Of these, the most important was rice, which had been the backbone of Cambodian exports since the 1920s. There was no way of escaping the past or the reality of resources: Rice exports became the key element in the Four Year Plan. Pol Pot placed an almost metaphysical value on rice, associating it intimately with the recently empowered rural poor. Even before the plan was promulgated, the party had launched the slogan "Three tons [of unhusked rice] per hectare," which soon became a national goal. The slogan itself, without acknowledgment, echoed a campaign launched in China by Vice Premier Hua Guofeng toward the end of 1975. The target figure of 3 tons per hectare suggests that the Cambodian leaders had not worked out any agricultural slogans or policies of their own and that what was good enough for China would suffice for Cambodia as well.

This hastiness and lack of thinking are not surprising. Hardly any of the leaders of the party had ever planted, transplanted, or harvested rice to feed a family. Although they knew that the target of 3 tons per hectare could not be achieved through uncoordinated storming attacks, even within the framework of the plan it was unrealistically high. Before 1970, yields in Cambodia had averaged less than 1 ton of unhusked rice per hectare. Most of this was of mediocre quality, produced on family-owned plots without fertilizer or machinery. The party's slogan demanded that Cambodia's average yield be tripled at once, not in response to superior technology or material incentives but as testimony to a collectivized revolutionary will and the transferability of military zeal into the economic sphere. "Can we accomplish the Plan or not?" Pol Pot asked rhetorically. "The answer is that we can accomplish it everywhere; *the evidence for this* is our political movement" (emphasis added).[9]

The northwest—comprising the provinces of Battambang and Pursat—was where the agricultural sections of the plan were to have the most effect. In a draft of the plan, a party spokesman referred to this zone as a "number one battlefield" for economic growth. In that zone, land scheduled for two rice crops was to increase from 60,000 hectares in 1977 to 200,000 hectares in 1980, making up 40 percent of the national total of double-cropped land. Over 140,000 hectares of uncultivated or unproductive land were to be brought under cultivation. All in all, the northwest was scheduled to provide 60 percent of Cambodia's rice exports between 1977 and 1980.

Most of the work in the northwest would be done by more than one million April 17 people who had been evacuated from Phnom Penh and from the city of Battambang into rural areas in the zone. Over the next two years, these men and women were forced to hack rice fields, canals, dams, and villages out of malarial forests. Tens of thousands of them died from malnutrition, disease, executions, and overwork. These deaths, when they became known, distressed the authorities in Phnom Penh only to the extent that they indicated that "enemies" were at work behind the scenes. New people, because they were so numerous and "class enemies" of the revolution, were expendable. Many survivors recall a chilling aphorism directed mockingly at them by cadre: "Keeping [you] is no gain. Losing [you] is no loss."[10]

By dramatically increasing rice harvests throughout Cambodia, Pol Pot hoped the country would produce 26.7 million tons of paddy over the lifetime of the plan, recreating what he assumed had been the state-directed plenitude of Angkorean times. Massive irrigation works, it was thought, would make these developments feasible. About half of the production was to be kept aside for seed, food, and "reserves and welfare." The exported surplus would earn $1.4 billion in foreign exchange. The income, in turn, was to be used to purchase farm machinery, tools, fertilizer, and insecticide to increase agricultural production. Roughly two-thirds of the income was to be redirected to the zones producing the rice, with the remainder held in reserve for national priorities. Defense expenditures were expected to reach $37 million over four years, with the southwestern and northwestern zones, bordering Thailand, receiving $23 million of that figure. At a later stage, additional foreign exchange would be used to finance industrial development.[11]

Unfortunately, paddy production was much lower in 1976–1977 than expected, particularly in the northwest, where most of the reserves intended to feed the people were designated as surpluses by beleaguered cadre and taken to unknown destinations. Some of the rice was exported to China. By the end of 1976, most "new people" in the northwest were badly undernourished. The situation deteriorated in 1977, when thousands more starved to death while others became ineffective because of illness and insufficient food. Reports of these conditions took time to reach the "Higher Organization," and since disagreement with the organization amounted to treason, the reports

were never critical of the plan or its framers. Instead, the news transmitted up
the line was always good, causing false optimism at the top even as rice production faltered and rural workers died.[12]

More than half the tables in the Four Year Plan referred to the rice campaign. Other crops—such as jute, corn, coconuts, tobacco, and cotton—were
mentioned but received less emphasis. After all, the income these crops
would produce ($29 million) was barely 2 percent of the income expected to
be earned from rice. In general, those portions of the plan that did not deal
with rice seem hastily written and poorly conceived. The text, it seems, was
tailored to fit the priorities of the party's leaders, who had placed their bets
on rice.

Agricultural infrastructure received glancing attention. Production of
"natural fertilizer" (human and animal waste) was to rise from 5.6 million
tons in 1977 to 8.9 million tons in 1980, although how the increase would be
accomplished was unstated. Factories were expected to come into being to
produce several thousand irrigation pumps. Where the material to make the
pumps would come from or how the funding and labor were to be acquired
was not specified. Another table notes that in 1979 Cambodia would "buy a
factory that produces DDT," although how this would be accomplished or
paid for is not mentioned. Similarly, there were references to the urgency of
expanding numbers of draught animals and other livestock and to increasing
fisheries, with little attention paid to financing, manpower requirements, vet-
erinary medicine, or the minimization of risk. Pol Pot's idée fixe was rice: "If
we have rice, we have everything," Radio Phnom Penh had said as early as
May 1975. The impression one gets from reading the plan is its faith in revolutionary zeal. Weighed against the plan's disastrous results, this "zeal" might
be seen as synonymous with amateurism, ignorance, and wishful thinking.[13]

The plan then dealt with proposed industrial and technological developments. Light industry, to be financed by agricultural exports, was to come
first. The plan said little about what products would be favored or where the
raw materials or labor force would come from. Instead, it suggested that industries be established "producing goods for everyday use, such as . . . clothing, mosquito nets, blankets, mats, shoes, hats, tables, cupboards, chairs,
plates, pots, pans, spoons, water bowls, pitchers, . . . cups, toothbrushes,
toothpaste, combs, scissors, soap, towels, medical equipment, muslin, cotton
wool, alcohol, knives, axes, sickles, ploughs, tailoring, leather, *etc.*" (emphasis
added). These jumbled "industries" were scheduled to produce "60 to 100
percent" by 1980. No priorities or allocations of resources were mentioned.

More space was devoted to "The Plan to Build Heavy Industry" than to
any other section, even though heavy industrialization would not be set in
motion until the Four Year Plan was complete. In speaking about it, the leaders of the party seem to have been mesmerized by a vision of the future that
included a thriving industrial sector serviced by an expanded proletariat. Fac-

tories with smoking chimneys, after all, appeared alongside rice fields on the country's coat of arms, and a third of the candidates to the National Assembly had run as "workers." This expansion would be accomplished regardless of resources, finances, or feasibility. Here again, the leaders' ignorance of industry and their refusal to use experts or take advice meant that their proposals were doomed to failure, except insofar as they could be accomplished by technical assistance from other countries. In large measure, this is just what happened—Chinese and North Korean aid concentrated on refurbishing prerevolutionary industries and building new ones. In addition, the plan talks about unverified petroleum deposits, coal mining ("If there's any coal, we'll find it"), and building an "iron-smelting factory of overseas standard," even though no exploitable deposits of iron ore exist in the country. Cambodia has never had the resources to sustain industrialization.[14]

The remainder of the plan seems hastily flung together. Under "Trade," for instance, "imports" consist of "screws and nuts, spare parts, agricultural and industrial machinery, necessary goods for the livelihood of the people, and goods for national defense." Under "Tourism" came the laconic note: "Must organize: hotels, water, electricity, . . . places to relax." The section on health and welfare stressed the importance of traditional healers (kruu khmer) working with local medical remedies. This preference reflected the triumphalism of the regime, echoed the policies of "barefoot doctors" in China and was seen as a way of saving money. The results of the poorly conceived medical program were disastrous. Survivors' memories teem with grisly accounts of arrogant, untrained medical practitioners in the countryside—many under fifteen years old—and of the regime's insistence on prerevolutionary (indeed, precolonial) cures, without emphasizing hygiene or heeding diagnoses. In many areas, people who were ill received fewer rations than those who were able to work. Once again, achieving public health was conceived in terms of storming attacks. Under "General Hygiene," for example, the plan proposed to "instigate a mass movement for general hygiene in every field" but provided no details.

The plan underscored the importance of accelerating collectivization, a program that was seen as synonymous with society's well-being. Collectivization, it was thought, would raise the people's living standards: "In 1977 there are to be two desserts per week. In 1978 there will be one dessert every two days. Then in 1979, one dessert every day, and so on." This macabre pledge is the only material incentive mentioned in the plan.

One aspect of collectivization not mentioned in the plan was the policy of forcing people to eat together in large dining halls rather than as families. This policy, which went into effect in 1977 and was arguably the most unpopular one in Democratic Kampuchea, deprived families of food and opportunities for cooking and casual conversation. According to a spokesman, "the capitalist framework"—which included relatives eating together—still existed in China and North Korea and had postponed revolutionary success in those otherwise admirable countries. "So long as the capitalist system exists," he said, "it will . . . become an obstacle to the socialist revolution."

The connection between families, private property, and counterrevolutionary ideas was made in the nineteenth century by Marx's colleague Friedrich Engels. Twentieth-century Khmer, however, never understood how families eating together endangered progress or how people with access to less than $100 per year in prerevolutionary times were "capitalist" or "bourgeois." It is generous to assume that communal eating, as a policy, was intended to benefit ordinary Khmer. It seems more likely, however, that it was intended as a means of strengthening the organization's surveillance and control over the people.

The shortest section of the document—covering three pages in Khmer—dealt with "culture, literacy, art, technology, science, mass education, and propaganda and information." The low priorities given to culture, literacy, and art reflected the rejection of traditional culture by the former school-teachers who wrote the plan as well as their slavish imitation of Chinese models. Turning their backs on "2,000 years of history" also meant turning their backs on the many-faceted Cambodian culture that had developed over these millennia for the pleasure (Communists would say the "mystification") of privileged and ordinary people alike. High culture that was accessible to peasants included complex dances, instrumental and vocal music, highly developed decorative skills (evident in woven textiles, bronze work, wood carving, and Buddhist temple paintings), and a long tradition of oral and written poetry—to say nothing of the "feudal" grandeur of Angkor. It also included sophisticated works of Buddhist teaching and exegesis and a wide-ranging collection of ethically oriented poems, known as *chbab*.

The leaders of Democratic Kampuchea, bewitched by the defeat of the Americans and by slogans like "Three tons per hectare" may have thought there would be little time and energy to devote to these peripheral aspects of existence until the problems of the economy had been solved. This is a generous reading. More likely, they were contemptuous or fearful of the private pleasures that culture, in a wide sense, had always offered to ordinary Khmer.

To be sure, Cambodia's poor peasants had survived without science, technology, literacy, mass education, and propaganda and information for hundreds of years. They had drawn pleasure, comfort, and cohesion, as the Communists did not, from their daily lives, building these up from such ingredients as families, religion and rituals, friendships, informal traveling (*dao lenh*), eating and gossiping together, and sharing in often backbreaking work. They would probably not have used the word *vapp 'thoa* ("culture") to describe what they were doing, but they would have enjoyed culture "from above" when they attended Buddhist ceremonies or poetry recitations or welcomed royalty to their villages.

Cambodia's rural poor may have been ripe for revolution, but many were stubborn and unwilling to accept the sacrifices (or unable to perceive the benefits) involved in overturning their prerevolutionary lives. The exceptions were landless peasants, teenagers, and those who had accepted Marxist-Leninist teaching. In the leaders' view, the peasants' "empty hands" gave them a head start toward utopia. The peasants themselves would have preferred to have more materials to work with, and to keep most of their cultural baggage—even or perhaps especially when "culture" came to them from other, supposedly "higher," levels of society. In this context, there is something ominous, even repulsive, about outsiders to poverty and rural life fashioning for rural people a twentieth-century state from nothing, while forbidding them the benefits that might have accrued from education, science, and technology and cutting them off from the pleasures they derived from family life.[15]

Revolutionary culture broke sharply with the past. A party spokesman discussing the plan went so far as to say: "If we chose [prerevolutionary] 'culture' [as a basis for education] it would lead to a life and death disaster for the Party." These ideas echoed those in vogue in China at the time. The only manifestations of culture mentioned in the plan were revolutionary poems and songs—although "books for reading" are mentioned earlier in the text as components of everyday life, along with the "*light study* of politics and culture" (emphasis added). The songs and poems, in turn, would "describe good models . . . in the building of socialism."[16]

The plan's proposals for education noted that "half study, half work" would be a watchword (as in China), that primary education would commence "from 1977 onwards," and that secondary education would proceed "simultaneously . . . *to some extent*" (emphasis added). The once bookish leaders of the party were intrigued by the idea of illiterate praxis. In fact, although some basic textbooks were printed under Democratic Kampuchea, few primary schools and no secondary schools seem to have been opened until 1978. Although the plan's proposals for secondary curricula were stillborn, those for history are nonetheless of interest. History would consist of "the revolutionary struggle of the people, the revolutionary struggle for the nation, the revolutionary struggle for democracy, the revolutionary struggle for socialist revolution and the struggle to build socialism."[17]

The closing pages of the plan reiterated the party's importance for Cambodia and the party center's importance for the party. "The decisive factor is the Party. . . . If the Center pervades everything, the Party will pervade everything . . . and so will the army and so will the people."

With hindsight, it is easy to criticize the Four Year Plan as slapdash, naive, and uninformed. It can almost be seen as a ritual performance, part of Cambodia's becoming an authentic Communist state. A reading of the plan gives the impression that it was written so that "socialist" Cambodia could resemble other socialist countries—which prided themselves on their plans—rather than with a serious view of improving the material welfare of the Cambodian people. It was an abrupt, muddled, and perhaps desperate attempt by Pol Pot to "grasp the wheel of history"—a favorite Red Khmer locution—to gain control of Cambodia's future.

The Crisis of September–October 1976

At the beginning of September 1976 Mao Zedong died, and on September 18, coinciding with the funeral services in Beijing, Pol Pot paid a glowing tribute to him, stating publicly for the first time that Cambodia was run by a "Marxist-Leninist" organization and adding that there was much to be learned from Mao's theoretical writings. This is the only reference in Pol Pot's writings where he admits that he read Communist literature.[18]

Two days later, the party secretary in the northeast, Ney Saran (Ya), was arrested as a traitor. Another party stalwart, Keo Meas, was arrested on September 25. By then, Pol Pot's own resignation as prime minister had been announced, on the grounds of his ill health. He was replaced by Nuon Chea. Because Pol Pot resumed work in October and Nuon Chea was never chastised, the resignation may have reflected genuine ill health. Perhaps it was connected in an obscure fashion with the succession crisis in China. More likely, however, Pol Pot resigned to confuse and encourage enemies in the party who could be crushed once they came into the open. That the resignation was announced over Radio Phnom Penh, known to be monitored abroad, suggests that he hoped to spread some of this confusion among foreign powers.[19]

Toward the end of September, the political crisis gathered momentum. Its basis was an apparently trivial difference of opinion about the founding date of the Cambodian Communist party. In its September issue, the party's youth magazine published a ten-page article praising the party's twenty-fifth anniversary, locating its beginnings in 1951, during the First Indochina War. The article was out of step with Pol Pot's thinking, although it was probably "planted" by him to smoke out his opponents. As we have seen, party documents from 1974 had already referred to the 1960 congress as the "first," foreshadowing a revision of party history favoring Pol Pot; also, the March 1976 meeting of the standing committee had noted in this regard, "Do not use 1951—make a clean break." In October 1976, after Keo Meas and Ney Saran had gone to S-21, a thirty-one-page article traced the party's beginnings to its "first" congress in 1960, noting that "we must rearrange the history of the Party into something clean and perfect"—that is, without a Vietnamese, pre–Pol Pot component.[20]

It is unlikely that Keo Meas, who was under house arrest, had been plotting to overthrow Pol Pot. Ney Saran's case is more ambiguous, for his surviving confession is very fragmentary and he was known to have maintained extensive contacts with the Vietnamese after 1975. His name was the only one mentioned as a traitor by Pol Pot when he was interviewed by Nate Thayer in 1997. Keo Meas was probably purged because he retained a following among those radicalized in the 1950s who were unhappy with Pol Pot and the extreme policies embodied in the Four Year Plan. Ieng Sary later spoke of a "coup d'état" in September 1976, but if there was one it does not seem to have involved any military forces: No important military cadre were brought into S-21 between September and the end of the year. It is more likely that Pol Pot moved against the two defenseless senior party figures to terrorize the clients they had built up over the years and to tighten his own grip on the party's apparatus.

Originally, Pol Pot had planned to announce the Four Year Plan, and probably the existence of the party, at nationwide ceremonies celebrating the party's anniversary on September 30, 1976. The ceremonies did not take place, however, and the party's existence was kept secret for another year. The Four Year Plan was never promulgated. Instead of celebrating the party's 1976 anniversary, Pol Pot spent his time from then on, judging from his speeches and the dossiers at Tuol Sleng, extirpating enemies inside the party and dealing with a hostile Vietnam.

Purges in Democratic Kampuchea, 1975–1977

The most extensive documentary source for a study of Democratic Kampuchea, and its most unsettling legacy, is the archive of 4,000 confessions assembled between 1975 and early 1979 at the regime's interrogation facility at Tuol Sleng. The facility occupied the site of a former high school in the southern section of Phnom Penh. Documents in its voluminous archive suggest that some 14,000 men, women, and children passed through S-21 between the end of 1975 and early 1979. All but a handful were questioned, tortured, and put to death. In 1975, only 200 prisoners were registered. In 1976, 1,622 prisoners were registered, while in 1977 over 6,300 prisoners were brought in. Although the files for 1978 are incomplete, it seems that at least 5,000 prisoners were registered that year. Only half a dozen of them emerged alive—for some reason, the alternatives to the death penalty of imprisonment or "re-education," employed so liberally in Communist Vietnam and China, were never seriously considered in Cambodia. The 4,000 confessions make melancholy reading. Some are only three or four pages long; others consist of dossiers covering several hundred pages. All of them admit crimes against the party, often couched in terms of membership in foreign intelligence agencies. The confessions follow Soviet precedents set by Stalin's purge trials in the 1930s and the show trials of high-ranking party cadre in eastern Europe after World War II. In fact, it may well be that the party's leaders considered Stalin's purges essential to consolidating his grip on the Soviet Communist party in the 1930s and chose his methods to hold on to power themselves.[21]

People using the archive experience the emotional drain of encountering so much pain, so much cruelty, so many innocent lives destroyed.[22] Another problem with the confessions is related to their usefulness as historical sources—all of them, after all, were extracted under torture and none of the prisoners were ever considered innocent. Many of the texts display what seems like genuine devotion to the Communist party of Kampuchea. At least some of the victims (but which ones?) were innocent of plotting against the party, whereas others (impossible to determine) were guilty of disloyalty, knew people who were, or knew people accused of being disloyal. As autobiographies, many of the documents are unreliable, although the personal data they contain concerning prerevolutionary careers are probably fairly accurate. Because the prisoners had to admit an all-embracing guilt, the texts are not helpful in determining or demonstrating a person's subversion of the party, although the longest confessions were probably those of people suspected, rightly or wrongly, of the most serious crimes. Some of these confessions, in turn, appear to have been culled after 1979. The primary value of the documents en masse is as evidence of the continuing phobias of the party's leaders. Taken as a whole, the confessions are a bleak testimony to the extent to which the Red Khmer were riddled with brutality and distrust. What the party found threatening or disloyal, however, constantly changed. Its enemies, like all counterrevolutionaries, were moving targets.[23]

S-21 was an officially supported operation, and it was in the interests of the bureaucrats there to retain the confidence of their leaders. This meant that confessions, files, and conspiracies had to be concocted at Tuol Sleng and sent by S-21's director, Kaing Kek Ieu (Duch) to his superior Son Sen (Khieu), who sent them along to K-1, the party headquarters. Some of these confessions were handwritten; those considered especially interesting were often typed, with several carbon copies. Accusations in confessions were cross-referenced with other documents. Files grew; more and more suspects were brought in, processed, interrogated, and "smashed" *(komtec)*. In the zones, three independent accusations that someone was a member of the U.S. Central Intelligence Agency (CIA)—that is, was counterrevolutionary in the eyes of another party member—were sufficient for an arrest, and if questioning raised further doubts, the prisoner was brought into Tuol Sleng. Factory workers nearby, who had a vague idea of what was going on, described the interrogation center as "the place [where people] went in and never came out *(konlaenh choul min dael chenh).*"

The staff at S-21 consisted of more than one hundred men and women. Interrogators were generally young peasants with little education; many had been messengers or combatants in *dombon* 25 in the closing stages of the

Tuol Sleng. Photo by Bruce Sharp. Copyright by Bruce Sharp.

An interrogation room at Tuol Sleng. When Vietnamese troops arrived in Phnom Penh on January 7, 1979, the bodies of the final victims were still shackled to the bed frames in these cells. *SOURCE:* Ministry of Information and Culture, Phnom Penh. Copyright 1991 Bruce Sharp.

civil war. Some of them had taken up their work at the center after only a few weeks of political training. Typists, archivists, photographers, electricians, and transcribers were also employed by the bureau, as were several former teachers, who could frame the interrogations, "obtain answers for the Party" (as one of them put it), and analyze trends. The most notorious of these former teachers was the director of S-21, Duch, a Sino-Khmer from Kompong Thom, formerly in charge of security in the special zone. By keeping his superiors happy and those who worked for him afraid, he survived the DK period, unlike at least sixty of his staff, who were executed on a variety of charges.[24]

In late 1975 and early 1976, those brought in to be questioned and smashed tended to be either former Lon Nol soldiers, Cambodians educated in North Vietnam, stray foreigners, or former revolutionaries who had made life difficult for cadre in the countryside. In May 1976 a military unit stationed in Phnom Penh, Division 170, exploded some ordnance—either in error or as part of a demonstration—near the party's headquarters. The soldiers, it seems, wanted to be demobilized and allowed to return home. Their commanders were also rounded up and questioned. The most important of these was the political commissar Prom Sombat (Chan Chakrei), a thirty-three-year-old former monk who soon was designated by the Roman numeral "I" in S-21 in a "conspiracy" that extended by the end of the year to twenty coded figures. Chakrei confessed to working for the CIA, the Vietnamese, and the Khmer Serei ("Free Khmer"), a pro-American, anti-Sihanouk grouping that had been active in prerevolutionary times. Some of these admissions (but which ones?) may have been true, but Chakrei also claimed, as he was told to do, that the Khmer Serei had Soviet and Vietnamese Communist backing. This absurd connection was typical of the statements Duch demanded and then transmitted to Pol Pot and other leaders.

Chakrei's arrest prompted Duch to compose memoranda to a "Respected Older Brother" (probably Son Sen) pointing out what he saw as the collusion of the Vietnamese Communists and the CIA in conspiracies against the party. These links became the leitmotif of confessions in 1977 and 1978. Cadre in the eastern zone came under special scrutiny, because—as Steve Heder has suggested—the eastern zone cadre, led by the party secretary there, Sao Phim, wanted to assume a more vigorous defensive military posture toward Vietnam than the party's leaders wanted. Pol Pot and his colleagues were still hoping that Vietnam would collapse under its own weight.[25]

Purging Friends

In September 1976, when Ney Saran and Keo Meas were brought to Tuol Sleng, procedures had not yet been routinized and it seems likely that both men thought they might eventually be released. They were both, after all, old friends of Brother Number One. Their relationships with the party leader dated back to the early 1950s. Their confessions contain evidence of anguish, surprise at being arrested, and in Keo Meas's case, genuine affection for Pol Pot.

Keo Meas had been a militant in Phnom Penh in the 1950s. He had also spent time in Office 100 and had gone to Vietnam and China with Saloth Sar in 1965–1966. Sar was then using the code name "Pouk." Meas had returned to Vietnam as a liaison officer in 1968 and had served alongside Khieu Thirith in Hanoi and Ieng Sary in Beijing.

His confession consists of several letters to "Pouk" (Pol Pot) protesting his innocence and desperately trying to rekindle friendship and explain the "1951–1960" controversy. On September 24, for example, he recalled a conversation in 1964 when Pol Pot had told him: "In France there were some Khmer who could never be genuine Khmer." This fragmentary reference, perhaps to Thiounn Mumm, was not followed up as Meas succumbed to more punishment, claimed to be a loyal Khmer, and tried to keep Pol Pot's attention ("I wrote you a letter several months ago: did you ever receive it?"). In 1966, perhaps on the way home from China, Pol Pot had told him, "Our Cambodia wants to get away completely from Vietnam and the Soviets." Meas had agreed, but his confession became more agitated as he was accused of founding a new, pro-Vietnamese party. "I feel these accusations are absurd," he wrote. "They are incomprehensible. I . . . did nothing of the sort . . . This is extremely serious. If comrade Pouk doesn't forgive me, then my road can lead only to death." There was no word from his old friend.[26]

Ney Saran had also been intimate with Pol Pot in Office 100 and had been active in the northeast during the civil war. Only fragments of his confession survive; they are of macabre interest. Ten days after his arrest, Saran appended a note to his confession alleging that "there was no compulsion while writing . . . However, I want to make it clear that from September 28 on, I have responded after being severely tortured." The sentences were crossed out by Duch, who noted: "Don't use this . . . word. You don't have the right to report such matters to the Organization." Soon after, however, Ney Saran, perhaps incredulous at the party's involvement in squeezing false admissions from him, noted: "If you want to force me to respond, then torture me and I will."

This was too much for Duch. In a memorandum on October 1 to his subordinate in charge of the interrogation, he wrote of a meeting that morning with "the Organization about the documents you provided [about Ney Saran]." Duch continued: "The Organization decided that if this man continues to hide his traitorous linkages . . . he should be executed and not allowed to play games with us any more. . . . The Organization considers [his behavior] to be looking down on the Party." The rest of the memorandum authorized Duch's subordinates to "use the hot method for prolonged periods" on Ney Saran, adding that "even if it kills him this wouldn't be a violation of the Organization's rules." Saran was interrogated for another week before being put to death.[27]

In Duch's mind—and probably in Pol Pot's—Keo Meas and Ney Saran fitted into a pattern of conspiracy stretching back to the 1950s. Before the end of the year, others of their background who were arrested included former Central Committee member Keo Moni, who had come from Hanoi in 1970;

several officials in the eastern zone; and former Pracheachon members. The Cambodian ambassador to Hanoi, Sien An, who had been in Paris with Pol Pot and at the Lycée Sisowath with Ieng Sary, was summoned home for consultations, arrested, and put to death. So was his wife, whose confession asserted that he had learned about "Marx-Lenin" from Ieng Sary while studying with him years before. Friendship or long association with leaders of the party, it seems, did not guarantee survival. Nor was loyalty perceived as a two-way street.[28]

Pol Pot and the "Microbes"

Toward the end of December 1976, as the dossiers piled up at S-21 and presumably in his desk as well, Pol Pot convened a study session for party cadre. His speech on this occasion revealed his disillusionment—it teemed with references to "enemies" and "traitors," setting the tone for purges in 1977. The triumphant optimism of Pol Pot's earlier speeches had disappeared, leaving in its place a more muted, menacing tone. One passage from the speech referred to a "sickness in the Party":

> We cannot locate it precisely. The sickness must emerge to be examined. Because the heat of the people's revolution and the heat of the democratic revolution were insufficient . . . we search for the microbes (*merok*) within the party without success. They are buried. As our socialist revolution advances, however, seeping into every corner of the Party, the army and among the people, we can locate the ugly microbes. They will be pushed out by the . . . socialist revolution . . . If we wait any longer, the microbes can do real damage.[29]

The menace, Pol Pot went on to say, lay in contradictions inside the party between collectivism and individualism, between the party leadership and anyone who opposed it. "If we try to bury them," Pot warned, "they will rot us from within." Individuals could be cauterized from the body politic by the "heat of the revolution," constant vigilance, and continuous class warfare so long as the party's leaders scrutinized everyone's life histories and retained control over "storming attacks." But even with this documentation, how could the "enemies" be identified? Pol Pot was not especially helpful:

> Are there still treacherous, secret elements buried inside the Party, or are they gone? According to our *observations over the past ten years* it's clear that they're not gone at all. This is because they have been entering the Party continuously. Some are truly committed; some waver in their loyalties. Enemies can easily seep in. They remain—perhaps only one person, or two people. They remain (emphasis added).[30]

Pol Pot said nothing about acting on the strength of his "observations," but those he looked at as he spoke must have felt uneasy. The crisis, he said, made working in secret even more essential. In this context, Pol Pot justified his decision not to announce the existence of the party to the outside world:

> The situation inside the country is sufficiently developed for the Party to come into the open. . . . Friendly parties have requested our Party to emerge. . . . Enemies also want us to emerge so they can observe us clearly, and so they can proceed to accomplish their long-term objectives. The emergence of the Party poses the problem of defending the leadership. Back in September and October [1976] we had thought to emerge, but since that time documents have revealed that enemies have tried to defeat us. . . . If the Party were to emerge, additional contradictions would develop *between certain people* (emphasis added).[31]

Did Pol Pot believe that some of these "enemies," or "certain people," were within reach of his voice? He was in no hurry to identify them or to specify their crimes. Did he know who they were? He had to pretend that he did, but he was obviously nervous, and he communicated his unease to his audience. Who could be trusted? they must have asked themselves. The person next to me? Why? They must also have known that he, not they, controlled the apparatus of terror that kept the Communists in power. In other words, they had more to be frightened of than he did.

The party, Pol Pot continued, had grown too rapidly and contained many untrustworthy people. There were not enough reliable cadre: Only half the collectives in the country had party members in charge of them, and in some areas April 17 people had been given positions of responsibility. Pol Pot blamed these "capitalists" for shortfalls in production. It was time, therefore, to expand and cleanse the party so that the pace of the revolution would accelerate. This could be done by struggling "against classes of any sort in Cambodian society," by reexamining life histories, by transferring cadre among zones, and by stressing the virtues of collective eating, labor, and decisionmaking.

Punishing the Intelligentsia

In January 1977 two high-ranking party figures—Touch Phoeun and Koy Thuon (Khuon)—were arrested in Phnom Penh. Thuon, an easterner and former lycée teacher with long experience in the north, held the post of secretary of commerce but was probably under surveillance. Touch Phoeun, a Lycée Sisowath graduate who had studied in France in the 1950s, was effectively in charge of public works.[32]

Both men had moved comfortably for years in party circles and had friends outside the party. They knew Ney Saran, Chan Chakrei, and others who had been purged; these connections eventually "proved" that they should be arrested as well, burning the "strings of traitors" *(khsae kbot)* formed by those arrested earlier. Both of them had probably attended the December meeting

and would have been two of the "certain people" Pol Pot mentioned as plotting against the party. As their interrogators wore them down, Thuon and
Phoeun admitted forming "CIA networks" made up of party colleagues, former students, and friends. A major consequence of their arrests was a purge
of their acquaintances, many of whom made up the intelligentsia of the party.
In Duch's 1978 roundup of conspirators against the regime, he singled out
intellectuals "who pretended to be progressive and infiltrated the revolution
to gather information"—the last phrase echoing Pol Pot's tautologous suspicion that bringing the party into the open would allow its enemies to observe
it. Soon after, it was the turn of cadre in the northern zone who had worked
with Koy Thuon. Thirty-two of these men were brought into S-21 in early
1977.[33]

While Touch Phoeun and Koy Thuon were being questioned and the
northern zone was being purged by cadre brought in from the east, Pol Pot
visited the northwest. A former combatant, Chhit Do, recalled encountering
him in Siem Reap at a "meeting about purification of the power structure in
Kampuchea." Do added, "He seemed like a nice guy when he talked, but
what happened afterwards was not nice."[34] "What happened afterwards" in
much of the north and northwest was the replacement of local military and
political cadre, who were purged, by cadre brought in from the southwest
controlled by Ta Mok. Southwestern cadre, like Ta Mok himself, had the
reputation of being especially harsh and zealous. They soon became Democratic Kampuchea's cutting edge. The failure of "new people" to deliver the
bonanza demanded by the party leadership was thought to be deliberate. The
cadre who had presided over the disaster were "objectively"—in the termi-
nology of the party—"wreckers," "enemies," and "traitors."

By the middle of 1977, what Anthony Barnett has called the "bureaucracy
of death" at S-21 was working smoothly. The prison had become an essential
part of the regime. More confessions were typed rather than handwritten;
tape recorders came into use; and the improved filing system allowed for
cross-references among confessions. Inevitably, more "conspiracies" were
found. S-21 gained momentum and became impossible to stop. Its documents fed the leadership's paranoia. Documents also led to more arrests, arrests produced more documents, and so on. In 1977–1978, those pulled in included many people quite close to the leaders themselves. Experienced,
high-ranking cadre like Siet Chhae, Ruos Mau, Sua Va Sy, and Mau Khem
Nuon were swept up, along with their relatives and people who knew them.
Since many of them worked closely with Pol Pot, the secretary's other close
associates acquainted with the "traitors" were also put to death. The talent
pool for carrying out a revolution was drying up. So were the possibilities of
anyone trusting anyone. As Pol Pot and his colleagues tightened their grip,
their perceptions became blurred. They were obsessed with purifying the
party and imposing "socialism." They lost sight of other priorities—if they

had ever entertained them. It is barely possible that their goals could have been achieved—though at an enormous cost—had the party leadership not embarked, as it did in mid-1977, on an open-ended confrontation with Vietnam.[35]

Personal Details

Hardly any details of Pol Pot's personal life in Democratic Kampuchea emerge from available sources. We know that he was heavily guarded, changed residences frequently, and seldom appeared in public. The exact locations of his residences are unknown, but one informant who prefers anonymity placed Pol Pot's principal house "near the Independence Monument" in a group of villas surrounded by a high fence—his Kremlin or Hidden City. Ironically, this was the part of the city near the palace where Saloth Sar (and Sihanouk, for that matter) had grown up in the 1930s. We know that the residence had running water and electricity because maintenance workers were purged and put to death when power failures occurred. Staff attached to it included drivers, guards, mechanics, typists, and cooks. Many of these, interestingly, were from tribal minorities, suggesting that they had held positions of trust since the 1960s.[36]

Pol Pot was always fearful of assassination. When he addressed party gatherings, those attending were strip-searched before going into his presence. Pol Pot was frequently ill, and recurring gastric problems led him to think his cooks were trying to poison him. He probably spent much of his time, as he had always done, reviewing files and talking with his close associates. Out of his depth, with an entire country to manage, he must have worked into the night to get on top of dossiers assembled for him at S-21 and flowing up from the various ministries and zones. These provided his vision of the world— with Cambodia surrounded by enemies and the country itself seen as concentric circles with the party leadership at the center.

In late 1976 Khieu Ponnary and Khieu Thirith's mother arrived in Cambodia from France. Her daughters failed to visit her for two months, although Thirith sent her children to see their grandmother, who, like Nuon Chea's mother, disliked the revolution and resented its attacks on family life. When Thirith and Ponnary's nonrevolutionary sister, Thirath—also a former school-teacher—died of illness in early 1977, Thirith thought she had been killed and demanded an investigation. Thirith and Son Sen's wife, Yun Yat, had minor posts in the government, as did Ieng Sary's children and some of his cousins-in-law. Yun Yat, along with only half a dozen high-ranking officials, had access to confessions from S-21. Khieu Ponnary, on the other hand, held no official positions and seems to have been ill much of the time. At one meeting in 1978, when she was assisted onto the dais, she was cheered by those attending as the "mother of the revolution" (me padevat). After that, she disappeared from view.

It was widely believed that she had become insane. The effects of this illness and of her absence on Pol Pot are impossible to assess.[37]

War with Vietnam

As we have seen, clashes with Vietnamese forces had followed the Red Khmer's seizure of power in 1975. Islands had been occupied and recaptured by both sides, and Vietnamese troops were slow to withdraw from Cambodian territory, particularly in the northeast. At the heart of these disputes lay wounded Cambodian pride, suspicions of Vietnamese patronage, and disagreement over the sea border between the two countries. The last component was crucial, since sizable petroleum deposits were known to exist offshore. The Cambodians wanted the Vietnamese to honor the agreements they had made with Sihanouk in the 1960s concerning Cambodia's "existing frontiers." The Vietnamese, however, were no longer willing to do this because "new phenomena" (the petroleum deposits) had overtaken their promises. The Cambodians saw this response as a betrayal and refused to negotiate.

Another issue between the two countries was Vietnam's intentions toward "Indochina," a term that always made Cambodians uneasy. Vietnam's oftproclaimed "special relationship" with Laos, in place by 1976, smacked of hegemony to the Khmer. So did the "fraternal" relations that the Vietnamese Communists claimed to enjoy with their Lao and Cambodian comrades. Many Khmer found this friendship menacing, just as most Vietnamese were nervous about similar offers of intimacy from the Chinese. It is possible to exaggerate the psychological dimension of the conflict at the expense of its economic and political dimensions, but it seems clear that Pol Pot's harping on independence-mastery was part of a doomed effort to escape Vietnamese patronage and advice. Feeling himself empowered (and knowing he was allied to China), he gave vent to his hatred of the Vietnamese and encouraged everyone else in Cambodia to do the same.[38]

Scattered, unpublicized skirmishes and incursions took place throughout 1975–1976 on both sides of the border. Chou Chet later wrote of Vietnamese "nibbling attacks . . . along the border" in 1976 and of more substantial incursions into the northeast. Red Khmer authorities kept a close watch on these occurrences, as a telegram from the military commander in the east to "Brother Pol" in November 1975 indicates. By the middle of 1976, incidents became less frequent. Relations between Vietnam and Cambodia remained correct but cool, even as hostility toward Vietnam became a theme of Communist study sessions in 1977 and collusion with Vietnam the leitmotif of confessions extracted at S-21.[39]

By the end of 1976, it seems, Cambodia's leaders had obtained assurances of increased military aid from China, without which they would have been unable and unwilling to mount offensive operations against Vietnam. This aid came because China's leaders, after Mao's death, renewed their interest in regional politics and because China's own relations with Vietnam were deteriorating.

It is not certain when or why Cambodia—or Vietnam, for that matter—decided to step up the pace of hostilities. Evidence suggests that the first large-unit Cambodian attacks were instigated by the Red Khmer in the southwest. What the Vietnamese had in mind for Cambodia at this point is impossible to unravel. Analyzing the early stages of the war is made more difficult by the fact that before the closing days of 1977, neither side admitted publicly that a war was taking place.

The shift toward a more aggressive Cambodian policy came in early 1977 when a directive from "870," the party's standing committee, enjoined regional cadre to round up ethnic Vietnamese and turn them over to state security. There were few Vietnamese in Cambodia in 1977. Most of them had been repatriated under Lon Nol or after April 1975. Those who remained, often Vietnamese women married to Khmer, were hunted down and killed. In March, military forces in the east were taken off agricultural duties and moved en masse to frontier regions, foreshadowing an assault. Soon after, in the southwest, several cross-border attacks occurred, timed to coincide, it seems, with the second anniversary of the liberation of Saigon. The Vietnamese towns of Chaudoc and Hatien were shelled by Khmer artillery, and small-unit attacks, initiated by the Khmer, took place along the border, inflicting heavy casualties on civilians and an unprepared militia. In a tragic irony, many of those killed were ethnic Khmers whom Democratic Kampuchea in its propaganda proposed to liberate from the Vietnamese. For the time being, none of the attacks was publicized by either side. A Vietnamese proposal for a cease-fire in June 1977 was turned down, and units in the eastern zone were secretly advised to prepare for large-unit offensive actions.[40]

Pol Pot's anxiety about Vietnam increased in July 1977 when Vietnam signed a treaty of friendship with Laos. By then, documents from S-21 had confirmed Pol Pot's suspicions that the Cambodian Communist party was riddled with Vietnamese agents who had undermined Cambodia's economic revolution and were endangering the leaders of the party. The documents focused on "enemies" in the eastern zone, where fighting against the Vietnamese was being pursued with the greatest vigor. In August and September, Cambodian artillery units bombarded Vietnamese territory, and there were several incursions near Tay Ninh. The most significant of these occurred when elements of a Red Khmer brigade deeply penetrated the province, massacred hundreds of civilians, and hauled prisoners and livestock back across the border. The attack may have been an attempt by eastern zone cadre, under Sao Phim's leadership, to prove their loyalty to the party center. It also demonstrated commendable aggressiveness, which Pol Pot would point out in his upcoming discussions in Beijing. Vietnamese probes allegedly took place at the same time, "all along the border."[41]

Although the new leadership in China was happy to use Cambodian forces to punish the Vietnamese, they were unhappy that the Cambodian Communists continued to conceal the party's existence and to claim independence from the international Communist movement. Clearly, the Chinese, perhaps along with the North Koreans, had been the "friends" whom Pol Pot had mentioned as having urged him to bring the party into the open in 1976. After Keo Meas's execution in 1976, there seem to have been few domestic pressures to do so. It seems likely that the Chinese increased their pressure on Pol Pot as hostilities with Vietnam grew. In any case, Pol Pot announced the existence of the Communist party of Kampuchea in a five-hour speech recorded for Radio Phnom Penh on September 27, 1977, just as his armies were plunging into Tay Ninh. By the time it was broadcast three days later, to commemorate the party's seventeenth anniversary, Pol Pot had been in China for two days.[42]

In the days preceding the speech, banners were prepared in government bureaus proclaiming the existence of the party, and freshly typed copies of the "Internationale" were circulated to be memorized in time for the party's birthday. There is no evidence that celebrations extended into the countryside.[43]

Coming into the Open

Pol Pot's speech encapsulated his ideas about Cambodian history and the Communist party of Kampuchea. He saw Cambodia's history in terms of its inexorable progress from a slave society through feudal and capitalist phases to 1960, when the national democratic revolution broke out soon after his elevation to the Central Committee. Here Pol Pot was following the schema of evolution, supposedly applicable throughout the world, that had been sketched by Marx and elaborated by Stalin. A distinctive element in Pol Pot's reading of history was that so few people were mentioned. His own name does not appear in the speech; nor does Sihanouk's or those of any of his colleagues except the trusted Nuon Chea and Khieu Samphan. Those singled out by name—Lon Nol, Sim Var, Sirik Matak, U.S. ambassador John Dean, and so on—are almost all defeated, absent enemies of the party. Living enemies (Vietnam; traitors inside the party), party leaders, and potential allies (Sihanouk; China) remain hidden.

The most detailed section of the speech deals with the national democratic revolution (1960–1975). Its twenty-nine pages trace the fortunes and strategies of the Communist party of Kampuchea without mentioning any intellectual roots or any assistance from foreign powers—independence-mastery, perhaps. Instead, it lists several allegedly independent decisions reached at the 1960 congress and stresses several of Pol Pot's *idées fixes*. One of these was that landlords formed an essential component of "feudal" Cambodian rural life. The corollary was that the elimination of landlords would eliminate injustice. In fact, as we have seen, landlordism was rare in Cambodia. Another of Pol Pot's ideas was that total collectivization would be welcomed by "more than 90 percent" of the Khmer people. A third was that "contradictions" abounded in Cambodian society (even when nearly everyone was a contented supporter of the party). Cambodia's history could be perceived in terms of these contradictions and the class struggle leading up to the empowerment of the rural poor: "We all know the Angkor of past times. Angkor was built during the slave period. It was our slaves who built it under the yoke of the exploiting classes of that time, for the enjoyment of the king. If our people were capable of building Angkor they can do anything."

Pol Pot concluded his speech by discussing the post-1975 period. He suggested that the revolution began to have shortcomings only after its success. He referred to an "infamous handful of reactionary elements" still at work in Cambodian society, but said they numbered only "2 percent" of the population (perhaps 140,000 men and women); the remaining 98 percent, a "vast, productive force," had been liberated into the revolution. No mention is made of the party's Four Year Plan, although Pol Pot added that since 1975 living standards had fallen for "only 5 percent" of the population and had risen to "the level of middle peasants" for the rest—testimony that flies in the face of hundreds of interviews with survivors. In his discussion of foreign policy, Pol Pot noted that "the political system of Democratic Kampuchea . . . does not permit us to aggress." By reading between the lines, we can see that Pol Pot was contrasting Cambodia with Vietnam.[44]

Soon after the speech was broadcast over Radio Phnom Penh, congratulations arrived from North Korea, China, Vietnam, Laos, and Romania. The Vietnamese national radio noted, heavy-handedly, that the Vietnamese had "always considered their *special relationship* with . . . Kampuchea as their sacred cause" (emphasis added). With friends like that, Pol Pot may have mused, what would Cambodia do for enemies?

When his speech was broadcast, Pol Pot had been in Beijing for two days. Elegantly attired in a Chinese-style suit, he appeared in public for the first time as Cambodia's prime minister and secretary of the Communist party of Kampuchea. Was the trip as triumphal as it looked, or was he making a virtue of necessity? It was reminiscent of Sihanouk's trips to China in the 1960s when the prince had sought help to protect Cambodia against the pro-American South Vietnamese regime. Pol Pot's public emergence was the price he paid, willingly or not, for Chinese help in his own confrontation with Vietnam. History was repeating itself. Democratic Kampuchea had a little more than a year left.[45]

CHAPTER EIGHT

———————— ■ ————————

Coming Apart, 1977–1979

Pol Pot in China and North Korea

On September 28, 1977, when Pol Pot arrived in Beijing, 100,000 spectators, many carrying paper Cambodian flags, were brought in to line Changan Avenue on the way to the Gate of Heavenly Peace. The lavish preparations and choreographed crowds resembled those that Sihanouk had ordered in Phnom Penh for important foreign visitors during his years in power. It was the first time Pol Pot had been treated in this fashion.[1]

At the airport, the Khmer delegation was met by the Chinese premier Hua Guofeng and Deng Xiaoping. Photographs of the encounter, the first available of Pol Pot, enabled foreign analysts to confirm that Pol Pot was Saloth Sar. He was accompanied by Ieng Sary, Vorn Vet, Thiounn Thoeun (the DK minister of health), and several junior staff members.

The Cambodians stayed in China until October 4, when they departed for North Korea. Their time was taken up in both places with ceremonies, banquets, and speeches. Although Pol Pot did not refer specifically to Vietnam in his speeches, he did stress the inviolability of Cambodia's frontiers and its national sovereignty. He also restated his admiration for Mao Zedong and for Mao's ideas of continuous revolution and class warfare. Hua Guofeng, in reply, praised Democratic Kampuchea for its "correct line . . . relying on the masses, upholding independence and persisting in armed struggle," while a Chinese editorial referred to China's friendship with Cambodia as "unbreakable"—a word reserved until then for Beijing's alliance with Albania. As Nayan Chanda has suggested, Pol Pot may have felt that the leftist faction on the ascendancy in China would support his radical internal policies and his confrontation with Vietnam. In fact, the Chinese leadership probably had mixed feelings about Pol Pot—admiration for his zeal and courage on the one hand, uneasiness about his naive triumphalism on the other.[2]

Privately, Pol Pot spoke about the conflict with Vietnam. As he had told his own standing committee the year before, he believed the growing strength of pro-Chinese Asian Communist parties—including those of Thailand, Burma, Malaysia, and Indonesia—worked in Cambodia's favor. He expressed confidence in victory. Presumably, one reason he had made this trip was that he believed Chinese help would make his forces invulnerable or would force the Vietnamese to be cautious. He never considered the alternatives of defeat, compromise, or negotiation.[3]

Another reason for Pol Pot's trip was to display the "human face" of his country and to counter charges emerging in Thailand and the West of human rights violations, terror, and starvation in Cambodia. To this end, the Chinese released a glossy magazine—*Democratic Kampuchea Is Moving Forward*—to coincide with the visit and a documentary filmed earlier in the year. Both depicted crowded work sites, thriving industries, and newly constructed irrigation dams; the well-fed workers were usually smiling. Other aspects of "opening up" included inviting sympathetic visitors to Cambodia and seeking diplomatic relations with Burma, Thailand, and Malaysia—the countries where Pol Pot claimed privately that revolutionary movements were on the march.[4]

In North Korea, Pol Pot was decorated by Korea's leader, Kim Il Sung. On the day he arrived, the North Koreans broadcast a biographical sketch about him, the first to reach the outside world. The sketch gave his year of birth as 1925. His primary schooling was dated from 1930 to 1935 and "primary and middle" schooling from 1940 to 1948. From 1937 to 1939, it seems, Pol Pot worked on his parents' farm. "Prior to World War II," the text continued, "he developed a love for the fatherland and people and—through discussions about patriotic struggle and progressive books—a hostile feeling toward the nation's enemies." "Progressive books" in pre-1940 Cambodia would have been difficult to find, but a studious, future-oriented youth (and a stint as a farmworker, which none of his brothers remembered in the 1980s or 1990s) were suitable ingredients of a revolutionary persona.[5]

From 1949 to 1952, the sketch maintained, Pol Pot "participated in organizing a Marxism-Leninism team among college students" in an unidentified country before heading into "jungle areas . . . during the armed struggle against France." The sketch then listed the posts Pol Pot held in the Communist party of Kampuchea between its congress in 1960 and his election as prime minister sixteen years later. From his own people, however, Pol Pot remained concealed. The biography was not rebroadcast in Khmer.

Cambodia's War with Vietnam

When the Khmer delegation returned to Phnom Penh, it learned that Vietnamese forces had recently crossed into Cambodia in retaliation for Cambo-

Pol Pot (left) in Beijing, October 1977, with Chinese Premier Hua Guofeng.

dian attacks on Tay Ninh. The Vietnamese had clearly timed some of their attacks to coincide with Pol Pot's visit to China to indicate their displeasure and reveal their military strength.[6] The attacks by either side were still kept secret from the outside world. To understand why war broke out between Cambodia and Vietnam, we must look at the history and geopolitics of the region and at how the region was affected by the Sino-Soviet split and by deteriorating relations between China and Vietnam.

Since the seventeenth century, if not before, the major foreign policy concern of most Cambodian rulers has been Cambodia's relations with Vietnam. Cambodia's accessibility, low population, and desirable resources have made it a tempting target for the Vietnamese. At the same time, the cultural division between Cambodia and Vietnam, until recently, was one of the widest in Southeast Asia. For centuries, Vietnamese disdain and Khmer distrust have colored relations between the two nations and thwarted mutual understanding.

Pol Pot and his colleagues were nurtured in the Communist movement by the Vietnamese. The Cambodian Communist party took the form it did under Vietnamese guidance to back up Vietnam's war with the United States. With Cambodia's own victory, the Red Khmer declared their independence from Vietnam, expunging Vietnam from party histories and making brutal raids across the frontier. The evidence suggests that Cambodia's leaders had always resented Vietnamese patronage. With victory, they considered themselves invulnerable because of the purity of their revolution and because of Chinese and Korean support.

To the Vietnamese Communists, Cambodia was never especially important, except as a zone to protect southern Vietnam from capitalist Thailand. Correct but cool relations with the Red Khmer were adequate for the Vietnamese, who faced massive tasks of reconstruction and political unification after their war with the United States. With Red Khmer intransigence about the borders in 1976, followed by subversion among the Cambodian minority in southern Vietnam and military attacks the following year, Cambodia became a problem that called for a politico-military solution by Vietnam. Given the balance of forces, Cambodia's humiliation became a matter of time.

Cambodian-Vietnamese antagonism was also part of a larger picture. Sino-Vietnamese relations had been deteriorating for several years. China felt insulted by having an ally of the "revisionist" Soviet Union on its southern border; Vietnam was insulted by having a Chinese ally to the west. Sino-Vietnamese relations, in many ways, resembled Vietnamese relations with Cambodia. Vietnamese distrust of China was fueled by a sense of persecution that resembled Red Khmer responses to Vietnam. The Cambodians saw nineteenth-century precedents for imperialistic Vietnamese behavior, much as the Vietnamese saw millennial precedents for Chinese attempts to dominate them. Similarly, traditional Chinese views of Vietnam's unruliness and unreliability paralleled those that Vietnam harbored about Cambodia. To compound the irony, Pol Pot's scramble for overseas patronage (like Vietnam's) resembled moves taken by Cambodia's King Norodom in the 1860s when he welcomed the French protectorate, and later by Sihanouk and Lon Nol when they faced up to what they saw as a Vietnamese threat to their survival. Pol Pot told visitors in 1978 that he was "building socialism without a model," but like his predecessors he was a victim of Cambodia's past and its location. He and his colleagues were surrounded and outnumbered by the Vietnamese. Throughout its history, he thought, only outsiders had ever saved Cambodia from Vietnamese encroachment. Like Sihanouk and Lon Nol, Pol Pot miscalculated the lengths to which foreign powers would go to rescue him from defeat.

As Cambodia and Vietnam edged toward sustained hostilities and a diplomatic break, high-ranking officials scurried between Beijing, Hanoi, and Phnom Penh. These visits accomplished little, although Chinese vice premier Chen Yonggui's trip to Cambodia is of anecdotal interest.

Chen Yonggui was a Politburo member with good Maoist credentials (he had once written a paper titled "Self-Reliance Is a Magic Wand") who visited Cambodia toward the end of 1977. Ostensibly, he came to teach Cambodians about the Dazhai (Tai Chai) agricultural work brigade in northern China, which he had supervised in the 1960s and which had been praised repeatedly in "Learn from Dazhai" campaigns. During his trip he toured agricultural sites—accompanied everywhere by Pol Pot—and praised Cambodia's domestic policies as "entirely correct." He said almost nothing in public to support Cambodia's conflict with Vietnam.[7]

Pol Pot's presence at Chen Yonggui's side suggests, however, that he did everything he could to display his respect and his desperate need for Chinese military assistance. Pol Pot's unexpected appearances with Chen in the countryside must also have been intended to demonstrate to cadre that he was in command of the country and had powerful friends.

Nearly everything we know about Chen's visit is filtered through official statements and radio broadcasts, but a brief, humorous moment came to life in Chou Chet's confession, written four months later, which showed an unrehearsed Pol Pot and a revolutionary tableau fraying at the edges.

Chou Chet (Si), party secretary in the western zone, was a fifty-three-year-old revolutionary who had worked with Pol Pot in Phnom Penh in the 1950s but had escaped the purges of 1976. In late 1977, he was recovering from a series of illnesses, perhaps related to his fear of being purged, when Brother Number One showed up at his office in Kompong Chhnang. As Chet recalled in his confession, Pol Pot told him that

> Ta Chai [Chen Yonggui] was going to come on a tour soon. I was asked to arrange for him to tour Kompong Chhnang. . . . When I heard that Ta Chai was going to come to tour my zone, it was an honor to receive him, so I worked day and night, going everywhere. When I received [Chen Yonggui] I was ecstatic, and forgot to think about Brother Number One, [Vorn Vet] and [Ieng Sary]. I walked right up in the front row, even in front of Brother Number One. The words I spoke were not appropriate for a revolutionary leader. They were not diplomatic. . . . As soon as Ta Chai had gone down to look at the paddy while he was still worn out from his train trip I nevertheless immediately requested his friendly advice. At that point, Brother Number One laughed.[8]

The scene Chou Chet described might have come straight from the pages of *Democratic Kampuchea Is Moving Forward.* The morning of December 10, the cortege carrying the Chinese visitors, Pol Pot, and other high-ranking party figures pulled into the Phnom Popok cooperative in Kompong Chhnang after traveling less than 10 kilometers from the nearby railroad station at Romeas. Parked alongside the sedans bearing the guests and high officials was a Chinese-made truck (or perhaps a pair of jeeps)—its cargo of security guards was already deployed around the site. The top cadre from the zone, in laundered peasant costumes and neatly knotted cotton scarves (*krama*) had been standing around for several hours. The work site and the well-fed, smiling workers had been chosen and cleaned up in advance. The nearby plot of Chou Chet would have been of high quality, close packed, and golden, filling a squared-off 1-hectare plot. Soon after the visitors arrived, the workers were to thresh the paddy in a Dazhai-style storming attack, perhaps to the rhythm of a revolutionary song. Everyone waited for a few words from Pol Pot and "Ta Chai" to set the tableau in motion. Instead, they were treated to a ragged, impromptu performance by Chou Chet as the middle-aged revolutionary, overwhelmed by the presence of a vice premier of China—and perhaps scared witless by Pol Pot—broke in, chattering and stumbling over himself and causing Pol Pot to laugh indulgently.[9]

The comedy evaporated a few months later when Chou Chet was arrested and ordered to concoct a narrative of his lifelong betrayal of the party. Buried inside his voluminous "confession" was a perceptive assessment of Democratic Kampuchea. This was cast in the form of a conversation Chou Chet had allegedly had with a Vietnamese agent in late 1976. In reality, the remarks probably reflect what he had been picking up from unhappy colleagues in the party. He wrote: "[I said that] the current regime was a highly dictatorial one, too rigid and severe, one that overshot the comprehension and consciousness of the people. Therefore a lot of people were muttering and moaning about how they were doing a lot of work and getting little back for it, how they couldn't get together with their families, couldn't rest, never had any fun, and so on."[10]

It is impossible to say whether Pol Pot was aware of such widespread discontent. Perhaps he saw fighting with Vietnam as a way of producing solidarity and lessening unrest. He probably saw Vietnamese "aggression" as connected with "treasonous elements" inside the Cambodian Communist party. People who disagreed with Red Khmer policies were "enemies"; enemies, generically, were labeled as CIA, KGB, or Vietnamese. Those who agreed with the leadership, or kept their heads down, stayed alive—for the time being.

The War Begins

The Vietnamese attacks of December 1977 were the most serious so far. Their forces penetrated more than 20 kilometers inside Cambodia in some places and reached the city of Svay Rieng. The *Livre noir* claims that the Vietnamese committed fifty thousand troops to the incursion. They probably hoped that the exercise would force Cambodia to desist from its own operations (several thousand troops in small units had plunged into Vietnam earlier in December, leaving the frontier undefended) and to agree to a cease-fire.[11]

On December 31, 1977, while Vietnamese units were still on Cambodian soil, Democratic Kampuchea broke off diplomatic relations with Hanoi, broadcast a catalog of Vietnamese "aggression," and opened its own propaganda war. The decision to break relations had been taken on December 25, when the Central Committee decided to send troops from the capital to reinforce the areas that had been attacked. Preparing the documents used to announce and justify the break occupied officials in the Ministry of Foreign Affairs (B-1) for a stretch of forty-eight hours.[12]

After another week of fighting the Vietnamese withdrew, taking thousands of prisoners, as well as civilians to whom they had offered shelter in Vietnam. Radio Phnom Penh treated the withdrawal as a "historic victory"—and so did the *Livre noir*, in an attempt to conceal the fact that Pol Pot and his military commander, Son Sen, had left the frontier undefended. To cover themselves further, the two men asserted privately that "enemies" in the party had allowed the Vietnamese units to withdraw. The stage was set for a purge of the eastern zone, where the Vietnamese had penetrated deepest and where senior Cambodian cadre had long been suspected of dragging their feet in implementing the party's policies. Before the purge began, but probably after deciding to set it in motion, Pol Pot visited the zone to congratulate military leaders on their heroism. The tactic of lulling people before attacking them was one he used often.[13]

The Vietnamese had invaded Cambodia intending to spur negotiations; instead, it was as if they had poked a beehive with a stick. Cambodia's leaders were now convinced that Vietnam wanted to swallow their country. They began preparing for a holy war. In January and February 1978, Red Khmer units swept repeatedly into lightly defended parts of Vietnam, massacring villagers, burning houses, and disrupting commercial life. At other times the Red Khmer lobbed artillery shells across the frontier. Vietnamese offers for talks were brushed aside. In a speech on January 17, 1978, Pol Pot cited "world opinion" and said: "The majority of it has been confident that [we] would . . . defeat and wipe out the Vietnamese for [we] had already defeated the U.S. imperialists." He was hoping that he had interpreted Chinese opinion correctly and that more aid would be coming from Beijing.[14]

U.S. officials saw the conflict in terms of the Sino-Soviet split. On January 8, 1978, U.S. presidential adviser Zbigniew Brzezinski referred to it as a "proxy war" between the USSR and China. In February the Chinese accelerated shipments of military aid to Phnom Penh and stepped up their propaganda against Hanoi. In Vietnam, the government began harassing ethnic Chinese residents and strengthened its alliance with the USSR. The Vietnamese also decided on a political solution to the Cambodian "problem," a solution that involved encouraging opponents of Pol Pot to revolt against him. They also began training Cambodians in Vietnam to take part in military operations and to form the nucleus of a new regime. By mid-February 1978 Radio Hanoi was referring to Cambodia's policies as "barbaric," as reflecting "bigoted nationalism" and "medieval rural thinking." At this point, it seems, Hanoi's plans for Cambodia began to resemble the intricate fantasies that Duch and his subordinates at S-21 had been concocting since the middle of 1976.[15]

Opening Up

Pol Pot's response to Vietnam's actions was to seek friends overseas, to welcome visitors to Cambodia, to make cosmetic improvements in people's standards of living, to grant an ambiguous political amnesty to April 17 people, and to proceed with the extirpation of enemies. His new policies included a more welcoming attitude toward visitors. Between November 1977 and the end of 1978, official delegations arrived from Burma, Malaysia, Thailand, Romania, Yugoslavia, and the Scandinavian countries. A television and news reporting team came in from Yugoslavia, and delegates from pro-Chinese Marxist-Leninist parties arrived from several countries, including Australia, Belgium, Denmark, France, Italy, Japan, Norway, and the United States. The visitors were taken to see Angkor and selected agricultural sites. Most of them had audiences with Ieng Sary; some had meetings with Nuon Chea and Pol Pot. In addition, greetings were now exchanged by mail between Red Khmer leaders, chiefs of state, and pro-Chinese Communist parties on national days and in response to offers of political support. As part of this opening up, Democratic Kampuchea began publishing materials in French and English as well as in Khmer.

During this period, Pol Pot was more accessible than ever before. In these controlled encounters, he was invariably pleasant but not especially revealing. At the same time, as Pol Pot selected the topics for one set of visitors or another, he revealed a good deal about his preoccupations.[16]

To a Yugoslavian television team that visited Cambodia for ten days in March, Pol Pot provided a brief biographical statement: "You are the first people to know my biography," he told them with a smile. Once again, as in his Korean press release, he concealed his palace connections, his real name, and his privileged education, but this time he admitted studying in Europe and working in Yugoslavia. He added that after coming home he had taught "history, geography and civics in a private school." During that time, he said, "Lon Nol's police followed my activities. They knew me, but they did not know exactly who I was." Turning to his policies, he mentioned that "we wish to do away with all vestiges of the past." His former student from Chamraon Vichea, Soth Polin, at that point driving a taxi in Paris, recognized him at once when the interview was broadcast over French television. So did his old mentor Keng Vannsak. One of the Yugoslavs remarked to a friend that in all the footage they shot, Pol Pot was the only person who was smiling.[17]

To build socialism and to defend Cambodia from Vietnam, Pol Pot and his colleagues needed all the cooperation they could get. To attack the major enemy (Vietnam) they had to unite with lesser ones, such as Cambodians in contradiction with the party. This meant relaxing the hostility extended to "new people" and ending the quarantine that had been applied to Cambodians who had returned from abroad ostensibly to help the revolution. Several hundred well-educated men and women, mostly university students, had come home from France, the United States, and elsewhere in 1976–1977. Many of them were sympathetic to the revolution, but those whose credentials were dubious—which included everyone who had come from the United States—were executed soon after they arrived. The survivors were sent to work in factories and, at the end of 1976, to perform rural labor in a special camp in western Kompong Cham. Conditions in the camp were harsher than anything they had known before but easier than those in most of the country. Many intellectuals were humiliated at not being given work appropriate to their education. Others resented being lectured on "Max-Lenin" (as the names appear, unexplained, in many party texts) by near-illiterates. In mid-1978 some of the returnees were brought into Phnom Penh, given better food, and lionized by Ieng Sary and Khieu Samphan. Fifteen of them were selected in October to form the faculty of a technological university under Thiounn Mumm. Three hundred students, aged ten to sixteen, were enrolled. Plans were set in motion to reintroduce money and a mixed economy in 1979.[18]

As part of Cambodia's opening up, primary schools now appeared in many cooperatives. Survivors recalled that the children of "new people" were not enrolled. Workmanlike, well-printed textbooks in geography and basic mathematics came into use. In some areas, people were allowed to wear brightly colored clothing (if they could find any) instead of the black pajamas that had clad the nation in 1975–1977. Here and there, workers were also given more time off. In May 1978 the differential classification of citizens into "full-rights citizens," "candidates," and "depositees" that had been in effect since 1975 was abolished and in the following month some categories of enemies were amnestied—although most Cambodians were too busy and unwell by then to notice. No measures were taken to relax rules about collectivized eating, to revive religious practices, or to strengthen family relationships at the expense of those of such collective units as cooperatives, work brigades, and military formations. Instead, the regime's paeans to collective living became even more strident, and claims were made that the country's collective strength would prevail over the individualistic character of Vietnam.[19]

At about this time the party's Central Committee circulated a study document to cadre that gave details of an amnesty affecting many suspected enemies who remained at large. Those involved were people who had allegedly joined the CIA, the Vietnamese, and the KGB at various times in the past. In the topsy-turvy world of S-21, these nonexistent men and women, it was suggested, were known to the party, which was now prepared to forgive them. The amnesty affected different categories of offenders in different ways.

Those who had worked for foreign intelligence services between 1946 and 1967—that is, between the beginning of the First Indochina War and the onset of armed struggle—were forgiven provided they had engaged in no traitorous activities since then. Those who committed offenses during the armed struggle (1967–1970) were similarly let off, as were those whose crimes fell between 1970 and 1975. In effect, the document amnestied people with connections to the Sihanouk and Lon Nol regimes. However, those who since April 1975 had "obstinately persisted in uniting to fight the Communist Party of Kampuchea, the workers' and peasants' state power, socialism or collectivism, who fought the Cambodian people and Democratic Kampuchea . . . will be indicted, for they have chosen to join the traitors." Those targeted were members of the party.[20]

For a regime that prided itself on "storming attacks" and "smashing enemies," forgiveness was unfamiliar, but a commentary on the decree published in *Tung Padevat* provided a chilly rationale for slowing the purges and letting possible offenders off. People who had offended the party since 1975 and now agreed to "go all out to improve themselves and perform their tasks," it seemed, would not be punished: "This is in accord with the Party's *line of saving human beings*, because if we attack one [person, normally] it doesn't affect just one, it affects four or five persons. We therefore want to increase the number of our friends while reducing the number of our enemies" (emphasis added).[21] This unsettling passage corroborates the suspicion that arises from analyzing confessions at S-21 that perhaps three-quarters of the people brought there were indicted not for their activities but for their associations. Because of the small number of trained cadre in the Cambodian Communist party, the likelihood that members were acquainted with each other was high; knowing an enemy, or being related to one, was sufficient grounds for being put to death.

The Red Khmer may have thought that the amnesty would restore confidence in their regime by producing a sense of well-being that had been lacking. Perhaps they thought it would encourage people who disliked the regime to unite against Vietnam. A less generous reading would be that the amnesty was intended to flush out those enemies who, after being "forgiven," remained counterrevolutionaries. Those who were genuinely innocent, in other words, had nothing to fear. For those who were guilty—thousands of moving, unidentified targets—it was only a matter of time.

Attacking Enemies

Despite the successful purges of 1977, which are referred to glowingly in many party texts, there were still "microbes" embedded in the army, the cooperatives, the ministries, and elsewhere that were spreading ideas of "privatism" among the population. Some of these ideas, it was asserted, were "systematically left"; others were "systematically right." Vigilance would reward the party, which was said to have "as many eyes as a pineapple." In early 1978 a policy of seeking new autobiographical statements was set in motion. By the end of the year, "April 17 people" came under scrutiny again. The regime's repressive machinery had a life of its own and could not decelerate or change direction just because an "amnesty" had been proclaimed.

S-21, in fact, was probably the best-run office in the country. In the first half of 1978, the center welcomed 5,760 prisoners for interrogation, torture, and execution—roughly as many as in all of 1977. A similar number were arrested between June and December. Most of these were connected with purges of the east, which began in May 1978 and continued through October, sweeping up military personnel, "new people," and those who lay in the expected path of a Vietnamese invasion. The party secretary of the zone, Sao Phim, committed suicide in June; his brother-in-law Muol Sambath (Nhim Ros), secretary of the northwestern zone, was then arrested and brought to Tuol Sleng. By the middle of 1978, the party replaced many of the troops who had failed to drive out the Vietnamese with units drawn from the center and southwest who were considered loyal. A former cadre described the process to Stephen Heder two years later: "Then we became traitors. We had done everything correctly and then they came and killed everybody. They said we were doing the opposite of what we were doing. We fought the Vietnamese and they killed us for not fighting the Vietnamese."[22]

Over the next few months, the military infrastructure of the eastern zone was torn apart in a purge reminiscent of those that swept through the Soviet army in the 1930s. Perhaps as many as 100,000 people—a large proportion of them cadre, soldiers, and their families—were gathered up and put to death. A similar operation, on a smaller scale, occurred in the northeast, an old base area where cadre from the southwest replaced local people in 1978. In both zones, hundreds of thousands of others were evacuated toward the north and northwest to keep them from being captured by the Vietnamese. Casualties in the course of the evacuations were horrendous.

The catastrophe in the east has been studied by Ben Kiernan and recalled by many survivors. It is significant because Pol Pot had finally alienated himself from his own revolutionary origins, which lay in the east; from his association with Sao Phim, which went back to the days of Office 100; and from his long-term relationship with Vietnam and the Vietnamese Communist party. In purging the east, Pol Pot was cleansing his own history. Perhaps he blamed the "east"—an amalgam of Vietnam and his own gullibility—for the troubles besetting his country. Certainly it was more severely punished as a region than any other—and more amply represented when the People's Republic of Kampuchea (PRK) established itself with Vietnamese assistance in 1979.[23]

Other high-ranking figures executed in 1978 included Vorn Vet, deputy prime minister for the economy; Chou Chet, secretary of the western zone; and Muol Sambath, secretary of the northwestern zone. All three men had been intimately associated with Pol Pot and Nuon Chea in the 1950s. In Phnom Penh, confessions at the end of 1978 began to implicate Son Sen, the chief of the general staff, a member of the party center, and the man responsible for S-21. In July he had visited China as minister of defense. That his name should crop up as an acquaintance of military men and party veterans being purged is not surprising, but the possibility that he was plotting against the party is remote. All the same, the flames burning through the party were drawing closer to the center, and had the Vietnamese held up their attack, it is likely that Son Sen and others near the top would have been "called to study."[24]

Did Pol Pot consider these former associates genuinely guilty? Stalin's biographer, Robert Tucker, in dealing with the Soviet purges of the 1930s, asked a similar question: "Why was Stalin driven to believe things he had no grounds for believing about the huge number of people who were victimized?" Tucker argued that "only by believing in the victims' treasonous designs . . . could [Stalin] come to terms with their failure to share his grandiose beliefs about himself." There is not enough evidence to form a similar indictment of Pol Pot, but it is conceivable that he viewed people with different strategic views or those unwilling to extinguish personal ambition as traitors to the amalgam of revolution and party with which he and Nuon Chea ("the organization") identified themselves. The existence of enemies was necessary for class warfare, which was essential in Maoist theory for the transition between socialism and communism. Contradictions among the people impelled the party forward. To maintain momentum, instability was essential. The party's leaders nourished themselves on suspicion, and they prided themselves on their ability to uncover plots. Those suspected of treason provided the instability the nation needed to move forward, but whether any of them were truly guilty is difficult to ascertain.[25]

A Cult of Personality?

In the second half of 1978, scattered evidence suggests that Pol Pot was being edged toward a personality cult that, had his regime lasted longer, might have transformed his taciturn, clandestine style of government into a more personalistic one and deepened continuities with previous, nonrevolutionary regimes. Like many Communist leaders—Mao, Castro, and Tito spring to mind—Pol Pot had to contend with pressures for deification by some of his colleagues and supporters, who were the beneficiaries of the revolution. After all, it had been his clear-sighted strategies and tactics that had wrested control of Cambodia from the United States and its feudal puppets; it was

Brother Pol who had uprooted enemies from the party, encouraged vigilance, built the alliance with China, and masterminded the Four Year Plan. Colleagues in the party held him responsible for the achievements of the nation. Others found it prudent to say so, because of his frequent resorts to terror and because they wanted to retain their posts.

In 1977–1978 the terms by which Pol Pot was known in confessions became more rarefied. From "Brother Pol" or "Brother Number One," the prime minister (never referred to by that title) became known as "Uncle Secretary" *(om lekha)*, "the party center" *(mocchim pak)*, "the leading apparatus" *(kbal masin)*, and "the organization" *(angkar)*. By the middle of 1978, large photographs of Pol Pot were put up in communal dining halls throughout the country—and his own brothers discovered that little Sar, whom they had last seen in the 1950s, was in charge of the country. In some documents, references to his "clear-sighted leadership" began to replace those that attributed leadership to the party.[26]

The cult of personality never became full-blown, however, because self-advertisement did not come easily to Pol Pot and the frequent exposure that such a cult would have entailed would have compromised his obsession with security. Conceivably, he felt that a certain amount of visibility had tactical advantages in uniting the country against Vietnam. These may have been pointed out to him by Chinese and North Korean advisers, who came from societies where hero worship was the norm.

The most concrete evidence for a cult of personality are the oil portraits of Pol Pot found at S-21 in early 1979. Some of these are head and shoulder portraits; one, copied from a photograph taken in 1973, shows him with his back to a waterfall. According to Ong Thong Hoeung, who worked at the Genocide Museum established on the site, the portraits had been painted from photographs by a prisoner who was held at S-21 for more than two years before he "escaped" in January 1979. Visitors to the prison in 1979 also found molds for concrete busts of Pol Pot. At least one of these busts—all of which were slightly larger than life size—was cast in silver. According to the Australian journalist John Pilger, the busts were designed by another survivor at Tuol Sleng.[27]

Speaking to David Ashley in 1996, the S-21 survivor Vann Nath, who had painted several portraits of Pol Pot from photographs while still a prisoner, recalled that toward the end of 1978 there were plans for a more grandiose sculpture in Pol Pot's honor:

We had to design a revolutionary monument with the design first taken to Nuon Chea who approved it and it was then supposed to be taken to Pol Pot for his approval. The monument was like those in China and Korea and featured Pol Pot in front of a line of people with his right hand stretched skywards and his left arm grasping a copy of the revolutionary works, the red book. Pol Pot was the only figure depicted as a particular individual. Behind him were a number of people indicating the progress of the revolutionary struggle, beginning with axes and knives and ending with abundance, with guns and B-40s [rocket launchers]. [The administrator of S-21] said that the plan was to destroy the temple at Wat Phnom and replace it with the monument. If the Vietnamese hadn't invaded, I think that's what would have happened.[28]

Compared with the elaborate cults surrounding Stalin, Mao, and Kim Il Sung, the well-orchestrated anti-personality cult orchestrated by Ho Chi Minh, and the adulation whipped up to honor Sihanouk and Lon Nol, there is something tentative, offhand, and almost poignant about the photographs, statues, and portraits of Pol Pot. It is likely that officials in S-21 had the prisoners make the statues and portraits without being asked to do so. When the regime collapsed, Pol Pot swiftly resumed his anonymity. We can imagine his feelings of relief. Even in his years in power, no biography of Brother Number One was ever broadcast over Radio Phnom Penh or published in *Tung Padevat*. No photographs of him appeared in party literature. No anecdotes of his childhood, his teaching career, or his time in the maquis entered popular folklore via speeches at political meetings. There were no plays or songs about him and no published "thoughts." On the other hand, considering the totality of his control over the party, his stifling of dissent, and his purging of anyone whose popularity he saw as threatening, it is clear that while he backed away from a cult honoring himself, he discouraged anyone else from seeking publicity and nearly everyone from sharing power. It is likely that he saw popular Communist figures like Hou Youn and Sao Phim as threats to his authority. Once again, the parallels with Stalin are suggestive, but Pol Pot's half-warm, half-cool impersonal style was recognizably Khmer. His assaults on "individualism," with their unspoken undertones of Buddhist teaching, were probably sincere.

Nuon Chea's anonymity may also have been an inspiration to him. During the DK era, Brother Number Two never revealed anything about himself in public. In his statements to the visiting Danish delegation, Chea suggested— echoing one of Pol Pot's phrases—that "secret work is fundamental"; he added that "the leadership apparatus must be defended at any price . . . as long as the leadership is there, the Party will not die." "Secret work" included moving unexpectedly to different houses, using messengers, living under guard, testing food for poison, and so on. To illustrate the importance of anonymity, Nuon Chea, unconsciously perhaps, fails to mention Pol Pot— good evidence, from another angle, that no cult of personality was in effect in Cambodia at that time.[29]

Except for Nuon Chea, Pol Pot was the least accessible Cambodian leader since World War II. Given the extent of the two men's power between 1975 and 1979, we must assume that their inaccessibility was deliberate. Being hidden provided security and room for maneuver. In a sense they both spent their lives as secret agents, even when they were in charge of seven million

COMING APART, 1977–1979   151

people. Their concealment kept their enemies off balance and convinced their followers and friends that they were working full-time for the revolution. This was probably true, especially since the essence of the revolution, as Chea told the Danes, was keeping themselves in power. Their self-effacement, however, had different effects. Pol Pot's was a key element in the loyalty and affection he commanded from those who managed to get close to him at various points in his career. Many Cambodians who came into his presence found him charismatic because he embodied the ideals of conduct—self-control, elegance, kindheartedness—that had been drummed into them for years. Foreigners, brought up to admire (or at least to single out) individuals as "personalities," found him exasperating, hypocritical, and elusive. Nuon Chea eschewed publicity altogether. Aside from a stray reference to his "emotionalism" from the 1980s and reports that when he was in power he favored the inhabitants of his native village in Battambang, he left no personal traces.

In September 1978 Pol Pot convened a national congress of the party. It lasted a week and was attended by about sixty people. Brother Number One sat at the dais, flanked by Nuon Chea and Ta Mok, the secretary of the southwest who had provided cadre to replace those purged in other zones. Pol Pot's speech "outlined a new four year plan to oppose the Vietnamese." In the context of "building the nation," he "outlined a need to create model cooperatives" that would be more or less self-sufficient. Pol Pot set a target for one-third of the country's cooperatives to be self-sufficient by 1980. On the eve of Democratic Kampuchea's collapse, Pol Pot was still "learning from Dazhai"—or lulling his audience into thinking he was.[30]

About this time, Pol Pot also spoke to some of the returned intellectuals at a seminar in Phnom Penh. One returnee told Marie-A. Martin:

He spoke *for two days*. He wished the state to be first in all domains and to become the model for non-aligned states. He wanted its [agricultural] yields to exceed those of Japan. He said Cambodia was an under-developed country, that it needed to wake up rapidly, make progress, make a great leap. At first we were a little surprised, and then we were hooked (*on s'est accroché*) by his skillful words" (emphasis added).[31]

Pol Pot had been mesmerizing small audiences in this fashion for over twenty years, and continued to do so well into the 1990s. His ability to enchant his listeners was a crucial part of his equipment as a leader. In 1991 a Cambodian official who remembered his speeches said that what was striking was his "everyday" (*samanh*) manner of speaking, "like a father speaking to his children."[32]

Many survivors recalled celebrations throughout Cambodia to mark the party's anniversary in 1978. They remembered having enough (and in some cases even too much) to eat. In Phnom Penh, Chinese and Albanian films

Pol Pot (right) with Chinese opera troupe, the dancers in Cambodian attire, Beijing, October 1977.

were shown and special meals were provided for government workers. Pol Pot's speech for the occasion was delivered at the Olympic Stadium and later published in *Tung Padevat*. It dealt with the inevitability of a Vietnamese defeat, the clear-sightedness of the party, the virtues of collectivism, and the need to build a socialist revolution. "If we open the door to capitalism," Pol Pot declared, "we will lose the country." Under the party, he continued, the people's livelihood had improved dramatically for "90 percent of the population." Men and women who had once had neither land nor food and who had "sold their sons and daughters to other people [now] eat three times a day; sweet desserts and sugar are readily available." Because "99 percent of the people" were united with the party, the remaining contradictions were unimportant. The problem of subsistence had been solved, Pol Pot stated, but he cited no figures and said nothing about rice exports. Efforts could now concentrate on other crops and on developing industry.

The next few pages of the speech, like those that dealt with industry in the Four Year Plan, were marked by triumphant wishful thinking. Several industries listed as "newly established" were ones from the Sihanouk era refurbished with Chinese and North Korean money and technicians. Those concerned with industry must have felt relieved to hear Pol Pot praising these developments. Over the next two months, however, the directors of factories and the minister of industry and his superior, Vorn Vet, were purged. Presumably these officials had missed the change in tune from an agriculturally based "Great Leap" to one based on industry and were blamed for the failure of Cambodia's factories to perform by international standards. Pol Pot closed his speech by cheering the party's anniversary. He promised his listeners "many new developments" over the next few years, adding that "friendly countries" would contribute to Cambodia's security.[33]

The speech was Pol Pot's explanation for the successes of his regime. The war with Vietnam was mentioned in terms of Cambodia's inevitable victory. Vietnam, Pol Pot said, had failed to learn the lessons of history, as taught by "Napoleon, Hitler and the American imperialists"—who had gone down to ignominious defeat. The audience probably believed him or vigorously pretended that they did. Many of them owed their empowerment to him. Perhaps, like Lon Nol, Pol Pot felt himself invulnerable. Perhaps, like Sihanouk, he was gambling that something (Chinese "volunteers"? the collapse of Vietnam?) would turn up. In any event, he was out of touch and concealing or blanking out a good deal of what he knew. As he spoke, his own troops were driving hundreds of thousands of people out of the eastern zone and hundreds of eastern zone cadre were being interrogated and executed at S-21. Cambodian troops in the east and southwest were being pounded by Vietnamese fighter bombers. Some territory in the east had already been taken by the Vietnamese. The young uneducated Cambodians entrusted with Chinese military equipment were being trained to use it at a breakneck pace. Many of them—tank drivers, pilots, mortar operators—died from injuries suffered in accidents. In early November, Pol Pot asked a Chinese delegation for "volunteers." The Chinese counseled self-reliance and increased their material assistance. Pol Pot's regime had three months to go.[34]

Pol Pot on Display

During the second half of 1978, Brother Number One gave several interviews to foreign visitors. Most of these were published and rebroadcast over Radio Phnom Penh. Some were translated into French and English at the Ministry of Foreign Affairs. Predictably, the interviews display Pol Pot as a benign patron presiding over a united front. On two occasions, however, in the closing days of his government, he gave interviews to outsiders hostile to the regime. One was to a pair of American journalists in late December; the other was to Prince Sihanouk at the beginning of 1979.

The Americans, Elizabeth Becker and Richard Dudman, were the first nonsocialist journalists to visit Democratic Kampuchea. They arrived in Phnom Penh in mid-December accompanied by a radical academic, Malcolm Caldwell, from the University of London. Dudman and Becker had lived in Cambodia and reported on the war in the early 1970s. Caldwell had been an active supporter of Democratic Kampuchea since its foundation and had spoken and written widely in its defense. Dudman and Becker were selected because Khmer officials saw the value of being covered by nonsocialist media and hoped for evenhanded treatment (which they received). The officials also took it for granted that the journalists were employed by the omnipotent CIA and prepared surveillance reports on them during their visits. Caldwell, on the other hand, was a "friend." The main effect of this was that he was granted an individual audience with Pol Pot, while Becker and Dudman were granted one together.[35]

The two reporters had submitted questions to Pol Pot in advance, and the prime minister's consolidated reply (which struck Dudman as a "filibuster . . . so that he would not have to answer our questions . . . which were rather pointed") answered some of the issues they had raised. The audience took place in the government guest house, formerly the Résidence Supérieure, in the northern part of the city. Dudman and Becker were driven there in a large Mercedes. Both of them recalled that Pol Pot, wearing a silvery Chinese-style suit, sat in an armchair on a slightly raised platform. Thiounn Prasith, who had been their guide on tours of the countryside, was also on the dais, with Ieng Sary and another translator; these three men remained standing.[36]

Becker found Pol Pot "elegant, with a pleasing face, not handsome but attractive. . . . Physically, he had a strong, comfortable appearance. . . . His gestures and manner were polished, not crude." Dudman thought that Pol Pot was "rather slight physically, not stocky like most Cambodians." Dudman also found the situation overly controlled and was "not especially impressed" by Pol Pot, although, like Becker, he noticed his elegant, manicured, "almost spidery" hands. Both reporters were exasperated when Pol Pot said nothing about human rights abuses, Sihanouk, or the identities of his colleagues—the questions begging for answers in the United States. Instead, after an exchange of pleasantries and some juice served in hollowed-out oranges ("There were flies everywhere," Dudman recalled), Pol Pot embarked on an hour-long monologue that traced the history of Vietnamese aggression and Cambodian righteousness. He said nothing of his domestic programs, the purges, or Vietnamese military successes. He failed to mention the party. He insisted that Vietnam was without international support and that its government was near collapse. He never raised his voice: "At the most," wrote Becker, "he nodded his head slightly or flicked his dainty wrist for emphasis." He spoke of the "Warsaw Pact" as threatening Cambodia and mused that this might provoke a counterattack from the anti-Soviet North Atlantic Treaty Organization (NATO). Perhaps he was spinning fantasies until the interview was over. Perhaps he hoped the journalists were in a position to obtain American military support for Cambodia. In view of the warm treatment the United States gave Romania's pro-Chinese, anti-Soviet dictator, Nicolae Ceausescu (who had recently visited Phnom Penh), Pol Pot's reading of possibilities was less farfetched than it appeared.

At the end of the monologue, Becker and Dudman were able to ask a few questions. Most of these were brushed aside. In response to one about his colleagues in the government, Pol Pot said that it would not be a good idea to name them, as they might soon be fighting a guerrilla war. Years later, Becker wrote that she was "grateful when the interview ended." At least for her, the sense of unreality that Pol Pot's talk exuded was overwhelming.[37]

After Becker and Dudman were driven back to their guest house, Caldwell returned to the Résidence Supérieure. There he and Pol Pot, roughly the same age, talked about agricultural policies and socialist economics. Caldwell returned to Becker and Dudman overjoyed with the revolutionary's frankness and friendly manner. Chatting with Becker, Caldwell compared Cambodia to his beloved Scotland. The three separated around 11:00 P.M. to write up their notes and prepare for their departure from Cambodia the next day.

Two hours later, in a confusing sequence of events, a group of armed Khmer stormed the guest house and in the ensuing fracas Caldwell and at least one of the intruders were shot and killed. Two middle-ranking cadre eventually confessed to the crime at S-21, indirectly implicating Son Sen, but the facts of the case remain obscure. One unlikely explanation is that Pol Pot ordered Caldwell killed before the Scottish radical could condemn Cambodia's revolution. Caldwell's discussion with Pol Pot was friendly, and Caldwell remained convinced only hours before he died about the justice of the Cambodian cause. It is more likely, as Stephen Heder has suggested, that Caldwell was murdered by opponents of Pol Pot to embarrass the regime. A third possibility—that Caldwell was a casualty in a personal feud among low-ranking cadre—should also be considered.[38]

On December 24, Becker, Dudman, and the coffin containing Caldwell's body left Phnom Penh, as scheduled, for Beijing. The following day, the Vietnamese launched a massive attack on Cambodia. Fourteen divisions—some 100,000 troops—were involved. The well-trained, heavily armed Vietnamese sliced into Cambodia at several points, isolating the units thrown against them. They were supported by helicopters, fixed-wing aircraft, and heavy artillery units. Cambodian troops fought courageously and sustained heavy losses but were outmaneuvered and outgunned. On December 29, Pol Pot greeted a Marxist-Leninist delegation from Canada. He told them in a three-hour interview that the Vietnamese faced "imminent defeat," adding that the "Warsaw Pact" was involved in the war. By January 1, 1979, the sound of artillery fire was audible in Phnom Penh, rattling the windows of Sihanouk's cottage. On January 2, Vietnamese commandos crossed the Mekong on rubber rafts in an attempt to kidnap the prince. They were mowed down by Cambodian troops, and Sihanouk was immediately evacuated to the northwest for three days. By then, Vietnamese forces controlled seven Cambodian provinces east of the Mekong.[39]

Sihanouk returned to Phnom Penh on January 5, the same day that Pol Pot issued a stirring statement calling for a "people's protracted war [against] Soviet international expansionism and the Warsaw Pact." Late that afternoon, Khieu Samphan visited the prince to say that Pol Pot had invited him to tea. When Sihanouk's Mercedes pulled up to the Résidence Supérieure, the prime minister came to the door to greet him with a "slight bow." The two men were dressed in short-sleeved white shirts and dark trousers—the costume Saloth Sar had favored years before in Chamraon Vichea. On several occasions, Sihanouk described Pol Pot that evening as "charismatic" and a "perfect host." The prince told Nayan Chanda later that "Pol Pot is very brutal, but it seems he did not hate me very much. He was really very charming."[40]

Sihanouk and Pol Pot spent four hours together. They began with small talk. While sipping orange juice, they recalled their previous encounter in 1973. Pol Pot, using submissive royal pronouns—to Sihanouk's delight—apologized for not calling on the prince since the liberation of Phnom Penh. He pleaded too much work; Sihanouk agreed politely. Pol Pot then suggested that the prince travel to the United Nations, via Beijing, to plead the cause of the regime. A Chinese jet would leave Phnom Penh with Sihanouk and his entourage on January 6. Sihanouk accepted the assignment. Pol Pot then gave the prince a long, optimistic briefing about the military situation using an enormous map. He promised to "liquidate" Vietnamese forces within two months. At that point, he added, he would be happy to welcome Sihanouk back to Phnom Penh. The rendezvous and the two performances were over. Sihanouk was taken home in the Mercedes. His wife and mother-in-law were delighted to see him. They had assumed he had been killed.

The prince's flight departed on time the following afternoon, less than twenty-four hours before Vietnamese forces reached the outskirts of Phnom Penh. It was the last plane to leave the city. Along with Sihanouk, it carried most of what remained of the diplomatic corps. Chinese aid personnel had been evacuated by train several days earlier. On January 6 it was the turn of several government ministries; others were given orders to leave the next day. At 8:00 A.M. on January 7, hundreds of minor officials were loaded onto a train. They included some of the returnees, one of whom, Y Phandara, later recorded his memories of the scene. Wounded troops brought in from the hospitals and anyone who could climb onto the carriages crowded around him. Soon after the train departed, around 9:00 A.M., Phandara "saw two helicopters coming from Phnom Penh and heading in the same direction as we were. I watched them disappear over the horizon." The helicopters were carrying Pol Pot and his close associates to exile in Thailand and an uncertain future. It was an ignominious departure, reminiscent of American ambassador John Gunther Dean's in April 1975, barely a week before the first "liberation" of Phnom Penh.[41]

CHAPTER NINE

■

"Grandfather 87," 1979–1998

The Vietnamese invasion of Cambodia caused hundreds of thousands of Cambodians to run, but very few could escape as neatly as Pol Pot managed to do. DK troops numbering over 30,000 men and women, accompanied by perhaps 100,000 villagers and conscripts, retreated through the forests into northwestern Cambodia as Vietnamese armies swept up the major roads and occupied the towns. Thousands of Cambodians died in combat and from malaria and malnutrition in the exodus. By the end of 1979 most of what was left of Democratic Kampuchea's army was encamped in malarial forests close to the Thai-Cambodian border. Pol Pot's whereabouts for most of that year are unknown.

In the wake of the invasion, Communist cadre fled their villages and work sites to join the retreating columns or to resume their lives elsewhere. Those who delayed their departure were often cut to pieces by enraged inhabitants. Hundreds of thousands of liberated people soon took to the roads themselves, looking for relatives, native villages, houses, and possessions. Thousands of them died as they crisscrossed the country on foot. Others, exhausted by hardship and drawn by rumors of prosperity in Thailand, headed west. In the chaos that ensued, much of the 1979 rice crop went unharvested, and famine broke out in many parts of the country.[1]

Meanwhile, in Phnom Penh the Vietnamese had established a satellite Cambodian government that called itself the People's Republic of Kampuchea. Its high-ranking officials were a mixture of DK cadre who had fled to Vietnam in 1977–1978 and Khmer who had been in exile there since the 1950s. Over the next few years, the regime also gave a few bureaucratic positions to noncommunist survivors of the Pol Pot era, but its main efforts in 1979–1980 were to bind the new government closely to Vietnam and prevent Pol Pot from regaining power. Until 1989, when the Vietnamese withdrew their forces, the People's Republic was protected by up to 200,000 Vietnamese troops and overseen by Vietnamese cadre. When the Vietnamese took over, the ordinary Cambodians offered little or no resistance. It was as if they had been bankrupted by the previous regime; politically, the Vietnamese were their receivers.

The new regime quickly dismantled some of the most offensive aspects of Democratic Kampuchea. By mid-1979 it had permitted or reestablished markets, schools, hospitals, freedom of movement, and family farming. In 1980, money and Buddhism were reintroduced, although access to the monkhood was restricted to people over fifty. Political pluralism and freedom of expression were discouraged, but most Cambodians were too preoccupied with reconstructing their lives and families to notice. Most of them saw the new government as a sharp contrast to that of Democratic Kampuchea. Many of those who detected a Marxist-Leninist agenda in the regime's pronouncements and were unhappy about it found it easy to escape to Thailand. Others who fled believed that Cambodia had become a colony of Vietnam. Still others swallowed their pride, concealed their views, and worked alongside the Vietnamese to bring Cambodia back to life. The new government attracted aid from the Soviet Union and its allies and from India, but it remained desperately poor. The PRK was deemed to be ineligible for development assistance, because Democratic Kampuchea retained Cambodia's seat at the United Nations—the only government-in-exile to be so honored. The Vietnamese occupation of Cambodia led the United States, China, and other powers hostile to Vietnam to punish Cambodia for Vietnam's action.[2]

By the end of 1979, Pol Pot had emerged from hiding long enough to be photographed in a fortified camp in eastern Thailand. He remained in the area through the 1980s. In 1990 the camp was known as Office 87, echoing the code name "870" that had formerly designated the Central Committee. Occasionally, Pol Pot moved his headquarters into Cambodia. From these bases he supervised the rebuilding of the DK army.

When the fighting died down toward the end of 1979, more than 100,000 Red Khmer, perhaps half of them combatants and support personnel, had slipped or stumbled into Thailand, where they were housed for a time with mostly hostile Khmer refugees in hastily established refugee camps. By the middle of 1980, DK forces and those living under their protection had been regrouped into tightly disciplined camps of their own. As many as 300,000 Cambodian refugees from other camps were eventually granted asylum in other countries, and they set off to start new lives overseas. Roughly the same number drifted into the camps in the 1990s and were unable to find shelter in foreign nations. Those in DK camps were not allowed by their mentors to be interviewed for resettlement or even to leave the camps.

In some respects, Pol Pot's time in hiding on the frontier echoed his briefer exile along the Vietnamese border from 1963 to 1965. On both occasions, he depended on foreigners for his survival, while Cambodian cadre visited him regularly for instruction and advice. The contrasts between the two periods are more important than their similarities. In 1963, holed up in Office 100, Saloth Sar had fewer than 20 people with him. Sixteen years later, he commanded the remains of a national army and perhaps 100,000 followers. In 1963–1965 he was a hostage of the Vietnamese, themselves absorbed in fighting a major war. After 1979 he was still dependent on foreign assistance, but it came from far more powerful and more prosperous patrons— China, Thailand, and the United States.

These powers supported him because they shared his hostility toward Vietnam. In January 1979, two weeks after the fall of Phnom Penh, the Thai government, fearful of a Vietnamese invasion, struck a deal with China. The Thai would offer shelter to the Red Khmer (whom the Chinese would supply with weapons and equipment) if the Chinese would drop their support for the Thai Communist party, a guerrilla movement that had been troubling the Thai military for years. The United States, whose friendship with China had become a cornerstone of its Asian policies, did nothing to undermine this agreement and supported the seating of Pol Pot's delegation to the United Nations. In doing so they ingratiated themselves with China and perpetuated an anti-Vietnam stance that many in Washington assumed was popular with the American public. Most countries allied to the United States and China— including the Association of Southeast Asian Nations (ASEAN)—fell in line behind those powers. By the middle of 1980, a motley collection of Communist-led refugees had been sorted into a government-in-exile, and a battered army was on its way to becoming an effective fighting force.[3]

For Pol Pot, foreign patronage and personal security meant that he could rebuild his military strength, reorganize his followers, and plan to return to power. To refuse foreign help without a territorial base would have been to commit political suicide, so he exchanged independence-mastery for the opportunity to stay alive. Ideologically, the loss of independence was not particularly painful in the circumstances, since his main objective—throwing the Vietnamese out of Cambodia—was shared by his major patrons.

The Discovery of Democratic Kampuchea's History

News about atrocities in Democratic Kampuchea had been growing since 1977 when an analysis of refugee reports and DK radio broadcasts was compiled by François Ponchaud, a French missionary fluent in Khmer. His perceptive, passionate book *Cambodia: Year Zero* was welcomed by many when it appeared but was greeted with skepticism by those who thought it was serving the anticommunist purposes of the United States. After 1979, however, most of Ponchaud's findings were confirmed. What emerged from his book and from subsequent accounts was horrifying to people who had thought of Cambodia, if at all, as peaceful, glamorous, and remote. Before the year was out, the interrogation center S-21 was being turned into a Genocide Museum by the People's Republic of Kampuchea. In 1980 the first confessions from S-21 were brought out of the country by Western scholars. By then, it was clear to all but a handful of diehard supporters of Pol Pot that Cambodia's revolution had been a disaster with few beneficiaries and millions of victims. On the heels of a ruinous civil war, the regime's faulty analyses of Cambodian society, its utopian policies, its disdain for people, its amateurish technology, and its brutal methods had come close to destroying the country.[4]

What were the human costs? Conservative estimates of the number of men, women, and children who died between 1975 and 1979 as a result of DK policies run between 800,000 (or 1 in 10) and one million (or 1 in 8) inhabitants of the country. These figures do not include those killed in the fighting with Vietnam. Most of the deaths were due to malnutrition, overwork, and untreated or wrongly diagnosed diseases. They can thus be traced to the "storming attacks" espoused by the regime, its empowerment of so many illiterate young people, its failure to punish their transgressions, and the notions of conspiracy and betrayal that dominated party leaders' thinking.

Perhaps 100,000 men and women, and probably more, were executed without trial. In rural areas, most of the killings occurred when young cadre enforced what they understood to be the will of the organization. Some of these executions, perhaps most, were impulsive overreactions. The 14,000 men and women brought into Tuol Sleng, on the other hand, were "smashed" more carefully, sometimes over several months.

Despite his disingenuous denials to Nate Thayer in 1997, there is no doubt that Pol Pot knew about S-21 and monitored its progress. He probably had information about the killings, malnutrition, and horrendous conditions in the countryside as well. In the 1970s and 1980s, Pol Pot saw himself as a wartime leader and was unable or unwilling to perceive anyone's death in terms of real suffering. Instead, he saw the deaths in terms of the exigencies of the party, by 1975 inseparable from his own, or as brought about by "enemies." The victims were thought of as "strata" rather than as human beings. Pol Pot later blamed the "excesses" of Democratic Kampuchea, which he minimized, on the Vietnamese and their agents—people with "Cambodian bodies and Vietnamese minds" who had betrayed the revolution. When pressed by journalists to estimate the deaths that had resulted from his policies, he became evasive, mentioning "several hundred" victims on some occasions and "several thousand" on others.[5]

The PRK capitalized on the horror generated by events when it brought Pol Pot and Ieng Sary to trial, in absentia, in August 1979. Eloquent evidence poured into the tribunal, and the two men were condemned to death, a sentence suggested by the lawyer ostensibly working in their defense. In the 1980s, human rights activists in the West tried repeatedly to bring Pol Pot to trial at the International Court of Justice in the Netherlands. They failed, however, because the Thai were unwilling to hand him over and because his patrons in Washington and Beijing were more interested in punishing Vietnam than in bringing Pol Pot to justice.[6]

For a while, Pol Pot was a media sensation. Some observers saw him as a "genocidal fascist" and compared him to Hitler. Others labeled him a "genocidal Communist" like Stalin; one journalist referred to him as a "moon-faced monster." These comparisons had little explanatory power, but by the end of 1979, "Pol Pot" had become a household word, synonymous with genocide, chaos, and everyone's worst fears of "communism."

Nonetheless, he held on to many of his supporters. To his cadre and combatants, he could do no wrong. The leadership in Beijing, for their part, while distancing themselves from his "excesses," saw him as a nationalist, an ally, and a revolutionary. The Thai found him cooperative and a good performer militarily. As information about his years in power proliferated (and peaked, perhaps, with the powerful film *The Killing Fields* in 1985), Pol Pot became an embarrassment to his American patrons, but they lacked the courage to abandon him, enmeshed as they were in a net of *realpolitik*.

Concealing Democratic Kampuchea

By 1981 worldwide revulsion against Pol Pot and impatience among noncommunist Cambodian refugees with Vietnam's prolonged occupation led the United States and its allies to sponsor the formation of an anti-Vietnamese coalition government that could replace the Red Khmer delegation at the United Nations and provide a noncommunist coloring to the anti-Vietnamese resistance. In December 1981, while the preliminaries to these arrangements were taking place, the Communist party of Kampuchea was officially dissolved following a decision by its Central Committee. However, since none of the committee members were purged and several retained the positions they held before the party was dissolved, it seems likely that the dissolution was a charade for overseas consumption. Indeed, a defector in 1989 stated that new members had been recruited into the party as recently as 1984.

The coalition "government" was formed in the middle of 1982. It was dominated by DK officials because of Democratic Kampuchea's patrons and military prowess; the other two factions were led by Prince Sihanouk, who lived for the most part in exile in Beijing, and by a prerevolutionary prime minister, Son Sann, who had lived for many years in France. Support for the noncommunist factions came from Cambodian refugees in Thailand and the West. Democratic Kampuchea retained the foreign affairs portfolio (the only meaningful one for a government-in-exile), and its diplomats remained on duty at the United Nations. Pol Pot's trusted lieutenant Khieu Samphan (who became the prime minister of Democratic Kampuchea in 1979) was the faction's spokesman overseas, joined from time to time by Son Sen, who had been responsible for S-21 between 1975 and 1979. Samphan spoke of his newly discovered attachment to capitalist economics and said that he had been forced to work under Democratic Kampuchea against his will. The story pleased people who wanted to give Democratic Kampuchea a "human face," but it failed to persuade those familiar with Samphan's long, intimate, continuing relationship with Pol Pot and Ieng Sary and his association with the purges in Democratic Kampuchea.[7]

The leaders of the three factions despised each other, and the leaders of the Phnom Penh government despised all three. Pol Pot's troops did most of the fighting against the Vietnamese, particularly in the rainy season from April to October, when roads became impassable for Vietnamese trucks and tanks. The Red Khmer troops were better trained, better equipped, and better motivated than most of those raised by Sihanouk and Son Sann, but they were unable to secure any Cambodian territory for long and were repeatedly driven back over the frontier by Vietnamese forces aided by troops from the People's Republic of Kampuchea. Arms for the three factions were provided by China with Thai cooperation, while financial and political support for the noncommunists came from Thailand, China, and the United States. The United Nations High Commission for Refugees helped construct a string of refugee camps in Thailand along the frontier to house and feed all Cambodians, including the Red Khmer. The camps, in turn, were controlled by the factions and provided manpower for their military forces.[8]

Repentant Optimist, 1979–1981

In December 1979 Pol Pot gave several interviews to journalists from Japan, Sweden, China, and the United States. The most extensive one was carried out by four sympathetic Japanese newsmen who met with him "at his camp in the Kampuchean jungle" for two days. The mood he conveyed "with an unceasing smile on his face" was one of studied optimism. He denied that his forces had been driven out of Cambodia, claiming that over fifty thousand of them were operating "like a mesh" on Cambodian soil. These troops, he said, had recently "put out of action" a similar number of Vietnamese.

"Asked about murders in his country when he was in power, Pol Pot said, 'Only several thousand Kampucheans might have died [sic] due to some mistakes in implementing our policy of providing an affluent life for the people.'" He added that the Vietnamese were "shifting the blame to him" for the "millions" of deaths they had recently inflicted. From 1976 to 1978, "there had been six coups d'état against his government. 'If we had [not?] executed the plotters, several thousand people would have died,' he said." The translation leaves it uncertain whether the plotters were executed or not. Pol Pot's only regret about his years in power was abolishing money—"a drastic measure." In passing, he admitted for the first time that he had originally been named Saloth Sar.[9]

A few days later Pol Pot greeted an American Broadcasting Corporation television team and used the opportunity to plead for help to drive the Vietnamese out of Cambodia, where, he said, they were waging a "war of genocide." In a revealing passage, Pol Pot said he found them "more ferocious" than Hitler: "Hitler killed the Jews and those who opposed him. Vietnam kills those who oppose it and innocent people who will not join it."[10]

Soon after, following a Central Committee meeting, DK radio announced that Pol Pot had resigned as prime minister and had turned the job over to Khieu Samphan. Although the rationale for the changes was not announced, it seems likely that they responded to public relations imperatives. Having Pol Pot out in the open was a liability. Until 1997, after he had fallen from power, he granted no further interviews to the press. Efforts by journalists over the years to talk to him or to take his picture were unsuccessful. In 1990 an American television network, through Thai intermediaries, offered Pol Pot $300,000 for an interview. He refused.[11]

In a talk to some of his supporters in Phnom Malai in January 1981, however, Pol Pot seems to have dropped his guard for a moment. One of his supporters, interviewed later in the year, provided this account:

> Pol Pot spoke as the representative of the military. He said that he knows that many people in the country hate him and think he's responsible for the killings. He said that he knows many people died. When he said this he nearly broke down and cried. He said he must accept responsibility because the line was too far to the left, and because he didn't keep proper track of what was going on. He said he was like the master in a house who didn't know what the kids were up to, and that he trusted people too much. For example, he allowed [Chhim Samauk] to take care of central committee business for him, Savan to take care of intellectuals, and [Sao Phim] to take care of political education . . . These were the people to whom he felt very close, and he trusted them completely. Then in the end . . . they made a mess of everything . . . They would tell him things that were not true, that everything was fine, but that this person or that was a traitor. In the end they were the real traitors. The major problem had been cadre formed by the Vietnamese.[12]

It was a masterly performance. Pol Pot's tearful regrets, while probably convincing to his listeners, were insufficient to make him leave politics or to ask any of his former associates in Democratic Kampuchea to resign. Perhaps he was genuinely sorry that so many people had died when he had commanded the state; nonetheless, his faith in the cause to which these lives had been sacrificed (even when it was "too far to the left") was unshaken. That his naïveté, idealism, or incompetence had permitted so many deaths did not unnerve him, although he begged the question why someone so easily deceived, and by so many, should remain in power. Moreover, his chagrin at being told "things that were not true" is difficult to square with his own tactical handling of the truth on issues as elementary as his own life story. Finally, for someone formed on the Vietnamese frontier in 1953–1954 and trained by the Vietnamese in the 1960s, his identification of the "major problem" as stemming from "cadre formed by the Vietnamese" is almost a Freudian slip.

This talk, like so many others by Pol Pot, seems to have accomplished its purpose: to serve communism, to secure and deepen his listeners' loyalty to him, and to anchor their devotion to his cause. The source added that Pol Pot "seemed very nice. He . . . treated me like an equal." Once again, in a succession of role models stretching back through Tou Samouth, Thiounn Mumm, and Khvan Siphan, Pol Pot had displayed a common touch so rare among Cambodia's authority figures as to be singled out for praise by those who listened to him.

Dropping Out of Sight, 1981–1986

From 1981 until the end of 1986 no speeches or writing can be traced with certainty to Pol Pot. We have only two photographs of him from this period and no anecdotes. Except for a stretch in the hospital in China in 1985—when rumors circulated in Bangkok and elsewhere that he was terminally ill—we know that he remained for most of the time in heavily guarded camps. His work involved transforming what remained of Democratic Kampuchea's army into a guerrilla force before building up larger, more heavily armed units when political warfare had proved successful. Until 1985 he had overall command of the armed forces. In August of that year, however, his "retirement" was announced to coincide with his sixtieth birthday. He became the director of the Higher Institute of National Defense—about which nothing is known—and held this position until he "resigned" in 1989. He probably remained secretary of the Communist party, such as it was, until 1997, and he certainly continued to play an advisory role to the Red Khmer's politico-military apparatus, but he was always concealed from view. Throughout the 1980s he mystified and frightened his opponents because his invisibility echoed that of many magically endowed Cambodian heroes in traditional literature. Like his guerrilla armies, he could appear (and disappear) at the times and places he chose.

Throughout the decade most Cambodians over twenty were terrified that Pol Pot would return to power. These fears, which immobilized many of these people, probably suited Pol Pot. He "came back" to Cambodia with every unexpected noise, every band of guerrillas stealing through villages at night, and every exploded antipersonnel mine. Thousands of these Chinese mines, each about the size of an apple, were planted by his forces (and by the Phnom Penh regime and by his colleagues in the coalition) all over Cambodia—in rice fields and markets, along paths and outside of villages. The mines, concealed an inch or two beneath the surface, exploded when the weight activating them (usually someone's foot) was lifted. All the victim heard was a loud "click." The explosions left thousands of Pol Pot's "enemies"—soldiers, farmers, women, and children—dead or maimed. Like those he said were unjustly targeted by the Vietnamese, these casualties were mostly "innocent people who refused to join" his movement. In 1990–1991, eighty patients a week, randomly maimed by mines, were being treated in Cambodia's overcrowded, poorly equipped hospitals. Pol Pot remained indifferent to their suffering. The incidence of maiming continued at a high level throughout the 1990s.[13]

Throughout these years, Pol Pot spent his time in the company of true believers. He was protected from unpleasant news and from the contradictory, nonpolitical changes that swept through the world in the 1980s. There were three major occurrences in his personal life. His wife, Khieu Ponnary, suffered what appears to have been a nervous breakdown and was hospitalized in the early 1980s in Beijing. In 1985 Pol Pot remarried after obtaining Ponnary's permission to do so. His second wife, Mea Son, also known as Muon, was in her late twenties at the time and came from a peasant background. In 1986 she gave birth to Pol Pot's first child, a daughter named Sith. After he died, Mea Son told Nate Thayer that Pol Pot had been "a very good husband . . . Since I married him, I never saw him do a bad thing." The nuclear family lived together in Office 87; his wife and daughter were with Pol Pot when he died. Defectors in the 1980s reported that Pol Pot was affectionate with his little daughter and sometimes carried her in his arms on his way to and from cadre training sessions. In his interview with Thayer, he spoke warmly of her.[14]

Summing Up for the Defense

The obscurity surrounding Pol Pot lifted slightly in 1988, when a thirty-nine-page document prepared in December 1986 was smuggled out of a DK camp and fell into the hands of the U.S. Embassy in Bangkok. Originally a talk to party cadre, the wide-ranging text surveyed the history of Democratic Kampuchea, analyzing its "victories and mistakes." Although the document is anonymous, its style and tone point to Pol Pot as its author. The rhetoric of the document suggests that it was a keynote address to a study session.

Pol Pot's brief history of Democratic Kampuchea (the party was never mentioned) had few surprises, but his rhetorical methods and conspiratorial cast of mind, as well as his rationalizations for "mistakes" *(khoh chhkong)* are very interesting.[15] Much of the text attacks the views of "others" *(ke)*. These others are unspecified, but the noncommunists in the coalition, as well as outside powers critical of Democratic Kampuchea's record of human rights abuses, are clearly meant. By 1986 the noncommunists in the coalition enjoyed considerable support from Cambodians overseas and in refugee camps in Thailand. Pol Pot warned his listeners about this development. The "others," it seems, had been spreading pernicious propaganda against Democratic Kampuchea, attacking its leadership and even urging the removal of "P.P.," although "there has never been a question of dismissing N.S. [Sihanouk] or S.S. [Son Sann]." These pressures had weakened support for the faction among inhabitants of Cambodia, whom the Communists were eager to recruit. Pol Pot urged cadre to create an "ideology force" with which to defeat the Vietnamese and the "others," so that they, the cadres, could be "masters of the political and ideological battlefield." At no point in the talk is the coalition treated as a viable political group; its other members were not to be trusted—"others" never are.

Pol Pot's exposition of united front tactics was crisp and cynical. To "protect the Cambodian race," a range of actions was permitted "in line with the political slogan of Nation, Democracy and Livelihood. We use Livelihood [that is, maintaining decent standards of living] as the means of drawing in people from the base areas; Democracy to mobilize middle stratum people, like students and intellectuals; and Nation to mobilize upper level people of the front as widely as possible." Pol Pot's listeners would not have been surprised that there was no indication that Democratic Kampuchea, when and if it returned to power, would honor the three-part slogan any more than it would honor any other commitments or favor anyone whose social origins were "incorrect." Pol Pot's listeners knew that the slogan, like everything the Red Khmer did, was a means to an end. The name of the game was regaining power.[16]

Turning to the history of Democratic Kampuchea, Pol Pot noted that in 1975 "for the very first time in more than two thousand years of history people from base areas [*pracheachon mul'than*] had taken charge of state power." This empowerment of the poor had never happened in the world, he added, "aside from the Paris Commune in 1871," which had been "taken over by capitalists" soon after.[17] Nothing was said about the party's educated leaders, none of whom (except perhaps Ta Mok) could be characterized as a "base person." Instead, the impression Pol Pot left was that people like his listeners had genuinely taken power in Democratic Kampuchea. If defectors' evidence from the 1990s can be a guide, those listening to him in 1986 would have been in their late twenties and early thirties, mostly from poor peasant backgrounds, who had been soldiers (*yothea*) since the early 1970s and had risen to become battalion and brigade commanders. Many of them had been recruited in the southwest in the early 1970s.

To combat criticism and raise morale, Pol Pot noted that Democratic Kampuchea's years in power could be examined in terms of "our victories" and "our mistakes." The first outweighed the second. Democratic Kampuchea had been strategically and tactically correct—"right on target," in the speaker's phrase. The Four Year Plan, for example, "was moving along nicely, considering that we had so little capital. . . . [W]e strove to meet our schedule so that the Vietnamese would not catch up with us and be our master." Pol Pot said nothing about the plan's collapse or its enormous human costs.[18]

Turning to "mistakes," Pol Pot said that "there were a sizable number of these, both large and small. There were political mistakes, organizational mistakes and mistakes due to ourselves in Democratic Kampuchea, from top to bottom." None of them is specified, and responsibility is never focused on an individual, a political group, a region, or a policy. The major mistake, he said, was unavoidable and thus not a mistake at all: "Base people, assuming state power for the first time . . . had little experience; three years was too short a time [for them] to gain experience." Inexperienced people ("poor and blank"), of course, had been favored by the regime precisely because they were not contaminated by the past. Pol Pot said nothing about his own (and everyone else's) inexperience at administration. Instead, he noted that "from top to bottom, we were *somewhat excessive* [*loeus loh*]" (emphasis added). Examples of excess were not forthcoming; the audience, glancing momentarily at their feet or fingernails perhaps, knew perfectly well what he meant. They were the people who had committed or authorized the "mistakes." Seven years later, there was no time for regrets. After all, Pol Pot remarked, "in the history of the world there has never been a country that made no mistakes."

The "brief look at world histories" that followed was an exercise in exoneration to keep "enemies and others from altering [*bongvae bongvil*] the history of Democratic Kampuchea"—presumably by emphasizing its human rights abuses or its erstwhile links with the Communist bloc. Echoing some of the triumphalist hyperbole of the 1970s, the passage implied that Democratic Kampuchea (which in 1986 controlled no territory, collected no taxes, and paid no bills) was still the finest *nation* in the world. One after another, the Soviet Union, China, Vietnam, the United States, Great Britain, France, and Australia (!) were examined in thumbnail fashion and found wanting. Pol Pot noted the "difficulties" the Soviet Union had encountered from 1917 to 1935 (that is, up to the eve of Stalin's purges). China's economy, after thirty-seven years, was still at a "low stage." Vietnam, racked by civil war, was experiencing "insoluble problems" because it was considered to be "the poorest country in the world." Pol Pot then asked, "And as for America, France, England and Australia, are they good?" Hardly. They were to be despised because their "original identities" were those of "land swallowers, race destroyers, megacolonialists . . . and human rights violators." Pausing for effect, Pol Pot continued: "The true character of Democratic Kampuchea is far higher than this collection of nations. Democratic Kampuchea has never once gone to usurp or gone to invade [*teu rumlop . . . teu chhlean pean*] anyone."[19]

The notion that Cambodia was purer than other nations and more sinned against than sinning has been shared by all Cambodian regimes since inde-

Pol Pot being interviewed, January 1980, Thailand. Photo by David Schwab. Courtesy of the Bettman Archive.

pendence—with the exception of the People's Republic of Kampuchea and its successor states which have stressed the need for living on the same planet as Vietnam. Indeed, Pol Pot's performance, calculated to make his audience feel good, was reminiscent of Sihanouk's addresses in the 1960s, with the obvious difference that Pol Pot's own ego, life history, and ambitions were not as prominently on display.[20]

In the final section of the speech, Pol Pot attacked the concept of "important personalities" (israqchun), citing the case of Napoleon, "whose bones have been placed inside a monument called Invalides"—a sly, schoolmasterish touch. "What was Napoleon's character? He gained power in a coup, had

Pol Pot in Thailand, early 1980. Photo by David Schwab. Courtesy of the Bettman Archive.

himself named emperor, and invaded all the countries of eastern and western Europe, spreading unlimited calamity—without the slightest moral feeling."[21]

Pol Pot then cited four nineteenth-century Cambodians who had resisted the French and noted that they had not been able to liberate the country. He paused again before continuing: "Between these heroes and Democratic Kampuchea, which one is better? . . . Democratic Kampuchea is far better than any of these historical heroes. We can say that during the history of Kampuchea for more than two thousand years the virtues, qualities, true character and value of Democratic Kampuchea are the best."

One interesting feature of the peroration is that Pol Pot, the embodiment of Democratic Kampuchea—mentioning himself only in passing ("P. P.") and never using the word "I"—was asking his audience to compare the state whose triumphs and future he embodied with a handful of discredited nineteenth-century figures and a cruel emperor from France. "Democratic Kampuchea," like the speaker himself, was humbler and more ethical than "land swallowers and megacolonialists." Even with its "mistakes," he said, Democratic Kampuchea had performed better than other socialist countries. The outcome of the comparisons was spelled out by Pol Pot whose own "true character, victories and mistakes" were the same as those of his audience. Having become virtuous, his listeners no longer needed to change and they no longer possessed a past that they needed to abandon. Without using the term (or saying "I") Pol Pot was describing his own enlightenment. In doing so, he revealed his insouciance about what was happening elsewhere in the world. Was it conceivable that Pol Pot and the battalion and brigade commanders were really prepared to administer a nation in the 1990s?

As so often in the course of Pol Pot's career, we witness an arranged occasion where he was on display and not on display, where he was in control but pretended not to be, where he posed as an equal but held life and death power over everyone who heard him, and where a genteel turn of phrase concealed a tendency toward violence, self-righteousness, and terror of which his listeners certainly approved.[22]

Solving the Cambodian "Problem," 1986–1991

In the late 1980s the Cold War diminished in intensity and the power balance shifted slightly on mainland Southeast Asia. The shift accelerated efforts by Cambodian factions and foreign powers to end Cambodia's civil war and reach a comprehensive political solution. There were several reasons for the shift. The most important was probably the erosion of Communist hegemony in eastern Europe in response to Mikhail Gorbachev's liberalization policies in the Soviet Union. The Chinese regime was also moving cautiously toward a market economy, geared in economic terms to its alliance with the United States. In Thailand, meanwhile, power shifted slightly away from the military faction toward commercially minded civilian politicians who saw no profit (except for the military) in supporting an open-ended civil war or permanently alienating Vietnam.

The effects of these changes were felt in Vietnam, in Cambodia, and along the Thai-Cambodian frontier. One effect was that economic and military assistance from the Soviet bloc to Cambodia and Vietnam began to diminish and the costs for Vietnam of keeping a large army in the field in Cambodia increased. Another was that Vietnam was also seeking to move toward a market economy, like China, and wanted to spend less of its resources on defense. Finally, its leaders hoped that withdrawing their troops from Cambodia would soften the stance the United States had taken in the matter of diplomatic recognition. Over the 1980s the number of Vietnamese troops in Cambodia gradually decreased. In September 1989 the last eighty thousand were ceremoniously withdrawn. The units that remained secretly behind consisted of technical personnel that the People's Republican Army lacked.[23]

The troop withdrawal, ironically, strengthened the government in Phnom Penh, which began, cautiously at first, to respond to popular pressure to relax government controls on the economy and to permit a wider range of Buddhist practices. In legislation passed shortly before the Vietnamese withdrawal, people were allowed to sell and purchase real estate, Buddhism was made the state religion, and age restrictions on entering the Buddhist monkhood were lifted. The three gestures were popular and impossible to rescind. Perhaps as a counterweight to these reforms, Pol Pot's definitive "retirement" was announced in 1989.

The response of coalition troops to the Vietnamese withdrawal was to attempt to capture significant portions of Cambodia to form a politico-economic base. In 1990, coalition troops occupied the ruined town of Pailin in the northwest and, more important, assumed control over the surrounding gem fields. Sales of rubies and sapphires in Thailand gave the coalition forces capital with which to purchase military equipment and supplies. More income came from selling timber and forest products to Thai entrepreneurs along the border. By 1992, in fact, the DK faction, supposedly part of a coalition government in Cambodia, had built up an impressive portfolio of foreign investments—with revenue from timber, jewel mining, and real estate—valued at over $100 million, making the faction financially independent. Its leaders continued to operate profitable ventures in Thailand and along the frontier with well-positioned Sino-Thai entrepreneurs. Thai military support for the Red Khmers, of course, has been crucial since 1979. Militarily, 1989–1990 was a standoff between coalition and Phnom Penh forces.

Meanwhile, negotiations between the two gathered momentum. Some of the pressure for these negotiations came from France, Australia, and Indonesia, which were eager to break the logjam imposed by China, Thailand, and the United States. These patrons, in turn, put pressure on the coalition to reach some sort of compromise with the government in Phnom Penh, whose prime minister, Hun Sen, had drawn a good deal of support—albeit reluctantly at first—from the Cambodian émigré community.

By 1989 it was customary to think of Cambodia as involving four factions capable of negotiating among themselves rather than two "governments" conducting an open-ended civil war. Vietnamese advice to Phnom Penh seems at first to have been to wait out developments, as Vietnam itself was doing. In effect, this meant working to dismantle the coalition and continuing to demonize Pol Pot. The DK faction, in turn, worked to delay a political solution until its forces had made inroads in rural areas. The stalemate was broken in 1990–1991, however, when the unravelling of communism in Europe encouraged Vietnam and China, which remained Communist, to press their warring Cambodian clients to accept a compromise that would give some power to China's clients and would not endanger the continuing existence of a Communist regime in Vietnam.

Between 1987 and 1990, conferences and meetings were held by faction members at sites in France, Thailand, and Indonesia. Pressures mounted on the four Cambodian factions to reach some kind of agreement. Sihanouk's faction and the Red Khmer were pushed to abandon an open-ended civil war that might have ended in their favor. Son Sann's anti-monarchic, anti-Communist faction was forced to cooperate further with people whose ideological positions it found difficult to accept. The State of Cambodia, as the regime in Phnom Penh now called itself, had to abandon its demonization of the DK regime, for the time being, and relinquish some of its national sovereignty to the United Nations. In this fast-breaking game, Pol Pot said nothing in public, although he seems to have surfaced briefly in June 1991 when negotiations between the factions in Pattaya, Thailand, reached a crucial stage. His presence there, while hidden from outsiders, indicated that his subordinates (including his ostensible superiors like Khieu Samphan) were unable or unprepared to make important decisions without consulting him. Democratic Kampuchea abandoned its flag and shelved its bloodcurdling national anthem; the People's Republic of Kampuchea changed its name to the State of Cambodia and altered its flag. The Permanent Five members of the United Nations Security Council (France, China, the USSR, the United States, and Great Britain) promised their support for a political compromise, and the United Nations offered to dispatch a team to Cambodia to monitor the transition to an elected, pluralistic government. In 1991 a Supreme National Council for Cambodia was formed whose members came from the three coalition factions and the State of Cambodia. It was envisaged that the council would take up residence in Cambodia, pending national elections and under UN protection, toward the end of 1991. These arrangements gathered momentum following the multinational Cambodian Peace Agreement, signed in Paris in October 1991. In the midst of the turmoil, if defectors' reports are to be believed, Pol Pot was guardedly optimistic, "smooth and clean," and unperturbed.

The UNTAC Period

Over the next two years, the United Nations Transitional Authority in Cambodia (UNTAC) was assembled to supervise the disarming of factions, the resettlement of refugees, and the preparations for national elections. More than 25,000 people were involved, and over $3 billion were spent on the operation, the most expensive of its kind in the history of the United Nations.[24]

The Red Khmer responses to the Paris agreements and the UNTAC presence were so inconsistent as to suggest that the party's leaders were unable or unwilling to deal with such an open-ended, unprecedented state of affairs. The party's leaders had almost no experience operating in the open. In late 1991 and early 1992, nonetheless, the Red Khmer's behavior suggested that they genuinely hoped that UNTAC would, as it promised, dismantle the infrastructure of the State of Cambodia, providing a "level playing field" (not a phrase they would have used) for the Red Khmer. Son Sen and Khieu Samphan were dispatched to Phnom Penh to negotiate toward the end of 1991 but left soon after riots were orchestrated against them by the Phnom Penh regime.

In May 1992, Son Sen was removed from the Central Committee and forbidden to consult with UNTAC officials, probably because he supported further participation in the peace process, which Pol Pot and his immediate colleagues now saw as a ruse intended to destroy their movement. Always suspected for his intellectual arrogance and his Vietnamese upbringing by Ta Mok, Son Sen remained out of favor and was assassinated at Pol Pot's orders in 1997—the event that removed Pol Pot from power.[25] In late May 1992 (whether before or after Son Sen's dismissal is unclear) the Red Khmer refused UN inspectors access to the areas they controlled, thereby expressing their unwillingness to disarm their forces. For the time being, the triumvirate of Pol Pot, Nuon Chea, and Ta Mok, which had controlled the Red Khmer movement since the late 1970s, remained in charge and unwilling to negotiate with the "Vietnamese puppets" in Phnom Penh.

During the UNTAC period, Red Khmer forces made several brutal attacks on Vietnamese civilians living in Cambodia, killing over a hundred and wounding many more. Perhaps the leadership hoped that these massacres would set off a wave of anti-Vietnamese violence, just as they hoped that their boycott of the UN-sponsored elections would produce massive absenteeism among Cambodian voters. Both assessments were based, as David Ashley has suggested, "on a grossly over-optimistic idea of the movement's political and military strength," a frame of mind that had buoyed up the leadership for many years.[26] The Communists did little to impede the UN presence, however, or to disrupt the national elections that occurred under UN supervision in July 1993. This inconsistent behavior in the UNTAC period reveals an incapacity or unwillingness to adjust to the evolving power relations and alterations in the Khmer economy that had taken effect since the Vietnamese withdrawal and were transforming Cambodia on a daily basis. Instead, Red Khmer radio broadcasts, closely monitored and often written by Pol Pot, delivered a steady flow of anti-Vietnamese polemics, whereby Vietnamese were still in charge of politics in Phnom Penh and UNTAC, for all intents and purposes, was working to serve Vietnamese interests, which had remained unchanged since time immemorial.[27]

"Grandfather 87"

Scattered sightings, recollections, and rumors in the late 1980s and early 1990s provided glimpses of Pol Pot—carrying his baby daughter, being hospitalized in Beijing, or traveling between military bases in a white van with blackened windows. Attempts by journalists to get closer than this, until Nate Thayer's journalistic coup in 1997, did not succeed. A posed family photograph, seen by chance by James Pringle in a photography shop in Beijing in 1989, revealed that Pol Pot's hair had whitened since the photographs taken ten years before, but that was as close as any journalist managed to get.[28]

Reports from defectors in the 1990s suggest, however, that Pol Pot's ideas about Cambodia, about himself, and about his faction's returning to power remained unchanged. His modus operandi was the one he had perfected in the 1950s. To understand Pol Pot in this period, it is important to recall that he had been teaching, in one way or another, for thirty-five years without a break.

Defectors described Pol Pot's headquarters—Office 87—as an oval compound a few kilometers inside Thailand near the city of Trat. The "zone," measuring roughly 300 by 500 meters, was surrounded by two barbed wire fences guarded by more than one hundred Cambodian troops. Access was controlled by Thai army units. The compound contained a house for Pol Pot, a separate one for his wife and daughter, six barracks for visiting students, a kitchen, and a cafeteria. Small cabins for his bodyguards surrounded Pol Pot's house. Of all prerevolutionary Cambodian institutions, Office 87 most closely resembled a Buddhist monastic compound. The study sessions, for that matter, resembled Buddhist retreats. Extending the comparison, Pol Pot can be seen as a kind of "forest monk" adept at meditation.[29]

In this controlled environment "Grandfather 87," as Pol Pot came to be called, conducted periodic study sessions for Red Khmer battalion, brigade, and division commanders. The sessions lasted for fourteen days. Students were in class eight hours a day; they were also expected to study for five additional hours and to attend a political meeting every evening. The session ended with two days of feasting before students returned to their military units. In the sessions, high-ranking Red Khmer, including Son Sen, Ta Mok, Khieu Samphan, and Nuon Chea, gave lectures dealing with their areas of expertise. Pol Pot was everyone's favorite: "Funny and warm with students; he lectured without notes," a former student recalled. In his lectures, Pol Pot spoke of Democratic Kampuchea regaining power. He also proposed tactics for the months to come. Depending on external circumstances as Pol Pot interpreted them, the tactics ranged from political to military and back again. After 1988 the emphasis fell on political warfare and preparing to compete in national elections. After the Paris agreements, "Office 87" shifted back onto Cambodian territory.[30]

Pol Pot's teaching techniques varied from lectures to sharp, Socratic question-and-answer sessions that recalled monastic styles of teaching. Roger Normand, drawing on defectors' interviews, described one of these sessions as follows:

> In March 1988, while teaching about the domestic situation inside Cambodia, he abruptly stopped the lesson and asked, "What can we do to make the people love us?" Several brigade and division commanders suggested exposing the corruption of other factions and demonstrating the Red Khmer's patriotism; others maintained that the key was economics. . . . Pol Pot kept shaking his head, dissatisfied. Then a battalion commander in the back row raised his hand and responded, "We must put ourselves in the same position as the poorest of the poor, then the people will crowd around us and love us." "Yes," cried the teacher, delighted that one of his lowest ranking students had answered correctly. "Yes! Yes!"[31]

From his Communist training, Pol Pot kept a future orientation, a sense of fraternity, and an obsession with secrecy, tactics, and organization. Early intellectual influences—Marx, Lenin, Stalin, Mao—were no longer mentioned; nor were the words "party," "socialism," or "revolution." More important, Pol Pot said nothing about how a reborn and rededicated Cambodia would fit into Southeast Asia in the 1990s or beyond. The world he described was changeable insofar as friends and enemies changed, but inside his head, it seems, it was not a different world from the world of the 1960s and 1970s. In this sense, Pol Pot's vision of the world in terms of contending good and evil forces resembled the timeless, uncontextualized vision imparted by Indian epic poems like the *Mahabharata* or by Buddhist teaching.

His indoctrination was simplified and rhetorical. There were no references to written sources. Pol Pot was absorbed by "Cambodia" and by the idea of restoring what he believed to be the only authentic and virtuous regime that the country had ever known. Like an abbot in a forest monastery taking charge of a retreat, he sought to purify his students' minds of extraneous

Pol Pot at Thai border. Photo by Jehangir Gazdar. Copyright 1979. Courtesy of Woodfin Camp & Associates.

ideas that would detract from their obtaining independence-mastery. Tightly disciplined, short of sleep, and subjected to hours of sermons, self-criticism, and discussion, the battalion, brigade, and division commanders were expected to pass their newly acquired enlightenment down the line to their units and then into the villages of Cambodia until revolutionary consciousness (with the word "revolutionary" concealed) had "seeped in" throughout Cambodia, making the nation invulnerable to attack.

In 1990 a defector told Christophe Peschoux of the effectiveness of Pol Pot's speeches: "Pol Pot makes a strong impression on those who hear him for the first time; after that, they want to come back. . . . Those who attend his seminars feel enlightened by his teaching, his explanations and his vision. . . . He's like a father to us . . . Everyone would like to be able to offer some years of their lives so that he could live longer."[32]

Like many previous Cambodian leaders, Pol Pot viewed the prospect of political pluralism with alarm and saw contending politicians as "enemies" who were preventing Democratic Kampuchea from renewing the 98 percent consensus it had enjoyed before 1979. In a revealing passage in 1985, he spoke about the party: "Although we have dissolved the Party, those who have been ordained [he shows a closed fist] are still loyal to the Party. Of 80,000 pure Party members, we hope and expect that at least 50 percent remain loyal to their vows. Remember our strength!"[33]

Two years later, in a peroration to his students, Pol Pot spoke in more detail than usual about his own continuing role:

Comrades, I am very regretful that you have not yet reached a high level of understanding. I worry that other factions will gain power, so though I am old and would like to retire, I must continue with all my strength to build up your knowledge. Do not underestimate yourselves, but also guard against apathy and overconfidence. Everyone must work hard in the political area, to reach a higher level [of understanding] than I have reached. If you fail in this regard, I will not die peacefully.[34]

The former student recounting this speech recalled that when it was over, many listeners wept and others pledged to fight on—to the death if necessary—to bring Pol Pot's dream to fruition. The idea that their mentor "had not yet reached a high level of understanding" would have struck them as appropriately modest—the way a holy man should talk—and, in view of his evident enlightenment, untrue.

In 1995, a former military cadre, interviewed by David Ashley, recalled another study session with Pol Pot, which occurred before the Paris talks:

Once during a week-long session in Thailand . . . I asked about the 75–78 period, because people would always ask me about why he killed so many people. He said the situation was very confused, we did not yet have laws or order, we were like children just learning to walk . . . He said, "I was responsible for everything so I accept responsibility and blame but show me, comrade, one document proving that I was personally responsible for the deaths."[35]

In late 1997, several months before Pol Pot's death, one of his former bodyguards, Sim, spoke about him to the journalist Terry McCarthy, recalling the period 1993–1994, before his crippling stroke and before he moved to Anlong Veng. McCarthy wrote:

Sim led the way uphill to the remains of Pol Pot's house and pointed out a large rock at the edge of a nearby cliff. "This is where he would come and sit in the evening," said Sim. "When he was depressed he would call me, and I would come sit with him. He drank expensive ginseng tea and he kept a bottle of Thai whiskey and he would talk about developing the country for the poor people."[36]

The Implosion of the Red Khmer, 1994–1998

In the Paris peace agreements of October 1991 Pol Pot's patrons had abandoned him for good, but for several years the effects of this abandonment failed to sink in. Pol Pot and his colleagues played for time. Cambodia and its politicians have always been easy for larger powers to "drop" or "pick up." Its leaders have often been deluded about the permanence of these powers' patronage or the genuineness of their support. Pol Pot in this sense was the most recent in a long line of docile or unwary Cambodian leaders forced or eager to accept foreign domination. In spite of, or perhaps because of, his talk of independence-mastery he was always dependent, after 1963 at least, on others for support. In the DK era, this dependence was a function of Cambodia's perennial vulnerability and, ironically, the flaws of its "independent" Communist movement. Over the years, the declaration by Cambodian leaders that their country was in effect an island has pleased some of their listeners and has endowed many with extraordinary zeal, but at the end of the twentieth century Cambodia is still what it has been for several hundred years: a small country surrounded by Thailand and Vietnam, and more recently, by a voracious capitalist world. A more interesting question, which is impossible to answer, is how and why the dream of Cambodia's power and isolation, in the face of overwhelming evidence to the contrary, has persisted for so long among so many Khmer.

As the Red Khmer faded in vigor and importance, they retained their capacity to frighten people and some of their viability as a guerrilla force. Red Khmer units continued their vicious hit-and-run attacks on Vietnamese civilians and in 1995 kidnapped and killed three foreign tourists taken from a train. The movement's leaders used their racialist hostility to Vietnam to explain their behavior and as a way of overriding survivors' memories of the past. In their public statements, they no longer presented the DK era as a period of massive social experimentation. The "three-year period," as they called it, became a noble-minded holding action that saved Cambodia from being "swallowed" by Vietnam. A Red Khmer spokesman, speaking in 1990, explained that "if we were Communists, that would mean we would be on the side of the Vietnamese"—an intriguing contortion of history.[37] Moreover, "if we had not carried out our struggle," Pol Pot told Nate Thayer seven years later, "Cambodia would have been another Kampuchea Krom in 1975." He was referring to the Mekong delta in southern Vietnam, which came under Vietnamese control in the seventeenth century. He repeated the statement in April 1998, shortly before he died.[38]

In 1993–1994 the coalition government cobbled together in Phnom Penh between the royalists (known by their French acronym FUNCINPEC), who had won the election, and Hun Sen's Cambodian People's Party (CPP), which had governed the country since 1979, pursued a cautious policy of reconciliation with the Red Khmer, which, with similar caution (or cynicism), hung onto the united front policy that had delivered so few dividends to them—aside from peace—in the UNTAC period. In 1994, however, the Phnom Penh authorities declared the Red Khmer "illegal" and resumed military operations against them.

It was at that point, we can say with hindsight, that the Red Khmer movement began to come apart. Altering their tactics in the areas under their control, Pol Pot and his colleagues introduced a policy based on the dictatorship of the peasantry. Now that they lacked foreign support, the leaders were making a virtue of necessity. They also hoped to lay the groundwork for victory by "purifying" their followers and recreating the conditions of the armed struggle against Sihanouk and Lon Nol. A former military cadre told David Ashley in 1997 that the new policy was "Pol Pot's autonomous decision, based on his experience . . . He went back to seek the old road again."[39] The savage policy introduced heavy penalties for trading with other zones and was very unpopular in the Pailin region, which bordered on a relatively populous area of Thailand and which had become prosperous in the 1990s from the exploitation of mineral resources. Buddhist temples and markets that had sprung up in Red Khmer areas were closed, personal belongings were collectivized, and plans were drawn up to limit people's agricultural holdings. The movement's prolonged contact with the outside world, its leaders thought, had infected it with the world's corruption. Characteristically, the blame was attributed to outsiders. The Red Khmer were doing poorly, a 1994 document asserted, because "enemy elements" had taken over "90 percent [of people's] views, politics, livelihood, economics, ethics and so on." Unable or unwilling to cope with an open, multifaceted world, Pol Pot and his colleagues turned the clock back and tried to restart the only war that they had won. Fortunately for the rest of the country, the conditions that had accompanied their victory in 1975 had all been overtaken by events.

The effect of the new policies on their followers was catastrophic. The prospect of renewed socialism, mandatory poverty, and endless warfare pushed thousands of them out of the movement. A former cadre told David Ashley in 1996:

> After the elections, the leadership started talking about fighting "til the end of the world," until the next generations. After the elections there was no clear idea of how the war would end or what we were fighting for. . . . Pol Pot and the others were very good at making theory in terms of the 10-point elements, the 8-this, the 6-that, and all the rest of it, but when it came to the basic question of how to end the war they didn't have an answer.[40]

Toward the end of 1995, it seems, Pol Pot suffered a stroke that affected the left side of his body and severely impaired the sight of his left eye. By then, Ta Mok was effectively in charge of what remained of the Red Khmer, but Pol Pot was still consulted on major issues. In the meantime, the partners in the coalition in Phnom Penh, Hun Sen and Norodom Rannaridh, were feuding openly. To bolster their own positions and to undermine each other, they competed for defectors from the Red Khmer. Hun Sen was luckier. In August 1996 Ieng Sary abandoned more than forty years of radicalism and defected to Hun Sen on the conditions that he receive a royal pardon and could remain in his fiefdom in Pailin. Talking with journalists, human rights workers, and scholars over the next twelve months, he adroitly distanced himself from the horrors of the DK regime. Then was then, he said repeatedly. Now is now. Troops sent from the Red Khmer stronghold of Anlong Veng to attack him deserted en route. Over the next two months, the Red Khmer lost thousands of seasoned followers and two of their three principal base areas. As the movement imploded, Pol Pot moved against Ta Mok (who had become second in command, replacing Nuon Chea, in 1995), Nuon Chea, and Son Sen, accusing them of contacts "with the Vietnamese" (i.e., Hun Sen) and placing them under house arrest in Ta Mok's former headquarters in Anlong Veng.[41]

At that point, Pol Pot attempted to form a new movement, with new associates, including a military cadre named Saroeun who had fallen out with Ta Mok in 1996. Using these new subordinates, Pol Pot embarked on his long march into the past. "Because Pol Pot had his own problems with national society and international society," the military cadre Khem Nguon explained to Nate Thayer in July, "he continually led the movement into darkness, into a black hole from which there was no way out."[42]

By the middle of 1997, Pol Pot had run out of time and space. His last few weeks in command were terrifying, and his behavior blotted out the image of easy-going charisma that he had cultivated, largely by operating in secret, for so long. Saroeun, presumably acting on his orders, murdered several members of an unarmed delegation sent from Phnom Penh in February 1997 by FUNCINPEC, seeking allies. Saroeun also had "about twenty" cadre murdered at Anlong Veng and saw to it that the houses of people suspected of loyalty to Ta Mok were burned down.

On June 9, 1997, at midnight, Pol Pot ordered Saroeun and some followers to assassinate Son Sen, whom Pol Pot suspected of contacting "the Vietnamese" via family members connected with the CPP. The brutal murders of Son Sen, his wife, and several relatives, including small children—fourteen people in all—angered cadre at Anlong Veng who had not yet taken sides in the feuding at the top. "After seeing the bodies," Ta Mok loyalist Khem Nguon told Nate Thayer in July, "all our comrades, the entire movement in Anlong Veng, saw that Pol Pot's action in killing Son Sen was improper, wrong, and barbarous." Along with Ta Mok and Nuon Chea, fence-sitters like Khem Nguon could be next. Opposition to Pol Pot's actions began to coalesce at Anlong Veng, and military units hitherto loyal to him deserted to Ta Mok. On June 13, Pol Pot fled with his family and a handful of supporters. Unable to walk any distance, he was carried in a green Chinese-issue army hammock, slung on a bamboo pole. The group was recaptured on June 16. Pol Pot was "near death." On June 17 Red Khmer Radio denounced him as a traitor.[43]

The next ten months were all that remained of his life. Ironically, he was more frequently on view in this period than at any time since the 1970s—first at a show trial staged by Ta Mok at Anlong Veng on July 25 and later in three interviews forced onto him by his captors with the American journalist Nate Thayer, Thai newspapermen, and a Cambodian correspondent.

Toward the end of June, after Pol Pot had been captured, FUNCINPEC officials renewed the negotiations with Ta Mok that the deposed leader had struggled to prevent. The prospect of Ta Mok's hardened forces arrayed alongside troops loyal to FUNCINPEC seems to have unnerved Hun Sen. On July 5–6 he presided over a brutal coup in the capital and elsewhere in which over a hundred FUNCINPEC members were killed and the royalist party was effectively removed from power.

In this confusing context, a bizarre spectacle took place at Anlong Veng when Pol Pot and three of his associates were brought before a people's tribunal, charged with treason. The American journalist Nate Thayer, who had cultivated contacts with the Red Khmer for several years, was invited to the event, accompanied by a television cameraman. It seems likely that the Red Khmer remnants hoped that by putting Pol Pot on trial, and allowing Thayer to film it, they could attract international support, but as Thayer wrote later, "the carefully orchestrated performance evoked the image of a grainy black-and-white film clip from China's cultural revolution" and recordings of the trial indicate that the occasion was a vintage piece of Red Khmer theater. As the crowd shouted slogans such as "Defeat for the contemptible traitors! Defeat! Defeat!" and "Defeat for the traitor Pol Pot, whose hands are soiled with blood!" in the open-air meeting hall, Thayer focused on the accused: "Slumped in a simple wooden chair, grasping a long bamboo cane and a rattan fan, an anguished old man, frail and struggling to maintain his dignity, was watching his life crumble in utter, final defeat."[44]

Unsurprisingly, perhaps, Pol Pot was not accused of any crimes committed in the 1970s or 1980s in which many of those in the audience and among his accusers were implicated. Instead, he was charged with murdering Son Sen, with taking people's property, ordering their houses burned down, and urging his exhausted followers into an open-ended war. These activities drew accusations dredged up from slogans used for the Red Khmer's opponents: "barbarous," "fascist," "narrow-minded," and "corrupt."

The former leader of the Khmer Rouge, Pol Pot, is led to a seat by a Khmer soldier at his trial in the Cambodian jungle on July 25, 1997, during which he was denounced as the mass murderer of his own people. Copyright 1997 Nate Thayer, and Tom Keller & Associates LLC.

Throughout the trial, as representatives of different "strata" put the case against him, Pol Pot never looked at his accusers and was never asked to speak. His silence as the accusations flowed over him eerily recalled his proud refusal to rebut Le Duan in Hanoi in 1965 and his years of taciturnity as he consolidated his power. When the trial was over, he was helped to his feet and guided, walking with difficulty, to a white Toyota van.

If it were not for what had happened in the 1970s, the brutal final months of his time in power, and the interviews he gave before his death, it would be tempting to close his biography at this point, with the sight of a frail old man stumbling off into what were to be ten months of closely guarded isolation. The ferocity of his actions in 1996–1997, however, suggests that his conduct in the 1970s, although concealed from view, had been similarly ruthless. Son Sen was not the first of his colleagues he had ordered killed. His capacity for terror, in fact, may have done as much to hold the Red Khmer together as did his genteel charisma and revolutionary zeal. The interviews, in turn, allow us to overhear him sifting through the ashes of his career, still seeking a place in history.

Thayer returned to Anlong Veng in mid-October 1997 and was granted two hours alone with Pol Pot and an interpreter—the first interview that

Pol Pot sits and listens as he is denounced as a murderer of his countrymen at a trial in the Cambodian jungle on July 25, 1997, in proceedings that found him guilty and sentenced him to life under house arrest. Copyright 1997 Nate Thayer, and Tom Keller & Associates LLC.

Brother Number One had given anybody since 1979. Thayer's questions pin-pointed the DK era. "As you know," he said, "most of the world thinks that you're responsible for the deaths of hundreds of thousands of innocent Cambodians who didn't deserve to suffer." Pol Pot replied: "I'm going to reply. I'm going to tell you clearly. I would like to tell you that I came to carry out the struggle, not to kill people. Even now, and you can look at me, am I a savage person? My conscience is clear."

Thayer pressed on, asking Pol Pot to acknowledge that he had "made very serious mistakes" during his time in power. Pol Pot replied deftly, in a schoolmasterish fashion: "There are two sides to it, as I told you. There's what we did wrong, and what we did right. The mistake is that we did some things against the people . . . but the other side, as I told you, is that without our struggle there would be no Cambodia right now."

After securing what he thought was his place in history, Pol Pot was more interested in talking about his illness and his family and about his times in

Pol Pot on his way to his interview with journalist Nate Thayer in October 1997. Copyright 1997 Nate Thayer and Tom Keller & Associates LLC.

Pol Pot is escorted away from the interview with Nate Thayer in October 1997 in Anlong Veng, Cambodia. Copyright 1997 Nate Thayer, and Tom Keller & Associates LLC.

Paris and Yugoslavia than about his time in power. He told Thayer about his stroke in 1995, his boredom under house arrest. He mentioned his daughter fondly but seemed prepared to die. When the interview ended, he said, "I feel very, very tired," but could not resist a parting sentence, as he was helped into the Toyota van. "I want you to know," he said, "that everything I did, I did for my country." Perhaps as he drove away, another Red Khmer adage occurred to him, one that cadre had used with the movement's enemies. "The wheel of history turns relentlessly," it runs. "Don't put your hand or foot in it or they will surely be cut off."[45]

Over the next few months, Pol Pot's health declined, and so did the fortunes of the people holding him prisoner. In March government forces drove the Red Khmer out of Anlong Veng into a makeshift base, nine miles away, just inside Cambodia from Thailand. Pol Pot lived, under guard, in a roughly built three-room house.

On April 15, 1998, he tuned in as usual at 8:00 P.M. to the Khmer language broadcast of the Voice of America. The lead story was a report, sourced to Nate Thayer, that his captors had decided to turn him over to a tribunal to face charges of crimes against humanity. The effect of the broadcast may have been fatal. On April 16, after Pol Pot had died, Ta Mok described the sequence of events to Nate Thayer: "He was sitting in his chair waiting for the car to come. But he felt tired. His wife asked him to take a rest. He lay down on his bed. His wife heard a gasp of air. It was the sound of dying. When she touched him he had already passed away. It was at 10:15 last night."[46]

Pol Pot's body was shown to journalists on April 16 and 17, twenty-three years to the day after the Red Khmer had marched triumphantly into Phnom Penh. On April 18, he was cremated beneath a pile of rubbish and personal possessions in a jungle clearing 500 yards inside Cambodia. No senior figures attended the cremation; neither did his wife or daughter. A Red Khmer cadre spoke to reporters after the ceremony was over. "Most people are happy because Pol Pot is finished," he said. "There is no more Khmer Rouge, no more bad reputation."[47]

Speaking to a Khmer reporter from Radio Free Asia on April 17, Ta Mok delivered a more brutal epitaph. "Pol Pot has died," he said, "like a ripe papaya. No one killed him, no one poisoned him. Now he's finished, he has no power, he has no rights, he is no more than cow shit. Cow shit is more important than him. We can use it for fertilizer."[48]

Pol Pot died in the sort of ignominy he had inflicted on millions of Khmer, under conditions almost as dehumanized as those encountered by his victims. It was rough justice, and at his death he was difficult to mourn.

What was his legacy? What had he looked for, and what had he accomplished in his years in power? A vision like his—of an autarkic, all-powerful Cambodia—has probably flickered in the minds of other Cambodian leaders since the decline of Angkor in the fifteenth century. Some of them had succumbed to it and had sought patrons (and clients) who could help them bring the vision to life. Others, the majority perhaps, weighed the vision against Cambodia's resources, the cost of leaping into the dark, and their own mundane priorities. In post-Angkorean Cambodia, antiheroic behavior for leaders and ordinary people alike made sense. One price of antiheroism—and this, for a time, played into the Communists' hands—was a stoic or resentful acceptance of hierarchies that paid no attention to "lesser" people except insofar as they could serve and feed the rich and powerful.

Pol Pot belongs among the visionary leaders of Cambodian history. At some stage in his life—perhaps in Paris, perhaps earlier—he reacted against the subservience and quietude of the Cambodian people. The royal family's indolence depressed him. His distress at Cambodia's dependence on Vietnam and France was probably genuine; he shared it with other Cambodian intellectuals at the time. In the early 1950s he came to see communism as a set of empowering and liberating techniques that could be applied to Cambodia to remove the handicaps of hierarchy, injustice, and subservience. The crucial role to be played by intellectuals like himself in this process meant that the actual priorities of Cambodia's poor, which would have centered around their families, their religion, and their leisure time, were disregarded for the sake of supposedly larger goals. In Saloth Sar's case, the vision of society seems to have been colored by a more personal one. He probably saw the Communist movement as an avenue through which he could find and express his personal identity, partly in terms of exercising power over others, so as to control the future.

The personal cost of these choices for Pol Pot is impossible to assess. Between the 1960s and the mid 1980s, as far as we can tell, he rejected the comforts of family life. At many stages in his career, particularly after 1975, he rejected compromises and consensus. Although in 1981 he was almost in tears because he had "trusted too many people," he sent hundreds of people he had worked with to their deaths, and toward the end of his life, aside from his wife and daughter, he probably trusted no one at all. He never stepped from the path he chose to follow in the 1950s and never spoke in detail about the price the Cambodian people paid to be subordinated to his vision of Cambodia and, after 1977, his abiding hostility toward Vietnam. Altering or abandoning his vision was impossible for Pol Pot. Perhaps in his final years he was fearful of the consequences—psychological and physical (in terms of his safety)—of any sweeping admission of responsibility or guilt. Self-pity, pride, and self-deception kept him from confronting what he had done and what had happened to Cambodia in the process. Whatever he thought in private, he told Nate Thayer—and thereby "history"—that his conscience was clear.

Foreign powers who exploited his vanity for their own reasons bear a responsibility for much of the suffering in Cambodia and among Cambodian refugees in Thailand and elsewhere after 1979. So do the Red Khmer, who put Pol Pot's visionary notions into practice after 1975 and through accident or design sent hundreds of thousands of their fellow citizens to their deaths. Many of these men and women have said that they were obeying the "organization," and Pol Pot himself has suggested that the violence, like everything else, was a response to revolutionary imperatives and pressures on the country from abroad.

In the end, however, the man who died on the Cambodian frontier in 1998 must be held responsible for what happened in Cambodia after April 1975. Perhaps, as he sat at night in his clearing in the forest, he had a faint perception (or a bleak, horrifying vision) of the sufferings he had inflicted. Perhaps he did not. He told his bodyguard that from time to time he was depressed. Was this because of what he had done, or because everything he'd done had failed? There is no way of telling, although in his last interviews self-pity seemed to outweigh self-knowledge. The story of his life traced his submission to a vision of history, of Cambodia, and of himself, where "personal responsibility," like so much else, was burnt away in the exigencies of revolutionary transformation and holding on to power.

We are left with the ashes of an old man in a clearing in the forest, with the country that he damaged so severely, and with the memories of his time in power that haunt survivors on a daily basis. Pol Pot blamed the failure of the revolution on others. Perhaps he was right. Perhaps he did trust too many people. Perhaps his vision was too incandescent for others to accomplish. The failure of the revolution, however, like his ignominious death, is not the point. As his life came to an end, this seventy-three-year-old man was alone with the fact, whether he realized it or not, that because of his inhuman policies and his unswerving love of power, more than a million Cambodians, or one in seven, died in less than four years, pointlessly and often in great pain.

Chronology

1925	Saloth Sar born in village of Prek Sbauv, Kompong Thom province, French Protectorate of Cambodia.
1927	King Sisowath Monivong crowned king of Cambodia.
1930	Indochina Communist party (ICP) founded in Hong Kong. Until 1950s, membership almost entirely Vietnamese.
1937	Khmer-language newspaper *Nagara Vatta* (Angkor Wat) founded in Phnom Penh.
	Saloth Sar enrolls in Ecole Miche, a private primary school in a Phnom Penh.
1940	France defeated by Germany. New, neutral government takes office in Vichy.
1941	Franco-Thai War. Thai assume control of two Cambodian provinces. Cambodian king, Sisowath Monivong, dies. Saloth Sar's sister, Saroeun, one of the king's concubines, is at his deathbed. Monivong's nineteen-year-old grandson, Norodom Sihanouk, chosen by French, replaces him.
	Japanese troops take up positions in much of Indochina. French retain administrative control.
1942	Anti-French demonstration in Phnom Penh. Instigators miscalculate Japanese support and are arrested by French.
	Saloth Sar enrolls as a boarder in Collège Sihanouk in Kompong Cham.
1945	French administrators are imprisoned throughout Indochina and Japanese encourage local rulers to declare independence. King Sihanouk does so. In May exiled nationalist leader Son Ngoc Thanh returns to Cambodia and becomes foreign minister.
	After coup in Thanh's favor on eve of Japanese surrender, Thanh acts as prime minister before French return to Cambodia in force and arrest him.
	After spearheading independence movement in Vietnam, ICP ostensibly dissolves in interests of fostering united front. Party in fact remains clandestinely in existence.
1946	French permit Cambodians to draft a constitution and form political parties. One of these, the Democrats, attracts wide support.

In northern Vietnam, fighting breaks out between French troops and Vietnamese forces led by clandestine ICP under Ho Chi Minh. First Indochina War begins.

1947 Saloth Sar graduates from Collège Sihanouk. In Phnom Penh he meets Ieng Sary; the two work as volunteers in Democrats' election campaign.

1948 Sar fails entrance examination to Lycée Sisowath and enrolls in Ecole Technique in Phnom Penh.

1949 Sar awarded scholarship to study radio-electricity in France; he reaches Paris in September.

Communist regime takes power in China.

1950 Korean war breaks out.

From Paris Sar spends a month as a volunteer worker in Yugoslavia.

Ieng Sary arrives in Paris and introduces Sar to leading Khmer intellectual, Keng Vannsak.

1951 Supposedly "national" Communist parties are founded in Cambodia, Laos, and Vietnam. Inspired by Vietnamese, who prepare statutes for them, these parties, whose existence is kept secret from outsiders, back up Vietnamese war of national liberation.

In Paris Sar moves to apartment in rue Letellier and begins attending Marxist discussions convened by Keng Vannsak. Others in group include Ieng Sary, Mey Mann, Thiounn Mumm, Son Sen, Rath Samoeun, and Hou Youn.

In August several Khmer Marxists in France (but not Saloth Sar) attend Communist-sponsored youth festival in Berlin and learn about Khmer People's Revolutionary party (KPRP).

1952 Sihanouk, supported by French, dissolves Democrat-dominated National Assembly in Phnom Penh. Move angers radical students in France. Writing as "Original Khmer," Saloth Sar publishes an article attacking royalty in Cambodia.

Sihanouk launches Royal Crusade for Independence, stealing initiative from Democrats in Cambodia.

Sar's scholarship is withdrawn for academic reasons. He lingers in Paris for several months and volunteers to seek information in Cambodia about Communist-led resistance there. In this period he joins the French Communist party.

1953 Sar returns to Phnom Penh. After several months testing Thanhist and other noncommunist alternatives, he joins a Vietnamese-Khmer unit on the Vietnamese border and becomes a member of the ICP. He meets his future mentor, Cambodian cadre Tou Samouth.

French grant independence to Cambodia but retain command over French troops still in country.

1954 Geneva Conference imposes political settlement of First Indochina War. For Cambodia, provisions include national elections within a year. Over 1,000 Communist-affiliated Khmer guerrillas are evacuated to newly established Communist state in northern Vietnam.

	Saloth Sar returns to Phnom Penh, goes into hiding using a pseudonym, and works to support radical candidates in Cambodian elections.
1955	Sihanouk abdicates the throne and forms political movement aimed at dissolving political parties. Democrats, who had hoped to win elections, thrown into disarray.
	In rigged elections, Sihanouk's Sangkum movement sweeps all seats. Democrats and Communist-front party, Pracheachon, draw over 100,000 votes. Saloth Sar works for these two parties, from concealment.
1956	Saloth Sar takes up career teaching at private collège in Phnom Penh; marries Khieu Ponnary, a teacher at the Lycée Sisowath; works secretly as a Communist militant alongside Tou Samouth, Nuon Chea, Ieng Sary, and a handful of others. During this period, Communists in Cambodia operate as members of an unnamed party.
1959	Ostensible leader of clandestine party, Sieu Heng, defects to the government, abandons radicalism.
1960	Probably under orders from Vietnam, twenty-one Khmer radicals meet secretly for three days in Phnom Penh to form the Workers' party of Kampuchea (WPK); newly formed Central Committee includes Tou Samouth (secretary), Nuon Chea, Saloth Sar, and Ieng Sary, among others.
	Sihanouk's father, Suramarit, named king in 1955, dies; Sihanouk becomes chief of state.
	National Liberation Front (NLF) founded in South Vietnam as political arm of struggle aimed at dislodging pro-American South Vietnamese regime.
1962	Tou Samouth disappears, presumably killed by Sihanouk's police; several members of Pracheachon imprisoned; Saloth Sar becomes acting secretary of Central Committee, bypassing more senior candidate, Nuon Chea.
1963	When their names appear on a list of supposed "Reds" published by Sihanouk's government, Saloth Sar, Ieng Sary, and Son Sen—all members of WPK Central Committee—flee to eastern Cambodia. Nuon Chea, not named by Sihanouk, stays behind in capital. Before leaving Phnom Penh, Sar is named secretary of WPK Central Committee.
	South Vietnamese president Ngo Dinh Diem is overthrown and assassinated; U.S. president John F. Kennedy is assassinated three weeks later.
	Sihanouk ends U.S. military aid program and seeks rapprochement with Vietnamese Communists and "neutral" solution to Second Indochina War, which had broken out in 1960.
1964	Saloth Sar spends year in "Office 100," a Vietnamese-controlled base located sometimes inside Cambodia, sometimes over the border in Vietnam.

1965   As Vietnam War intensifies, Saloth Sar and a WPK delegation visit
         Hanoi, where Sar presents WPK's political program to his Viet-
         namese counterparts. The text is sharply criticized by the Viet-
         namese for its failure to stress international factors.
         U.S. combat troops begin landing in Vietnam.
         Sihanouk makes secret agreement with Vietnamese Communists, al-
         lowing them to station troops in Cambodia in lightly populated
         areas in east.

1966   Cultural Revolution inaugurated by Mao Zedong in China.
         Saloth Sar embarks from Hanoi on a visit to China. After his rough
         treatment in Vietnam, he is comparatively warmly received and
         befriended by the former head of Mao's secret police, K'ang
         Sheng.
         Sar returns to Cambodia via Hanoi, secretly changes name of WPK
         to Communist party of Kampuchea (CPK). Office 100 shifts to re-
         mote northeastern province of Ratanakiri.
         For first time since 1955, National Assembly elected from slate of
         candidates not handpicked by Sihanouk; assembly names Lon Nol
         as prime minister; Sihanouk is enraged.

1967   Peasant uprising against Sihanouk regime breaks out at Samlaut in
         northwest and is savagely repressed. In the aftermath of the re-
         pression, CPK decides to inaugurate a policy mixing armed and
         political struggle. Throughout the year, Sihanouk continues re-
         pression of local Communists.

1968   On the eve of the Vietnamese Communist Tet offensive in Vietnam,
         CPK unit overruns government post in Battambang and captures
         several weapons. Incident later celebrated as inaugurating armed
         struggle.

1969   Fearing further Communist inroads, Sihanouk renews diplomatic re-
         lations with the United States. Fighting between his army units
         and CPK guerrillas continues in the northeast.
         Toward end of year, Saloth Sar visits Hanoi for consultations; he is
         away from Cambodia for six months.

1970   Sihanouk voted out of office by the National Assembly while he is
         visiting the USSR. Prince proceeds to Beijing, where he pledges to
         fight on. Vietnamese prime minister, Pham Van Dong, accompa-
         nied by Saloth Sar, flies in to offer support. Prince agrees to form a
         United Front government in exile to overthrow the pro-American
         regime established by Lon Nol.
         U.S. and South Vietnamese forces briefly invade eastern Cambodia.
         Vietnamese Communist forces retreat to the west. CPK guerrillas,
         claiming they are loyal to Sihanouk, gain thousands of supporters.
         Saloth Sar returns from Vietnam and sets up his headquarters in rural
         Kompong Thom.
         Lon Nol declares that Cambodia has become a republic. His forces
         are beaten in several engagements with the Vietnamese.

1971   Trained by Vietnamese and by Cambodian cadre brought from
            northern Vietnam, CPK forces gain combat experience. Lon Nol
            offensive (Chenla II) is smashed toward end of year.

1972   At Paris peace talks between U.S. and Vietnam, Vietnamese agree to
            a cease-fire. They also plan to withdraw their forces from Cambo-
            dia. News alarms CPK leadership, who refuse to honor a cease-fire
            and become resentful at being abandoned by the Vietnamese.

1973   U.S. bombers drop tens of thousands of tons of bombs on CPK posi-
            tions, stall CPK offensive on Phnom Penh, inflict thousands of
            civilian casualties, and force tens of thousands into cities. Bombing
            stops in August under pressure from U.S. Congress.

            During bombing, Sihanouk visits northern Cambodia and Angkor
            Wat and is hypocritically welcomed by CPK leaders, who have no
            intention of allowing him any political power. Socialist measures,
            including collectivization of agriculture, adopted in some areas un-
            der CPK control.

1974   As Lon Nol regime approaches collapse, CPK "storming attack" on
            Phnom Penh is beaten back.

1975   CPK offensive begins January 1. Floating mines in Mekong stop
            river traffic bringing rice and ammunition to Phnom Penh.

            In March, Lon Nol flies into exile. U.S. Embassy evacuates its per-
            sonnel.

            April 17, CPK forces occupy Phnom Penh and Battambang. Inhabi-
            tants of all cities ordered into countryside to take up agricultural
            work.

            Saigon falls to Vietnamese Communists three weeks later.

            When city is empty, Saloth Sar returns—after twelve-year absence.

            "Revolutionary Organization" takes power in Cambodia. Radical
            measures (abolition of money, markets, private property; closing of
            monasteries and schools) take effect at once.

            In secret discussions with Vietnamese, Cambodians refuse to negoti-
            ate their frontier, fearful that Vietnamese will adjust sea frontiers
            to profit from known petroleum deposits offshore.

1976   Constitution of Democratic Kampuchea (DK) proclaimed. Prime
            minister, announced in April, is a "rubber plantation worker"
            called Pol Pot. Sihanouk resigns as chief of state and spends next
            two-and-a-half years under house arrest in Phnom Penh.

            DK national security police open their interrogation and torture fa-
            cility in the Phnom Penh suburb of Tuol Sleng.

            Four Year Plan introduced to CPK cadre.

            Mao Zedong dies in China. At memorial ceremony, Pol Pot admits
            for first time that Democratic Kampuchea follows Marxist-Lenin-
            ist ideology. CPK's existence still concealed.

            Pleading ill health, Pol Pot "resigns" as prime minister and is replaced
            temporarily by Nuon Chea. Almost immediately, purges begin
            against veteran members of CPK thought to be pro-Vietnamese.

1977	Hostilities, probably instigated by Democratic Kampuchea, break out along frontier between DK and Vietnamese forces.
	CPK purges in first half of the year wipe out most intellectuals in the party, who are accused of CIA affiliations.
	Just before state visit to Beijing, Pol Pot reveals existence of CPK in long speech setting out its history; speech says nothing about purges in party or about hostilities with Vietnam.
	Photographs of Pol Pot in China and biographical information he provides allow Cambodia watchers to identify him as Saloth Sar.
	Pol Pot feted in China as ally against "revisionist" (pro-Soviet) Vietnamese. China promises military aid. Meanwhile, fighting between Vietnamese and DK forces intensifies.
	Vietnamese army invades and occupies much of eastern Cambodia for two months.
	On December 31, Democratic Kampuchea breaks off diplomatic relations with Vietnam.
1978	Purges expand to include cadre in eastern zone, where much of fighting with Vietnam occurred. Hostilities continue.
	Democratic Kampuchea struggles to "open up," welcoming some state visitors and sympathetic journalists. On several occasions, Pol Pot allows himself to be interviewed.
	In December, Vietnamese launch major offensive.
1979	Pol Pot sends Sihanouk to the United Nations to argue DK case.
	Phnom Penh falls to Vietnamese. Pol Pot escapes to northwest. Vietnamese forces occupy most of country following blitzkrieg attack.
	Chinese and Thai agree to support Democratic Kampuchea. Thousands of DK soldiers find shelter along Thai border.
	People's Republic of Kampuchea (PRK), a regime set in place by Vietnam, stages trial of Pol Pot and Ieng Sary and condemns them to death.
	In December, before resigning as prime minister, Pol Pot gives his last public interview.
1981	CPK Central Committee announces party's dissolution, but none of its top members resign and party's infrastructure, especially in army, remains in place. Significantly, Pol Pot retains military posts, as in 1970–1975.
1982	Coalition government of Democratic Kampuchea formed, consisting of anticommunist factions, Sihanouk, and Democratic Kampuchea. Coalition retains DK seat at United Nations and accepts military aid from China and some Association of Southeast Asian Nations (ASEAN) powers.
1983–1987	Vietnamese forces control military balance of power. Pol Pot, based in Thailand, occasionally seeks medical treatment in China.
1985	On the occasion of his sixtieth birthday, Pol Pot "resigns" from all his positions. In fact, he remains powerful as the secretary of the CPK and as a teacher.

Pol Pot remarries (date uncertain) and his second wife, of peasant background, bears him a daughter.

1988   Vietnamese withdraw forces from Cambodia. Negotiations for political settlement gather momentum.

1991   A comprehensive settlement, signed in Paris, provides for interim government in Cambodia under United Nations supervision. In negotiations in Thailand leading up to Paris meeting, DK delegation seeks Pol Pot's advice by telephone on several occasions before agreeing to concessions. When DK representatives Son Sen and Khieu Samphan return briefly to Phnom Penh, Sen reports secretly to "87" (Pol Pot) about conditions there but claims in public that Pol Pot has "ceased all his duties."

1992   DK faction refuses UN request that it disarm, ceases cooperating with UN Transitional Authority. Son Sen demoted. DK spokesmen claim that government in Phnom Penh is still controlled by Vietnamese.

1993   DK faction boycotts national elections, which are won by royalist party (FUNCINPEC). Results contested by CPP, Hun Sen's party, and compromise is reached whereby Cambodia is governed by a CPP-FUNCINPEC dyarchy, presided over by two prime ministers.

1994   CPK introduces harsh policies in zones under its control, aiming to reignite revolutionary fervor. Policies backfire as thousands of supporters defect.

1997   Ieng Sary defects to the Hun Sen government in Phnom Penh.
Two months later, Hun Sen stages a coup d'état against FUNCINPEC. Soon afterwards, Son Sen and several members of his family are murdered under Pol Pot's orders.
Pol Pot is purged by rivals in the CPK hierarchy and put on trial for treason in a Khmer Rouge encampment. Trial is filmed by U.S. journalist Nate Thayer, who interviews Pol Pot in October.

1998   Pol Pot dies on April 16 of heart failure and assorted ailments in Khmer Rouge encampment on the Thai-Cambodia border

Appendix 1:
Non Suon's Biography of Pol Pot

What follows is drawn from the Tuol Sleng confession of the veteran CPK cadre Non Suon (alias Chey Suon), who was arrested in November 1976 while serving as Democratic Kampuchea's secretary of agriculture. Non Suon, of peasant background, had joined the Khmer Issarak in the 1940s and was a prominent member of the Pracheachon movement after independence. Arrested by Sihanouk's police in 1962, he was released in 1970 and immediately joined the maquis. In the course of composing his confession extracted at Tuol Sleng, Non Suon wrote biographical sketches of several high-ranking party members. The relative accuracy of the sketches suggests either that he had access to written autobiographies circulated in the upper reaches of the CPK or, as is more likely, that he had attended self-criticism sessions in the 1970s where high-ranking party cadre provided autobiographical data. Although Non Suon's assessment of several other CPK figures, such as Ta Mok and Son Sen, are openly critical, his assessment of "Brother Secretary," given the circumstances under which it was written, is unsurprisingly supportive, although it is clear that Non Suon saw little of him after his own imprisonment in the 1960s.

The sketch of Pol Pot was composed on November 21, 1976, almost a year before Pol Pot himself gave out any biographical data about himself. The translation is by Steve Heder.

The Brother Secretary of the party lived in a middle [peasant] family in Kompong Thom. He studied at a technical school in Kompong Cham province. In 1945, when the Japanese moved into the country (sic) he returned to live with his family in Kompong Thom. During 1949 or 1950—I can't remember exactly—he went to further his education in France. In 1954 he returned from France and joined the armed struggle movement in the Eastern Zone. When the cease-fire took place in Cambodia he returned in late 1954 to live in Phnom Penh in order to carry out the clandestine struggle movement.

In Phnom Penh, Elder Brother fulfilled major party assignments, such as:

1. He assembled progressive elements in the city and enrolled them in the Democrat Party in order to attack and eliminate . . . the Son Ngoc Thanhists the Democrat Party. The diehards fled and joined the Sangkum. Only the

diehard Um Sim and some of his lapdogs remained and continued their activities [in support of Son Ngoc Thanh].

2. He made a crucial contribution to the Pracheachon Group's formulation of its statutes and its immediate political program. He also made arrangements to insure that the Democrat Party did not put forth candidates for election in the same constituencies as the Pracheachon Group. As the balloting drew near there were exchanges of opinion with him about stepping aside in favor of the Democrat Party in those instances when the Democrat Party was stronger than the Pracheachon Group, so as to win in the overall tally against the Sangkum Reastr Niyum.

3. He created the newspapers *Democracy, Worker, Friendship, Unity*, and others, which illuminated the path of political struggle for the people in the city and the countryside. At the same time he also created French-language newspapers.

4. He conducted agitation among students, intellectuals, workers, and laborers in the city in order to carry out strikes and uprisings opposing American imperialism and its lackeys such as Dap Chhuon, Sam Sary, and Son Ngoc Thanh, and in attacking the American Embassy.

Inside the party, the Brother Secretary fulfilled the following vital assignments:

He formulated the statutes of the Communist party of Kampuchea.
He formulated the strategic and tactical lines of the National Democratic revolution.
He formulated the united front policy of uniting forces.
He created the Communist Youth League of Kampuchea organization and the Democratic Women of Kampuchea organization.
He conducted brief or extended Party conferences and study sessions according to the time available for urban and rural cadres.

When he left for the bases [in 1963]:
In the countryside, Brother fought against subjugation by the revolutionary organization of Vietnam. He surmounted the hardship of the forests and mountains to fulfill revolutionary tasks, proceeding from a stance of independence-mastery and self-reliance. He conducted a civil war, starting with his bare hands and proceeding [to armed struggle] once we had weapons with which to attack the enemy. During the five year war [1970–1975] Brother fashioned many of the Party's lines: the military line, the economic line, the united front line, etc. He had a firm grasp on the Cambodian situation. . . .

When he lived in the city [i.e., before 1963] he did not live in comfort or abundance. Some of the time he taught by the hour in a private school in order to make profits for the revolution. Generally speaking, Brother Secretary lived in the most ordinary and common way, without any frivolity, carousing, or ostentation. It was his habit to wear nothing more [pretentious] than a short-sleeved shirt.

It was manifest from his origins and from his practical activities in the city and the countryside that he remained composed no matter what problem arose. He was able to resolve domestic and international contradictions correctly and well and was able to gather many friends while isolating the enemy. . . .

Brother Secretary of the Party is a forceful Party member politically, ideologically, and organizationally. He is the iron rudder of the ship of Kampuchea leading Kampuchea to its destiny of making socialist revolution and building socialism and advancing toward permanent communism in Kampuchea.

Appendix 2:
Khmer Personnel at
"Office 100," 1963–1966

1. *Om* (uncle) Pol: Pol Pot
2. *Bong* (elder sibling) Van (alias Penh): Ieng Sary
3. *Bong* Kham (alias Bong Ki, Bong Khieu): Son Sen
4. *Bong* Neu: Chan Chakrei?
5. *Bong* Phea: Ieng Thirith, wife of Ieng Sary
6. *Bong* At: Yun Yat, wife of Son Sen
7. *Pu* (uncle) Ya (aka Phu): Ney Saran, administrator of Office 100
8. *Bong* Pung: Keo Meas
9. *Bong* Tum: Siet Chhae
10. *Mit* (Comrade) Pang: Chhim Samauk
11. *Mit* Phoeun: identity unknown
12. *Mit* Ret: identity unknown
13. *Yey* (Aunt) Li: Im Naen, wife of Chou Chet

Working in the Printery

14. *Mit* Yon: identity unknown
15. Lin: Sok Knol

Working in the Cookhouse

16. Hul: identity unknown
17. Phon: identity unknown

Working in the Infirmary

18. *Mit* But: Kheang Sim Hon
19. Ing Chheng Im

Deputy Administrator Office 100

20. *Mit* Sdaong: identity unknown*

Undefined Tasks

21. *Mit* Yin: identity unknown
22. *Komar* (young man) Vung: identity unknown

* Nuon Chea, "History," identifies Sdaong as a bodyguard of Pol Pot.
Sources: Cornell Microfilm reels from S-21 archive 42.21, 53.27, 138.11, and 142.2.

Notes

Chapter One

1. See Ben Kiernan, *How Pol Pot Came to Power* (London, 1985; hereafter *HPP*), and other materials in Bibliographic Essay, pp. 243ff., and Ben Kiernan, *The Pol Pot Regime* (New Haven, 1995).

2. I refer especially to Nate Thayer's October 1997 interview with Pol Pot himself, summarized in Thayer, "Day of Reckoning," *Far Eastern Economic Review (FEER)*, October 30, 1997; the unpublished interviews with former Red Khmer cadre conducted since 1995 by David Ashley; and Stephen Heder's unpublished interviews with Ieng Sary and Mey Mann. I am grateful to Ashley and Heder for transcripts of their interviews and to Thayer for extensive conversations about his encounter with Pol Pot.

3. Before he fell from power in 1997, Pol Pot toyed with the idea of presiding over a biographical project that would, he hoped, secure his place in history. According to Nate Thayer (personal communication), he recruited a young Khmer Rouge cadre, Tep Kunnal, for the project and over several months Kunnal filled nine notebooks with data provided by his mentor. The notebooks, he told Thayer, were accidentally destroyed during the government assault on the Red Khmer base of Anlong Veng in 1998, shortly before Pol Pot died.

4. See David P. Chandler, *The Tragedy of Cambodian History: Politics, War, and Revolution Since 1945* (New Haven, Conn., 1991).

5. See François Ponchaud, "Social Change in the Vortex of Revolution," in Karl Jackson, ed., *Cambodia, 1975–1978: Rendezvous with Death* (Princeton, N.J., 1989); Soth Polin, "La diabolique douceur de Pol Pot," *Le Monde Diplomatique*, May 18, 1980; and Roger Normand, "At the Khmer Rouge School: The Teachings of Chairman Pol Pot," *Nation*, September 3, 1990.

Chapter Two

1. See U.S. Foreign Broadcast Information Service (hereafter FBIS), *Daily Reports*, October 4, 1978, and Nate Thayer, "My Education: How Saloth Sar Became Pol Pot," *FEER*, October 30, 1997, where Pol Pot insisted on a January 1925 birthdate: "January—I remember because my mother wrote it in chalk on the wall of the house, next to the cupboard."

2. According to Saloth Sar's older brother Loth Suong, one sister died in childbirth and two brothers died before 1975. Another brother, Saloth Chhay, died in the exodus from Phnom Penh in April 1975. Saloth Sar's given name means "white" in Khmer and may have been chosen because of his relatively light complexion.

3. Author's interviews with Tap Meak (February 1990), Loth Suong, and Suon Kaset Sokho (October 1987, May 1989, June 1990). After 1975, Meak was evacuated to Battambang and did not survive the Democratic Kampuchea period. Like Sar's other relatives, she enjoyed no special privileges at that time. (Youk Chhang's interview with Saloth Roeung, March 1997).

4. In his North Korean biography and in his later interview with Yugoslavian journalists, Pol Pot claimed to have been under monastic discipline for four years. His brother, however, was adamant about the shorter period.

5. James Gerrand, personal communication. See also Vu Can, *Kampuchea: The Nightmare Is Over* (Ho Chi Minh City, 1982), pp. 29–36. Saloth Sar's younger brother, Saloth Nhep, told Jon Swain, who interviewed him in Prek Sbauv in 1989, "As a child [Saloth Sar] was a lovely boy, very gentle"; and Christine Chameau, "Brother's Tears of Recollection and Resignation," *Phnom Penh Post*, April 24–May 7, 1998, a special issue commemorating Pol Pot's death. Saloth Nhep told Chameau that as a boy, Saloth Sar was "gentle and did not like to pick a fight with others. He was as nice as a girl."

6. See Khy Phanra, "La communauté vietnamienne au Cambodge à l'époque du protectorat français, 1863–1953" (Thesis, University of Paris, 1974). I am grateful to Thiounn Mumm for sending me a copy of this interesting study.

7. For visitors' impressions of Phnom Penh in the 1930s, see François de Croiset, *La côte de jade* (Paris, 1938), pp. 64–71; and Guy de Pourtalès, *Nous à qui rien n'appartient* (Paris, 1936), pp. 142ff. See also Pierre-Lucien Lamant, "Phnom Penh," in P. B. Lafont, ed., *La peninsule indochinoise: Etudes urbaines* (Paris, 1991), pp. 59–102.

8. On the ballet, interviews with Suon Kaset Sokho (1987–1990) and Eileen Blumenthal (1991).

9. Suon Kaset Sokho, who danced in the ballet in the 1950s, described the dancers' quarters—which she visited but never lived in—as a "rather hectic, filthy little village." Conditions were worse in Monivong's time.

10. See David P. Chandler, "Seeing Red: Perceptions of Cambodian History in Democratic Kampuchea," in David P. Chandler and Ben Kiernan, eds., *Revolution and Its Aftermath in Kampuchea* (New Haven, Conn., 1983), pp. 34–56.

11. See David P. Chandler, *A History of Cambodia* (Boulder, Colo., 1983; 2nd ed., updated 1996), Chapters 6 and 7.

12. For an astute analysis of this period, see Milton Osborne, *The French Presence in Cochinchina and Cambodia: Rule and Response* (Ithaca, N.Y., 1969).

13. See Benedict Anderson, *Imagined Communities* (London, 1982).

14. Some French authorities viewed the institute and its innovative director, Suzanne Karpelès, with suspicion. In the 1940s, many monks who had been affiliated with the institute joined Cambodia's embryonic Communist movement.

15. For a discussion of *Nagara Vatta*, see Bunchhan Mul, *Kuk Niyobay* [Political prison] (Phnom Penh, 1971). Monireth's remark is from author's interview with Sim Var (November 1987). *Nagara Vatta* ceased publication in July 1942, following the monks' demonstration and Pach Chhoeun's imprisonment (see below). See Ben Kier-

nan and Chanthou Boua, *Peasants and Politics in Kampuchea, 1942–1982* (London, 1982), pp. 114–126. Khieu Ponnary's early career from author's interviews with So Bun Hor (February 1989), Chheam Van (November 1987), and Suon Kaset Sokho (May 1988).

16. On Saloth Roeung, Youk Chhang's interview with her. For an analysis of the succession, see Milton Osborne, "King-Making in Cambodia," *Journal of Southeast Asian Studies* 4 (1973): 169–185; and Norodom Sihanouk, *Souvenirs doux et amers* (Paris, 1981), pp. 69–72.

17. Information on this period is drawn from author's interviews in January 1990 with Chhay Yat, Laeo Chheng Heat, and Major General Pel Nal, who all attended the Collège Sihanouk with Saloth Sar in the 1940s. See also Stephen Heder's unpublished interviews with Khieu Samphan's brother Khieu Seng Kim and with Khvan Siphan (1975). Heder recently analyzed Samphan's survival in Democratic Kampuchea, suggesting that he was heavily implicated in the Communist purges against intellectuals and other associates of Pol Pot in 1977–1978. See Stephen Heder, *Khieu Samphan and Pol Pot* (Clayton, Australia, 1991).

18. On Khvan Siphan, see interviews above and Heder's interviews of 1975. Siphan, originally a primary school teacher, later taught at lycées in Phnom Penh, became a school inspector, and served as a senator under the Khmer Republic. He died during the DK period. I am grateful to Justin Corfield for biographical data and for the information (from an anonymous source) that Saloth Sar played violin in the school orchestra.

19. On Sar's friendship with Lon Non, see author's interview with Chhay Yat. On Lon Non in 1975, see interviews with Chhay Yat and Pel Nal. Other students at the school during this time who later became prominent include Um Sim, the Khmer Republic's last ambassador to the United States, and Phung Ton, the rector of the Faculty of Law in Phnom Penh.

20. For details, see Chandler, *Tragedy*, Chapter 2.

21. See *Cambodge*, July 28, 1948. Many of those who sat with him at the examinations—e.g., Khieu Samphan, Kol Siphuong, and Sien An—proceeded to the lycée. In his interview with Yugoslavian journalists in 1978, Pol Pot said that his failure to get into a lycée led him toward a technical education. See FBIS, *Daily Reports*, April 22, 1978.

22. On Ieng Sary's early life, see author's interviews with Thach Ren (November 1986) and Pung Peng Cheng (April 1987).

23. On Prince Yuthevong, see author's interviews with Thonn Ouk, Son Sann, Chheam Van, and the late Sim Var.

24. On the constitution, author's interviews with Thonn Ouk (November 1986) and the late Sim Var (May 1988). Both men took part in the negotiations. On Ieng Sary's early career, see interviews with Keng Vannsak and Brigadier Thach Ren (a distant cousin) (November 1986), Sisowath Arayavady (June 1989), and Pung Peng Cheng (May 1988).

25. On this period in the history of Cambodian radicalism, see Kiernan, *HPP*, pp. 58ff.; and Chandler, *Tragedy*, Chapter 1.

26. According to Chheam Van, prime minister in 1948–1949, many of those selected for scholarships were of "mediocre" academic ability but enjoyed connections with the party (author's interview, November 1987). The Democrats were also in-

volved in arranging Ieng Sary's scholarship in 1950, after he had led a series of anti-French, pro-Democrat demonstrations followed by a strike at the Lycée Sisowath. Of the twenty students who sailed to France with Sar, about half pursued technical studies. Steve Heder's interview with Mey Mann, March 1997.

27. See Royaume de Cambodge, Ministère de l'Education, *Contrôle des étudiants boursiers: Carnet 1, France* (microfilm), Echols Collection, Cornell University Library, Ithaca, N.Y.

28. On the dinner celebration, see *Cambodge*, August 18, 1949. In *Cambodge*, September 2, 1949, Saloth Sor [sic] is listed as going to study at "the National Professional School in Limoges or Toulon." There is no evidence that he enrolled in either school. Instead, he went directly to Paris and stayed there for the next forty months.

Chapter Three

1. Two readable memoirs by former Communist militants are E. Leroy Ladurie, *Paris-Montpellier* (Paris, 1982); and Alain Besançon, *Une génération* (Paris, 1987). See also Dominique Dessanti, *Les staliniens* (Paris, 1975); Annie Kriegel, *The French Communists* (Chicago, 1972); and Jeanine Verdès-Leroux's penetrating study, *Au service du parti: Le parti communiste, les intellectuels, et la culture, 1944–1956* (Paris, 1986).

2. See Louis Malleret, *L'exotisme indochinoise dans la littérature française depuis 1860* (Paris, 1934), especially pp. 183–192. Penny Edwards's work in progress at Monash University makes a detailed study of French representations of "Cambodge" and "Angkor" in the colonial era. See also Bruno Dagens, *Angkor: La forêt de pierre* (Paris, 1989).

3. Royaume de Cambodge, Ministère de l'Education, *Contrôle des étudiants boursiers: Carnet 1, France*, provides information on Sar's arrival, departure, his failure to pass examinations, and his address in Paris.

4. Biographical information on Thiounn Mumm from author's interviews with him (May 1988, June 1989, February 1990). See also Kiernan, *HPP*, pp. 29–30; and Stephen Heder's unpublished interview with Thiounn Mumm (1980), which mentions his friendship with Saloth Sar.

5. From author's interviews with Keng Vannsak (October 1986, May 1987); and Kiernan, *HHP*, pp. 121–123, drawing on interviews with Vannsak.

6. From author's interview with Pierre Brocheux (May 1987). Brocheux joined the French Communist party as a lycée student in Paris in 1950.

7. See FBIS, *Daily Reports*, March 22, 1978, "Interview with Pol Pot." See also *Khmer nisut* [Khmer student] 11 (January 1951): 36 (I'm grateful to Thiounn Mumm for lending me a copy of this issue); and V. Vinterthaler, *In the Path of Tito* (Tunbridge Wells, U.K., 1972), pp. 218ff., describing the "self-management" reforms introduced by Tito in the summer of 1950.

8. *Khmer nisut* 11 (January 1951): 36. Ieu Yang returned to Cambodia in 1951 and supported Son Ngoc Thanh's abortive bid for power. Later he became a republican politician in Phnom Penh. *Le démocrate* (Phnom Penh), August 31, 1950, confirms the presence of "eighteen Cambodian students" in Yugoslavia. The enthusiasm of the article suggests that Sar and the others went to Zagreb with the Cambodian Democrats'

knowledge and approval. Keng Vannsak (author's interview, May 1987) said that Saloth Sar, whom he encountered in 1951, never mentioned his time in Yugloslavia.

9. For details, see Chandler, *Tragedy*, Chapter 3.

10. Michael Vickery, *Kampuchea* (London, 1986), pp. 60–62, and notes to these pages, pp. 182–183. See also Kiernan, *HPP*, pp. 83ff.; and Gareth Porter, "Vietnamese Communist Policy Toward Kampuchea, 1930–1970," in Chandler and Kiernan, eds., *Revolution and Its Aftermath in Kampuchea*, pp. 57–98.

11. Kiernan, *HPP*, p. 79, mentions this meeting. Nguyen Thanh Son's speech, in French, is in France, Service Historique des Armées de Terre (hereafter SHAT Archives), Chateau de Vincennes, 10H 284 (Divers Cambodge, 1949–1950). On Son, see Porter, "Vietnamese Communist Policy," p. 65. See also Khmer Peace Committee, *Khmer Armed Resistance* (n.p., 1952), which notes that "Toussamoth" [Tou Samouth, a colleague of Son's] is "an authoritative priest." Christopher Goscha's ongoing research will do much to clarify the relationships between the Vietnamese and Cambodian Communist movements in this period.

12. Pol Pot interview with Nate Thayer. "I was not a bad student," he told Thayer. "I was average . . . I studied just enough to keep my scholarship." Interestingly, Pol Pot, talking to Thayer, named no role models from this period. The room that Keng Vannsak found for him was at 31 rue Letellier. In 1996, Ieng Sary's protégé Suong Sikoeun referred to the quartier as "a nice area occupied by the children of good families" and said that "Pol Pot spent his time playing music and cards." House numbers have changed since 1951, but it is possible that the two-story structure at number 29 (with the Café Brazza on the ground floor) was "31" in the 1950s. I am grateful to Lionel Vairon for this detective work. Saloth Sar passed the room along to a former schoolmate at the Collège Sihanouk, Khieu Komar, in 1952. Keng Vannsak quotation from his wife (personal communication). Mey Mann quotation from *Asiaweek*, July 29, 1989, p. 17. Mann was interviewed in a DK refugee camp on the Thai-Cambodian border and again in Phnom Penh in 1997. Pierre Brocheux remembered him as a conscientious member of the CPF in Paris in the early 1950s.

13. See Elizabeth Becker, *When the War Was Over* (New York, 1986), p. 74; and author's interviews with Suon Kaset Sokho (May 1987). Ponnary returned home after her sister's wedding to resume her teaching career.

14. Steve Heder's interview with Mey Mann. On the discussion groups, see Kiernan, *HPP*, pp. 119ff.; author's interviews with Keng Vannsak and Thiounn Mumm; and François Debré, *Cambodge: La révolution de la forêt* (Paris, 1976), pp. 81ff.

15. Others affiliated with the group included Khieu Komar, Thiounn Prasith, Ok Sakun, and Kenthao de Monteiro. As a philologist, Keng Vannsak spent many years attempting to modernize the Khmer language by finding or coining terms appropriate to twentieth-century life. Although Vannsak failed to say so, it seems likely that another text discussed by the group would have been Stalin's *History of the Communist Party of the Soviet Union*, from which Saloth Sar may well have drawn some of his ideas about conspiracies inside the Cambodian Communist movement and the postrevolutionary continuation of class struggle. See Andrew G. Walder, "Cultural Revolutionary Radicalism: Variations on a Stalinist Theme," in William Joseph et al., eds., *New Perspectives on the Cultural Revolution* (Cambridge, Mass., 1990), pp. 41–62; and Robert C. Tucker, *Stalin: The Years in Power* (New York, 1990), pp. 530ff. Sar's reading of French Communist literature in Paris probably had suggested Stalin, rather than

Ho, as a role model. See E. H. Carr, "A Great Agent of History," in T. H. Rigby, ed., *Stalin* (Englewood Cliffs, N.J., 1966), pp. 133–142. A Cambodian who attended the study sessions but wished to remain anonymous suggested that the Cambodian-language meetings angered Vietnamese in the CPF who "wanted to control the Khmer."

16. Debré, *Cambodge*, p. 82.

17. Kiernan, *HPP*, p. 121; Marie-A. Martin, *Le mal cambodgien* (Paris, 1989), p. 105; and interviews with Keng Vannsak (May 1988) and Thiounn Mumm (February 1990). In 1997, Mey Mann told Steve Heder: "This was the first time that anyone in Paris had learned anything concrete" about the Issarak. "We were all operating in the dark. Our only source of information was through that Vietnamese delegation." Those who attended the conference included Hou Youn, Thiounn Prasith, Thiounn Mumm, and five others. The flag was resurrected in 1979 by the People's Republic of Kampuchea (PRK). In 1989 the lower half of the flag became blue (just as the "NLF" [National Liberation Front] flag in southern Vietnam was a North Vietnamese flag with its lower half blue). The five-towered yellow motif, perhaps a Khmerization of Vietnam's five-pointed star, remained the same. Debré, *Cambodge*, p. 84, reported that students returning from Berlin were even more action oriented than they had been before. According to Thiounn Mumm, "Saloth Sar did not go because he had been to Yugoslavia" (interview with Steve Heder, April 1980).

18. For a helpful chronology of events affecting the French Communist party in the early 1950s, see Dessanti, *Les Staliniens*, pp. 250–267. See also Philippe Robrieux, *Histoire du PCF*, 4 vols. (Paris, 1985–1990); and Irwin Wall, *French Communism in the Era of Stalin* (Westport, Conn., 1964), Chapter 5. On p. 119, Wall referred to 1949–1953 in the CPF as "years of blunder and vacillation." "Springtime" quotation from author's interview with Jacques Vergès (October 1987). Restaurant information from author's interview with Pierre Brocheux (May 1987).

19. From author's interview with Thiounn Mumm.

20. Khmer Peace Committee, *Khmer Armed Resistance*, p. 7, refers to the assassin as a "Khmer patriot."

21. See Chandler, *Tragedy*, pp. 57–61; and Kiernan, *HPP*, pp. 98ff.

22. Individuals radicalized by these events included Hu Nim and Vorn Vet in Cambodia (Kiernan, *HPP*, p. 118). Thonn Ouk, a prominent Democrat then in Paris, noted the radicalizing effect Sihanouk's coup had on Cambodian students there (author's interview, October 1987).

23. A French translation of the essay appears as an annex to Serge Thion and Ben Kiernan, *Khmers rouges!* (Paris, 1981), pp. 357–361. Keng Vannsak identified "Original Khmer" as Saloth Sar in conversations with Ben Kiernan. *Khmer daom* has overtones of ethnic authenticity and racial purity (author's interview with Khing Hoc Dy, October 1991), but this does not seem to be its overriding meaning. See Marie-A. Martin, *Khmer doeum* (Paris, 1997), a book about the Pear or Porr; and R. Baradat, "Le Samre ou Pear: Population primitive de l'ouest du Cambodge," *Bulletin de l'Ecole française d'Extrême Orient* 4 (1941). I am grateful to Vannsak for a copy of the original Khmer version. See also Serge Thion, "The Cambodian Idea of Revolution," in Chandler and Kiernan, eds., *Revolution and Its Aftermath in Kampuchea*, pp. 16–17.

24. Forty years later, Pol Pot was quoted in the *Bangkok Post* (February 22, 1993) as referring to Sihanouk as "more than 90 percent paranoid due to all sorts of hedonism, corruption, and debauchery." The Khmer wording is not available, but I suspect that

Pol Pot was not referring to paranoia so much as to a mental unbalance that he traced to Sihanouk's fondess for excess.

25. The word for "soldier" or "recruit" (transliterated here as *pol*) is spelled and pronounced differently in Khmer from "Pol," Saloth Sar's pseudonym. Intriguingly, Saloth Sar used the name "Pol" (or "Paul") on at least one occasion in Paris (author's interview with Keng Vannsak, May 1987). It is conceivable that the nickname dated from his time at Ecole Miche, where students, regardless of their religion, were given saints' names (like "Paul") by their Catholic teachers (Suon Kaset Sokho, personal communication). According to Thel Thong (personal communication), the name "Pol Pot is not unusual. 'Pol' is a common rural surname, and 'Pot' a widely used given name—like John Jones or Bill Smith."

26. Steve Heder's interview with Mey Mann, March 1997.

27. See Nayan Chanda, *Brother Enemy* (New York, 1986), p. 58. A 1973 history of the Cambodian Communist party asserted that in its early days, the party had included ten members of the Communist party of France. Saloth Sar was almost certainly one of them, but none had returned from France when the Cambodian Communist party was founded in 1951. Some of the others were Sien An, Rath Samouen, Sok Knol, Hou Youn, Mey Mann, and Ieng Sary.

28. Nearly all of Sar's formal training as a Communist, such as it was, occurred after his return to Cambodia in 1953. His mentors there would have been either Vietnamese or Cambodians who had received their training from the Vietnamese.

29. See Bruce Mazlish, *The Revolutionary Ascetic* (New York, 1976), especially pp. 92ff.

30. Debré, *Cambodge*, p. 86. This quotation suggests that Saloth Sar planned to model his personal style on that of Stalin rather than on those of other Communist leaders. For final quotation, Thayer, "Day of Reckoning."

Chapter Four

1. From Loth Suong's interviews with Stephen Heder (1981) and with author (1990).

2. Kiernan, *HPP*, pp. 122–123; and from author's interviews with Keng Vannsak (1986). In 1953 Sar probably still considered Son Ngoc Thanh a genuine nationalist. Steve Heder's interview with Saloth Chhay (March 1975). Chhay died under Democratic Kampuchea. In a November 1974 interview with the Australian journalist Niel Davis, Chantaraingsey, whom Saloth Sar may have known from his childhood, recalled that when Sar visited him in 1953, "he was already working with the Vietnamese." I am grateful to Steve Heder for his notes from these two interviews.

3. Chanda, *Brother Enemy*, p. 58. See also W. Burchett, *The China-Cambodia-Vietnam Triangle* (London, 1981), p. 54, which relies on another interview with Pham Van Ba.

4. For Pham Van Ba's recollection and the DK statement from 1980, see Kiernan, *HPP*, p. 123; and Khieu Thirith's complaint in 1981 in Becker, *When the War Was Over*, p. 91. See also Thirith's interview with Becker (October 1980), Echols Collection, Cornell University Library, Ithaca, N.Y., which mentions "Saloth Sar's sad experiences with the Viet Minh," and the confession of Meas Mon (Keo Samnang), which

tells of Mon's participation in 1953–1955 in a military unit on the border that was "half Vietnamese and half Khmer." (All confessions are in the Tuol Sleng Archives, Phnom Penh.)

5. Stephen Heder's manuscript interview with Chea Soth (1981); and Kiernan, *HPP*, p. 60. Chea Soth survived the Pol Pot period and became a minister in the PRK. In 1953 Tou Samouth held several military and political titles including chief of the territorial organization, assistant chief of the party cadre committee, and chief of the Issarak Front (see SHAT Archives, 10H 5613).

6. In his interview with Steve Heder, Mey Mann said that "Grandfather Tou established residence in a house in Tuol Svay Prey on a piece of land purchased by Saloth Sar." This part of the capital, where Saloth Sar taught school, later became infamous as the site of Democratic Kampuchea's interrogation and extermination center known at Tuol Sleng.

7. Vorn Vet's confession (typed version), p. 3, states that Saloth Sar brought Thuok into the Cambodian Communist party at the end of 1954.

8. Ibid.; Kiernan, *HPP*, pp. 154ff. Sien An, Rath Samoeun, and Yun Soeurn were purged under Democratic Kampuchea. See also Carlyle Thayer, *War by Other Means* (Sydney, 1989), pp. 16–17. Nuon Chea's draft history of the Communist party of Kampuchea, prepared in 1997 (hereafter "History") mentions a figure of 1,500–2,000 evacuees. I am grateful to Nate Thayer for a copy of this document, and to David Ashley for a translation.

9. From author's interview with Thiounn Mumm (May 1988). Chheam Van, Mumm's brother-in-law, recalled meeting Saloth Sar at this time and discussing politics. On at least one occasion, Saloth Sar used the name "Pol" (or "Paul") in France (author's interview with Keng Vannsak, May 1987).

10. See Kiernan, *HPP*, pp. 156ff.; author's interview with Thiounn Mumm; and Non Suon's confession (September 1976). Mumm met Keo Meas in East Berlin in 1951. The Pracheachon Group was founded in early 1955. U.S. Embassy Phnom Penh, Telegram 57, February 3, 1955, refers to new directorate of Democrats as a "left-wing element strongly permeated by Communist taint."

11. From author's interview with Chhay Yat (February 1990). Yat claimed that at this time Saloth Sar was a "humanitarian" rather than a hard-line Communist.

12. From author's interviews with Keng Vannsak, Thonn Ouk, Sim Var, and Thiounn Mumm. See also Non Suon's confession; and Philippe Preschez, *Essai sur le démocratie au Cambodge* (Paris, 1961), pp. 57ff.

13. See *Khemara*, December 22, 1954 (Michael Vickery's notes).

14. See *Neak Cheat Niyum* (The Nationalist), October 18, 1955—a month after the election (Michael Vickery's translation).

15. For details, see Kiernan, *HPP*, pp. 159ff. See also Great Britain, Public Records Office, FO 371/117126–117127, reports from British Legation in Phnom Penh, 1955; and author's interviews with Keng Vannsak (November 1986) and Thonn Ouk (May 1987).

16. Justin Corfield (personal communication) examined the original (not microform) copies of *Cambodge* in this period and discovered that the first published results of the election showed that the Sangkum had lost five seats. Before the edition was circulated, these results were "corrected" to a unanimous victory by pasting a slip of paper with other figures over the original results. Nuon Chea, "History," wrote of the

1955 elections that those who voted for the Pracheachon were "arrested and imprisoned and their wives had to sell rice and land to find the money to get their husbands
released. Some people had their stomachs cut open and their eyes stabbed with bayo-
nets."

17. Pol Pot, "Long Live the 17th Anniversary of the Communist Party of Kampuchea," speech delivered September 29, 1977 (English translation; Chicago, 1977),
p. 22. Steve Heder has pointed out that these "repressive tools" were supposedly to be
swept aside by the revolution. See also Vorn Vet's confession, pp. 3–5, where he stated
that the results of the election "demoralized" him.

18. See author's interviews with Lim Keuky (November 1997), Chea Samy (October 1990), Suon Kaset Sokho (June 1990), Chheam Van (November 1987), Pel Nal
(January 1990), and You Sambo (July 1989). Some sources asserted that Ponnary was a
dedicated revolutionary; others doubted that she was ever a party member. Siet Chhae
in his confession said that Ponnary brought him into the Cambodian Communist
party in 1959.

19. From author's interview with You Sambo (July 1989). The phrase *s'aat s'om* also
cropped up in my interview with Ith Sarin (November 1988), when he spoke of his
admiration for Cambodian radicalism in the 1960s. The term was also used to describe the uncorrupted Communist society promised by the revolution (see Tiv Ol's
confession, 1977). *S'aat s'om* translates into French as *propre* (Alain Daniel, personal
communication).

20. On the foundation of Kambuj'bot, see author's interview with Thonn Ouk.
Among the Communists who taught there were Ieng Sary, Hou Youn, and Khieu
Samphan. Chamraon Vichea was located in a set of humble buildings near the Lycée
Yukhanthor, not far from Tuol Sleng. I am grateful to Sok Pirun and Om Narong for
information about it.

21. From author's interview with Chhay Yat.

22. From author's interview with Soth Polin (October 1988) and from Polin's letter
to author (November 1989). See also Polin's "La Diabolique douceur de Pol Pot."

23. From author's interview with Om Narong (March 1991). Narong's older
brother told him in the 1960s that it was "inevitable" that Cambodia turn Communist, although he was not a radical himself. Still another former student, who prefers
anonymity, remembered Sar's geography classes as "prudent and conscientious,"
adding that Khieu Ponnary had a reputation at the time of being far more categorical
and intolerant than her husband (author's interview, January 1992).

24. Steve Heder's interview with Mey Mann, July 1997. Mey Mann added: "The
secret was not its name, but that it was nameless, which made its secrecy very deep."
See also Kiernan, *HPP*, pp. 177ff.; and Becker, *When the War Was Over*, pp. 100–101.
Thiounn Mumm, interviewed in 1988, remembered meeting Saloth Sar "in empty
fields at night" in 1954–1955. According to Khieu Kannarith, Cambodian officials in
the early 1990s occasionally referred to each other in private correspondence by code
names and numbers, years after coming to power (author's interview, October 1990).

25. Author's interview with Pel Nal, who befriended Sary and Thirith in Paris; and
author's interview with Khing Hoc Dy (October 1991). Mey Mann, who saw a good
deal of Sar and Sary at this time, told Steve Heder that "when Ieng Sary came back to
Cambodia, Sar told me to be wary of him because he was the kind of person who didn't
know how to take orders. It was my impression that Saloth Sar and Ieng Sary didn't get

along. Indeed, it seemed as if they couldn't stand each other. The problem with Ieng
Sary, according to Sar, was that he wasn't prepared to do immediately what the party
decides." This memory is of interest when set against the Vietnamese formulation of
the DK period as one dominated by the "Pol Pot-Ieng Sary genocidal clique" and also
when viewed from the angle of Sary's 1997 defection. Mey Mann also recalled that
Ieng Sary, born in southern Vietnam, was more vocally anti-Vietnamese than others
in the movement at this time.

26. Information about Nuon Chea's early career is from Hin Sithan in an October
1990 letter to me (conveying information gathered from Chea's surviving siblings);
from Nuon Chea's "History"; Non Suon's confession; author's interviews with Suon
Kaset Sokho (whose late husband was Nuon Chea's cousin); and conversations with
Somsak Jeemtearaskul. On Sieu Heng, see U.S. Embassy Phnom Penh, Airgram A-
23, February 17, 1972.

27. On rural/urban responsibilities, see Kiernan, *HPP*, pp. 172–173. In his September 1977 speech, Pol Pot asserted that Nuon Chea had been put in charge of urban
affairs after 1955, not in 1963. Presumably this legerdemain was effected to place "Pol
Pot" retroactively in charge of the peasant sector, which was more honorable twenty-
two years later.

28. Kiernan, *HPP*, pp. 169–248. See also the confessions of Chhim Samauk, Keo
Meas, and Saom Chea; and Becker, *When the War Was Over*, pp. 94–105. A 1973 party
history states: "Because there had not been any indoctrination, criticism or self-criticism sessions, and no directives on organization, liberalism was born in each individual [party member] which had a bad effect on the masses."

29. Nuon Chea, "History," which adds: "After Sieu Heng's betrayal, Tou Samouth
didn't do any new work because he was old and also didn't understand much" (*ot sou
yu'l eichung*). This uncorroborated assertion is obscure; Samouth at this stage was still
in his 40s. On Sieu Heng, see author's interview with Ty Sophen; and Kiernan, *HPP*,
pp. 186ff. See also Saom Chea's confession (April 1978). Vorn Vet's confession, p. 9,
declares that "in the Sihanouk era, the masses stopped believing in the revolution."

30. *Réalités cambodgiennes* (hereafter *RC*), October 16, 1959; *L'Observateur*, October
13, 1959.

31. See George McT. Kahin, *Intervention* (New York, 1986), pp. 110ff.; and Porter,
"Vietnamese Communist Policy Toward Kampuchea," in Chandler and Kiernan, eds.,
Revolution and Its Aftermath in Kampuchea, pp. 57–98.

32. Pol Pot, "Long Live the 17th Anniversary," p. 23. In his "History," Nuon Chea
claims to have taken draft statutes of the new party to show to Vietnamese Communist officials in Tay Ninh (South Vietnam) before the September meeting. "The Vietnamese were unhappy," he wrote thirty-seven years later, "because they saw that we
had the ability to raise a strategic-tactical line and make [party] statutes by ourselves."

33. On Son Ngoc Minh's attendance at the Vietnamese congress, see U.S. Central
Intelligence Agency, "Communism and Cambodia" (n.d. [probably 1971]), p. 29. Nei-
ther Sihanouk's police nor U.S. intelligence services were aware of the subsequent
Cambodian meeting.

34. Pun Than's confession quotes Keo Meas in 1960 as saying, "We must become a
Workers' Party, like Vietnam." On regional responsibilities, see Serge Thion's inter-
view with Ouk Boun Chhoeum (September 1981). See also Thomas Engelbert and
Christopher Goscha, *Falling Out of Touch: A Study on Vietnamese Communist Policy To-*

ward an Emerging Cambodian Communist Movement, 1930–1975 (Clayton, Australia, 1994), which indicates that the program advanced at the 1960 meeting suggested that the party "must also be prepared to adopt a non-peaceful form of struggle"—a phrase that falls short of "armed struggle."

35. See U.S. Embassy Phnom Penh, Airgram, A-93, August 23, 1962; and *RC*, August 17, 1962, in which Sihanouk is reported as saying that "a few months ago" his intelligence services obtained a message "from Viet Minh authorities, addressed to Cambodian cadres." The document urged the party not to present candidates for the 1962 election, adding: "Our best interests are served by relying on young intellectuals who sympathize with our movement." This text, which may have been captured in the raid that resulted in Tou Samouth's death in July 1962 (see below), might also have been the document "from 1961" referred to in Pol Pot's anti-Vietnamese polemic, *Livre noir*, and characterized as "excelling in confusion" (see Democratic Kampuchea, Ministry of Foreign Affairs, *Livre noir: Faits et preuves des actes d'agression . . . du Vietnam* [Paris, 1978]).

36. See U.S. Embassy Phnom Penh, Telegram 471, January 15, 1962, and Telegram 477, January 17, 1962.

37. Nuon Chea, "History." After Samouth's disappearance, Nuon Chea went underground: "I never went anywhere during the day. I never went to eat noodles in a shop. I was never happy like other people. That's why my children said to me: 'You're like a rat in a hole.'" See also Kiernan, *HPP*, p. 241; and author's interview with Tea Sa Bun (September 1990). The confessions of Ruos Mau (Say) (September 1977) and Som Chea (March 1978) both asserted that Samouth was abducted from "Lon Nol's house" in a car. Som Chea added that party members stabbed Samouth to death on the outskirts of Phnom Penh. Serge Thion, "A propos de Tou Samouth," *Srok khmer*, May 1987, summarized the evidence available up to that point. Cambodian official Ouk Boun Chhoeum told Thion in 1981 that he believed Samouth was betrayed by a fellow Communist who had been working for Sieu Heng and had been arrested, interrogated, and killed "after 1975." Heng was assassinated on Nuon Chea's orders in April 1975 after Communist forces occupied Battambang (from author's interview with Ty Sophen, February 1989). An argument against Heng's complicity would be that cadre brought to Tuol Sleng on trumped-up charges would have been eager to blame their treachery on Sieu Heng, one of the few genuine and well-known deserters from the party. Had Heng handed Samouth over to Lon Nol, it seems likely that others in the Communist network would have been arrested soon after. On balance, evidence points to Samouth being picked up, unrecognized, in a police raid and then killed after a fruitless interrogation.

38. Vorn Vet's confession (typed version), p. 15. Nuon Chea, in his "History," also blames Samouth's bodyguards, but his assertion may have been colored by his knowledge of the S-21 confessions.

39. From author's interview with Sok Chuon (June 1990). Michael Vickery (personal communication) recalled that Saloth Sar was known as a progressive among fellow schoolteachers. Chhim Samauk's confession mentions secret study sessions in the suburb of Beng Trabek. For an analysis of the interplay between Buddhist and Communist styles of teaching, see François Ponchaud, "Social Change in the Vortex of Revolution," in Jackson, ed., *Cambodia, 1975–1978*, pp. 172ff. Sok Chuon claimed that at this time Nuon Chea was also well known as a propagandist.

40. From author's interviews with Oeur Hunly (September 1989) and Sok Pirun (November 1989); and Siet Chhae's confession. Party members held their own closed sessions. Pun Than's confession lists those regularly attending such sessions in Phnom Penh in 1958–1959.

41. On the Siem Reap demonstrations, see *RC*, March 8, 1963. See also Khieu Samphan, *Cambodia's Economic Development*, ed. and trans. by Laura Summers (Ithaca, N.Y., 1979), p. 17; and author's interviews with Ith Sarin (November 1988) and Thel Thong (August 1987). On Lon Nol's list, see Kiernan, *HPP*, pp. 202 and 242 (n158). Chou Chet fled Phnom Penh a week earlier, according to his confession.

42. See Engelbert and Goscha, *Falling Out of Touch*, p. 64. The money had been given to Chea by Vietnamese colleagues in the Indochina Communist party and was intended to buy a house for an ICP cadre in Phnom Penh. This intriguing tale of double-dealing may explain why Chea was reluctant to follow Sar into the forest in 1963 and also suggests, in view of Chea's long career, an overwhelming, self-abasing loyalty to the party. Vietnamese Communists accepted Sar's promotion, referring to him by 1964 as Anh Hai ("eldest brother")—a position probably occupied by Ho himself within the Vietnamese party. Sar was also known to the Vietnamese as Hai Thien ("the good-natured one").

43. Nuon Chea, "History." According to his confession, Siet Chhae was removed from party work after the promulgation of the list; he followed Sar to Office 100. On Saloth Sar's conversation, see author's interview with Keng Vannsak (October 1986). See also "Interview with Comrade Pol Pot," March 1978, p. 22 (uncatalogued item in Tuol Sleng Archives, Phnom Penh).

44. See Robert Jay Lifton's persuasive article "Protean Man," *Partisan Review* (Winter 1968): 13–25. Throughout his career, Pol Pot seems to have associated clandestinity with success.

Chapter Five

1. The label "Khmers rouges," coined by Sihanouk, was never used by members of the Communist movement to describe themselves. I have borrowed the last phrase from Timothy Carney, "The Unexpected Victory," in Jackson, ed., *Cambodia, 1975–1978*, pp. 13–35.

2. For a discussion of the politics of this period, see Chandler, *Tragedy*, Chapter 6.

3. See the confession of Chhim Samauk (Pang) (July 1977). See also the confession of Siet Chhae (Tum) (November 1977): "Meeting the Brothers at Office 100, I could see how combative they were in their work. Even if they were feverish they worked. I saw the Brothers writing documents themselves, and also stenciling them themselves." Office 100, clearly a Vietnamese base, may also have been a Vietnamese designation. In 1970 the Vietnamese had five rear service groups (RSGs) operating along the Cambodian frontier. One of these, based in Svay Rieng, was known as RSG 100. Conceivably, a unit bearing this number had operated farther north in 1963. By 1970 RSG 100 had over two thousand Vietnamese troops under its command. I am grateful to William Turley for this information. See also the confession of Ney Saran (Ya), which locates the camp in 1964 "at Daom Chambak in Tay Ninh province [in Vietnam], within 10 kilometers of the border." Appendix 2 lists personnel at Office 100, as recorded in several confessions from Tuol Sleng.

4. In his confession of December 1978, Kheang Sim Hon (But) asserted that Saloth Sar at one stage taught him to sing the "Internationale." See also Im Naen's and Som Chea's confessions. Chea came to Office 100 from Phnom Penh in 1964. Chou Chet was never at that base, but his confession corroborates Im Naen's. Poignantly, Naen's faithful service as a cook was transmuted in her confession into a series of botched attempts to poison various "brothers."

5. Vorn Vet's confession (typed version), p. 17; and Kiernan, *HPP*, p. 211.

6. Pol Pot, "Long Live the 17th Anniversary," p. 37. A 1974 party history mentions a "second" party congress of early 1963, adds that the party "gathered strength" in 1964, and fails to mention any activities in the succeeding two years.

7. Vorn Vet's confession (typed version), p. 15.

8. See Kiernan, *HPP*, p. 220; Vorn Vet's confession (typed version), p. 17; and Becker, *When the War Was Over*, pp. 120–121. The composition of the delegation was kept secret from the Vietnamese media (Serge Thion, personal communication). Vorn Vet was informed of Sar's trip to China by Nuon Chea, who took command of Office 100 but spent some of the time in Phnom Penh. Day-to-day control of the camp fell to Ieng Sary, according to several confessions, suggesting that Ieng Sary did not accompany Saloth Sar to China. On Um Neng's participation, see Chhim Samauk's confession.

9. On Saloth Sar's lectures, see Serge Thion (personal communication); and Keo Moni's confession (December 1976). Keo Moni referred to Sar as a "representative of the Party Center." On party names, see Kiernan, *HPP*, p. 220. On Cambodians in Vietnam, see U.S. Embassy Phnom Penh, Airgram A-165, November 11, 1965; and the confession of Kol Thai (January 1976). Samoeun and Soeurn both returned to Cambodia in 1970. Samoeun disappeared before 1975; Soeurn was executed as a traitor in 1976 (Kiernan, *HPP*, p. 401). According to Steve Heder (personal communication), Keo Meas's confession suggests that Cambodians integrated into the Vietnamese armed forces became and remained members of the Vietnam Workers' party, while those who were civilians were affiliated with the Cambodian movement headed by Son Ngoc Minh.

10. See *Livre noir*, pp. 26 and 50. For an analysis of the text, see Serge Thion, "The Ingratitude of Crocodiles," *BCAS* 12, 4 (1980): 38–54.

11. Engelbert and Goscha, *Falling Out of Touch*, p. 74. According to Nuon Chea's history, "when Saloth Sar returned, he said that the Vietnamese weren't happy because (1) our party had gone to contact the Chinese party; (2) Saloth Sar didn't call Ho Chi Minh 'uncle' (*om*). He called him 'Comrade chairman' (*sommit protean*)."

12. *Livre noir*, p. 27. In "Interview of Comrade Pol Pot to [sic] the DK Press Agency" (1978), Pol Pot asserted that he had given Vietnamese troops permission at this time to sojourn in zones controlled by Cambodian Communist forces. But no such zones existed before 1969, and the Vietnamese troops that were in Cambodia were there with Sihanouk's permission, not Saloth Sar's. The Communists' decision to combine armed and political struggle was not made until late 1967. By 1978 Cambodia was at war with Vietnam, and Pol Pot's resentment at years of Vietnamese condescension was intense. He was probably convinced that he had confronted them successfully in 1965–1966. Serge Thion noted that no Vietnamese documentation about the visit has been released ("Ingratitude of Crocodiles," p. 42). Such documents might well vindicate Pol Pot's assertion in 1978 that he had been treated as a "son" or a "lit-

tle brother" and confirm the close relations between the two parties that the Vietnamese took pains to deny after 1977. Engelbert and Goscha, in *Falling Out of Touch*,
pp. 71ff., citing Vietnamese Communist sources, make it clear that Le Duan was enraged by the naïveté of the CPK documents presented by Sar in Hanoi. Duan criticized the documents in detail. A Vietnamese account of the confrontation, cited by
Engelbert and Goscha, closes at page 75 with the sentence: "Saloth Sar left the meeting without saying anything at all." After the humiliation, Sar lingered in Hanoi for
several months. The depth of his rancor and his sense of helplessness are easy to
imagine.

13. Carney, "Unexpected Victory," p. 245 (n15). See also Kiernan, *HPP*, pp. 220ff.
As evidence of Sino-Vietnamese collaboration at this time, a Cambodian Communist
party member from Hanoi supervised a study session in late 1966 for Cambodians
and their "Chinese brothers."

14. Lin Biao, "Long Live the Victory of the People's War!" *Peking Review*, Septem-
ber 3, 1965, p. 22. See also Stuart Schram, *The Thought of Mao Tse-Tung* (Cambridge,
U.K., 1989), pp. 171ff.; and Paul J. Hiniker, *Revolutionary Ideology and Chinese Reality:
Dissonance Under Mao* (Beverly Hills, Calif., 1977), pp. 209ff. For a sympathetic ac-
count of China at this time, see David Milton and Nancy Dall Milton, *The Wind Will
Not Subside* (New York, 1976), pp. 95ff. On K'ang Sheng, see David Apter and Tony
Saich, *Revolutionary Discourse* (Cambridge, Mass., 1996), pp. 280ff.; John Byron and
Robert Pack, *The Claws of the Dragon* (New York, 1992); Roderick MacFarquhar, *The
Origins of the Cultural Revolution*, Vol. 3. (Oxford, 1997), pp. 291–294; and Roger
Faligot and Remi Kauffer, *The Chinese Secret Service* (London, 1989), which claims (at
p. 410), without citing a source, that Pol Pot "took training courses with K'ang
Sheng's special services in 1965 (sic) and 1969." See also Hu Yao-ping, "Problems
Concerning the Purge of K'ang Sheng," *Issues and Studies* (June 1980): 74–100;
Michael Schoenhals, "The Central Case Examination Group, 1966–1979," *China
Quarterly* (March 1996): 87–110; and Michael Schoenhals, "Mao's Great Inquisition:
The Central Case Examination Group, 1966–1979," special issue of *Chinese Law and
Government* (May-June 1996). The CCEG, functioning throughout the DK period,
may well have provided some inspiration for S-21. Until his death, K'ang Sheng was
closely associated with it.

15. Several confessions link the shift of Office 100 to U.S. bombardment.

16. See Chhim Samauk's confession; and Becker, *When the War Was Over*, p. 469.
See also Sok Knol's confession and author's interview with Sok Knol's brother, Sok
Sambath (July 1989).

17. See Robert Cribb, ed., *The Indonesian Killings, 1965–1966: Studies from Java and
Bali* (Clayton, Australia, 1990). The parallels between Sihanouk and Sukarno and between Lon Nol and Suharto were not lost on the major actors.

18. On Red Khmer relations with these tribes, see Becker, *When the War Was Over*,
pp. 122–124; and Siet Chhae's and Chhim Samauk's confessions. Siet Chhae commented: "I could see that the national minority youths were very good, working class
and natural." On Communist attitudes, see author's interviews with Thiounn Mumm
(May 1988), Keat Chhon (November 1987), and Ong Thong Hoeung (May 1988).

19. On this period of Pol Pot's life, see Sara Colm, "Pol Pot: The Secret 60s,"
Phnom Penh Post, April 24–May 7, 1998, drawing on extensive interviews. For a list of Pol
Pot's bodyguards in 1977, many of whom were tribal people, see Keat Chau's confes-

sion. On Marx's view of such an undifferentiated society, see Maurice Bloch, *Marxism and Anthropology* (Oxford, 1982), pp. 10ff.; and Michael Thompson et al., *Cultural Theory* (Boulder, Colo., 1990), pp. 147ff. In 1976 Pol Pot's bodyguard was a tribesman named Thoeun (see Kheang Kim Hon's confession, p. 10). See also the confession of Ket Chau in 1977, which gives the names of two Tapuon and two Jarai tribesmen who worked as bodyguards for "the Organization" (that is, Pol Pot). See also David Ashley's interview (September 1997) with Phi Phuon, an ethnic Jarai who served as Saloth Sar's bodyguard from 1967 to 1975.

20. See Frank Smith, *Interpretive Accounts of the Khmer Rouge Years: Personal Experiences and the Cambodian Peasant World View* (Madison, Wis., 1989). Cambodian refugees often spoke of the Pol Pot era as fulfilling the Buddhist prophecies of disaster *(put tumniay)* that they had absorbed as children or as monks. Ong Thong Hoeung recalled lectures by Ieng Sary in 1977–1978 in which he admired tribespeople because "they dared to sacrifice their lives to save their chiefs." Hoeung also said that much of Pol Pot's favorable reputation among the Khmer came from his "travels through the forests . . . like someone in a Cambodian legend" (author's interview, February 1990). Colm, "Pol Pot," quotes a former bodyguard: "We carried Pol Pot [in a hammock] because he was a big man, *neak thom.* He'd lie down in the hammock and not walk. More than 10 or 20 people a day would carry him up and down the mountains. When they carried him, if they brushed him against a branch, they'd beat the porter." See also Solange Thierry, "*Brai* et *Himavant,* les thèmes de la forêt dans la tradition khmère," *Cambodge* (special issue of *Asie du Sud-est et monde insulindien*) 13, 1–4 (1982): 121–134.

21. For a detailed narrative of the uprising, see Kiernan and Boua, *Peasants and Politics,* pp. 166–205. Nuon Chea's "History" suggests that Communists in Phnom Penh, of whom he was the leader, followed the rebellion much more closely than did those in Ratanakiri.

22. See Hu Nim's confession in David Chandler, Ben Kiernan, and Chanthou Boua, eds. and trans., *Pol Pot Plans the Future: Confidential Documents from Democratic Kampuchea, 1976–1977* (New Haven, Conn., 1988), pp. 245ff.; and the confession of An Seng Hen (Chun) (December 1977): "In 1967 our revolutionary movement reached a boiling point throughout the country . . . Sihanouk shouted his opposition to the movement on the radio . . . government officials everywhere lost their positions." The fact that these popular intellectuals were unwilling, unable, or forbidden to join their superiors in the northeast had important repercussions. Nuon Chea, in his 1997 history of the CPK, noted that "in 1967 there was a revolt in Samlaut but this movement was not yet ripe *(tum)* so the party decided to quiet it down first. The people revolted and we contributed *(ruom psom)* too." Nuon Chea's stance is consistent with Communist practice, whereby the party, theoretically infallible, assumes full responsibility only for success.

23. See Kiernan, *HPP,* pp. 256ff.; the confession of Ruos Mau; author's interview with In Nath (June 1987); and Debré, *Cambodge,* pp. 111ff. Phnom Vay Chap was known in Communist circles as a "mountain of heroes" (see Chandler, Kiernan, and Boua, eds. and trans., *Pol Pot Plans the Future,* pp. 290–291).

24. See the confession of Muol Sambath (Nhim Ros) and confession of Kong Sopal (Kuu). See also *Tung Padevat* (August 1975): 36–37: "In March-April 1967 an armed uprising took place in Battambang, brought on by contradictions on a national scale

as well as by local contradictions, but the Party ordered that [fighting] cease so as to draw lessons from these contradictions and from this armed struggle." See also *Tung Padevat* (December 1976–January 1977): 44: "The Party Center said: 'Desist for a moment. Wait until the struggle can occur on a national scale.'" Chou Chet's confession asserts that the uprising occurred "under the impetus of party leaders in the northwest," suggesting a fissure between party veterans in Battambang and the leadership in the northeast. On Kuu, see Vorn Vet's confession, p. 18. Kuu survived the DK period but disappeared after 1979 (Steve Heder, personal communication). In the *Livre noir*, p. 28, Pol Pot asserted that following the Samlaut uprising, the Vietnamese were "overcome with panic"; he added (p. 47) that the Vietnamese told the Red Khmer to stop the armed resistance "after the outbreak at Samlaut." The party's orders calling off the resistance may have reflected Vietnamese fears of alienating Sihanouk as well as their own prudence. See captured Red Khmer notebook in Indochina Archives (Douglas Pike Collection), University of California, Berkeley (hereafter Pike Archives), which asserts of Samlaut that "even though victorious, our people agreed to lay down their arms and return to their farmlands."

25. See Kiernan and Boua, *Peasants and Politics*, pp. 180–181; Chandler, *Tragedy*, Chapter 5; Kiernan, *HPP*, pp. 277ff.; Vorn Vet's confession; and author's interview with Sok Chuon (June 1990).

26. Pol Pot, "Long Live the 17th Anniversary," p. 38.

27. See Kheang Sim Hon's confession. On conditions toward the end of 1967, see Bu Phat's confession. Kiernan, *HPP*, p. 181, asserts that "by December 1967, word had been passed around that the Samlaut rebellion was about to enter another phase"; this rumor may have reflected decisions taken at the study session. In 1978 the *Livre noir* noted (p. 34) that if the party "had not carried out armed struggle, it would have been condemned to disappear." According to Engelbert and Goscha, *Falling Out of Touch*, Saloth Sar wrote to the Chinese authorities in October 1967, in a letter intercepted by the Vietnamese, that "we are preparing the implementation of a people's war which has moved toward an unstoppable point." He also praised "the line of people's war which Chairman Mao has pointed out in terms of independence, sovereignty and self-reliance"—turns of phrase that must have been distressing to the Vietnamese. Nuon Chea, "History," claims that the decision to implement armed struggle was taken by Communists in Phnom Penh acting under his leadership.

28. Kiernan, *HPP*, pp. 268ff.; Kiernan and Boua, *Peasants and Politics*, pp. 182ff.; and author's interview with Ty Sophen (February 1989). On Bay Damram, see "Speech by Representative of the Party at the Ninth Anniversary of the Revolutionary Army," *Tung Padevat* (December 1976–January 1977): 38–39; and Nuon Chea, "Statement of the CPK to the Communist Worker's Party of Denmark, July 1978," *Journal of Communist Studies* (March 1987): 26ff. Nuon Chea dated the decision to start armed struggle to a "Central Committee meeting" held in January 1968, shortly before the incident at Bay Damram. In his "History," however, Chea claims to have made the decision with several colleagues in Phnom Penh, without reference to authorities in Ratanakiri. His statement to the Danes fails to mention Samlaut. However, under Democratic Kampuchea the region containing Samlaut and Phnom Vay Chap was named "sector *(dombon)* 1," perhaps to honor its revolutionary credentials (see Michael Vickery, *Cambodia, 1975–1982* [Boston, 1983], p. 67).

29. On the Bowles visit, see Chandler, *Tragedy*, Chapter 5; and William Shawcross, *Sideshow: Nixon, Kissinger, and the Destruction of Cambodia* (New York, 1979), pp. 68–71.

30. On morale issues, Al Santoli (personal communication). See also CIA reports from 1969 (numbers excised) in Pike Archives (Cambodia, 1969); and Kiernan, *HPP*, pp. 282ff. Nuon Chea's "History" claims that Red Khmer forces at this time traded chickens for guns with Vietnamese quartered in Cambodia "because the Vietnamese were starving."

31. See Siet Chhae's confession.

32. See "Seckdei nai no'm 870" [Guidance from 870], *Tung Padevat* (January 1972): 12–37. The number "870" was used to designate the highest authority in the Communist party. See also Nuon Chea, "Statement of the CPK," p. 22: "We had no weapons to speak of and no aid from the outside. . . . Sometimes we had weapons but no ammunition. Sometimes even if we had no ammunition we carried weapons so as to frighten the enemy."

33. See Sok Nhanh's confession; and "Training Khmers in North Vietnam," CIA document in Pike Archives (Cambodia, March 1973). See also Kiernan, *HPP*, p. 280. Keo Meas stayed in Vietnam and China until 1975 and was purged in 1976. In December 1972, Son Ngoc Minh died of an illness in Beijing, where he had been transferred from Hanoi. He was revived as a hero in Cambodia after 1979—an avenue in Phnom Penh was named after him and his portrait appeared on 100-riel notes.

34. See Chandler, *Tragedy*, Chapter 5; Charles Meyer, *Derrière le sourire khmer* (Paris, 1971), pp. 283–385; and Martin, *Le mal cambodgien*, pp. 119ff.

35. On U.S. bombing, see Kiernan, *HPP*, pp. 285ff. See also "Notebook Entries August to September 1969 by [a Vietnamese] Cadre," Pike Archives (Cambodia, September 1969); and testimony of Chau Vari So, Pike Archives (Cambodia, January 1974). On the prelude to the coup, see Chandler, *Tragedy*, Chapter 5.

36. On Sar's visit to Hanoi, see Kiernan, *HPP*, pp. 297ff. Sihanouk was the only chief of state to attend Ho's funeral. Engelbert and Goscha, *Falling Out of Touch*, citing Vietnamese sources, date Sar's visit to November 1969, after Ho's funeral. At this time, apparently, Sar asked the Vietnamese to send the Cambodian Communists in Vietnam home to help the CPK in its confrontation with Sihanouk. The Vietnamese delayed doing so until Sihanouk had been overthrown.

37. See *Livre noir*, pp. 34ff.

38. See Chandler, *Tragedy*, Chapter 6; and Shawcross, *Sideshow*, pp. 118ff.

39. See *Livre noir*, p. 35; and author's interviews with Alain Daniel (November 1987) and So Bun Hor (October 1988).

40. See Kiernan, *HPP*, p. 312. A 1974 party history, p. 12, states that before the coup the Communists had been fighting "by ourselves," but that after March 1975 they received substantial aid from other countries, including Vietnam.

Chapter Six

1. Khieu Samphan was frequently called on to play this role, most recently in the early 1990s. See Heder, *Khieu Samphan and Pol Pot*.

2. Becker, *When the War Was Over*, pp. 153ff. On the NLF, Steve Heder pointed out (letter to author, August 1991) that similar front organizations had operated in Cambodia in the First Indochina War and in Laos until 1975. See also Teri Caraway, "The United Front Strategies of the Khmer Rouge" (B.A. honors thesis, Pomona College, California, 1989).

3. See the confession of Kheang Sim Hon (But) (December 1978), p. 20. But's confession was composed after the release of the *Livre noir*, which makes similar anti-Vietnamese assertions (p. 52). See Carney, "Unexpected Victory," p. 23; and Kiernan, *HPP*, pp. 310ff. Vietnamese training of Cambodian Communist-led troops continued through 1971. See Meas Mon's confession (June 1978), p. 25: "In 1971 the work of building up our strength was the responsibility of the Vietnamese who helped with all the arrangements, and provided clothing, weapons, and training."

4. *Livre noir*, pp. 48–49.

5. Chhim Samauk's and Kheang Sim Hon's confessions. An important aspect of the confessions that relates to Saloth Sar/Pol Pot is the numerous references to illness. On Cambodians coming south from Hanoi in April 1970, see the confession of Kol Thai (Vong) (January 1976); and U.S. Embassy Phnom Penh, Airgram A-165, November 8, 1971, reporting Yun Soeurn's departure from Hanoi "in April." See also U.S. Embassy Phnom Penh, Airgram A-179, November 30, 1971, and Airgram A-5, January 11, 1972.

6. Kheang Sim Hon's confession, p. 22; Prum Saeng's confession (January 1977). In 1971 Sary moved from Hanoi to Beijing. The photograph of Ieng Sary, Saloth Sar, and Nuon Chea in the forest printed in Ieng Sary, *Cambodge 1972* (Beijing, n.d.), probably dates from 1970. Discussing the photograph, Becker noted: "Of them all, Saloth Sar has the least memorable face, the least assertive stance. Even in front of the camera he hides" (*When the War Was Over*, p. 160).

7. See Ben Kiernan, "The 1970 Demonstrations Against Lon Nol," in Kiernan and Boua, *Peasants and Politics*, pp. 206–223.

8. Report Number 6, 028 0177 71, "Red Khmer Policy and Activity," captured in December 1970 (Pike Archives, June 1971). For a similar injunction, see *Tung Padevat* (September–October 1972): 10, which states that "the Party is attached organizationally to the masses. That is to say: surrounding the Party is the secret organization; and surrounding the secret organization is the mass organization, thick and close together (*s'ek skoh*). Thus, the Party is attached to the masses." Here and later, Saloth Sar referred to the leaders of the CPK as the "party" and its members as the "secret organization."

9. *Livre noir*, pp. 55–57; Koy Thuon's confession; and Hu Nim's confession, in Chandler, Kiernan, and Boua, eds. and trans., *Pol Pot Plans the Future*, p. 251. See also U.S. Embassy Phnom Penh, Airgram A-5, January 13, 1972, which states that Hu Nim, among others, conducted training sessions in Kompong Thom for Cambodians arriving from Vietnam in 1971; and Thion and Kiernan, *Khmers rouges!* pp. 166ff.

10. Kiernan, *HPP*, 327ff., based on interviews with participants; see Vorn Vet's confession (typed version), p. 32; Non Suon's confession. See also "Pisaoch muoy comnuon ompi ka ngie kosang pak, 1963–1971" [Some observations on the tasks of building the party, 1963–1971], *Tung Padevat* (September 1971). For Hu Nim's account, see Chandler, Kiernan, and Boua, eds. and trans., *Pol Pot Plans the Future*, pp. 256–257. See also Kenneth Quinn, "Political Change in Wartime: The Khmer Kra-

hom Revolution in Southern Cambodia, 1970–1974," *Naval War College Review* 28 (Spring 1976): 3–31. Quinn served as the U.S. Ambassador to Cambodia in 1996-1998. Steve Heder (letter to author, August 1991) pointed out that it was tactically in Vietnam's interest to emphasize the nationalist elements of the movement it mobilized to support its war against the United States and, eventually, to establish communism throughout Indochina.

11. "Pisaoch klah ompiii ka to't tu'l nung ka vay komtech a-Chenla II" [Some observations on the smashing of contemptible Chenla II], *Tung Padevat* (December 1971): 27ff. Documents captured in the southwest in early 1971 also failed to mention Vietnamese contributions (Kiernan, *HPP*, p. 322). But see the Red Khmer notebook in the Pike Archives (Cambodia, May 1971), which mentions "solidarity of the international liberation front" but notes that "foreign participation [in the revolution] is secondary." On the intrinsic superiority of the Khmer, see Chandler, "Seeing Red," pp. 34–56. Pol Pot, "Long Live the 17th Anniversary," says nothing about Vietnamese aid in 1970–1975.

12. See Kate Frieson, "Reluctant Comrades: The Peasantry and the Red Khmers, 1970–1975," unpublished paper, 1991; and "Seckdei nai no'm reboh 870" [Guidance from 870], *Tung Padevat* (February 1972).

13. See Shawcross, *Sideshow*, especially pp. 220–235; Walter von Marschal, *The War in Cambodia: Its Causes and Military Development* (London, 1975), pp. 112ff.; and U.S. Central Intelligence Agency, "The Short-Term Prospect for Cambodia (SNIE 57–73)." In May 1973 the Khmer Republic called for military volunteers. Only fifty-two young men signed up (U.S. Central Intelligence Agency, "The Situation in Cambodia, July 1973," Report 7333/73, p. 2). By then the republic's armed forces numbered more than 200,000.

14. Kiernan, *HPP*, pp. 331ff. For the eyewitness accounts, see Thion and Kiernan, *Khmer rouges!* pp. 43–97; Timothy Carney, *Communist Party Power in Kampuchea (Cambodia): Documents and Discussion* (Ithaca, N.Y., 1977), pp. 34–55 (a partial translation of Sarin); and Ith Sarin, *Sronoh proloeung Khmer* [Lament for my Khmer beloved] (Phnom Penh, 1973).

15. Carney, *Communist Party Power*, p. 9 (n45). See also "The Red Khmers' Organization and Activities" (Pike Archives, March 1974); and Kiernan, *HPP*, pp. 336ff. In September 1971 Sar and ninety other "Cambodian intellectuals" signed a twelve-page declaration attacking Lon Nol and supporting the United Front. For the text in translation, see Malcolm Caldwell and Lek Tan, *Cambodia in the Southeast Asian War* (New York, 1973), pp. 417ff. Sar identified himself as a "professor."

16. On Pol Pot's speaking style, see author's interviews with Richard Dudman (April 1991) and Soth Polin. As François Ponchaud has written, "Content was less important [in Communist sermons] than harmony of effect" (Jackson, ed., *Cambodia, 1975–1978*, p. 158). When Serge Thion visited the special zone in 1972, a Buddhist monk sympathetic to the party told him: "Religion is teaching. Teaching cannot disappear." The pedagogical thrust of Theravada Buddhism, and the notion that people can remake themselves by working to become enlightened, played into the hands of cadre, many of whom had been trained as monks or novices to believe in the efficacy of teaching and in the possibility, through study, of personal transformation. See Kiernan and Thion, *Khmers rouges!* p. 95. When he spoke to Yugoslavian journalists in

1978, Pol Pot took pains to leave the (false) impression that he had spent several years as a Buddhist monk.

17. See Porter, "Vietnamese Communist Policy Toward Kampuchea," pp. 57–98. Son Ngoc Minh, the titular head of the Cambodian Communist movement, died in December 1972 in Beijing, where he had been taken for medical treatment. His death loosened the links between the Cambodian Communists and Hanoi.

18. See Donald Kirk, "Cambodia 1973: Year of the Bomb Halt," *Asian Survey* (1974): 89–100; Shawcross, *Sideshow*, pp. 261–262; Becker, *When the War Was Over*, pp. 161ff. In a speech honoring the ninth anniversary of the Revolutionary Army in 1977, a CPK spokesman said that "had we stopped fighting [even] for a month, the enemy would have been able to catch his breath and strengthen his forces" (*Tung Padevat* [December 1976–January 1977]).

19. *Livre noir*, pp. 66ff., claims that last-minute pressure was applied by the Vietnamese on Saloth Sar in January 1973, paralleling U.S. pressures on Lon Nol. See also Chea, "Statement of the Communist Party of Kampuchea to the Communist Workers' Party of Denmark, July 1978," pp. 21–36. On page 23, Nuon Chea echoed the 1977 speech cited above.

20. See von Marschal, *War in Cambodia*, pp. 117ff; and Interrogation Report 058/74 (Phan Van Tay), March 1974, Pike Archives (Cambodia, April 1974), which catalogs disagreements in *dombon* 25. The dismantling of a parallel Cambodian Communist apparatus in Vietnam may have been interpreted by some Cambodians there and by some returnees as another Vietnamese betrayal, as Kiernan suggested in *HPP*, p. 359.

21. See Georges Boudarel, "La liquidation des communistes cambodgiens formés au Vietnam," *Problèmes politiques et sociaux* 373 (1979): 4–7; Kiernan, *HPP*, pp. 335ff.; Keo Moni's confession; confessions of Kol Thai (Vong) (January 1976); and author's interview with Ith Sarin (October 1988). See also U.S. Embassy Phnom Penh, Airgram A-179, "Conversations with Khmer Rouge Rallier Ieng Lim," November 20, 1971, and Airgram A-146, "Khmer Rouge Rallier Kum San," September 12, 1972. The extent of the purges before 1975 may not have been thorough. Chou Chet's confession reports that in "late 1976" there were still "about 100" returnees working in the southwestern zone office. Others, like Men Tul (Sat), retained their posts through 1977–1978, when they were purged. Still others, impossible to identify, undoubtedly covered their tracks and survived the entire period.

22. See Kenneth Quinn, "Political Change in Wartime," *Naval War College Review* 28 (Spring 1976): 3–31. His prescient report, originally a State Department airgram (in 1972–1974 Quinn was stationed in Chaudoc, just across the Vietnamese border from Takeo), had little effect on U.S. thinking about the Cambodian Communist movement.

23. On the bombing campaign, see Shawcross, *Sideshow*, pp. 280ff. and maps on pp. 266–267; Kiernan, *HPP*, pp. 349ff.; and Ben Kiernan, "The American Bombardment of Kampuchea, 1969–1973," *Vietnam Generation* (Winter 1989): 4–41. The arguments Shawcross presented have been disputed in the appendixes to Henry Kissinger, *Years of Upheaval* (Boston, 1982); but see Shawcross, "Additions to the New Edition," in *Sideshow*, pp. 409ff., and FBIS, *Daily Reports*, August 16, 1977, where a speaker asserted that the U.S. bombing campaign had produced "blood rancor, national anger and class indignation."

24. On Sihanouk's visit, see Monique Sihanouk, "Voyage historique au Cambodge en 1973," *Bulletin mensuel de documentation de . . . Norodom Sihanouk* (March–April 1987): 17–26. The U.S. Embassy in Phnom Penh was reluctant to believe that the prince had gotten to Angkor, but Cambodians in Siem Reap heard about the visit soon after Sihanouk departed (see author's interview with Sok Pirun; and Bruce Palling's interview with Chhit Do [1986] on file at William Joiner Center, University of Massachusetts, Boston). Do, a Red Khmer soldier at the time, was brought to Phnom Kulen to welcome the prince.

25. USLO (United States Liaison Office) Peking, Airgram A-8, "Sihanouk Interview with Stanley Karnow," May 17, 1973. For Hu Nim's description of the visit, see Chandler, Kiernan, and Boua, eds. and trans., *Pol Pot Plans the Future*, pp. 265–266. As far as I know, the 1973 albums contain the last published photographs of Khieu Ponnary. Others from 1972 struck Elizabeth Becker as "haunted": "The posed photograph cannot hide her condition: Ponnary is going mad in the service of her husband's revolution" (Becker, *When the War Was Over*, pp. 160–161). In the 1973 photographs, Ponnary looks listless and unwell. Nuon Chea does not seem to have participated in the visit. Sihanouk was lulled into believing that the "Three Ghosts" were in charge, as he later admitted in *Prisonnier des khmers rouges* (Paris, 1987), p. 229.

26. For Khieu Samphan's remark, see Shawcross, *Sideshow*, p. 281. According to Chhit Do, study sessions after Sihanouk's departure stressed that pleasing Sihanouk was still important, because "if he were disappointed he might go over to the Americans on his return to Beijing, and we would lose the war."

27. Kirk, "1973." Shawcross, *Sideshow*, pp. 295ff., argues that the heavy casualties suffered by the Red Khmer forces—perhaps as high as 25 percent killed in some units—drove some survivors mad. See von Marschal, *War in Cambodia*, p. 117 (n23); and Becker, *When the War Was Over*, p. 172. See also the triumphal "Chayo kongto'p padevat reboh pak kommunis" [Long live the Revolutionary Army of the Communist party], *Tung Padevat* (September 1975): "We were not afraid [of the American bombing], because for reasons of national honor and independence we had to struggle against it alone and regardless of the world." Sihanouk told Stanley Karnow that he had "advised our forces not to take Phnom Penh" because he did not want to endanger his mother, who was still there (USLO Peking, Airgram A-8, "Sihanouk Interview," p. 6).

28. Kiernan, *HPP*, p. 371; and Steve Heder to author (letter, August 1991). In 1974, when Red Khmer forces captured the former royal capital of Udong, north of Phnom Penh, they swept off more than ten thousand people. Reports of random executions by cadre surfaced at this time. See Donald Kirk, "Revolution and Political Violence in Cambodia, 1970–1974," in Joseph Zasloff and M. Brown, eds., *Communism in Indochina* (Lexington, Mass., 1975), pp. 215–230.

29. Kiernan, *HPP*, pp. 365ff. On rivalries between the southwest and *dombon 25*, see Vickery, *Cambodia, 1975–1982*, pp. 91ff.; and Chou Chet's confession.

30. See unpublished interviews conducted by Steve Heder with former DK cadre, p. 35: "On May 20, 1973, there were meetings everywhere to proclaim the co-operativization movement." See also Kiernan, *HPP*, pp. 369ff.; and Pol Pot, "Long Live the 17th Anniversary," p. 57. In 1982 the PRK designated May 20 as a national "day of hate," demonizing the previous regime while slyly drawing attention to the day when the Cambodian revolution had diverged publicly from Vietnam's (author's conversa-

tion with a Cambodian official, October 1990). The extent of the collectivization program in 1973 is unclear. Kate Frieson, after more than one hundred interviews with survivors from this period, obtained only scattered evidence that collectivization was widespread in 1973 (personal communication).

31. This fifteen-page document is contained in a microfilm titled "The Hu Nim and Tiv Ol files," deposited by Anthony Barnett in the Echols Collection, Cornell University Library, Ithaca, N.Y. Saloth Sar's name appears as Number 47 (just ahead of Hou Youn) in a list of fifty-seven party members. Khieu Samphan appears as Number 37, just before Ieng Sary. Vorn Vet appears as Number 52.

32. See the confession of Chhim Samauk (Pang). Sar's illness may have been exacerbated by exhaustion. In his confession (p. 79), Men Tul (Sat) stated that "Brother Number One in 1974 was sometimes in the northwest, the west, or the southwest, before returning to the east." Also, in his confession, Ni Muong (Yon), a subordinate of Chhim Samauk, reported frequent movements by Saloth Sar and Nuon Chea in 1974.

33. See "Summary of Annotated Party History," CPK document captured in 1973, translated by Timothy Carney; and "Prawat nei pak kommunis kampuchea" [History of the Communist party of Kampuchea], typewritten text, n.d. [probably 1974]. For comparisons of these texts, see Kiernan, *HPP*, pp. 364–365. See also "Chayo konto'p padevat reboh pak kommunis," pp. 24–64.

34. "Chayo konto'p padevat reboh pak kommunis," pp. 49–50. In a similar speech in early 1977, a party spokesman boasted that the Revolutionary Army, only "seven years old" in 1975, had "beaten the American army [sic] which is two hundred years old" (*Tung Padevat* [December 1976–January 1977]: 61).

35. See Chou Chet's confession; Pol Pot, "Long Live the 17th Anniversary," p. 46; Siet Chhae's confession; and Chhim Samauk's confession. The battles of 1974–1975 were very bloody. Fatalities on both sides often ran as high as 50 percent. See Vickery, *Cambodia, 1975–1982*, p. 69.

36. See Kiernan, *HPP*, pp. 415ff.; Carney, "Unexpected Victory," pp. 3ff.; and Chandler, *Tragedy*, pp. 247ff. See also George Hildebrand and Gareth Porter, *Cambodia: Starvation and Revolution* (New York, 1976), pp. 39ff., which praises the evacuation.

37. See U.S. Central Intelligence Agency, "National Intelligence Estimate: Prospects for Cambodia through August 1975" (Pike Archives); and Arnold Isaacs, *Without Honor* (Baltimore, 1983), pp. 252ff.

38. See Chandler, *Tragedy*, Chapter 7; Isaacs, *Without Honor*, pp. 276ff.; and Shawcross, *Sideshow*, pp. 361ff. William Duiker, *China and Vietnam: The Roots of Conflict* (Berkeley, Calif., 1986), p. 60 (n47), claims that "two Vietnamese divisions" participated in the final attack on Phnom Penh. See also K. Gough, "Roots of the Pol Pot Regime in Kampuchea," in L. Donald, ed., *Themes in Ethnology and History* (Meerut, 1987), p. 134, where Gough, drawing on interviews in Vietnam, claimed that Vietnamese artillery participated in the assault on Cambodia's capital. See also Burchett, *China-Cambodia-Vietnam Triangle*, p. 144, which claims that Sar visited Beijing and Hanoi in late 1974 to plead for military aid. None was forthcoming from China; the Vietnamese allegedly offered heavy artillery and a few gun crews. The visit is uncorroborated and unlikely given the travel times involved, but the requests might well have been made through diplomatic channels. Saloth Sar/Pol Pot always denied Vietnamese participation in the "historic victory" of April 1975.

2>251&h8*

39. See Chhim Samauk's confession; and Chou Chet's confession. Becker, *When the War Was Over*, p. 178, says that Sar entered the city "like a nocturnal predator [that] shuns daylight." See also Men Tul's confession, p. 51, which states that during this period Brother Number One "moved his quarters without warning every two or three days." See also Chandler, Kiernan, and Boua, eds. and trans., *Pol Pot Plans the Future*, p. 276.

40. See author's interview with Loth Suong and Chea Samy (October 1990); and Kate Frieson's interview with them (January 1990). Saloth Chhay had worked for a Republican journal in the 1970s. A Cambodian official who visited Saloth Sar's relatives in Kompong Thom in the 1980s claims that Sar's sister Saroeun, who had left the palace in 1941, received favored treatment, ordered by Saloth Sar, under Democratic Kampuchea. This information contrasts sharply with Sar's neglect of other family members and is not corroborated in Youk Chhang's interviews with Saroeun and her brother Saloth Nhiep.

41. On the massacre of the army officers, see author's interview with Ty Sophen (February 1989); and the confession of Cho Chhan (Sreng) (March 1977): "After the liberation of the entire country the Organization put forward a policy of successively exterminating officers, starting from the generals and working down to the lieutenants." In 1988 Pol Pot told assembled cadre that the "smashing" of Lon Nol's soldiers and officials had been deliberate, because they "represented imperialist strata" (Roger Normand, personal communication, drawn from his interviews with Red Khmer defectors).

42. On the *Mayaguez* incident, see Chandler, *Tragedy*, p. 257. Also see Roy Rowan, *The Four Days of* Mayaguez (New York, 1975).

43. On Sar's visit to Vietnam, see *Livre noir*, p. 72; and author's interview with Ngo Dien (October 1990). On Chinese aid, see Kiernan, *HPP*, p. 413. On Sar's photograph with Mao, see Y Phandara, *Retour à Phnom Penh* (Paris, 1982), p. 52. Phandara saw the photograph in the DK Embassy in Beijing in 1977.

44. See Laurence Picq, *Au delà du ciel* (Paris, 1984), Chapter 1.

45. See Steve Heder, "Kampuchea's Armed Struggle: The Origins of an Independent Revolution," *BCAS* 10, 4 (1978): 2–23; and *Livre noir*, pp. 71ff.

46. Taing Kim Men's interview (June 1989). I am grateful to Kate Frieson for a transcription of this interview, which we carried out together. Taing Kim Men noted that Sar's bodyguards were "minority people. When they spoke Khmer, I could hardly understand a word." Men saw Saloth Sar again in 1977, when Men was working near Pech Nil. Pol Pot visited his work site in a white Toyota van "that looked like an ambulance." Pol Pot remembered him from their previous meeting and called out to him "affectionately."

47. Author's interview with Thiounn Mumm. I am grateful to Ian Cummins for tracking down the Axelrod quotation for me. Compare Pol Pot's eulogy for Mao Zedong, September 18, 1976: "He dedicated his physical, moral, and intellectual strength to revolution. His whole life was dedicated to the revolutionary struggle" (FBIS, *Daily Reports*, September 20, 1976).

48. I am grateful to a Cambodian official for providing me with access to these texts in 1990. They are dated October 1975 (1 set); November 1975 (1 set); January 1976 (1 set); February 1976 (3 sets); March 1976 (7 sets); May 1976 (2 sets); and June 1976 (2 sets). See also "Decisions of the Central Committee on a Variety of Questions," an-

other text from March 1976, in Chandler, Kiernan, and Boua, eds. and trans., *Pol Pot Plans the Future*, pp. 1–8. Ben Kiernan obtained the Khmer original in 1986. The fate of documents recording Central Committee meetings after June 1976 is unknown, but the possibility that they were culled by the Vietnamese after January 1979 should not be dismissed out of hand.

49. *Ka prochum achhimtray thngai 9-10-75* [Meeting of the Central Committee permanent (group), October 9, 1975].

50. I am grateful to Steve Heder for identifying these figures.

51. See also minutes of meeting held on November 2, 1975, dealing in part with relations with Thailand. Biographical information on more than one hundred guards at S-21, the DK interrogation facility in Phnom Penh, suggests that most of them "entered the revolution" immediately before or after April 1975 and underwent brief courses of political training before being assigned to S-21. More than half of these guards came from *dombon 25*.

52. See Chandler, Kiernan, and Boua, eds. and trans., *Pol Pot Plans the Future*, pp. 1–8; and notes from Central Committee meeting of March 12, 1976.

53. See the minutes of the standing committee meeting on March 11, 1976. On the DK constitution, see David P. Chandler, "The Constitution of Democratic Kampuchea," *Pacific Affairs* (Fall 1976): 506–515; and Becker, *When the War Was Over*, pp. 218ff. For Sihanouk's account, see *Prisonnier des khmers rouges*, pp. 97ff.; and FBIS, *Daily Reports*, February 8, 1979: "I resigned as Head of State in April 1976. After trying to make me reverse my decision, they kidnapped me."

54. See the minutes of the standing committee meeting on March 8, 1976: *Ompi pannyha boh chnaot 20-3-76* [On the difficulties of the March 20, 1976, elections].

55. On the rules for the elections, see FBIS, *Daily Reports*, March 10, 1976. Sihanouk remembered voting in Phnom Penh; voting occurred in some rural areas as well. The Central Committee document of March 31, 1976, in Chandler, Kiernan, and Boua, eds. and trans., *Pol Pot Plans the Future*, pp. 1–8, notes that the "representatives," once elected, "will disperse to live with the people again" (p. 7).

56. See Bruce Palling's interview with Pech Kim Luon, a DK pilot who defected to Thailand in late April 1976. Luon said that the main speech on April 17 had been given by "Saloth Sar," but Khieu Samphan's speech was the one broadcast over Radio Phnom Penh. Luon claimed that Sar was the leader of Cambodia; he was unable to identify "Pol Pot." I am grateful to Ben Kiernan for a transcription of this interview. On the ambassador's statement, see Phandara, *Retour à Phnom Penh*, p. 56. Khieu Kannarith suggested that Sar used the pseudonym "Pol" on some occasions and "Pot" on others (author's interview, September 1990).

57. For a list of officers in Democratic Kampuchea in 1976, see Carney, "Organization of Power," pp. 100–102. Fourteen of the twenty-six people on this list were executed between 1976 and 1978. See also Chandler, Kiernan, and Boua, eds. and trans., *Pol Pot Plans the Future*, p. 7, where "Comrade Pol" is listed as the future prime minister.

Chapter Seven

1. Among survivors' accounts, see Pin Yathay, *L'utopie meurtrière* (Paris, 1980); Someth May, *Cambodian Witness* (London, 1986); and Martin Stuart Fox and Ung Bunheang, *The Murderous Revolution* (Sydney, 1985).

2. See Chandler, Kiernan, and Boua, eds. and trans., *Pol Pot Plans the Future*, for translations of eight confidential party documents from this period.

3. See "Statement of the Communist Party of Kampuchea," *Journal of Communist Studies* 3, 1 (March 1987): 19–36; quotation on p. 27. In a December 1976 speech, Pol Pot used similar language: "The methods of defense must be secret," he said. "Those who defend us must be truly adept. They should have practice in observing. They must observe everything, but so those being observed are unaware of it" (Chandler, Kiernan, and Boua, eds. and trans., *Pol Pot Plans the Future*, p. 211). He returned to the theme in his speech of September 28, 1977: "Secret work was the fundamental thing. It allowed us to defend the revolution [the leadership] and also allowed us to arouse the people" (Pol Pot, "Long Live the 17th Anniversary," p. 35).

4. Chandler, Kiernan, and Boua, eds. and trans., *Pol Pot Plans the Future*, p. 121. Steve Heder (letter to author, August 1991) wrote that, in Pol Pot's view, "to survive, the revolution had to move faster than its counterpart in Vietnam. Therefore, anyone who slows things down will prevent the revolution's survival and is objectively 'Vietnamese.'"

5. Hildebrand and Porter, *Cambodia: Starvation and Revolution*, p. 93.

6. FBIS, *Daily Reports*, December 21, 1975. Cambodia's break with its past (see, for example, "Over 2,000 Years of Cambodian History Has Virtually Ended," in FBIS, *Daily Reports*, January 2, 1976) was a break with hierarchical social arrangements, money, markets, religious practices, higher education, and so on. To achieve these goals, the regime decided to control people's access to information and food. Suspicious of enemies, the regime even tried to control courtship, "family-ism," and other remnants of the "old society" *(sangkum chas)*. For a perceptive discussion of DK ideas, see François Ponchaud, "Social Change in the Vortex of Revolution," pp. 159–178. Steve Heder (letter to author, August 1991) pointed out that the phrase "independence-mastery" resembles the Chinese slogan *di li zi zhu* ("Maintain independence and keep the initiative").

7. For Chinese inspirations for these views, see Zhang Chunqiao, "On Exercising All-Round Dictatorship over the Bourgeoisie," *Peking Review*, May 27, 1975; and David Zweig, *Agrarian Radicalism in China, 1968–1981* (Cambridge, Mass., 1990), especially pp. 16–31 and 190–204.

8. Chandler, Kiernan, and Boua, eds. and trans., *Pol Pot Plans the Future*, pp. 130ff. See the confession of Chan Mon, p. 29, which notes that the speed of the plan was disconcerting to those like Chan Mon who allegedly were plotting to undermine Democratic Kampuchea: "If the Plan succeeds by going swiftly, we will grow weaker."

9. For earlier references to the slogan, see Chandler, Kiernan, and Boua, eds. and trans., *Pol Pot Plans the Future*, pp. 20–21. In the First National Conference on Learning from Dazhai held in China in October 1975, Hua Guofeng set national targets of 200 to 250 kilograms of agricultural produce per *mou* (1/15 of a hectare)—that is, exactly 3 metric tons per hectare. See Jonathan D. Spence, *In Search of Modern China* (New York, 1990), p. 644; and Zweig, *Agrarian Radicalism in China*, pp. 66–67. On agriculture under Democratic Kampuchea, see Marie-A. Martin, "La riziculture et la maîtrise de l'eau dans le Kampuchea Démocratique," *Etudes rurales* 83 (July-September 1981): 7–44; and Martin, "La politique alimentaire des khmers rouges," *Etudes rurales* 99–101 (July-December 1985): 347–365. These studies show that although production increased in many areas under Democratic Kampuchea, some of the regime's pet ideas—such as the decree that all rice fields measure precisely 1 hectare regardless

of topography—had disastrous consequences. Martin also noted that although many DK irrigation works collapsed, several survived into the 1980s. See also Charles Twining, "The Economy," in Jackson, ed., *Cambodia, 1975–1978*, pp. 109–150. For the final quotation, see Chandler, Kiernan, and Boua, eds. and trans., *Pol Pot Plans the Future*, p. 130.

10. On life in the northwest as recorded by two "new people," see Pin Yathay, *L'utopie meurtrière*; and Someth May, *Cambodian Witness*. See also Vickery, *Cambodia, 1975–1982*, pp. 100–120. On the motto, see Henri Locard, *Le livre rouge de Pol Pot ou les paroles de l'Angkar* (Paris, 1996), p. 179.

11. See Chandler, Kiernan, and Boua, eds. and trans., *Pol Pot Plans the Future*, pp. 128ff. And see Kheang Sim Hon's confession (December 1978), which notes that in the northwestern zone, cadre were asked to set targets to be incorporated into the plan by the Central Committee in May 1976.

12. Twining, "Economy," p. 144, estimates that rice harvests in 1976 amounted to roughly half the pre-1970 averages. Even without the diversions of surpluses, with no imports this shortfall would have led to widespread starvation. See also Martin, *Le mal cambodgien*, pp. 170ff.; and Becker, *When the War Was Over*, pp. 246–247, reporting Khieu Thirith's tour of the northwest in 1976. Thirith was appalled by what she saw. On her return, she told Pol Pot that "agents had got into our ranks" and were wrecking the revolution. Her brother-in-law, convinced by this explanation, embarked on purges of the northwest in early 1977.

13. Chandler, Kiernan, and Boua, eds. and trans., *Pol Pot Plans the Future*, pp. 90ff.; FBIS, *Daily Reports*, July 25, 1975. François Grunewald (personal communication) has remarked how *foreign* these measures seemed to many Cambodian farmers—an ironic charge to level at the revolutionaries, who stressed the autonomy and "Cambodian-ness" of their proposals.

14. See also Twining, "Economy," pp. 132–137; and Martin, *Le mal cambodgien*, pp. 185ff.; and Marie-A. Martin, "L'industrie dans le Kampuchea Démocratique," *Etudes rurales* 89–91 (January-September 1983): 77–110. Approximately 80 percent of the factories operating in the DK era dated from before 1975. Goods manufactured included "Liberation" cigarettes (distributed to cadre), cotton cloth, jute bags, and bricks.

15. See FBIS, *Daily Reports*, June 18, 1976, which suggests that "the traitorous clique and exploiting classes were afraid and frightened by the spirit of collectivism" exhibited by peasants. These peasants, however, preferred to work alone or with relatives and thus they resented the imposition of collectivization by the government. FBIS, *Daily Reports*, March 13, 1978, nevertheless boasted that "all remnants of the work systems, production techniques, beliefs and individualistic ways of life . . . have been abolished by our . . . peasants."

16. For translations of DK revolutionary songs dating from 1975–1976, see Kiernan and Boua, *Peasants and Politics in Kampuchea*, pp. 236–238. Sihanouk, *Prisonnier des khmers rouges*, p. 131, refers to the songs broadcast over Radio Phnom Penh as "musical torture." Picq, *Au delà du ciel*, p. 146, says that Pol Pot wrote the words to the national anthem, although Pol Pot himself suggested collective authorship in "Long Live the 17th Anniversary," p. 48.

17. See Chandler, "Seeing Red," pp. 34–56.

18. For Pol Pot's two eulogies to Mao on September 18, see FBIS, *Daily Reports*, September 20, 1976. The writings of Mao mentioned by Pol Pot were "Analysis of Classes in Chinese Society" (1926); "Problems of Strategy in the Chinese Revolution" (1936); "On Protracted War" (1938); "On Contradiction" (1937); "On Practice" (1937); "On New Democracy" (1940); "On Chinese Revolutionary Culture, Literature and Art" (1942?); "On Correct Handling of Contradictions Among the People" (1957); and "On Class Struggle." See John Bryan Starr and Nancy Anne Dyer, *Post-Liberation Works of Mao Zedong: A Bibliography and an Index* (Berkeley, Calif., 1976). I have been unable to identify "On Class Struggle." Mao's "statement of 20 June 1970 supporting the Cambodian people" mentioned by Pol Pot is probably the statement issued by Mao on May 20, 1975. I am grateful to Serge Thion for providing this reference.

19. On the September 1976 crisis, see Ben Kiernan, "'Introduction' to Document 5," in Chandler, Kiernan, and Boua, eds. and trans., *Pol Pot Plans the Future*, pp. 164ff.; Becker, *When the War Was Over*, pp. 278–279; and David Chandler, "Revising the Past in Democratic Kampuchea: When Was the Birthday of the Party?" *Pacific Affairs* (Summer 1983): 283–300.

20. See Chandler, "Revising the Past"; FBIS, *Daily Reports*, October 31, 1978, a report from a defecting cadre broadcast over Vietnamese radio, recalled an order from the Central Committee in September 1976 decreeing the "1960" birthday of the party: "Anyone who joined the Party prior to that date should not consider himself a Party member."

21. See Robert Conquest, *The Great Terror* (New York, 1953), pp. 151ff.; and Tucker, *Stalin: The Years in Power*, pp. 441–478. Not all those executed were party members, but the damage suffered by the party can be inferred from the fact that its membership in 1975, before S-21 went into operation, was estimated to be only fourteen thousand men and women (Carney, "Organization of Power," p. 95).

22. For a detailed study of the S-21 archive, see Chandler, *Voices from S-21*. The best short introduction to S-21 is still one of the earliest: Anthony Barnett, Chanthou Boua, and Ben Kiernan, "Bureaucracy of Death," *New Statesman*, May 2, 1980, pp. 668–676. See also Becker, *When the War Was Over*, pp. 271–298; Vickery, *Cambodia, 1975–1982*, pp. 151–152; Ing Pech, "Tuol Sleng," *L'évènement du jeudi*, December 6–12, 1990, p. 318; and Steve Heder, "Khmer Rouge Opposition to Pol Pot: Pro-Chinese or Pro-Vietnamese?" (unpublished seminar paper, 1990). The following discussion, like *Voices from S-21*, draws on these sources, on conversations with Heder, and on S-21 documents kindly supplied by David Hawk in 1986–1987. For confession texts and related materials, I am grateful to Anthony Barnett, Timothy Carney, May Ebihara, Kate Frieson, Ben Kiernan, Judy Ledgerwood, and Michael Vickery. I am also grateful to the archival staff of the Tuol Sleng Genocide Museum and the staff of the Documentation Center–Cambodia in Phnom Penh for their help on my frequent visits to their respective archives.

23. The party itself was a moving target. An interrogator at S-21 noted in 1976: "The Party changes rapidly and frequently; [it] changes the prisoners we have to interrogate, the way of making up documents, the methodology of interrogation. We must adjust to the system in time, leaping along with the movement" (quoted in Chandler, *Tragedy*, pp. 287–288). Similarly, a 1977 *Tung Padevat* editorial demanded: "How are good, average, not good, risky, strong and not strong [cadre] to be judged?

They are to be judged by the movement ... [and] the masses will know when something is wrong that it isn't the Party, but this or that individual not putting into practice the Party line" (*Tung Padevat*, [October–November 1977]: 37; Heder's translation). Heder, in his "Khmer Rouge Opposition" likens the process of analyzing data from Tuol Sleng to "toying with a kaleidoscope, turning a jumble of data around and around in combinations until some patterns emerge that look like they might reflect something real."

24. For a discussion of the staff at S-21, see Chandler, *Voices from S-21*, Chapter Two. Over seventy S-21 workers were purged between 1976 and January 1979. Their confessions are of special interest. On Duch, see Chandler, *Voices from S-21*, Chapter Two; Vickery, *Cambodia, 1975–1982*, pp. 151–152; and Becker, *When the War Was Over*, pp. 272–273. In 1971 the French scholar François Bizot was detained for three months by the CPK near Udong. During that time, he was made to prepare three detailed autobiographical statements of the sort that later formed the bases for S-21 confessions. His interrogator was Duch, who impressed Bizot as "a man of principle" completely devoted to the revolutionary cause. Author's interview (July 1989).

25. See Chan Chakrei's confession; and *Chatupom nei paenka yothea* 76 [On the nature of the 1976 military plan], dated June 6, 1976. Heder's argument, contained in "Khmer Rouge Opposition to Pol Pot," is that although hundreds of prisoners were accused of being pro-Vietnamese, hardly any pro-Vietnamese sentiments or statements supporting the Vietnam Workers' party surface in the texts. It is possible that soldiers in Division 170 mutinied in large part for better living conditions and the right to get married. See *Vietnam Courier*, ed., *Kampuchea Dossier II* (Hanoi, 1978), p. 65; and Steve Heder to author (letter of August 1991). For a discussion of the 1976 purges, see Chandler, *Voices from S-21*, Chapter Three.

26. See Keo Meas's confession (September–October 1976).

27. See Ney Saran's confession (September–October 1976). The fact that only one copy of the memoranda survives in the S-21 archive suggests that they never left the prison.

28. See Non Suon's and Sien An's confessions. Suon's contains biographies of several party leaders, including Pol Pot; this is reproduced as Appendix 1. See also Hak Sien Lamy's confession (December 1976), which claims knowledge of Vietnamese plans to attack Cambodia militarily by the middle of 1976.

29. See Chandler, Kiernan, and Boua, eds. and trans., *Pol Pot Plans the Future*, pp. 177–216; and David P. Chandler, "A Revolution in Full Spate" (which discusses the speech), in David Ablin and Marlowe Hood, eds., *The Cambodian Agony* (Armonk, N.Y., 1987), pp. 165–179. The passage echoes Stalin's charge in 1933 that the "capitalists ... have managed to make their way into our Party," and Mao's similar statement, in 1976, that "the bourgeoisie is right inside the Communist party" (citations from Jeremy Paltiel, "The Cult of Personality: Some Comparative Reflections on Political Culture in Leninist Regimes," *Studies in Comparative Communism* 16, 1, 2 [Spring-Summer 1983]: 49–64).

30. Chandler, Kiernan, and Boua, eds. and trans., *Pol Pot Plans the Future*, p. 183.

31. Ibid., p. 204.

32. See Koy Thuon's confession, which appears to have been culled after 1979. Vickery, *Cambodia, 1975–1982*, pp. 148–149. Many confessions from 1977 refer to the prisoners' acquaintance with "Khuon." Perhaps, as with Hou Youn in 1975, Koy

Thuon's popularity was seen as a threat to Pol Pot, who seems to have been more comfortable with people like Nuon Chea, Khieu Samphan, and Ieng Sary, who had no power base outside the Central Committee. Ta Mok, with his powerful southwestern zone network of clients, would be the exception that proves the rule.

33. Hu Nim later claimed that at a more restricted gathering soon after, Pol Pot revealed the names of four men executed at S-21. Three of them (Chhuk, Chakrei, and Ly Phen) had links with the eastern zone (Chandler, Kiernan, and Boua, eds. and trans., *Pol Pot Plans the Future*, p. 303). See also Picq, *Au delà du ciel*, pp. 99–100. Those purged at this time, Picq wrote, "were people whom I knew and had admired."

34. Bruce Palling's interview with Chhit Do is corroborated in Chanda, *Brother Enemy*, p. 83. In April 1977 a week-long uprising broke out in Chikreng, Siem Reap. It was put down with heavy casualties. The uprising probably convinced Pol Pot that the party had genuine enemies in the region. See Thach Keo Dara, "Une révolte de la population," *Sereika* 28 (September 1978): 7–8; *Kampuchea Dossier II*, p. 65; and Vickery, *Cambodia 1975–1982*, pp. 126–127.

35. Chandler, *Voices from S-21*, Chapter 3; Becker, *When the War Was Over*, p. 250; Picq, *Au delà du ciel*, p. 104. Siet Chhae's confession refers to "measures taken in the north" by the organization in February 1977. In April, Siet Chhae himself was "gathered up" by the organization.

36. Interview with a Cambodian official (October 1990). See also the confession of Ket Chau (Sem) (March 1977); Chhim Samauk's confession; the confession of Chou Chet (Si); and author's interview with You Sambo. Ket Chau, a thirty-four-year-old from Kompong Cham, was forced to confess to five years of botched assassination attempts against Pol Pot. According to a former DK official who prefers anonymity, Pol Pot was housed in a compound with Nuon Chea and other high-ranking officials in 1975–1977 but moved to a secret location by himself in the middle of 1978. The official added intriguingly that in his opinion Nuon Chea and Pol Pot "cordially detested one another."

37. On Thirith, see You Sambo interview. On the persistence of familism in Democratic Kampuchea, see Serge Thion, "The Pattern of Cambodian Politics," in Ablin and Hood, eds., *Cambodian Agony*, pp. 149–164. Khieu Ponnary survived Pol Pot. In 1998 she was living in northwestern Cambodia in the zone controlled by Ieng Sary, who defected to the Phnom Penh government in 1996. The exact nature of her illness is impossible to determine.

38. See Heder, "Kampuchea's Armed Struggle," pp. 2–23; and Steve Heder, "The Kampuchean-Vietnamese Conflict," in David Elliott, ed., *The Third Indochina Conflict* (Boulder, Colo., 1981), pp. 21–67. For new phenomena, see *Far Eastern Economic Review (FEER)*, August 19, 1977. See also Chanda, *Brother Enemy*, pp. 84ff.; Alan Dupont, "The Vietnamese-Kampuchea Conflict, 1975–1979" (Master's thesis, Australian National University, 1980), pp. 8–9; and Pierre-L. Lamant, "La frontière entre le Cambodge et le Vietnam du milieu du XIXe siècle à nos jours," in P. B. Lafont, ed., *Les frontières de Vietnam* (Paris, 1989), pp. 156–187. For a detailed review of Cambodian relations with Vietnam since World War II, see Lionel Vairon, "Du Parti Indochinois à la "Triple Alliance Indochinoise," Doctoral thesis, INALCO, Paris, 1998.

39. On the 1976 fighting, see Vickery, *Cambodia, 1975–1982*, p. 190; and author's interview with Ha The Duc, a former Vietnamese soldier (May 1991). The telegram, dated November 11, 1975, reports Vietnamese troop movements along the eastern

frontier, referring at one stage to a "100-meter" incursion by a Vietnamese unit into Cambodia. Some of these incidents, as Lionel Vairon suggests, may have involved South Vietnamese non-Communist remnants. Others clearly involved Vietnamese government troops operating, perhaps without hostile intentions, on Cambodian soil. See Vairon, "Du Parti Indochinois," p. 103.

40. See Ben Kiernan, "Wild Chickens, Farm Chickens, and Cormorants: Kampuchea's Eastern Zone Under Pol Pot," in Chandler and Kiernan, eds., *Revolution and Its Aftermath*, pp. 1970ff.; and Becker, *When the War Was Over,* pp. 252 and 311ff. Vickery, *Cambodia, 1975–1982,* pp. 194–196, reviews the evidence. On Khmer casualties in Vietnam, see author's interview with Thach Tan (February 1988). For evidence of a Khmer probe into Vietnam on August 20, 1977, see the confession of Meas Mon (June 1978): "After the Vietnamese ran away [sic] my CIA group [sic] wandered around burning houses and matériel."

41. Kiernan, "Wild Chickens," pp. 172ff. On the public relations value of the enterprise, an idea drawn from Steve Heder, see Chanda, *Brother Enemy,* p. 195. On Vietnamese probes, see Robert Ross, *The Indo-China Tangle* (New York, 1988), pp. 155–156.

42. Pol Pot, "Long Live the 17th Anniversary," and FBIS, *Daily Reports,* October 4, 1977. See also Nayan Chanda, "The Pieces Begin to Fit," *FEER,* October 21, 1977.

43. Picq, *Au delà du ciel,* pp. 109–110. FBIS, *Daily Reports,* September 29, 1977, reports that with the emergence of the party, the "Internationale" was to be sung daily before the national anthem.

44. See "Learning from Our Four Year Plan," *Tung Padevat,* special issue (October-November 1977): 113–128, which suggests that in some way the unannounced, unexplained plan was still in effect. I am grateful to Steve Heder for a translation of the article.

45. On the Vietnamese broadcast, see FBIS, *Daily Reports,* September 30, 1977; also noted in Ross, *Indo-China Tangle,* p. 148.

Chapter Eight

1. For Pol Pot's visit to China, see Chanda, *Brother Enemy,* pp. 98ff. His visit coincided roughly with the first anniversary of the arrest of the Gang of Four and also, we know now, during a struggle for leadership between Hua Guofeng and Deng Xiaoping. Sihanouk, in *Prisonnier des khmers rouges,* pp. 217–218, seeing a film of the reception, commented forlornly that it "surpassed, in magnificence, anything I had ever received." The identification of Saloth Sar with Pol Pot came from comparing photographs and matching details provided in the thumbnail biography broadcast when he visited North Korea (discussed below).

2. See *Peking Review,* October 7, 1977, pp. 9ff. and 22ff.; Chanda, "Pol Pot Plays Up to Peking," *FEER,* October 14, 1977; and Chanda, *Brother Enemy,* pp. 101–102. Vorn Vet, identified as a member of the delegation in the *Peking Review,* said nothing about the visit in his 1978 confession. Thiounn Thoeun is identified in a photograph of the delegation in *China Illustrated,* December 1977. Lenin, in his attack on ultra-leftism, cited Engels's comment on the Blanquists in France in the 1870s: "What childish innocence it is to present impatience as a theoretically convincing argument!"

3. On the confidential discussion, see Chanda, *Brother Enemy*, pp. 100–101, drawing on documents produced at the Pol Pot/Ieng Sary genocide trial in 1979.

4. Becker, *When the War Was Over*, pp. 316–317. A similar upmarket periodical, the Khmer-language monthly *Kampuchea*, circulated among Cambodians in Europe. A Burmese delegation visited Democratic Kampuchea in mid-1977 to prepare for a visit by General Ne Win later in the year. Malaysian officials arrived in December 1977; their Thai counterparts followed in early 1978. Ross, *Indo-China Tangle*, p. 168.

5. The biography was broadcast over Radio Pyongyang. See FBIS, *Daily Reports*, October 4, 1977. The film of the visit was shown in Phnom Penh several months later (FBIS, *Daily Reports*, February 21, 1978). Kim Il Sung sent Sihanouk, via the delegation, a case of Korean apples. They were transmitted to the prince as a gift from Pol Pot. Sihanouk, *Prisonnier des khmers rouges*, p. 215.

6. For evidence of Vietnam's attack, not publicized by the Khmer, see Chanda, *Brother Enemy*, p. 196. From the Cambodian side, see Meas Mon's confession (June 1978): "We opened fire on 16 October 1977. The combat lasted for more than a month in Vietnam. No major results were achieved. . . . We attacked according to a CIA plan, not imagining . . . a breakthrough." For testimonies allegedly from prisoners, see Democratic Kampuchea, "Evidences [sic] of the Vietnamese Aggression Against Democratic Kampuchea," Phnom Penh, February 1978; and Khin Ka, "Laissons parler les soldats kampuchéens capturés," in *Kampuchea Dossier II*, pp. 75–81. These confessions had already been broadcast by Phnom Penh and Hanoi, respectively.

7. On Chen Yonggui's visit, see Chanda, *Brother Enemy*, pp. 203–204; and Ross, *Indo-China Tangle*, pp. 157–161. On Dazhai, see Milton and Milton, *The Wind Will Not Subside*, p. 75; and Mao Zedong, "Comment on Learning from Dazhai," *Peking Review*, October 6, 1972. The Dazhai campaign peaked in 1975, during Mao's decline, and sputtered out in 1980.

8. See Chou Chet's confession (Stephen Heder's translation). It is unclear if Chou Chet knew what "Dazhai" was. It is conceivable that Pol Pot, in a playful mood, merely told him that Tai Chai (in Khmer, "Grandfather Chai"), an important guest from China, would soon be visiting the zone.

9. The details are from FBIS, *Daily Reports*, December 12, 1977. Chen Yonggui helped with the threshing here and at "several places" along the railway during his journey to Kompong Chhnang. Arranging for the "impromptu" stops (more clean, well-fed workers, more well-maintained irrigation works) had obviously cost Chou Chet much trouble.

10. Compare this with Touch Phoeun's confession: "I became afraid that we could build Angkor Wat and then be unable to live in it." The litany of complaints, with starvation added, recurs in survivors' accounts of the "Pol Pot time." Chou Chet's career was similar to Pol Pot's: recruitment into the Indochina Communist party in 1951, work in Phnom Penh for the Pracheachon Group in the 1950s, flight into the maquis in 1963. Chou Chet's wife Im Naen cooked for Brother Number One in Office 100 in the 1960s and became a *dombon* secretary in 1977 (a rare post for a woman and indicative of her revolutionary status). The couple were close friends of Chhim Samauk (Pang), who also was purged in 1978 after serving for years as Pol Pot's *aide-de-camp*.

11. Dupont, *Vietnam-Kampuchea Conflict*, p. 16; Becker, *When the War Was Over*, p. 319; *Livre noir*, pp. 74–75; and Democratic Kampuchea, "Evidences," passim. See also *Tung Padevat* (May-June 1978): 9. The charge in "Evidences" that Vietnamese military units began to be subjected to anti-DK propaganda in September 1977, preparatory to a sustained attack, is corroborated by other sources. See also *New York Times*, December 25, 1977, reporting hostilities in "Parrot's Beak"; and FBIS, *Daily Reports*, December 28, 1977.

12. Picq, *Au delà du ciel*, pp. 114ff. For the text of these DK statements, see *Vietnam Courier*, ed., *Kampuchea Dossier I* (Hanoi, 1978), pp. 144–158. The last paragraphs in the Khmer text (not contained in the French-language official version) listed the same casualty figures for 1975, 1976, and 1977: enemy losses of "100 killed" and Cambodian losses of "4 killed or wounded." Chanda, *Brother Enemy*, p. 209, suggests that the break was intended to force Beijing's hand. Ross, *Indo-China Tangle*, pp. 161ff., documents Chinese foot-dragging in offering military support to Democratic Kampuchea. According to Chanda, until mid-February 1978 China was still hoping for a standoff or a negotiated solution. If Stephen Heder's suggestion that Vietnamese attacks had been provoked by Cambodian infiltrations of Vietnam that had left the frontier undefended are true—and he referred to an "overwhelming amount of evidence" (letter to author, August 1991)—it is possible that the break in relations and the appeal to China were desperate attempts to cover up an enormous strategic blunder for which Pol Pot was directly responsible.

13. For the regime's explanation of Cambodia's "victory," see FBIS, *Daily Reports*, February 2, 1978, which lists the four causes as the Communist party of Kampuchea's political line; the intrinsic virtues of conducting a people's war; the unity of the army and the party; and (significantly, in view of what happened later in 1978) "because we have conducted a vigorous, profound revolution [purge] in the ranks of the Party and the army." Vietnamese officials were convinced that Cambodia's break with Vietnam signaled increasing Chinese support for the Cambodians (Chanda, *Brother Enemy*, pp. 215–216).

14. On Pol Pot's visit, see R. A. Burgler, *The Eyes of the Pineapple: Revolutionary Intellectuals and Terror in Democratic Kampuchea* (Saarbrücken, 1990), p. 135, citing Stephen Heder's unpublished interview with a former cadre. See also *Tung Padevat*, special issue (December 1977-January 1978): 12: "In the southwest, for every two casualties on our side, the enemy had ten. The situation was similar in the east."

15. On prisoners, see *FEER*, March 31 and April 21, 1978; and Chanda, *Brother Enemy*, p. 215. In April a Polish journalist, Monikja Warnenska, visited a camp holding Cambodian prisoners and wrote: "At first when I saw them with chalk in their hands and their faces turning toward a blackboard, I did not understand what was going on. I asked the camp commander, 'What are they doing?' The camp commander replied: 'We are teaching them how to read and write.' How really strange it is that Cambodian soldiers had to wait until they were taken prisoner to learn the alphabet." The last word suggests that the prisoners were being taught to read and write in Vietnamese. FBIS, *Daily Reports*, April 5, 1978. I am grateful to Ms. Warnenska, whose name I misspelled in the first edition, for several interesting letters about her research.

16. Even in this opening-up phase, Pol Pot continued to play hide-and-seek. For example, in an interview broadcast over Radio Phnom Penh on April 12, an an-

nouncer read Pol Pot's replies to questions. On the other hand, every day at 6:00 A.M. an anonymous "spokesman for the Organization" broadcast "Moments of Training" *(neati oprum)*, which contained guidance for cadre and work teams throughout the nation. According to Ong Thong Hoeung (author's interview, February 1990), who was made to listen to the broadcasts daily, they were delivered by the prime minister himself. Sihanouk, *Prisonnier des khmers rouges*, p. 219, concurred.

17. Author's interview with Soth Polin (October 1989); Polin, "La diabolique douceur de Pol Pot"; author's interview with Keng Vannsak (May 1987).

18. See Phandara, *Retour à Phnom Penh*, pp. 243ff.; Martin, *Le mal cambodgien*, pp. 191ff.; Jan Myrdal, "Why Is There Famine in Kampuchea?" *Indochina Chronicle* 77 (February 1981); and author's interviews with Yem Nolla and Ong Thong Hoeung (May 1988). The returnees, suspected of having caught "the capitalist virus," were considered foreigners and placed under the supervision of the Ministry of Foreign Affairs. Touch Kamdoeun, a diplomat educated in France, confessed in 1977 that Cambodian students "in France learned to be happy like Europeans, and therefore how to oppress ordinary people." On schools, see Picq, *Au delà du ciel*, pp. 124ff. A side effect of the reforms was that "new people" became liable for military conscription (Becker, *When the War Was Over*, p. 326).

19. See "Seckdei nai no', reboh kanak machhim pak kommunis kampuchea . . . compu'h neaq kan chrolom" (Guidelines from the Central Committee of the CPK . . . toward misled people), typewritten text, dated June 20, 1978. I am grateful to David Hawk for providing me with a copy. See also Picq, *Au delà du ciel*, p. 166; Vickery, *Cambodia, 1975–1982*, p. 141; and author's interview with Heng Sen (June 1989).

20. See "Learning from Important Experiences," *Tung Padevat* (May-June 1978): 17–33. I have relied on Stephen Heder's translation. The raw pragmatism of the passage (that is, the way to make friends is not to kill people) marks the document as authentically Red Khmer.

21. See "Pay Attention to Sweeping Out the Concealed Enemy Boring from Within," *Tung Padevat* (July 1978): 5–25; quotation on p. 9 (Stephen Heder's translation). On p. 24, the speaker (almost certainly Pol Pot) returns to the theme that Vietnam, rather than Cambodia, is surrounded, adding on p. 44: "The Marxist-Leninist parties in North and South America and in France and Italy defend us. . . . They stand on the side of revolution. . . . They are excited and happy with our revolution." It is unclear whether Pol Pot was aware of the marginality of these groups.

22. Unpublished Heder interview, quoted by Burgler, *Eyes of the Pineapple*, p. 135.

23. Ben Kiernan, *The Eastern Zone Massacres* (New York, 1986); Fox and Bunheang, *Murderous Revolution*, pp. 129–153; and Becker, *When the War Was Over*, pp. 306–308, 320–323. The purges were concentrated in Kratie, Kompong Cham, and Svay Rieng. Heng Samrin, an eastern zone divisional commander, defected to the Vietnamese in May 1978. He became chief of state of Cambodia in 1979.

24. See Chandler, *Voices from S-21*, Chapter 3; and the confession of Chhay Kim Hor (December 1978). Had Son Sen been genuinely implicated in a plot, it would have been easy for him to disappear, either by being destroyed by the party or by taking refuge elsewhere after 1979. Instead, he held on to military positions under Pol Pot's exiled government and by mid-1991 was named a member of Cambodia's Supreme Executive Council, along with Khieu Samphan and representatives from other factions.

25. Tucker, *Stalin: The Years in Power*, p. 476. See also William A. Joseph, *The Critique of Ultra-Leftism in China, 1958–1981* (Stanford, Calif., 1984), p. 214; Zweig, *Agrarian Radicalism in China*, pp. 24ff.

26. See "The National Duties of Us All," *Tung Padevat* (July 1978): 1, which refers to the "correct and wise leadership of the CPK with POL POT at its head" (Heder translation). See also the untitled poem in *Kampuchea*, August 1978, p. 36, line 3, for the same formulation. Sok Bunthan (author's interview, July 1989) claimed to have seen a school textbook in 1978 with Pol Pot's picture on the cover. See also *New Straits Times*, March 6, 1990, where Loth Suong in an interview with Larry Jagan stated that his brother's portrait in the dining hall in Kompong Thom was bracketed by photographs of Mao Zedong and Kim Il Sung.

27. Author's interviews with Ong Thong Hoeung (February 1990), Khieu Kannarith (October 1990), and Vann Nath (January 1995). Hoeung identified the artist as Mok Sokhun, who had come back from France with Hoeung in 1976. Sokhun was arrested in December 1976 and held at S-21 until January 1979, when he "escaped." Presumably, much of his time was spent executing portraits and other paintings for the regime. On the sculptures, see John Pilger, *Heroes* (London, 1989), p. 394. Pilger interviewed the sculptor, Ten Chan, in Phnom Penh in 1979. See also *Vietnam Courier*, ed., *Kampuchea Dossier III* (Hanoi, 1979), p. 116. Thiounn Mumm told Sauv Kim Hong in 1980 that "from what he knew about Pol Pot, Pol Pot would never have ordered" the statues made (Heder interview with Hong).

28. David Ashley's interview with Vann Nath (May 1995). Wat Phnom is a small hill in the northern section of the capital. The mock-up of the statue has not survived. See also Christine Chameau, "No. 55 Delivers His Verdict on Pol Pot," an extended interview with Vann Nath, in *Phnom Penh Post*, November 7–20, 1997.

29. Some accurate biographical information about Nuon Chea appears in Non Suon's confession, suggesting that in the self-criticism sessions that all party members attended periodically, Nuon Chea had on at least one occasion provided a version of his life story. By 1978, some party members had blended Nuon Chea and Pol Pot in their minds to form "the organization." On Nuon Chea, see Roger Normand (personal communication, citing conversations with defectors); author's interviews with Hin Sithan (November 1987) and Ty Sophen (February 1989); and Suon Kaset Sokho's letter to author (November 1989). Sithan and Sophen spent the Pol Pot period in Wat Ko, Nuon Chea's home village, where Chea's mother exercised a strong influence over him. In 1975–1977, when she lived in Wat Ko, she was allowed to visit the Buddhist monastery daily. Four monks were kept on duty to receive her. They were almost certainly the only functioning monks in Democratic Kampuchea. In 1997, Nuon Chea allowed himself to be interviewed by Nate Thayer and provided Thayer with an interesting handwritten history of the Communist movement, but revealed very little about his personal life.

30. See U.S. Embassy Bangkok's telegram of Heder's interview with Sok Sim (Lonh), unnumbered, Pike Archives (Cambodia, January 1980).

31. Martin, *Le mal cambodgien*, p. 194. This may have been the seminar on education in October 1978 mentioned by Sauv Kim Hong to Stephen Heder (interview): "[Pol Pot] seemed to be a very good speaker, cogent and coherent."

32. Author's interview with a Cambodian official (September 1990). The word *samanh* has overtones of humility as well as everydayness.

33. On the celebrations in Phnom Penh, see Picq, *Au delà du ciel*, pp. 123–124. See also Peter Schier and Manola Schier Oum, *Prince Sihanouk on Cambodia* (Hamburg, 1980), p. 31: "China and Korea helped them to industrialize the country." See also Thiounn Mumm's unpublished interview with Stephen Heder (September 1980), where Mumm pointed to several major industrial developments in 1978—a new oil refinery, electric power stations, and a "big paper factory," among others.

34. See Chanda, *Brother Enemy*, p. 327; Picq, *Au delà du ciel*, p. 141; and Ross, *Indo-China Tangle*, p. 211. Ross, p. 214, noted that several Chinese delegations, including a troupe of acrobats, visited Cambodia in the closing months of 1978.

35. Becker, *When the War Was Over*, pp. 406–436. Dudman had been taken prisoner by a Vietnamese-Cambodian guerrilla unit in 1970. See his *Forty Days with the Enemy* (New York, 1971) and his reports in the *Sydney Morning Herald*, December 26–30, 1978, and January 1–4, 1979. See also Malcolm Caldwell and Lek Hor Tan, *Cambodia in the Southeast Asian War* (New York, 1973). Caldwell's writings on Democratic Kampuchea are collected in B. Hering and Ernst Utrecht, eds., *Malcolm Caldwell's Southeast Asia* (James Cook University, Australia, 1979), pp. 27–137. Ben Kiernan, *The Pol Pot Regime* (New Haven, Conn., 1995), pp. 446–447, also discusses the visit, citing Caldwell's notebooks.

36. The following paragraphs are drawn from Becker, *When the War Was Over*, pp. 430–433; author's interview with Richard Dudman (April 1991); Dudman's letter to author (March 1991); Stephen Webbe, "Who Is Pol Pot?" *Christian Science Monitor*, December 12, 1978; and Elizabeth Becker, "A Killing Machine with a Mission," *London Times*, September 14, 1989, where she writes: "I was seated to his right, organizing my notebook and trying to avoid his smile, which was . . . charming. Beware of stereotypes and bad photographs."

37. Pol Pot was planning for prolonged guerrilla resistance and a Vietnamese occupation. See Nayan Chanda, "Pol Pot Eyes the Jungle," *FEER*, December 15, 1978. The rapidity and success of the Vietnamese invasion probably surprised him.

38. Elizabeth Becker, "How a Western Radical Fell Victim to a Murderous Oriental Intrigue," *Guardian*, April 21, 1982; *When the War Was Over*, pp. 433–436; Picq, *Au delà du ciel*, pp. 145–147; author's interview with Ngo Pen (July 1989); and David Monaghan's letter to author (March 1991). Ngo Pen was present at the Pol Pot–Caldwell interview as an interpreter and spent the night preparing a translation. He recalled the interview as "friendly" and as dealing with "agriculture and economics." For a detailed discussion of the murder, see Burgler, *Eyes of the Pineapple*, pp. 151–152, 350–351. See also Kiernan, *The Pol Pot Regime*, pp. 448–450.

39. Sihanouk, *Prisonnier des khmers rouges*, pp. 312ff. Chanda, *Brother Enemy*, pp. 301ff., 339–340. See also Canadian Communist League (Marxist-Leninist), *Kampuchea Will Win!* (Montreal, 1979).

40. See "Statement of Comrade Pol Pot," January 5, 1979; Sihanouk, *Prisonnier des khmers rouges*, pp. 316–320; and Chanda, *Brother Enemy*, p. 302. Sihanouk later told James Pringle, "I was mesmerized. I knew [Pol Pot] was mad, but I couldn't stop listening" (author's interview with Pringle, February 1991). In 1990 Sihanouk told the Indochina specialist Philippe Devillers that "there are two charismatic people in Cambodia: Pol Pot and I" (Devillers, personal communication).

41. Phandara, *Retour à Phnom Penh*, p. 186. See also Picq, *Au delà du ciel*, pp. 151–153; and Chanda, *Brother Enemy*, pp. 316–317, 344ff. Ieng Sary, who left on the

same train, reached the Thai border, without shoes, on January 11 and Beijing three days later. Pol Pot's immediate destination is not known. He probably fled to Thailand with Nuon Chea.

Chapter Nine

1. See William Shawcross, *The Quality of Mercy* (London, 1984).

2. The most detailed account of the People's Republic of Kampuchea so far is Michael Vickery, *Kampuchea* (London 1984), which is favorable to the regime. See also Vairon, "Du Parti Communiste Indochinois," pp. 272 ff.; and Viviane Frings, *Le paysan cambodgien et le socialisme* (Paris, 1997). Evan Gottesman's work in progress should provide a valuable analysis of the period.

3. For details, see Chanda, *Brother Enemy*, pp. 348ff. Although ASEAN convened meetings throughout the 1980s to deal with the "Cambodian problem," its first official condemnation of DK occurred in February 1990. See Patrick Raszelenberg and Peter Schier, *The Cambodia Conflict: Search for a Settlement* (Hamburg, 1997), p. 299.

4. François Ponchaud, *Cambodia: Year Zero* (New York, 1978). Noam Chomsky and Edward Hermann, *After the Cataclysm* (Boston, 1979) includes a sustained attack on Ponchaud's findings, which have stood up better than those of Chomsky and Hermann, as far as the Red Khmers and their policies are concerned. On the metamorphosis of S-21, see Judy Ledgerwood, "The Cambodian Tuol Sleng Museum of Genocidal Crimes: National Narrative," *Museum Anthropology* 21 (Spring-Summer 1997): 83–98.

5. On the statistics of regime-related deaths in Democratic Kampuchea, see Michael Vickery, "How Many Died in Pol Pot's Kampuchea?" *BCAS* 22 (1988); and Marek Sliwinsky, *Une analyse demographique du genocide des khmers rouges* (Paris, 1994). See also Office of the Vice President of Democratic Kampuchea in Charge of Foreign Affairs [Khieu Samphan], "What Are the Truth [sic] and Justice about the Accusations against Democratic Kampuchea of Mass Killings from 1975 to 1978?" (n.p., July 1987); and Heder, *Khieu Samphan and Pol Pot*. Khieu Samphan's tendentious document admits to fewer than 3,000 deaths as a result of DK "mistakes," while 30,000 were falsely put to death by "Vietnamese agents"; another 11,000 were killed justifiably because they *were* Vietnamese agents. In 1980, the text asserts, "about 1.5 million died, victims of Vietnamese aggressors." The dogmatic hauteur of this document, amateurishly translated from French, suggests that it is vintage Khieu Samphan. In his interview with Nate Thayer in October 1997, Pol Pot referred approvingly to this document when he was asked about the magnitude of deaths under Democratic Kampuchea.

6. On the trial of Pol Pot and Ieng Sary, see Burchett, *China-Cambodia-Vietnam Triangle*, pp. 81ff. See also David Hawk, "International Human Rights Law and Democratic Kampuchea," in Ablin and Hood, eds., *Cambodian Agony*, pp. 118–148. Efforts to bring Pol Pot to trial redoubled in 1997 when he fell from power, and there is some evidence that his subordinates were willing to turn him over to such a tribunal in 1998.

7. See Heder, *Khieu Samphan and Pol Pot*. In 1988 Pol Pot told military cadre that his faction had joined the coalition "because after the Vietnamese invasion, we needed to gather them to us" (Roger Normand's notes).

8. For a discussion of these developments, see Ross, *Indo-China Tangle*. On the coalition government, see Jacques Bekaert, "The Khmer Coalition," *Indochina Issues* (September 1982). On the camps, see Michael Vickery, "Refugee Politics: The Khmer Camp System in Thailand," in Ablin and Hood, eds., *Cambodian Agony*, pp. 293–331. Vickery's essay describes conditions in the camps in 1980–1982.

9. See Sho Ishikawa, "I Want to Join with Sihanouk, Lon Nol," *Bangkok Post*, December 11, 1979; and FBIS, *Daily Reports*, December 19, 1979.

10. FBIS, *Daily Reports*, December 27, 1979. The visit occurred on December 11–12, 1979. There is something chilling about Pol Pot's reference to the Holocaust. He must have known that the Vietnamese, among others, had already compared him to Hitler. Who were "the Jews" in the Cambodian case? And who were "those who opposed" Pol Pot's regime, whose extinction in Nazi Germany he could understand? Who were the "innocent" people? To Swedish reporters who arrived the following day, Pol Pot remarked casually that "the number of people who died when our people made mistakes were only a few hundred" (FBIS, *Daily Reports*, December 21, 1979). By 1997 he had settled on "a few thousand."

11. On Pol Pot's resignation, see FBIS, *Daily Reports*, December 27, 1979. On the $300,000 offer, Nayan Chanda, personal communication with author.

12. Steve Heder's interview with an anonymous Cambodian, March 1981. I am grateful to Heder for his translation.

13. Author's interview with Mary-Kay Magistad (July 1989). See also Magistad, "The Khmer Rouge: A Profile," *Indochina Issues* (December 1988). On later statistics, Rev. John Dennis (personal communication).

14. On the dynamics of small groups such as Pol Pot's, see R. C. Raack, "When Plans Fail: Small Group Behavior and Decision Making in the Conspiracy of 1808 in Germany," *Journal of Conflict Resolution* 16, 1 (1977): 3–19. In September 1985, Pol Pot's retirement was announced, and on December 7, 1986, the *New York Times* reported rumors from Bangkok that he was terminally ill and undergoing medical treatment in Beijing. By 1989, however, "Grandfather 87" was sighted frequently and seemed in excellent health. On Pol Pot's remarriage, author's interview with James Pringle (February 1991), Thayer, "Final Reckoning." Nate Thayer, "Dying Breath," *FEER*, April 30, 1998; Seth Mydans, "In Death, Indignity for Despised Killer," *New York Times*, April 18, 1998; Peter Sainsbury, "An Uncertain Future for the Widow of a Despot," *Phnom Penh Post*, April 24–May 7, 1998; and David Ashley's interview with Suong Sikoeun (September 1996), who said that Ponnary, "who hasn't occupied any position since 1979" had not approved the marriage.

15. "Tao kunnthoa, theatupit nung tuo neati reboh kampuchea pratheaneathipodei yoeung yang na peel mun, peel poacchubon, nung to teu anakut?" [What are the virtues, qualities, nature, and responsibilities of our Democratic Kampuchea in former times, nowadays, and extending into the future?], typescript, dated December 8, 1976, 38 pages. I am grateful to Tony Jackson for a copy of the Khmer version.

16. Ibid., pp. 29–30.

17. Interrogators' notebooks from S-21, drawn from study sessions, also denigrate the revolutions in France, Russia, and China—which had all been in one way or another betrayed. See Chandler, *Voices from S-21*, Chapter Four.

18. Interestingly, the speech dates the birth of Democratic Kampuchea to "over thirty years ago"—that is, to 1955–1956, when Saloth Sar began working for the Communist movement in Phnom Penh.

19. Australia's presence in the blacklist may reflect Australian efforts in the early 1980s to seek a rapprochement with the government in Phnom Penh. The U.S. Embassy in Bangkok translated the final phrase as "has never violated or abused anybody," which suggests human rights abuses rather than aggressive international behavior.

20. See Justin Jordens, *A 1991 State of Cambodia Political Education Text: Exposition and Analysis* (Clayton, Australia, 1993). This text plays down the utopian (or quixotic) views of Cambodia's uniqueness and emphasizes its links with other countries such as Vietnam.

21. It is tempting to contrast what the audience knew of Pol Pot with his picture of Napoleon, who may have raised faint echoes in their minds of Lon Nol or Sihanouk. Pol Pot had not seized power in a coup; he had never had himself named "emperor"; and he had been defending Cambodia rather than attacking neighbors during his time in power. The humility he displayed in his talk (even as he stood before his audience as the embodiment of Democratic Kampuchea) was proof of the "moral feeling" that Napoleon, Lon Nol, and Sihanouk lacked. Pol Pot's failure to select less vulnerable, more self-effacing, or more contemporary heroes was probably a device to enhance his own persona.

22. The most detailed descriptions of Pol Pot in the late 1980s and early 1990s and of his effect on listeners are in Roger Normand, "At the Khmer Rouge School: The Teachings of Chairman Pot," *Nation*, September 3, 1990; a general picture of the movement emerges from Christophe Peschoux, *Enquête sur les "nouveax" khmer rouges: Essai de débroussaillage* (Paris, 1992). Peschoux's penetrating study, based on several months of fieldwork, shows how thoroughly the Red Khmer held to their tactical priorities and how, in private, they did not abjure the possibility of massive human rights abuses should they return to power. For people's impressions of Pol Pot after 1992, I have drawn on the interviews conducted with former Red Khmer cadre by David Ashley and Nate Thayer.

23. See Gary Klintworth, ed., *Vietnam's Withdrawal from Cambodia* (Canberra, 1990); Grant Evans and Kelvin Rowley, *Red Brotherhood at War*, rev. ed. (London, 1990), pp. 301ff.; and Vairon, "Du Partie Indochinois," pp. 377–381. All Vietnamese troops were withdrawn by 1991, but the Red Khmer faction, and many Cambodians living overseas, suspected that the State of Cambodia was still controlled by "agents" from Vietnam.

24. See, among many works dealing with this period, Michael Doyle, ed., *Keeping the Peace* (Cambridge, 1997); Trevor Findlay, *Cambodia: The Legacy and Lessons of UNTAC* (Oxford, 1995); and Stephen Heder and Judy Ledgerwood, eds., *Propaganda, Politics, and Violence in Cambodia* (Armonk, N.Y., 1996). See also David Ashley, "The End," *Phnom Penh Post*, April 24–May 7, 1998.

25. Findlay, *Cambodia*, p. 60; and Nate Thayer, "Shake-up of Khmer Rouge Hierarchy," *Phnom Penh Post*, February 28–March 10, 1994. Son Sen's dismissal was not publicized at the time. It is possible that the Red Khmer hoped for a royalist victory in the July 1993 elections and a favored place in postelection Cambodia. Such a stance, which underestimated the staying power of Hun Sen's Cambodian Peoples' Party

(CPP) would explain their failure to disrupt the elections when they took place and their attentiste policy for several months thereafter.

26. Ashley, "The End."

27. On the radio broadcasts, see Matthew Grainger, "The Voice of Pol Pot," *Phnom Penh Post*, April 24–May 7, 1998. Reflecting what may well have been a widespread popular view, a Cambodian told Serge Thion in the early 1990s that "the Vietnamese are most dangerous when they are invisible."

28. Author's interview with James Pringle (February 1991). One undated snapshot from the mid-1980s showed Pol Pot and his associates posed in a line; another shows them, uncharacteristically in business suits, posed in a garden in Pyongyang.

29. I have relied here on a map drawn by Roger Normand from defectors' descriptions of the camp. Over the next seven years, Pol Pot moved (or was moved) frequently.

30. This information is from Roger Normand's notes; from Peschoux, *Enquête*; from author's interview with Peschoux (September 1990); and from transcripts of interviews conducted with former Red Khmer cadre by David Ashley in 1995–1997. In the study sessions, the following topics were discussed: political situation; internal policy; building up military and civil forces; tripartite (coalition) politics; national and socialist viewpoints; virtue, morality, and the origins of the Cambodian nation; review lesson and self-criticism. Other speakers at the sessions included Son Sen, Ta Mok, Khieu Samphan, and Nuon Chea. Of these, Nuon Chea was the least popular, Ta Mok was the most feared, and Son Sen was almost as popular as Pol Pot.

31. Normand, "At the Khmer Rouge School," p. 200.

32. Peschoux, *Enquête*, pp. 73–74. In November 1996 a former cadre told David Ashley: "When speaking about an issue, Pol Pot was very good at explaining it in a very clear, lucid way which convinced you that he'd found a complete solution to the problem." The cadre added: "He speaks slowly, quietly, with a melodious voice."

33. Normand, "At the Khmer Rouge School," p. 201.

34. Ibid., p. 202.

35. David Ashley, interview with ex-division level cadre (May 1995). Interestingly, although the confessions of senior cadre imprisoned at S-21, and probably those of hundreds of lesser figures as well, were transmitted to Pol Pot (under the cover name of "*angkar*"), nothing in his handwriting is known to have survived among the hundreds of thousands of pages generated by the prison and currently accessible to scholars. Throughout his career, Pol Pot avoided leaving a paper trail.

36. Terry McCarthy, "The Butcher of Cambodia," *Time*, April 27, 1998.

37. Quoted by Sina Than, "Cambodia 1990: Towards a Peaceful Solution?" *Southeast Asian Affairs 1990* (Singapore, 1991), p. 87.

38. Thayer, "Final Reckoning"; and Eric Pape, "Pol Pot's Final Interview," *Phnom Penh Post*, April 24–May 7, 1998.

39. David Ashley's interview with I Chhean (January 1997); and David Ashley, "The End of the Revolution," unpublished paper, April 1997. I am grateful to Ashley for a copy of this insightful essay.

40. David Ashley's interview with a former Division 450 cadre (September 1996).

41. Material in these two paragraphs is drawn from Nate Thayer, "Next Generation," *FEER*, August 7, 1997; and from the verbatim translation of his July 25, 1997, interview with Khem Nguon, the incoming military commander who, along with Ta

Mok, engineered Pol Pot's show trial on the same day, discussed below. Khem Nguon's fluent narrative rings true but should be treated with caution as far as the timing of conversions and people's ascribed motivations are concerned.

42. This idea was echoed by an accuser at Pol Pot's trial in July 1997: "Looking backwards, Cambodia was dissolving into nothing."

43. Nate Thayer, "Brother Enemy No. 1," *Phnom Penh Post*, August 15–18, 1997, is a more detailed treatment than his "Brother Number Zero," *FEER*, August 7, 1997. For a summary of events in June–July 1997, see *Phnom Penh Post*, January 2–15, 1998.

44. Thayer, "Brother Enemy Number One." The slogans are taken from David Ashley's translation of cassette tapes recording the trial and Thayer's subsequent interview with Khem Nguon.

45. Thayer, "Day of Reckoning." I am grateful to Sok Pirun, a survivor of the Pol Pot era, for the mordant adage.

46. Nate Thayer, "Nowhere to Hide," *FEER*, April 23, 1998, and his "Dying Breath," *FEER*, April 30, 1998. See also Seth Mydans, "Pol Pot's Body Is Shown to Reporters," *New York Times*, April 17, 1998.

47. Seth Mydans, "Pol Pot Is Cremated; No Tears Are Shed," *New York Times*, April 19, 1998.

48. I am grateful to Judy Ledgerwood for a translation of this macabre interview.

Bibliographic Essay

Interviews by Author

These interviews were conducted in Australia, Cambodia, Canada, France, and the United States between 1986 and 1997. In listing them alphabetically, I have followed the accepted practice with Vietnamese and Cambodian informants of giving family names first (e.g., Ngo Dien).

François Bizot, Eileen Blumenthal, Pierre Brocheux, Sara Colm, Chhay Yat, Chheam Van, Alain Daniel, Richard Dudman, Ha The Duc, Stephen Heder, Hin Sithan, In Nath, Ith Sarin, Keat Chhon, Keng Vannsak, Khieu Kannarith, Khing Hoc Dy, Laeo Chheng Heat, Lim Keuky, Henri Locard, Loth Suong, Mary-Kay Magistad, Ngo Dien, Ngo Pen, Oeur Hunly, Om Narong, Ong Thong Hoeung, Oung Bophal, Pal Sam, Panh Menh Heang, Pel Nal, Christophe Peschoux, James Pringle, Pung Peng Cheng, Sa Bun, Sim Pal, Sim Var, Sisowath Aravady, Sisowath Ravivaddhana, So Bun Hor, Sok Bunthan, Sok Chuon, Sok Pirun, Suon Kaset Sokho, Soth Polin, Tang Kim Buon, Tea Sa Bun, Thach Ren, Thach Tan, Thap Heak, Thun Hen, Ty Sophen, Vann Nath, Jacques Vergès, Yem Nolla, You Sambo.

Interviews by Others

David Ashley's interviews with former Red Khmer cadre
Stephen Heder's interviews with Ieng Sary, Mey Mann, and Saloth Chhay
Bruce Palling's interview with Chhit Do
Nate Thayer's interviews with Nuon Chea and Pol Pot
Youk Chhong's interviews with Saloth Nhiep and Loth Soeung

Confessions from Tuol Sleng

Over four thousand confession dossiers have come to light at the DK interrogation facility at Tuol Sleng, Phnom Penh and in other documentary collections in the city. In 1991–1993 the S-21 archive was microfilmed under the auspices of Cornell University and became available to scholars after the first edition of this book was published. I have discussed the archive in depth in my book *Voices from S-21: Terror and History in Pol Pot's Secret Prison* (Berkeley, Calif., 1999). In 1990–1992 I consulted many confessions that cast light on Pol Pot's political career.

The confessions are listed by name, date, revolutionary pseudonym (if any), and position as given on the cover sheet of each text.

An Seng Heang (Chun; 1976–1977); military commander, 310th Brigade.
Bon Nan (Yi; 1978); secretary, *dombon* 505.
Bun Kung (Sombok; 1977); deputy, *dombon* 22.
Chan Mon (Tul; 1977); official, *dombon* 42.
Chan Sam (Sae; 1978); secretary, new northern region.
Chea Non (Suong; 1977).
Chea Soeun (1977); secretary, 703 Regiment.
Cheng An (1978); minister of industry.
Chhan Tres (Seng; 1976); female combatant.
Chhang Seng (1976); combatant.
Chhay Kim Hor (Hok; 1978); foreign ministry official.
Chhean (1978); secretary, *dombon* 22.
Chhim Samauk (Panh; 1978); Office of CPK Central Committee.
Chhun Hem (Sras; 1976); messenger, northern zone.
Chhun Sok Nguon (Som; 1976–1977); Kompong Som port director.
Chon Chay (1978); interrogator S-21.
Chou Chet (Si; 1977); secretary, western zone.
Hak Sien Lamy (1977); foreign affairs official.
Hang Phon (Sophy; 1978); chief of security, Koh Chey District.
Hem Sambath (Sambath; 1976); former soldier.
Heng Keum (1978); secretary, Division 5, eastern zone.
Heng Sany (Mak; 1977); Mey Saran's brother.
Hu Nim (Phoas; 1977); minister of information.
Im Naen (Ly; 1978); secretary, *dombon* 32, and wife of Chou Chet.
In Van (Souvan; 1977); combatant, 171st Brigade.
Keo Meas (1976); former Pracheachon member.
Keo Moni (1976); former Pracheachon member.
Ket Chau (Sem; 1977); chairman, Organization Office.
Kheang Sim Hon (But; 1978); *dombon* 104.
Khek Pen (Su; 1977); political commissar, *dombon* 4.
Kol Dorathy (1977); former student in France.
Koy Thuon (Khuon; 1977); minister of commerce.
Kong Sopal (Kuu; 1978).
Maen San (Ya; 1976); secretary, northeastern zone.
Mau Khem Nuon (Phom; 1977); secretary, CPK Political School.
Meas Chhuon (1978); secretary, *dombon* 21.
Meas Mon (Keo Samnang; 1978); military commander, eastern zone.
Men Tul (Sat; 1978); doctor, April 17 Hospital, Phnom Penh.
Mey Kimsan (n.d.); combatant.
Minh Thoeum (Heang; 1978); secretary, *dombon* 4.
Muol Sambath (Nhim Ros; 1978); vice chairman, State Presidium, and secretary, northwestern zone.
Neu Muy (1978); Vietnamese combatant.
Ni Muong (Yon; 1978); bodyguard and combatant, K-1.
Non Suon (Chey Suon; 1976–1977); Pracheachon member and minister of agriculture.

Oy Ngorn Ly (1977); interrogator, S-21.
Paen Cheuan (1978); secretary, Division 3, eastern zone.
Phi Nhe (1978); female rubber plantation worker.
Phuong (1978); rubber plantation worker.
Pin Nan (Yi; 1978); secretary, *dombon* 505.
Prum Pal (Vin; 1978); wife of Vorn Vet.
Prum Sambot (Chakrei; 1976); commander, Division 171.
Prum Seng (1977); wife of Sien An.
Pun Than (Chan; 1978); cadre from northeast.
Ruos Mau (Saay; 1977); party cadre, northwestern zone.
Sam Huy (Tal; 1978); DK official.
San Bun Hy (Khuon; 1978?); cadre from Kratie.
Sbauv Him (Euan; 1977); Division 310.
Sien An (1977); former ambassador to Vietnam.
Siet Chhae (Tum, 1977); secretary, *dombon* 22.
Soeu Van Si (Doeun; 1977); administrator, Office of the CPK Central Committee.
Sok Knol (Lin; 1978); party cadre, eastern zone.
Sok Suy (1978); Vorn Vet's daughter.
Sok Thuok (Vorn Vet; 1978); minister of industry.
Som Chea (1978); former secretary, *dombon* 25.
Suon Kaset (1976); former agricultural official.
Tauch Chaem (Sot; 1978); secretary, *dombon* 21.
Thach Pich (Vorn Chen; 1976); former Buddhist monk.
Tiv Ol (Penh; 1977); former teacher.
Touch Kamdoeun (1977); foreign ministry official.
Um Phim (1976); interrogator, S-21.
Uy Yun (Sin; 1978); cadre, Office of CPK Central Committee.
Yang Kan (Phors; 1978); wife of Cheng An.

Cambodia: General Works

The most recent general history is David Chandler, *A History of Cambodia* (Boulder, Colo., 1983; 2nd ed., updated 1996). On earlier times, see Claude Jacques's masterly *Angkor* (Paris, 1989). For the period from 1945 to 1979, the most detailed study is David Chandler, *The Tragedy of Cambodian History: Politics, War, and Revolution Since 1945* (New Haven, Conn., 1991). Russell R. Ross, *Cambodia: A Country Study* (Washington, D.C., 1990), is helpful, and so is Jean Delvert's magisterial *Le paysan cambodgien* (Paris, 1962). See also Remy Prud'homme, *L'économie du Cambodge* (Paris, 1969), and Marie-A. Martin, *Le mal cambodgien* (Paris, 1989). For the history of Cambodian radicalism, Ben Kiernan's pathbreaking *How Pol Pot Came to Power* (London, 1985; hereafter *HPP*) is indispensable. Books dealing primarily with Democratic Kampuchea (DK) are listed under the relevant chapter headings below.

Chapters 2–4 (1928–1963)

On Cambodian nationalism, see V. Reddi, *A History of the Cambodian Independence Movement* (Tirupati, 1971); Chandler, *Tragedy*; and Kiernan, *HPP*. The 1940s and

1950s are covered nicely in Philippe Preschez, *Essai sur la démocratie au Cambodge* (Paris, 1961). For a royal perspective, see Norodom Sihanouk and Jean Lacouture, *Indochine vue de Pékin* (Paris, 1971); and Sihanouk's often self-serving memoirs, *Souvenirs doux et amers* (Paris, 1981).

There is an extensive literature dealing with radicalism in France in the 1950s. See, for example, Alain Besançon, *Une génération* (Paris 1987); E. Leroy Ladurie, *Paris-Montpellier* (Paris, 1982); and Dominique Dessanti, *Les staliniens* (Paris, 1975). Jeanine Verdès-Leroux, *Au service du parti: Le parti communiste, les intellectuels, et la culture, 1944–1956* (Paris, 1986), is a penetrating analysis. See also Frank S. Meyer, *The Making of Communists* (New York, 1961); and Edward Upward, *The Spiral Ascent* (London, 1967), an interesting fictional account by a former British Communist. Janet Flanner, *Paris Journal, 1944–1955* (New York, 1988), is an excellent introduction to the ambience of the period. For Saloth Sar's time in Paris, see Kiernan, *HPP*; and François Debré, *Cambodge: La révolution de la forêt* (Paris 1976).

Sihanouk's years in power are dealt with perceptively in Milton Osborne, *Power and Politics in Cambodia* (Melbourne, 1973); and in Osborne, *Sihanouk Prince of Light, Prince of Darkness* (Honolulu, 1995). See also Roger Smith, *Cambodia's Foreign Policy* (Ithaca, N.Y., 1965); and Charles Meyer's hostile but enlightening *Derrière le sourire khmer* (Paris, 1971)—Meyer was an adviser to Sihanouk for fifteen years. Michael Field, *The Prevailing Wind* (London, 1967), is a more sympathetic account than Meyer's. There are several interesting essays about this period in Ben Kiernan and Chanthou Boua, *Peasants and Politics in Kampuchea, 1942–1982* (London, 1983).

Chapters 5–7 (1963–1977)

On the last years of Sihanouk's regime, see Meyer, *Derrière le sourire khmer*; Milton Osborne, *Before Kampuchea* (London, 1979); and J.-C. Pomonti and Serge Thion, *Des courtisans aux partisans* (Paris, 1971), which also covers Sihanouk's demise. Kiernan, *HPP*, has valuable insight into the fortunes of the Cambodian Communists in this period.

The most readable approach to the Lon Nol era is William Shawcross, *Sideshow: Nixon, Kissinger, and the Destruction of Cambodia* (New York, 1979), a scathing attack on U.S. policies. Sak Sutsakhan, *The Khmer Republic at War and the Final Collapse* (Washington, D.C., 1980), is a helpful military history. See also Justin Corfield, *Khmer Stand Up! Politics in the Khmer Republic* (Clayton, Australia, 1994); and Elizabeth Becker's persuasive analysis extending into the Democratic Kampuchea period, *When the War Was Over* (New York, 1986).

The evacuation of Phnom Penh and events in the succeeding months are treated sympathetically in George Hildebrand and Gareth Porter, *Cambodia: Starvation and Revolution* (New York, 1976) and humanely in François Ponchaud's pioneering account, *Cambodia: Year Zero* (New York, 1978). See also Becker, *When the War Was Over*; Bernard Hamel, *Du sang et de larmes* (Paris, 1977); and three memoirs, among many: Pin Yathay, *L'utopie meurtrière* (Paris, 1980); Martin Stuart Fox and Ung Bunheang, *The Murderous Revolution* (Sydney, 1985); and Someth May, *Cambodian Witness* (London, 1986). For the broadcasts of Radio Phnom Penh, which were monitored overseas, see U.S. Foreign Broadcast Information Service (FBIS), *Daily Reports*; and British Broadcasting Corporation, *Summary of World Broadcasts (Far East)*.

Chapters 8–9 (1977–1998)

Several analytical studies, memoirs, and anthologies are useful for studying the Democratic Kampuchea period and its aftermath. The most recent of these are David Chandler, *Voices from S-21: Terror and History in Pol Pot's Secret Prison* (Berkeley, Calif., 1999); and Ben Kiernan, *The Pol Pot Regime* (New Haven, Conn., 1995), which draws to a large extent on interviews conducted in the 1980s. Earlier analyses include Michael Vickery's *Cambodia, 1975–1982* (Boston, 1983); and Craig Etcheson, *The Rise and Demise of Democratic Kampuchea* (Boulder, Colo., 1984), an intelligent survey that, unlike Vickery's book, relies entirely on secondary sources. Becker, *When the War Was Over*, attempts a politico-cultural explanation for events, as does Martin, *Le mal cambodgien*. See also R. A. Burgler, *The Eyes of the Pineapple: Revolutionary Intellectuals and Terror in Democratic Kampuchea* (Saarbrücken, 1990), which approaches Democratic Kampuchea from a radical perspective.

In addition to the memoirs already cited, see Laurence Picq, *Au delà du ciel* (Paris, 1984), a moving account of life in Democratic Kampuchea by a Frenchwoman married to a DK official; Haing Ngor, *Surviving the Killing Fields* (New York, 1988); and Norodom Sihanouk, *Prisonnier des khmers rouges* (Paris, 1987). See also Vann Nath, *A Cambodian Prison Portrait: One Year in the Khmer Rouge's S-21* (Bangkok, 1998). The most recent estimate of deaths in Cambodia in the 1970s is Patrick Heuveline, "Between One and Three Million: Toward the Demographic Reconstruction of a Decade of Cambodian History, 1970–1979," *Population Studies* 52 (1998): 39–65.

Two useful anthologies of primary materials are Timothy Carney's pioneering *Communist Party Power in Kampuchea (Cambodia): Documents and Discussion* (Ithaca, N.Y., 1977); and David Chandler, Ben Kiernan, and Chanthou Boua, eds. and trans., *Pol Pot Plans the Future: Confidential Documents from Democratic Kampuchea, 1976–1977* (New Haven, Conn., 1988). See also Henri Locard, *Le petit livre rouge de Pol Pot ou les paroles de l'Angkar* (Paris, 1996).

Three collections of essays about Democratic Kampuchea are of interest: Serge Thion and Ben Kiernan, *Khmers rouges!* (Paris, 1981); David P. Chandler and Ben Kiernan, eds., *Revolution and Its Aftermath in Kampuchea* (New Haven, Conn., 1983); and Karl Jackson, ed., *Cambodia, 1975–1978: Rendezvous with Death* (Princeton, N.J., 1989). See also Serge Thion, *Watching Cambodia* (Bangkok, 1996), a stimulating collection of essays, many of which deal with the Pol Pot era.

On developments in China impinging on the Cambodian revolution, see William Joseph et al., eds., *New Perspectives on the Cultural Revolution* (Cambridge, Mass., 1990); Paul J. Hiniker, *Revolutionary Ideology and Chinese Reality: Dissonance Under Mao* (Beverly Hills, Calif., 1977); Stuart Schram, *The Thought of Mao Tse-Tung* (Cambridge, Mass., 1989); and Lynn White, *Policies of Chaos: The Organizational Causes of Violence in China's Cultural Revolution* (Princeton, N.J., 1989).

On Vietnam, see William Turley, ed., *Vietnamese Communism in Comparative Perspective* (Boulder, Colo., 1980), an interesting collection of essays.

The most detailed studies of the DK economy are three essays by Marie-A. Martin: "La riziculture et la maîtrise de l'eau dans le Kampuchea Démocratique," *Etudes rurales (ER)* 83 (July-September 1981); "L'industrie dans le Kampuchea Démocratique," *ER* 89–91 (January-September 1983); and "La politique alimentaire des khmers rouges," *ER* 99-101 (July-December 1985). See also Charles Twining, "The Economy," in *Cambodia 1975-1978*, ed. Karl Jackson.

On Vietnamese-Cambodian hostilities, see Robert Ross, *The Indo-China Tangle* (New York, 1988); Nayan Chanda, *Brother Enemy* (New York, 1986); Grant Evans and Kelvin Rowley, *Red Brotherhood at War* (London, 1983; rev. ed., 1990); and Lionel Vairon, *Du Parti Communiste Indochinois à la "Triple Alliance Indochinoise*, Doctoral thesis, INALCO, Paris, 1998.

The most detailed study of the People's Republic of Kampuchea is Michael Vickery, *Kampuchea* (London, 1986), which favors the regime. See also Viviane Frings, *Le paysan cambodgien et le socialisme: La politique agricole de la Republique Populaire du Kampuchea et de l'Etat du Cambodge* (Paris, 1997). On post-1985 developments in the DK faction, see Christophe Peschoux, *Enquête sur les "nouveaux" khmers rouges: Essai de débroussaillage* (Paris, 1992), a wide-ranging work based on several months of field research; and articles published in the *Far Eastern Economic Review* and the *Phnom Penh Post* by Nate Thayer, whose forthcoming book, *Sympathy for the Devil* (New York, in press) summarizes his work.

Index